Quick Reference: Creating Items and Files

To	Press
Create an appointment	Ctrl+
Create a contact	Ctrl+
Create a folder	Ctrl+Shift+E
Create a Journal entry	Ctrl+Shift+J
Create a meeting request	Ctrl+Shift+Q
Create a message	Ctrl+Shift+M
Create a note	Ctrl+Shift+N
Create a task	Ctrl+Shift+K
Create a task request	Ctrl+Shift+U
Create a new item of the same type as that currently displayed in Information viewer	Ctrl+Shift+N

Quick Reference: Moving Around in a Dialog Box

To	Press
Switch to next field	Ctrl+Tab
Switch to previous field	Ctrl+Shift+Tab
Move to next option or option group	Tab
Move to previous option or option group	Shift+Tab
Perform action assigned to selected box; select or clear selected check box	Spacebar
Move to item in drop-down list	Press key corresponding to first character of item in list
Select option; select or clear check box	Alt+underlined character
Open selected drop-down list	Alt+Down-arrow
Close drop-down list	Alt+Up-arrow, or Esc
Perform action of selected button	Enter
Cancel command and close dialog box	Esc

Quick Reference: Moving Around in a Text Box

To	Press
Move to beginning of text in box	Home
Move to end of text in box	End
Move by one character	Left-arrow or Right-arrow
Move by one word	Ctrl+Left-arrow or Ctrl+Right-arrow
Select from insertion point to beginning of text in box	Shift+Home
Select from insertion point to end of text in box	Shift+End
Select or unselect one character to left of insertion point	Shift+Left-arrow
Select or unselect one character to right of insertion point	Shift+Right-arrow
Select or unselect one word to left of insertion point	Ctrl+Shift+Left-arrow
Select or unselect one word to right of insertion point	Ctrl+Shift+Right-arrow

Quick Reference: Adding World Wide Web Information to Items

To	Press
Edit a URL within a message	Ctrl+Left mouse button
Specify a browser	Shift+Left mouse button
Insert a hyperlink	Ctrl+K (WordMail only)

Quick Reference: Applying Formatting to Text

Note: This reference does not apply to text formatted as Plain Text.

To	Press
Make selected text bold	Ctrl+B
Make selected text bulleted	Ctrl+Shift+L
Center selected text	Ctrl+E
Italicize selected text	Ctrl+I
Increase selected text indent	Ctrl+T
Decrease selected text indent	Ctrl+Shift+T
Left align selected text	Ctrl+L
Underline selected text	Ctrl+U
Increase font size	Ctrl+]
Decrease font size	Ctrl+[
Clear formatting	Ctrl+Shift+Z or Ctrl+Spacebar

Quick Reference: Working in Forms and Views

Note: "Item" in this table refers to an item (control) on a form, not to an Outlook item.

To	Press
Cancel current operation	Esc
Display ScreenTip for active item	Shift+F1
Expand selected group	+ (numeric keypad)
Collapse selected group	- (numeric keypad)
Select item	Enter
Enable editing in selected field (except in icon view)	F2
Move from item to item	Arrow keys
Switch to next tab	Ctrl+Tab or Ctrl+Page-down
Switch to previous tab	Ctrl+Shift+Tab or Ctrl+Page-up
Display address book	Ctrl+Shift+B
Dial phone number	Ctrl+Shift+D
Find	Ctrl+Shift+F
Next item	Ctrl+Shift+>
Previous item	Ctrl+Shift+<
Mark message as read	Ctrl+Q
Reply to message	Ctrl+R
Reply all to a message	Ctrl+Shift+R
Switch case of selected text	Shift+F3
Switch between folder list and Information viewer	F6 or Ctrl+Shift+Tab

Using

Microsoft® Outlook™

98

Gordon Padwick

with Bill Ray

A Division of Macmillan Computer Publishing, USA
201 W. 103rd Street
Indianapolis, Indiana 46290

Contents at a Glance

Using Microsoft® Outlook™ 98

Library of Congress Catalog No.: 98-84841

ISBN: 0-7897-1516-3

01 00 99 98   6 5 4 3 2 1

Interpretation of the printing code: the rightmost double-digit number is the year of the book's printing; the rightmost single-digit number, the number of the book's printing. For example, a printing code of 98-1 shows that the first printing of the book occurred in 1998.

Credits

Executive Editor
Jim Minatel

Acquisitions Editor
Jill Byus

Development Editors
Rick Kughen
Lorna Gentry

Technical Editors
Vince Averello
Kyle Bryant

Managing Editor
Thomas F. Hayes

Project Editor
Karen A. Walsh

Copy Editor
Julie McNamee

Cover Designers
Dan Armstrong
Ruth Harvey

Book Designers
Nathan Clement
Ruth Harvey

Indexer
C.J. East

Production Team
Betsy Deeter
Becky Stutzman

Graphics Image Specialists
Sadie Crawford
Wil Cruz
Tammy Graham

Contents

About the Authors

Gordon Padwick is a senior programmer analyst with SYS, a company that provides engineering support services to the U.S. Government and to private industry. He develops database and integrated applications based on Microsoft's Office suite. Padwick has worked with computers for more years than he cares to remember, and has had experience as an engineer and a manager in many hardware and software design projects. He has worked with Windows and Windows applications since Microsoft introduced the first version of Windows more than 10 years ago.

Prior to joining SYS, Padwick was an independent consultant who specialized in Windows applications. He has authored and contributed to many books about Windows applications, including *Special Edition Using Microsoft Outlook 97*, *Building Integrated Office Applications*, and *Platinum Edition Using Office 97*.

Padwick is a graduate of London University, has completed postgraduate studies in computer science and communications, and is a Senior Member of the Institute of Electrical and Electronics Engineers. He currently lives in southern California.

Bill Ray is a Microsoft Certified Solution Developer and a Product Specialist. He has contributed to several Que publications, including *Special Edition Using Visual Basic for Applications*, and *Special Edition Using Excel 97, Bestseller Edition*. He is a Senior Consultant for the Versicon Consulting Group of Shelton, CT, a Microsoft Solution Provider Partner. His work at Versicon has included the design and implementation of the Versicon Word for Windows Productivity Pack, a collection of templates and macros for the corporate environment. He also provides custom solutions using Microsoft Excel, Access, and FrontPage. Bill holds an M.A. in Music Education from Teachers College, Columbia University, and an M.S. in Computer Science from Union College. You can reach Bill at `bill.ray@versicon.com`.

About the Technical Editors

Vince Averello is a Microsoft Outlook MVP (Most Valuable Professional) and is a Microsoft Certified Professional. He is a Senior Programmer Analyst at Ernst & Young.

Kyle Bryant, owner of a Dallas-based PC network integration firm, has more than 15 years experience in the personal computer industry. He was an early advocate of the Microsoft Windows platform and continues to follow Windows technologies developments under Windows 95, Windows 98, and Windows NT.

Dedication

from Gordon Padwick
To Kathy, my wife and best friend.

Acknowledgments

from Gordon Padwick
Writing the acknowledgments page for a new book is one of my favorite tasks—for two reasons. It's usually the last thing I write, so I can heave a big sigh of relief that the task is nearly over. Also, it's my opportunity to look back over the past few months and gratefully remember the many people who have willingly helped me write the book.

My special thanks go to my co-author, Bill Ray, for writing Chapters 18 through 24. Without Bill's help, there would have been no way for me to get everything written in time.

I'm also indebted to many people, far too many to mention individually by name, who have replied to my questions. Whenever something wasn't clear to me and I sent a question by e-mail or posted a question on a newsgroup, I rarely had to wait more than a day to get the answer I needed.

My thanks also go to the many people at Que who have made this book possible. Jill Byus—acquisitions editor—directed the entire process of getting the book written. Lorna Gentry and Rick Kughen—developmental editors—helped me keep the subject in focus and made many constructive suggestions. Karen Walsh—project editor—managed the process of laying out pages and getting the book ready to print.

Two technical editors, Vince Averello and Kyle Bryant, have made an indispensable contribution to the book by catching my errors and omissions. Thank you, guys. Without your help I would soon accumulate several layers of mud on my face. If any errors remain, I accept full responsibility for them.

The many illustrations of what you can expect to see on your screen were captured with Collage Complete. Thank you, Nancy and Neil Rosenberg of Inner Media, for providing Collage Complete—it's an excellent product.

As always, I want to acknowledge my gratitude to my wife, Kathy, for her support and patience. She has willingly put up with me spending most evenings and weekends pounding away on my computer. Her encouragement has made it possible for me to finish this book almost on schedule.

We'd Like to Hear from You!

Que Corporation has a long-standing reputation for high-quality books and products. To ensure your continued satisfaction, we also understand the importance of customer service and support.

Orders, Catalogs, and Customer Service

To order other Que or Macmillan Computer Publishing books, catalogs, or products, please contact our Customer Service Department:

Phone: 1-800-428-5331
Fax: 1-800-835-3202
International Fax: 1-317-228-4400
Or visit our online bookstore: http://www.mcp.com/

Introduction

A little over a year ago, Microsoft introduced Outlook 97 and called it a desktop information manager. Now, a significantly enhanced Outlook 98 is available—Microsoft calls it a "messaging and collaboration client." That changed description says a lot about the new Outlook.

Yes, Outlook is still a desktop information manager—among the best you can find. But the emphasis now is on using Outlook to collaborate with other people.

This book's predecessor, *Special Edition Using Microsoft Outlook 97*, had a lot to say about using Outlook as a desktop information manager and also covered sending and receiving e-mail. This new book covers the same topics, updated to match the many improvements in Outlook 98, but also has a lot to tell you about collaborating with your colleagues, particularly if you use Microsoft Exchange Server for exchanging information.

Getting Started with Outlook 98

When you first install Outlook, you get what's called Internet Only E-mail Service—sometimes called Internet Mail Only (IMO)—which you can use to send and receive e-mail messages by way of the Internet and intranets. If you want to send and receive e-mail messages by way of other messaging systems (such as Exchange Server, Microsoft Mail, or cc:Mail), you must install Outlook's Corporate or Workgroup E-mail Service component. Corporate/Workgroup E-mail Service provides access to Internet e-mail as well as other messaging systems.

With one significant exception, the functionality of Outlook is similar whether you have Internet Only E-mail Service or Corporate or Workgroup E-mail Service. You have the same capabilities to maintain calendar, contact, and task information. The exception is using Outlook to send and receive faxes. The Internet Only service lets you use the new WinFax Starter Edition that Microsoft licenses from Symantec; the Corporate or Workgroup Service uses Microsoft Fax, the same as Outlook 97.

This book focuses on Outlook with the Corporate or Workgroup component installed. If you run Internet Only, you'll see differences in some menus. Of course, the information about Exchange Server and other messaging systems won't apply to you. Significant differences between Internet Only and Corporate or Workgroup are noted throughout the book.

If you work in an organization where a LAN with an e-mail system is already in use, you probably have Outlook 98 already set up and ready to go on your computer. The first part of this book, "Starting to Work with Outlook," is for you.

The four chapters in this section will get you started using Outlook 98 to send and receive e-mail, keep your personal calendar, organize your Address Book, maintain a to-do list, and remember all you've done. You'll also learn about finding your way around in Outlook.

If you've never used Outlook before, you'll find these four chapters particularly valuable. Even if you have used Outlook 97, I suggest you at least scan through these chapters to discover some things that are new in Outlook 98.

Who Should Read This Book

This book is for everyone who uses Outlook. Beginning users will find the first four chapters particularly useful. As they evolve, or want to evolve, into knowledgeable users, they'll be interested in much that's in the subsequent chapters.

People who have previous experience with Outlook 97 will find that this book brings them up-to-date with what's new in Outlook 98 and leads them into an understanding of matters that may not have been previously clear in their minds.

Those who have previously used another e-mail system will find this book provides a comprehensive introduction to e-mail and collaboration within the Microsoft Exchange environment.

Special Book Elements

- *Menu and dialog box commands and options.* You can easily find the onscreen menu and dialog box commands by looking for bold text like you see in this direction: Open the **File** menu and click **Save**.

- *Hotkeys for commands.* The underlined keys onscreen that activate commands and options are also underlined in the book as shown in the previous example.

- *Combination and shortcut keystrokes.* Text that directs you to hold down several keys simultaneously is connected with a plus sign (+), such as Ctrl+P.

- *Graphical icons with the commands they execute.* Look for icons like this in text and steps. These indicate buttons onscreen that you can click to accomplish the procedure.

- *Cross references.* If a related topic is a prerequisite to the section or steps you are reading, or a topic builds further on what you are reading, you'll find the cross reference to it after the steps or at the end of the section like this:

SEE ALSO

➤ *For information about how to display the Appointments view, see "Working with Views" on page 165.*

- *Glossary terms.* For all the terms that appear in the glossary, you'll find the first appearance of that term in the text in *italic*.

- *Sidebars.* Information related to the task at hand, or "inside" information from the author, is offset in sidebars so as not to interfere with the task at hand and to make it easy to find this valuable information. Each of these sidebars has a short title to help you quickly identify the information you'll find there. You'll find the same kind of information in these that you might find in notes, tips, or warnings in other books but here, the titles should be more informative.

Final Comment

As I always do in the books I write, I invite readers to send me their suggestions, comments, and questions. Send e-mail to me at

gpadwick@earthlink.net

I value all messages I receive and, so far, have been able to respond personally to each one.

I hope you enjoy and benefit from this book.

Gordon Padwick

Starting to Work with Outlook

Getting the Feel of Outlook

What is Outlook?

Outlook Today summarizes what's on your schedule

How to see the information that Outlook saves

Using Outlook to save items of information

Getting help while you're working with Outlook

Important words are defined in the glossary

Throughout this book, words and terms printed in italicized type are defined in the glossary at the back of the book.

What Is Outlook?

Outlook 98 Messaging and Collaboration Client is a versatile tool you can use to keep your business and personal life organized. You can use Outlook to

- Send and receive e-mail and faxes
- Share information with other people
- Participate in electronic meetings with groups
- Maintain your calendar
- Organize meetings
- Keep a personal to-do list
- Ask other people to take on tasks
- Build and maintain your address book
- Access pages on the World Wide Web
- Participate in Internet newsgroups
- Keep a journal of your activities
- Save instant notes

In a couple of words, Outlook is your information center. Use Outlook to share, access, and save information. Figure 1.1 illustrates some of the ways you can use Outlook.

Outlook is Microsoft's primary e-mail *client* (the software running on your computer) for services including e-mail, provided by *Exchange Server*. You can also use Outlook to send and receive e-mail from other messaging services, such as Internet e-mail (using any Internet service provider), Microsoft Mail, and cc:Mail.

If you have a fax-modem, you can use Outlook to send and receive faxes.

One of the great advantages to using Outlook is that all the messages you send and receive are saved in one set of folders, no matter which messaging service you use. By default, Outlook saves all the messages you receive in your Inbox folder and saves copies of all the messages you send in your Sent Items folder. You can, if you like, create your own hierarchy of folders in which to save messages you send and receive.

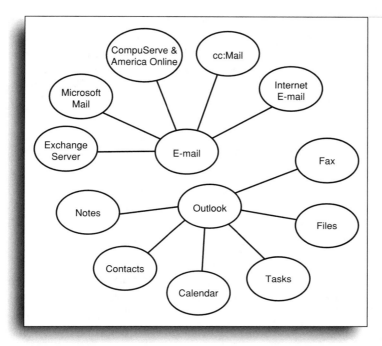

FIGURE 1.1

You can use Outlook for handling many types of information.

You use e-mail to send messages to, and receive messages from, other people. You can also share information by using *Public Folders* and *Net Folders*. Public Folders reside on a server and can be accessed by anyone who has the appropriate rights; Net Folders are folders you share by way of the Internet. Public Folders and Net Folders are a convenient way to share information with a group that may consist of just a few people or a large number of people.

Yet another way to use Outlook as an information tool is to participate in *newsgroups* on the *Internet* or on an *intranet*. Outlook uses facilities in Outlook Express for this purpose. To access newsgroups, open the **Go** menu and choose **News**. The first time you do so, Outlook asks you to select a folder where Outlook Express should keep your messages. The default is a folder named Outlook Express, but you can choose a different one if you prefer. You can also use Outlook as a starting point for browsing through Web sites on the Internet.

In addition, you can use *NetMeeting* to meet with one or more other people by way of the Internet or an intranet. NetMeeting goes beyond the basics of communicating by allowing other people to see what you are typing and, likewise, allowing you to see what they are typing. NetMeeting sessions can include any or all of the following:

- Audio and video
- Shared applications so everyone involved can see what others are doing
- Using NetMeeting as an electronic white board so other people can see what you draw and they can contribute to your drawing

Outlook keeps all the information you work with in a set of folders you can access from the Outlook window. From within Outlook, you can also easily access folders that contain information created by other applications. Outlook is compatible with the other applications in the Office 97 suite, and with many Office-compatible applications from companies other than Microsoft. You can easily incorporate documents and objects from other Office applications in your e-mail messages and other Outlook *items*.

The Many Faces of Outlook

Outlook for hand-held computers

At the time this book was written, Microsoft was talking about small versions of Outlook suitable for use on hand-held computers. When these versions become available, Microsoft will post information about them on its Web site.

Another name for Internet Only Support

Internet Only Support is also known as Internet Mail Only (IMO).

You might have noticed references to Outlook Express in previous paragraphs. Before we go any further, let me help you understand the various faces of Outlook you'll come across.

First, Outlook 98 (the successor to Outlook 97) contains most of the bells and whistles. Outlook 98 is the core product you can use for messaging and managing your information.

Corporate/Workgroup Support and Internet Only Support

You can install Outlook 98 in two modes: either *Corporate/Workgroup* Support or *Internet Only* Support. Corporate/Workgroup Support mode is "Outlook Complete;" Internet

Only Support mode is a slimmed-down version of Outlook that, as the name suggests, provides only the Outlook e-mail functionality that gives you access to the Internet. Both modes allow you to use Outlook as a Personal Information Manager.

Why would you want to install the Internet Only Support mode? If you're using Outlook only for Internet e-mail, newsgroups, and so on, this mode gives you all you need. It requires far less of your computer resources than the Corporate/Workgroup Support mode, loads and closes much faster, and is faster to use.

This book is primarily about Outlook 98 installed in the Corporate/Workgroup Support mode. If you're working at a computer on which Outlook 98 is installed, you can easily find out whether the installation is Corporate/Workgroup Support or Internet Only Support. To do so, open Outlook and then open the **Help** menu and choose **About Microsoft Outlook**. You should see a message box similar to that in Figure 1.2.

FIGURE 1.2
The second line in this message box contains the words **Corporate** or **Workgroup** if Outlook is installed in the Corporate/Workgroup Support mode.

If the second line in the message box tells you that you have the Internet Mail Only version installed, you won't be able to reproduce some of what's described in this book on your computer. You can easily switch to the Corporate/Workgroup Support mode by following the instructions in Appendix A, "Installing Outlook 98."

Outlook relies on Outlook Express

You'll notice that Outlook 98 calls up Outlook Express (a separate application) from time to time. Because you must have Internet Explorer 4.0 installed on your computer before you can install Outlook 98, and Internet Explorer 4.0 includes Outlook Express, there's no need to duplicate functionality within Outlook 98 that exists in Outlook Express.

Outlook Express

Outlook Express comes with Internet Explorer 4.0. Think of Outlook Express as a slimmed-down version of Outlook's Internet Only Support mode, but with some extras. If you're using only basic Internet capabilities (such as e-mail and newsgroups), Outlook Express probably contains all you need. If you need to interact with some of the more sophisticated Internet *protocols*, however, you must use Outlook 98.

Outlook Web Access

In addition to Outlook 98 and Outlook Express, you might come across references to *Outlook Web Access*, an Exchange Server component. You don't need to be concerned about Outlook Web Access unless you're an Exchange Server administrator. Outlook Web Access is included in Service Pack 1.0 for Exchange Server 5.0 and is a standard component of Exchange Server 5.5. Outlook Web Access, which contains a small subset of Outlook's functionality, provides direct Internet access to e-mail, calendar items, and data in Public Folders located on Exchange Server.

A First Look at Outlook 98

When you start Outlook 98, the first window you usually see is the Outlook Today window, shown in Figure 1.3. This window gives you an overview of what's waiting for you.

Displaying the Outlook Today window

If you don't see the Outlook Today window, open the **Go** menu and choose **Outlook Today**. See Chapter 5, "Controlling How Outlook Starts" for more information about displaying the Outlook Today window.

The Outlook Today window gives you a summary of your commitments for today and the next few days, informs you of how many unread messages are waiting for you, informs you of how many unfinished drafts of messages you have, and alerts you to your current tasks. You can click **Calendar** to display today's calendar immediately, **Mail** to open your Inbox where you see details of waiting messages, or **Tasks** to see a list of your tasks. If you want to look up a person's e-mail address or fax number, enter that person's name in the **Find a Contact** box and click **go**.

To make changes to how Outlook Today works, choose **Options** to display the window shown in Figure 1.4.

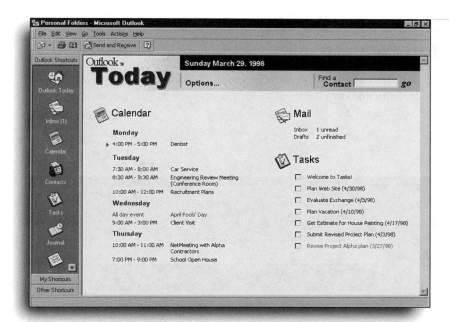

FIGURE 1.3
The Outlook Today window
gives you a summary of your
current schedule.

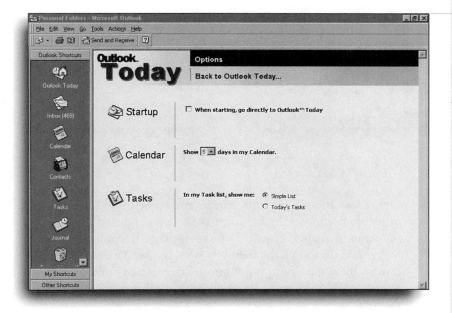

FIGURE 1.4
Select how you want Outlook
Today to display information
by making choices in this
window.

Understanding How Outlook Displays Information

Often when you're working with Outlook, you'll have an Information viewer on your screen, such as the one shown in Figure 1.5.

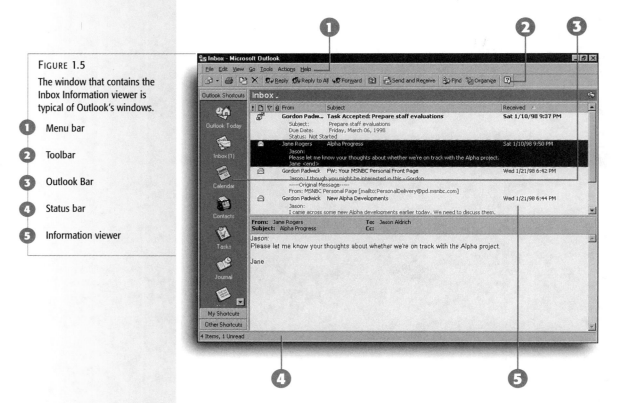

FIGURE 1.5

The window that contains the Inbox Information viewer is typical of Outlook's windows.

1 Menu bar

2 Toolbar

3 Outlook Bar

4 Status bar

5 Information viewer

Outlook's windows are similar in several ways to windows in other applications. The *menu bar* at the top contains the names of menus; you click a menu name to display a list of items in that menu, and then click the item you want to use. The menu names remain the same while you're using different parts of Outlook, but many of the items in those menus change according to what you're doing.

The *toolbar* immediately below the menu bar contains buttons you can click to access specific Outlook capabilities. Many of the buttons in the toolbar are different according to what part of Outlook you're using. If you want to know what a button does, just move the mouse pointer over the button and wait for a moment until a *ScreenTip* appears with a word or two of explanation.

The *status bar* at the bottom of the window tells you how many Outlook items are displayed, or are available to be displayed, in the window. At various times while you're using Outlook, the status bar displays additional information.

The *Outlook Bar* and *Information viewer* are unique to Outlook. The Outlook Bar contains three groups of shortcuts.

The first group, labeled **Outlook Shortcuts**, provides access to Outlook Today, to the six major parts of Outlook, and to your Deleted Items folder.

If you click **Outlook Today**, you see the Outlook Today window described earlier in this chapter. Click any of the other shortcuts to see what's in one of Outlook's folders displayed in the Information viewer.

For example, if you click the **Inbox** shortcut, the Information viewer displays what's in your Inbox folder, as shown in Figure 1.5. Similarly, you can click the **Calendar** shortcut to see what's in your Calendar folder (appointments, events, meetings), and so on.

Take a few moments now to click each of the shortcuts in the **Outlook Shortcuts** group of the Outlook Bar to gain an idea of how Outlook displays different types of information. Of course, if you're using Outlook for the first time after you've installed it, your folders will be empty, or contain only sample items supplied by Microsoft.

After you click the **Inbox** shortcut in the Outlook Bar, you see the contents of your Inbox folder—the folder that contains messages you've received and not deleted or moved to another folder. To see messages you've created, click the **My Shortcuts** button near the bottom of the Outlook Bar. Then you'll see

Advanced toolbar

The toolbar you normally see is the Standard toolbar. You can also display the Advanced toolbar by opening the **View** menu and choosing **Toolbars**.

Scrolling in the Outlook Bar

The number of shortcuts visible in the Outlook Bar depends on whether you have the Outlook window maximized and on the resolution you've selected for your monitor. If you can't see all the shortcuts in a section of the Shortcut bar, click the small arrow button at the top or bottom of the bar to scroll up or down.

another section of the Outlook Bar that contains these three shortcuts:

- *Drafts*. Displays the contents of your Drafts folder. The Drafts folder contains messages you've saved but haven't told Outlook to send.

- *Outbox*. Displays the contents of your Outbox folder. The Outbox folder contains messages you've told Outlook to send, but haven't yet been sent.

- *Sent Items*. Displays the contents of your Sent Items folder. The Sent Items folder contains copies of messages Outlook has sent to your local *postoffice*.

Using Outlook to Access Your Computer Environment

Click the **Other Shortcuts** button at the bottom of the Outlook Bar to display a section containing three or more shortcuts that provide access to your computer environment:

- *My Computer*. Displays a list of disk drives to which you have access (similar to the list displayed when you choose **My Computer** from the Windows desktop).

- *My Documents or Personal*. Provides access to your Personal folder (if you've just started to use Outlook you won't have anything in this folder).

- *Favorites*. Provides access to a folder that contains shortcuts to items, documents, folders, and Uniform Resource Locators (URLs).

- *Public Folders*. Provides access to Public Folders on your Exchange Server (only included in the Outlook Bar if your *profile* contains the Microsoft Exchange Server information service).

After you've displayed the My Shortcuts and Other Shortcuts sections of the Outlook Bar, you can return to the Outlook Shortcuts section by clicking the **Outlook Shortcuts** button at the top of the Outlook Bar.

Default folders in Windows 95 and Windows NT

My Documents is the default folder that Office applications running under Windows 95 use for saving documents. *Personal* is the default folder used by Office applications running under Windows NT for saving documents.

Saving URLs

When you use Internet Explorer 4.0 as your Web browser and save a Web site as a "Favorite," that site's *Uniform Resource Locator* (URL) is saved in the Favorites folder.

What is your profile?

Your profile is information that controls how Outlook works for you. Chapter 6, "Creating a Profile," explains profiles in detail.

Creating an Outlook Item

Outlook deals with *items* of information. Outlook has six types of items; each type of item is saved in a separate folder. The types of items and the locations in which they're saved are

- *Mail item*. A message you've created or received. Mail items you've received are saved in the Inbox folder; copies of mail items you've sent on their way to recipients' mailboxes are saved in the Sent Items folder. You can save a mail item you're working on, but are not ready to send, in the Drafts folder. Mail items that Outlook is waiting to send to recipients' mailboxes are saved in your Outbox.

- *Calendar item*. An appointment, event, or meeting. These items are saved in the Calendar folder.

- *Contact item*. Information about a person or organization is saved in the Contacts folder.

- *Task item*. A task you've planned for yourself or delegated to someone else is saved in the Tasks folder.

- *Journal item*. A record of something that happened is saved in the Journal folder.

- *Note item*. Some information you want to remember and, perhaps, use later. Outlook saves note items in the Notes folder.

- *Deleted item*. When you delete any item from a folder, it becomes a deleted item and it's saved in the Deleted Items folder.

To create an item (with the exception of a deleted item), display the Information viewer for that type of item and then click the left-most button in the toolbar. For example, to create a contact item that contains information about yourself, follow these steps:

Creating a contact item

1. Click the **Contacts** shortcut in the Outlook Bar to display the Contacts Information viewer.

2. Click the New Contact button ⬚▾ at the left end of the Standard toolbar to display the Contact *form* similar to that shown in Figure 1.6.

Customizing the Outlook Bar

The preceding brief account of the Outlook Bar refers to the Outlook Bar as it appears immediately after you install Outlook. You can add more sections to the Outlook Bar and also add shortcuts to each section.

Find out more about the Outlook Bar

Read Chapter 4, "Using the Outlook Bar," and Chapter 34, "Customizing the Outlook Bar," for more information about the Outlook Bar and how to customize it.

Saving files and shortcuts in folders

In addition to saving a specific type of item, each folder can also be used to save files and shortcuts to files.

FIGURE 1.6

The contact form is shown here after information has been entered into it.

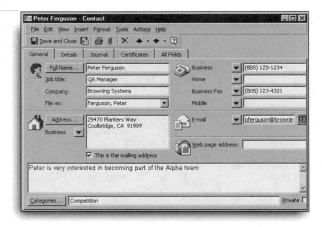

3. For the present, just enter basic information about yourself in the various text boxes on this form: your name, address, home phone number, and e-mail address.

4. When you've finished entering information, click the **Save and Close** button on the form's toolbar.

Whenever you want to create an item, Outlook provides a form for you to enter information.

Notice that when you save the new contact, the information you provided appears on an address card in the Contacts Information viewer, as shown in Figure 1.7.

Items in the Deleted Items folder are not created directly; they are created when you delete any other Outlook item. If you delete an Outlook item by mistake, you can move it from the Deleted Items folder back into its original folder. When you delete items from the Deleted Items folder, those items are permanently deleted.

SEE ALSO

➤ *For detailed information about using forms to create Outlook items, see page 141.*

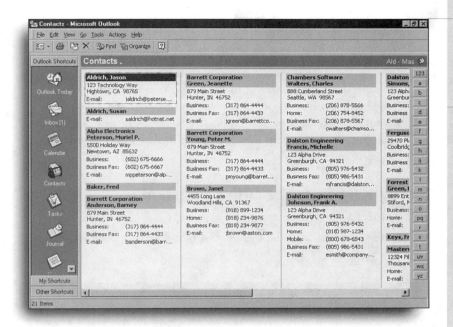

FIGURE 1.7

The Contacts Information viewer displays contact information
formatted as on an address
card.

Getting Help

Many sources of help are available for using Outlook. In addition to books (such as this one), you can turn to the following
sources for Outlook 98 Help information:

- An experienced colleague
- The Office Assistant—love it or hate it
- Online Outlook Help—the traditional help system
- Internet sites

Asking a Colleague

Despite all the resources provided by Outlook's built-in help and
all the information available in books and by way of the Internet,
your best source of information is a colleague or, perhaps, your
organization's support people. For most of us, it's much easier
(and faster) to explain a question to a person than to try to navigate our way through computerized search systems.

Nothing can replace having an experienced person sit down with you in front of your computer and work with you to solve a problem. Failing that, if you work for an organization that has a help desk, call that resource and have the help person talk you through what you're trying to do. If you don't have an experienced colleague and your organization doesn't have a help desk, however, all is not lost. The following sections of this chapter describe several ways in which you can find answers to your Outlook questions.

Getting Help from the Office Assistant

When you first start Outlook, you'll probably see the Outlook Today window with the Office Assistant superimposed, as shown in Figure 1.8.

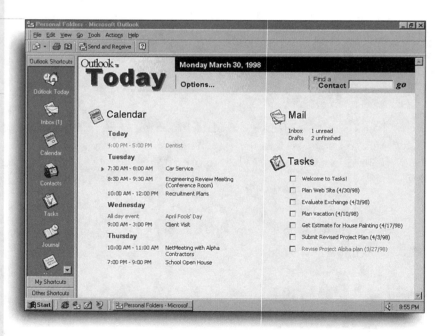

The first time you start Outlook you'll see Welcome to Microsoft Outlook in the Office Assistant balloon, followed by a list of subjects. Take the time to look at each of the subjects listed in the balloon. After you've done so, you can uncheck **Show these**

choices at startup so that Welcome to Microsoft Outlook doesn't appear the next time you start Outlook. Click **OK** to close the balloon and the Office Assistant.

At any time while you're using Outlook, you can click the Office Assistant button ⟨?⟩ in the Standard toolbar (or press Shift+F1) to bring up the Office Assistant.

Replace the text in the **What would you like to do?** box with the question you want to ask. For example, you could type What is an event, as shown in Figure 1.9. Then choose **Search**. Outlook searches its database for information about the subject in which you're interested and displays a balloon in which several topics are listed.

FIGURE 1.9

Enter your question in the Office Assistant balloon, using plain English.

Soon after you choose **Search**, Outlook displays an answer to your question. You can read the answer or print it for future reference. After you've finished, click the Close (**X**) button in the message box's title bar to close the window and return to Outlook.

If you want to use the Office Assistant again, click anywhere on it to display the balloon in which you can ask a question. To close the Office Assistant, click the Close (**X**) button on the Office Assistant title bar.

Do you want the Office Assistant to keep popping up, or would you rather ask for it when you need it? After you remove the check mark from **Show these choices at startup** in the balloon that's displayed when you first start Outlook, the Office Assistant still appears each time Outlook starts, showing the dialog box that invites you to ask a question.

If you prevent the Office Assistant from being displayed when Outlook opens, you can display it at any time by pressing F1, by choosing the Office Assistant button 🔲 on the toolbar, or by opening the **Help** menu and choosing **Microsoft Outlook Help**.

SEE ALSO

➤ *To prevent the Office Assistant from being displayed when Outlook opens, see page 90.*

Getting Traditional Help

To obtain traditional help with Outlook, open the **Help** menu to see a list of **Help** items, as shown in Figure 1.10.

FIGURE 1.10

The **Help** menu contains several sources of help.

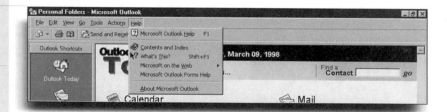

The first **Help** item, **Microsoft Outlook Help**, opens the Office Assistant.

Contents and Index displays the Help Topics dialog box that has three tabs:

- *Contents*. A list of online books that each contain information about broad topic areas. Choose the book you want to open and then choose topics within that book.

- *Index*. An index to topics on which help is available. Type the first few words of the topic in which you're interested or scroll through the list of index entries to find the information you need.

- *Find*. A means to search the entire Outlook Help system to find references to specific words or phrases. Type the word you want to find and then choose from the list of topics that contain that word.

It might take some time, but these three ways of locating information in Outlook's Help system usually lead you to what you need to know.

The third item on the **Help** menu is **What's This?**. After you choose this item, the mouse pointer changes to an arrow with a question mark next to it. Move this pointer onto any place in an Outlook window to see information about what you're pointing to.

Choose **Microsoft on the Web** to see a list of menu items that offer access to Microsoft Web sites and resources. If your computer has Internet access, you can choose among these menu items:

- *Free Stuff*. A frequently updated site from which you can download Outlook enhancements.
- *Product News*. News about Outlook and related products.
- *Frequently Asked Questions*. Tips and suggestions about using Outlook.
- *Online Support*. Access to Microsoft's KnowledgeBase where you can find answers to questions about Outlook and other Microsoft products.
- *Microsoft Office Home Page*. A regularly updated site that contains information about all members of the Office suite.
- *Send Feedback*. A Microsoft site to which you can send suggestions and comments and from which you can obtain assistance and information.
- *Best of the Web*. A site that contains suggestions for interesting Web sites to visit.
- *Search the Web*. A site at which you can choose a search engine, define the topic for which you want to search, and initiate a search for information on that topic.
- *Web Tutorial*. A tutorial about the Internet that contains sections named **Introduction**, **Surfing**, and **Advanced topics**.
- *Microsoft Home Page*. Regularly updated news, mainly about Microsoft and its products.

Microsoft Outlook Forms Help provides information you'll need when you create custom Outlook forms.

Choose the sixth item on the **Help** menu—**About Microsoft Outlook**—to display a box that contains information about the version of Outlook you're using. If you ever need to know your Product ID, you can find it here. You can choose the **System Info** button in this box to find information about your computer. Figure 1.11 shows an example of this information.

FIGURE 1.11

The Microsoft System Information dialog box contains detailed information about your computer.

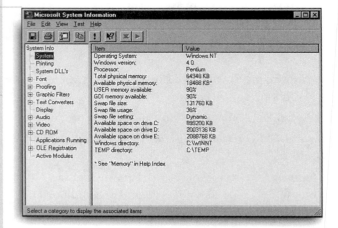

If you're using Outlook with Corporate/Workgroup Support and have set up Outlook to use Microsoft Mail for e-mail, the **Help** menu contains an item that provides help for Microsoft Mail.

If you've added add-ins to Outlook on your computer, you may see additional items in the **Help** menu, each offering help about a specific add-in.

Getting Help from Other Sources

The World Wide Web contains many sites that provide useful information about Outlook, Exchange Server, and related subjects. I won't attempt to list those sites here because site names and URLs frequently change, but one particularly useful site is

http://www.slipstick.com

This site not only contains regularly updated information about Outlook, but it also contains extensive references to other relevant sites.

You can use a search engine that provides detailed coverage of technical subjects (such as AltaVista) to search the Web for sites that interest you.

SEE ALSO

➤ *For information about using Outlook to find and open Web sites, see page 492.*

Communicating with the World

Sending and receiving e-mail

Participating in newsgroups

Sharing information in Net Folders and Public Folders

Surfing the Web

Chapter Assumptions

In this chapter, I assume you're sitting in front of a computer on which someone has already installed and set up Outlook, so you're all ready to go. If you're in the less fortunate position of having to set up Outlook for yourself, you'll have to dive into the chapters in Part II of this book before you can use Outlook.

I also assume that you have a *Corporate/Workgroup* installation of Outlook on your computer. If you have an Internet Only installation, you will not be able to use some of the features described in this chapter.

SEE ALSO

➤ *For an overview of Outlook's Corporate/Workgroup Support and Internet Only Support modes, see "The Many Faces of Outlook" on page 6.*

Sending and Receiving E-mail

Many people think of the Outlook 98 Messaging and Collaboration Client primarily as a means to send and receive e-mail, so we'll start with that aspect of Outlook's functionality.

In many ways, *e-mail* is like conventional *snail mail* (letters a mail carrier delivers to, and picks up from, the mailbox in front of your home). E-mail, however, is much faster than snail mail and, after you're set up to use it, much more convenient.

You create an e-mail message by typing it on your computer. If you want to get fancy, you can attach files that already exist on your computer to your messages. You address the message by choosing a *recipient* from one of the names in your address lists. Then you send it.

When you send a snail mail letter, you put that letter into a mailbox. A letter carrier picks up the letter and takes it to your local postoffice. That postoffice sends the letter on its way to the recipient's postoffice. From there, a letter carrier delivers the letter to the recipient's mailbox. Finally, the recipient retrieves the letter from the mailbox, opens the letter, and reads it.

Compare that with what happens when you send e-mail. Figure 2.1 illustrates the similarities between snail mail and e-mail.

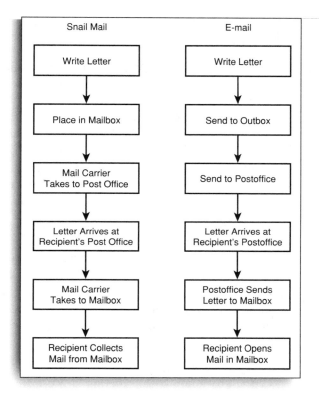

FIGURE 2.1
Many similarities exist between snail mail and e-mail.

After you've prepared a message in Outlook, you click the **Send** button to send it. The action of sending a message actually places it in a folder called your Outbox. The message waits in your Outbox until a connection is made to your local *postoffice*. As soon as that connection becomes available, the message moves to the postoffice (Outlook keeps a copy of the message in your Sent Items folder).

Let's pause here for a moment to understand what a postoffice is in the context of e-mail. If you're a member of a workgroup that uses a *peer-to-peer network*, one of the computers on the network runs the postoffice software system that routes messages between workgroup members. Your computer may be connected to a *LAN (Local Area Network)*, in which case a server exists on which messaging server software, such as Exchange Server, is running. Among many other facilities, the messaging software on the

Sending e-mail now

If your system is set up to connect to a postoffice at regular intervals, you don't have to wait for those connections to happen. You can tell Outlook to connect to a postoffice at any time.

server provides a postoffice to route messages among people who have access to the LAN.

Depending on how your system and peer-to-peer network or LAN is set up, you may have a continuous connection to your postoffice (while your computer is running and the network is up). If that's the case, messages you send to your Outbox are immediately sent on to the postoffice. Alternatively, your system may be set up to connect to the postoffice periodically, perhaps every ten minutes, every hour, or whatever. That's a lot better than waiting for the mail carrier to arrive once a day (never on Sundays and holidays) to pick up your snail mail.

What about Internet mail? As with other e-mail systems, the Internet uses postoffices to route mail between senders and recipients. If you have a direct connection to the Internet by way of your local LAN, the postoffice you use for Internet mail is probably on your LAN server. Alternatively, if you access the Internet by way of an *Internet service provider (ISP)*, that service provider probably provides an e-mail service that includes a postoffice. Your system is probably set up to connect to your Internet postoffice at regular intervals.

Let's go back now to considering how e-mail works. When a message you send arrives at your local postoffice, it's the post-office's job to do one of two things. If the message is addressed to someone who has an *account* on that postoffice, the postoffice places the message in that user's *mailbox*. If you've addressed the message to someone who has an account on a different post-office, your postoffice sends the message on its way to that user's postoffice where it is placed in the user's mailbox.

When a message arrives in your mailbox, it stays there until you access your mailbox. In some cases, a postoffice may alert you when mail arrives. Depending on the mail service you're using, you may be able to set up Outlook to do this. Again, depending on your system and network configuration, messages received in your local mailbox may be automatically moved into your Outlook Inbox, in which case Outlook Today tells you how many messages are waiting for you.

When you open Outlook and display your Inbox folder, you see a list of all the messages in your Inbox. You can select any message to display its contents in the Preview pane, or you can double-click the message to see it in the Message form.

SEE ALSO

➤ *For instructions on how to set the intervals at which your computer connects to postoffices, see page 109.*

Sending a Message

It's easy to compose and send an email message. Start by opening Outlook. You probably have Outlook Today displayed.

Preparing and sending an e-mail message

1. Click the New Mail Message button 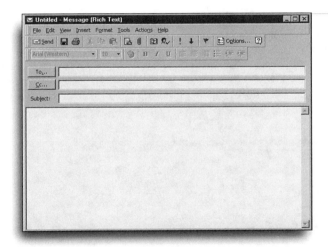 at the left end of the toolbar to display the Untitled – Message form shown in Figure 2.2.

FIGURE 2.2

Use the Message form to address and write your message.

2. Click **To** to display your list of contacts, such as the list shown in Figure 2.3.

3. Select the person to whom you want to send the message (be careful to select a person's e-mail address, not the person's fax address), choose **To** to move that person's name into the **Message Recipients** list, and choose **OK**. Now the Untitled – Message form contains the name of the recipient.

Message format

The words "Rich Text" in the Message form's title bar identify the format in which Outlook will send the message. Refer to "Choosing a Message Format" in Chapter 18 for information about message formats.

FIGURE 2.3

Choose the person to whom
you want to send your message from this list.

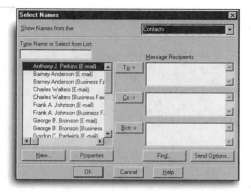

4. Move the insertion point into the **Subject** box and type the
subject of your message.

5. Move the insertion point into the large text box in the lower
part of the form. When you do so, the name of the form (in
its title bar) changes to the text you typed for the subject of
the message.

6. Type the text of your message. At this stage, the form should
look something like that shown in Figure 2.4.

7. Look over the message at this time. If necessary, you can use
normal editing methods to make corrections and changes.
When you're satisfied with it, choose **Send** in the toolbar.

FIGURE 2.4

The Message form looks like
this after you've created a
message.

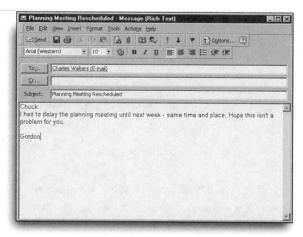

That's all there is to it. If you're curious, you can see what happened to the message you sent. You can find it either in your Outbox folder (if it hasn't yet been sent out to your postoffice), or in your Sent Items folder (if it has been sent to your postoffice). Choose the **My Shortcuts** section of the Outlook Bar, and then choose **Outbox** to see if the message is still in your Outbox, as shown in Figure 2.5, or choose **Sent Items** to see if it has been sent.

Messages in the Outbox are italicized

Messages waiting to be sent in the Outbox are displayed in italics. A message that is not italicized is an indication that Outlook has attempted to send the message but has not been able to do so.

FIGURE 2.5

A message waiting in your Outbox is displayed like this.

If the message is still in your Outbox and you want to send it now rather than wait for the next time Outlook automatically establishes a connection to the postoffice, just click **Send and Receive** in the Standard toolbar.

SEE ALSO

➤ *To create a list of contacts, see "Organizing Your Contacts" on page 48, and for more detailed information, see Chapter 15, "Creating a Contact List and Outlook Address Book."*

Receiving Messages

When you open Outlook, Outlook Today shows you how many messages you have waiting. Choose **Inbox** in the **Outlook Shortcuts** section of the Outlook Bar. The Inbox Information viewer lists all the messages in your Inbox folder, as shown in Figure 2.6.

If you think that some messages haven't yet been delivered to your Inbox folder, choose **Send and Receive** in the Standard toolbar. If any new messages arrive, you see them listed in the Information viewer.

Click any message listed in the Inbox Information viewer to see it in the Preview Pane in the lower half of the Information viewer. Alternatively, double-click a listed message to see it in the Message form.

Was your e-mail delivered?

Don't be mislead into thinking that your messages have been delivered just because they're listed in your Sent Items folder. All that means is that Outlook has sent those messages to your local postoffice. Many other steps are involved that your messages have to go through before they finally arrive at your recipients' postoffices.

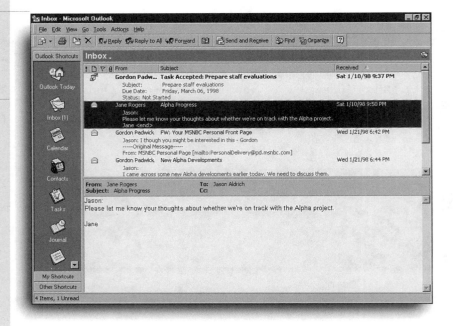

Choosing Your E-mail Format

If you previously used Outlook 97, you're probably familiar with choosing between using WordMail (Word for Windows) or Outlook's built-in editor (sometimes known as RichEdit) as the editor you use when creating e-mail. In Outlook 98, you can choose from four message formats:

- *HTML (the default).* Choose this format if you know your recipients have an e-mail client that supports HTML (the common language of the Internet). By using HTML, you can format your text (fonts, font sizes, colors, and font styles) and include graphics in your messages.

- *Microsoft Exchange Rich Text.* Choose this format if you know your recipients have an e-mail client that supports Rich Text. By using Rich Text, you have more control over fonts than is available in HTML.

- *Plain Text.* Choose this format if you don't know what your recipients use to receive your messages. This choice limits you to sending only text.

- *Microsoft Word.* Choose this format if you know your recipients have an e-mail client that supports Word 97. In this case, you can send messages that incorporate all of Word 97's formatting capabilities.

Just because you send a nicely formatted message doesn't mean recipients will see it that way. For example, if a recipient reads your message on an old terminal connected to a *legacy* main frame (many do), all that recipient sees are *ASCII* characters; for these people, you should use the Plain Text format. On the other hand, if you're sending messages to people who use the Internet, you can be sure they'll be able to see the formatting of messages you've created in the HTML format.

SEE ALSO
➤ *For detailed information about mail formats and how to change from one mail format to another, see "Selecting a Message Format" on page 293.*

Replying to a message

When you reply to a message you've received, or add comments to a message you're forwarding, Outlook attempts to use the same mail format as the original message. If that format's not available, however, Outlook resorts to the Plain Text format.

Communicating with Groups of People

In addition to e-mail, Outlook provides four other ways for you to share information with other people:

- Participating in newsgroups
- Using Public Folders
- Using Net Folders
- Participating in NetMeetings

The next few pages introduce you to each of these. You'll find detailed information about the first three in subsequent chapters of this book. See *Special Edition Using Microsoft Internet Explorer 4.0* for more information about NetMeeting.

Participating in Newsgroups

A *newsgroup* is a collection of messages accessible on a computer (*news server*). Many news servers act as the host for thousands of newsgroups. Each newsgroup focuses on a specific area of interest. For example, several newsgroups focus on various aspects of using Outlook. Many newsgroups deal with non-technical subjects such as politics, hobbies, human relationships, history, entertainment, finance, and so on.

To participate in a newsgroup, open the **Go** menu and choose **News**. Outlook calls up Outlook Express, establishes a connection to your default news server, and displays a window as shown in Figure 2.7.

FIGURE 2.7

Depending on the Outlook Express layout selected, you might not see all the components shown in this window.

1 Toolbar

2 Folder list

3 Tip of the day

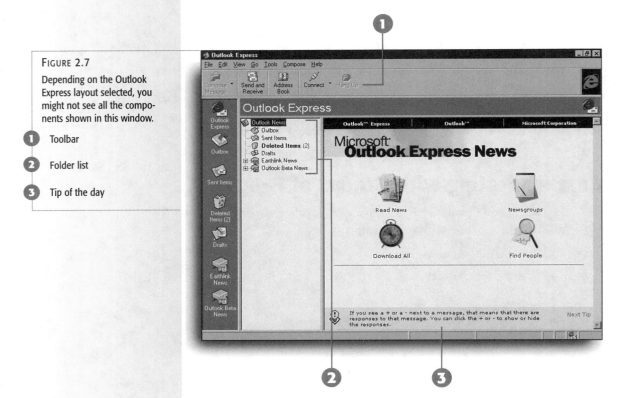

The Folder List section in Figure 2.7 includes the name of two news servers—Earthlink News and Outlook Beta News. Your Folder List probably has one or more news servers with different names listed.

If you've already subscribed to one or more newsgroups available in a news server, a box at the left of the server's name contains a plus sign. Click the plus sign (+) to display a list of newsgroups, and then select the newsgroup you want to access.

The left section of the Outlook Express window displays messages from the selected newsgroup in the upper pane. After you choose a message, the contents of that message are displayed in the lower pane, as shown in Figure 2.8.

If you haven't already subscribed to a newsgroup, or you want to look into a newsgroup to which you haven't subscribed, choose the news server and then click **News groups** on the toolbar.

Changing the size of panes

You can drag the vertical border between the left and right panes, and you can drag the horizontal border between the two panes at the right to change the size of those panes.

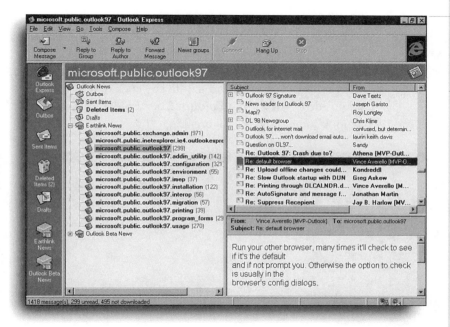

FIGURE 2.8

This is an example of how you see messages when you access a newsgroup.

After you've finished working with newsgroups, choose **File**, **Exit** in the Outlook Express menu bar to close Outlook Express and return to Outlook.

SEE ALSO
➤ For detailed information about working with newsgroups, see page 380.

Accessing Information in Public Folders

If you're using Outlook as a client for Exchange Server, you can access information in Exchange Server's Public Folders. These

Outlook as a client for Exchange Server

You must have Corporate/ Workgroup Outlook installed to use Outlook as a client for Exchange Server.

Exchange Server provides public
folders

You must have the Microsoft
Exchange information service in
your profile to access Public Folders.
If you don't have this information
service in your profile, you won't
have a Public Folders shortcut in
your Outlook Bar.

folders can contain files and shortcuts to files in addition to
Outlook items.

Accessing Public Folders

1. Choose the **Public Folders** shortcut in the **Other Shortcut**
section of the Outlook Bar.

2. If your folder list is not already displayed, open the **View**
menu and choose **Folder List** to display the folder list.

3. One of the items in the folder list is **Public Folders**. If necessary, expand the Public Folders list by clicking the **+** at the
left side of Public Folders in the folder list.

4. One of the items in the Public Folders list is **All Public
Folders**. If necessary, expand that list by clicking the **+** at
the left side of **All Public Folders**. Your **Folder List** should
now look something like Figure 2.9.

FIGURE 2.9

Select one of the listed Public
Folders to show its contents in
the right pane, as shown here.

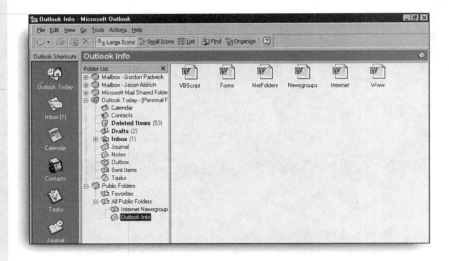

You can create Public Folders, and then save information in,
and read information from, those Public Folders from within
Outlook. Other people can save information in, and read
information from, the Public Folders you create, provided you
give them permission. Likewise, you can access Public Folders
other people have created provided they give you appropriate
permission.

To find out what permissions you have for a specific Public Folder, right-click the name of that folder to display a context menu and then choose **Properties** to display the Outlook Info Properties dialog box. Choose the **Permissions** tab of that dialog box to examine your permissions, as shown in Figure 2.10.

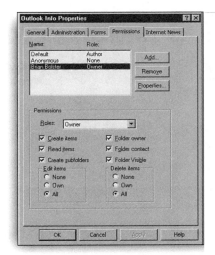

SEE ALSO

➤ *For detailed information about Public Folders, see "Using Public Folders," on page 370.*

Making Information Available in Net Folders

Just as you can use Public Folders to share information among Exchange Server clients, you can use Net Folders to share information among Internet and intranet users. To use Net Folders, you must have the optional Net Folders add-in component of Outlook installed.

You can use Net Folders to share e-mail messages, calendars, contacts, and tasks with other Outlook users and with people who don't use Outlook. Outlook users see the shared folders within Outlook on their computers in the same way they see their own folders. People who use a messaging client other than Outlook see e-mail messages you share in their Inboxes; they see items other than e-mail messages as e-mail attachments that are usually not readable.

SEE ALSO

➤ *For information about adding components to Outlook, see Appendix A, "Installing Outlook 98."*

➤ *For detailed information about using Net Folders, see "Using Net Folders" on page 497.*

Holding NetMeeting

You can use NetMeeting to hold teleconferences with other people. Your teleconferences can include

- Talking (Internet phone)
- Using two-way video
- Sharing documents and applications
- Collaboratively using applications
- Sending and receiving files
- Drawing on a shared whiteboard
- Sending messages in Chat

Of course, all participants in the teleconference must have NetMeeting installed on their computers.

Microsoft offers NetMeeting free as an independent application and bundles it with Internet Explorer 4. Because you get Internet Explorer 4 when you install Outlook 98, you also get NetMeeting.

Although NetMeeting is not an Outlook component, Outlook provides direct access to NetMeeting.

To start a NetMeeting, open the **Go** menu, move the pointer to **Internet Call**, and choose **Start NetMeeting** to display the Microsoft NetMeeting window. Use this window to start your NetMeeting.

Surfing the Web

Although surfing the Web isn't really a feature of Outlook, you can use Outlook as a convenient starting point. Open the **Go** menu and choose **Web Browser** to open Internet Explorer.

Outlook connects you to the Internet either by way of your LAN or by a dial-up connection and, all being well, you see your home page. From there, you're free to surf the Web.

Using Outlook as Your Personal Information Manager

Managing your calendar

Keeping a to-do list

Organizing your contacts

Journaling your activities

Saving miscellaneous information

Finding and organizing information

Managing Information

Having taken a quick look in Chapter 2, "Communicating with the World," at using Outlook 98 Messaging and Collaboration Client to communicate via e-mail, it's time to come back to home and take a look at using Outlook as your *Personal Information Manager* (PIM). In this chapter, you'll find a survey of how Outlook can help you manage your everyday activities.

As your Personal Information Manager, you can use Outlook to keep your calendar, address book, and to-do list close at hand.

As in Chapter 2, this chapter assumes Outlook is all set up and running on your computer.

Managing Your Calendar

You can use Outlook to help you organize your schedule for the coming weeks, months, and years. In your Outlook calendar, you can

- Block out times for appointments you have on specific days at certain times. These appointments can be one-time or recurring.
- Mark events such as birthdays, anniversaries, and other events that occur at regular intervals.
- Plan meetings at times when you and other people are available.

SEE ALSO

➤ *For detailed information about using Outlook's calendar, see Chapter 26, "Planning Your Time."*

Displaying Your Calendar

Returning to today

After you've selected another day, you can return to the current day by clicking **Go To Today** in the Standard toolbar.

Choose the **Calendar** shortcut in the Outlook Bar to display your calendar, similar to that shown in Figure 3.1.

FIGURE 3.1

When you first choose Calendar, Outlook displays the day view of the Calendar Information viewer.

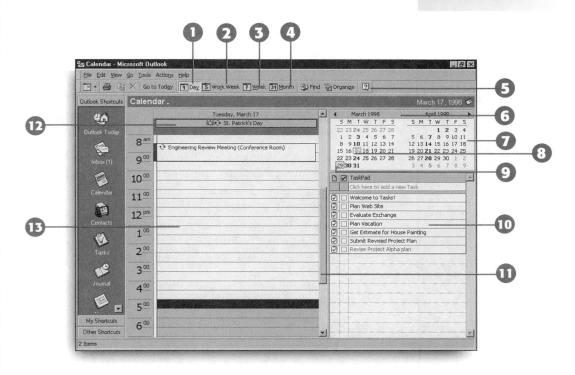

1	Day button	**8**	Selected day
2	Work Week button	**9**	Current day
3	Week button	**10**	TaskPad
4	Month button	**11**	Scrollbar
5	Standard toolbar	**12**	Event area
6	Scrollbar	**13**	Appointment area
7	Date Navigator		

Outlook initially shows the day view for the current day with appointments, events, and meetings marked. Appointments and meetings for which you've set specific times appear in the appropriate places in the appointment area. Events, which don't have a specific time, are listed in the event area at the top of the appointment area. You can display a different day by clicking that day in the Date Navigator.

The number of hours displayed in the appointment area depends on the resolution of your monitor and whether you have the window maximized. You can see additional hours by clicking the arrows at the top and bottom of the scrollbar at the right edge of the appointment area.

Outlook can display the Calendar *Information viewer* in many different *views*, some of which are supplied with Outlook and others you can create for yourself. Each view displays certain types of information in a specific format. The first time you look at the Calendar Information viewer, you see the day view. Subsequently, when you open the Calendar Information viewer, you see whichever view you most recently used.

To see some other views of your calendar, choose these buttons in the Standard toolbar:

- **Work Week** to see Monday through Friday in the appointment area
- **Week** to see Monday through Sunday in the appointment area
- **Month** to see a complete month in the appointment area
- **Day** to return to seeing a single day in the appointment area

By default, the Date Navigator pane shows two complete months (the current and following months) with today marked by a small square and the currently selected day with a gray background. You can display other months by clicking the arrows at each end of the scrollbar at the top of the Date Navigator. You can change the number of months displayed by dragging the left and bottom borders of the Date Navigator, as shown in Figure 3.2.

The TaskPad in the bottom-right of the Calendar Information viewer displays your current tasks.

How monitor resolution affects what you see

The Outlook Shortcuts section of the Outlook Bar displays six shortcuts at a time if your monitor is set for 800×600 pixel resolution. It displays only four shortcuts (and part of a fifth) if your monitor is set for 640×480 pixel resolution.

Changing work-week days

By default, Outlook considers Monday through Friday to be your work week. If your work week consists of different days, you can change this default by opening the **Tools** menu, choosing **Options**, choosing the **Preferences** tab, and choosing **Calendar Options**.

Displaying the TaskPad

When you select the month view, you'll probably find that Date Navigator and TaskPad are no longer visible. To make them visible, drag the right border of the appointment area to the left.

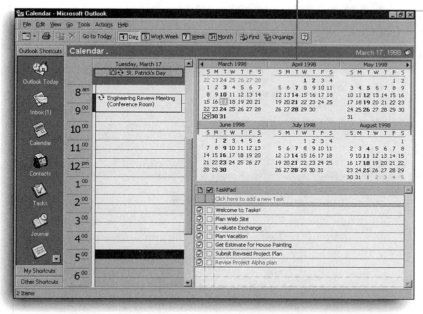

FIGURE 3.2

With the Date Navigator stretched to show more than two months, less space is available for the appointment area and TaskPad.

1 Six months are now shown in the Date Navigator

SEE ALSO

➤ *For detailed information about setting calendar options, see "Setting Calendar Options" on page 540.*

➤ *For detailed information about choosing calendar views, see page 165.*

➤ *For an explanation of current tasks, see "Keeping Track of Tasks" on page 45.*

Entering an Appointment or Event

To enter an appointment into your calendar, open the **Actions** menu and choose **New Appointment** to display the Appointment form. The form is shown with information about an appointment entered in Figure 3.3.

After you've entered the appointment information, choose **Save and Close** in the Standard toolbar to return to the Calendar Information viewer. Notice that the Date Navigator shows all dates on which you have appointments and meetings, including the one you just entered, marked in bold.

FIGURE 3.3

Information about an appointment has been entered in the Appointment form.

To review the appointment you just created, click that appointment's date in the Date Navigator; the appointment is displayed in the appointment area. The time you blocked for the appointment is marked, together with the name and location of the appointment, as shown in Figure 3.4. The bell symbol indicates you've asked Outlook to give you a reminder a certain time before the meeting. To see more information about the appointment, double-click the appointment in the appointment area; Outlook displays the Appointment form that contains information about the appointment you selected.

Marking events, such as someone's birthday, on your calendar is much like marking an appointment. Start by opening the **Actions** menu and choosing **New All Day Event**. Supply the information about the event in the Event form and choose **Save and Close** to return to the Calendar Information viewer. Use the Date Navigator to go to the date of the event you just entered. Notice that the event is displayed in the event area, as shown in Figure 3.5.

The Date Navigator doesn't show days on which you have marked events in bold, as it does for days on which you have appointments and meetings.

Entering recurring events

The preceding example shows how you enter a one-time event into your calendar. You can also enter events that recur at yearly, or other intervals.

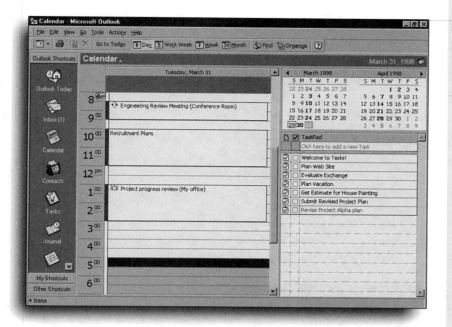

FIGURE 3.4
The appointment area shows
the subject, location, and time
of an appointment.

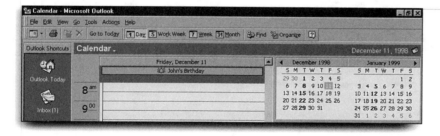

FIGURE 3.5
Events are displayed in the
event area at the top of the
appointment area.

SEE ALSO

➤ *For detailed information about using the Appointment form, see "Creating One-time Activities" on page 420.*

➤ *To set recurring appointments and events, see page 426.*

Keeping Track of Tasks

Tasks are those activities that you want to remember to do, or have asked someone else to do. Some tasks such as "Clean out the garage," don't necessarily have to be done by a specific date.

Other tasks, such as writing this book, do have to be completed by a specific date. For future tasks, such as "Buy Christmas presents," you may want to mark a date to start working on the task.

SEE ALSO

➤ *For complete information on tracking and assigning tasks, see Chapter 28, "Planning, Tracking, and Assigning Tasks."*

Entering a Task

To enter a task into your to-do list, begin by choosing the **Tasks** shortcut in the Outlook Bar. Outlook displays the Tasks Information viewer with all the tasks you've previously entered displayed, as shown in Figure 3.6. The first time you open this Information viewer, Outlook tells you There are no items to show in this view.

FIGURE 3.6

The Tasks Information viewer lists all the tasks you've previously entered and, where appropriate, each task's due date.

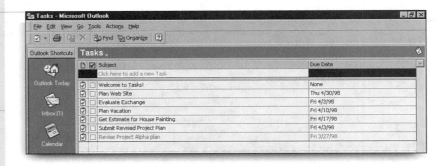

Outlook displays items in various views

By default, Outlook displays each type of item in a view that is appropriate for that item. Tasks are shown in the Simple List format.

Entering a new task

1. Click where you see Click here to add a new task and type a brief description of the task. As soon as you click, the text disappears, leaving the insertion point ready for you to start typing. Also, **None** appears in the Due Date column.

2. If you want to add a due date, click in the **Due Date** box (where None is currently displayed). Click the arrow that appears at the right end of that box to display the current month's calendar.

3. If the due date is in a subsequent month, click the arrow at the right end of the calendar's scrollbar as many times as necessary to move to the appropriate month.

4. Click the date on which the task is due. The calendar disappears and the selected date appears in the Due Date box.

5. Press Enter to move the new task into the list of tasks.

Displaying Tasks

After you've entered a task as just described, that task appears in the TaskPad in the Calendar Information viewer. That's because the task doesn't have a start date after today, so it is one of today's current tasks.

The TaskPad and the Tasks Information viewer both have two narrow columns at the left as shown previously in Figure 3.6. The first narrow column contains a symbol that indicates the status of the task (whether it's uncompleted, completed, assigned to someone else, and so on). The symbol you currently see indicates a task for yourself. The second narrow column initially contains an open box to indicate that the task is open (not completed). When you have completed the task, click the box; after you do so, Outlook places a check mark in the box and puts a line through the name of the task.

Tasks are displayed in black in the TaskPad and the Tasks Information viewer unless they are overdue, in which case they are displayed in red.

Completed tasks remain listed in the Tasks Information viewer until you delete them. By default, the TaskPad shows completed tasks until the first working day after their due dates. You can, however, modify the way Outlook selects the tasks to show in the TaskPad. For example, you can choose to include completed tasks.

SEE ALSO

➤ *For information about creating tasks and specifying start dates, see "Creating a Task for Yourself" on page 453.*

➤ *For information about changing what's displayed in the TaskPad, see "Changing the TaskPad View" on page 183.*

Organizing Your Contacts

Your business and personal activities probably involve contact with many people and organizations. You can use Outlook to remember postal addresses, e-mail addresses, phone numbers, fax numbers, and other information about these contacts. Subsequently, you can use Outlook to address letters, send messages to e-mail addresses, place phone calls, send faxes, and so on.

SEE ALSO

➤ *For detailed information about contacts, refer to Chapter 15, "Creating a Contact List and Outlook Address Book."*

Displaying Your Contacts

To begin working with contacts, choose the **Contacts** shortcut in the Outlook Bar. Outlook displays the Contacts Information viewer that, by default, shows the contacts you've already entered in Address Cards view (see Figure 3.7).

FIGURE 3.7

Outlook displays information about each of your contacts in a format similar to a conventional card index.

1 New Contact button

2 Address card

3 Scrollbar

4 Index buttons

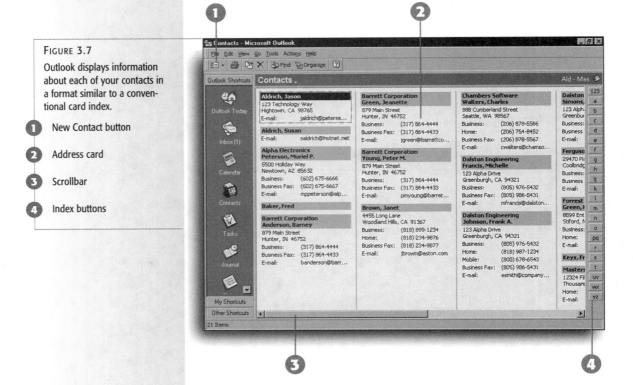

You may have hundreds of contacts entered, but Outlook can only display a few at a time. To move quickly to any contact, click the appropriate index button at the right side of the Information viewer. Alternatively, you can use your keyboard—just press the key corresponding to the first letter of the contact's name. You can also use the horizontal scrollbar at the bottom of the Information viewer to scroll through your contacts.

Entering Information About a New Contact

Each contact item can consist of information about a person or an organization. You must enter the person's or organization's name, or both. You can enter such additional information as addresses, phone numbers, and e-mail addresses.

Creating a new contact item

1. Click the New Contact button [icon] in the Standard toolbar to display the Contact form, shown in Figure 3.8. Information about a contact has already been entered.

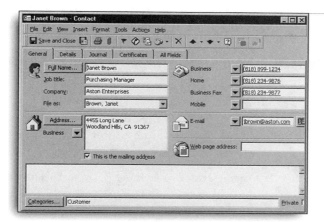

More about addresses

Outlook automatically creates a name in the **File as** box, based on the person's or organization's name. You can select the **File as** box and open a drop-down list that contains several **File as** names based on the person's name and the company name. Alternatively, you can enter any **File as** name you like, such as a person's nickname.

Outlook lets you enter three addresses for each contact. By default, the address you enter is the business address. Click the arrow at the right of the word **Business** to display a list of address names, and then choose the appropriate one.

FIGURE 3.8

Each contact item must contain the name of a person or organization. Other information is optional.

2. Enter information into the various boxes on the form. In addition to providing information in the named boxes, you can enter miscellaneous information in the large text box in the lower part of the form.

3. When you've finished entering information about the contact, choose **S**ave and Close in the form's toolbar.

After you choose **S**ave and Close, Outlook displays the information about the new contact in the Contact Information viewer. If you already have many contacts entered, you may have to choose the appropriate index button to see the card for the new contact.

SEE ALSO

➤ *For more information about creating contacts, see Chapter 15, "Creating a Contact List and Outlook Address Book."*

Editing a Contact

You can easily add, delete, or change information to an existing contact. To do so, double-click the contact you want to edit in the Contact Information viewer. Outlook displays the Contact form in which you can make changes to the existing information. After you've made the changes, click **S**ave and Close in the form's toolbar.

Using Your Contacts

This section describes some of the ways you can use contact information.

In the Contact Information viewer, click a contact to select it and then choose **Actio**ns; that menu contains several menu items you can choose to use information about the selected contact:

- *New **M**essage to Contact.* Choose this menu item to open the Message form in which you can create an e-mail message to the contact.

- *New **L**etter to Contact.* Choose this menu item to open Word's Letter Wizard that leads your through the process of writing and addressing a letter.

- *New Meeting with a Contact.* Choose this menu item to open the Meeting form in which you can create an e-mail message inviting the contact to a meeting.

- *__P__lan a Meeting*. Choose this menu item to open the Plan a Meeting dialog box in which you can look for a mutually convenient time for a meeting with that contact.

- *New __T__ask for Contact*. Choose this menu item to create a new task and send e-mail asking the contact to accept that task.

- *__C__all*. Choose this menu item to place a phone call to one of the contact's phone numbers. You must, of course, have a modem directly connected to a phone line to place a phone call in this way.

- *Call Using N__e__tMeeting*. Choose this menu item to start a teleconference with the contact.

Remembering What You've Done

You can use Outlook's Journal to keep an ongoing record of your daily activities. Outlook remembers some activities automatically; other activities you have to save manually. The Journal Information viewer displays activities in a continuous timeline view, as shown in Figure 3.9.

The Journal's timeline view groups items vertically by type, each group having a header that contains the group's name. Each group can be expanded (in which case all the items in that group are displayed) or collapsed (in which case all the items in that group are hidden). You can collapse an expanded group by clicking the minus sign at the left end of the group's header. Likewise, you can expand a collapsed group by clicking the plus sign at the left end of the group's header. You can use the vertical scrollbar at the right side of the Information viewer to scroll through Journal items.

You can choose the **Day**, **Week**, or **Month** buttons in the Standard toolbar to determine the range of time shown on your screen. You can also use the horizontal scrollbar at the bottom of the Information viewer to scroll backwards and forwards in time.

SEE ALSO

➤ *For more information about Outlook's journal, see Chapter 29, "Journaling Your Activities."*

FIGURE 3.9

The Journal's timeline view makes it easy for you to find something you did when you know the approximate date of the activity.

① **Day** button

② **Week** button

③ **Month** button

④ Horizontal scrollbar

⑤ Vertical scrollbar

⑥ Expanded group

⑦ Collapsed group

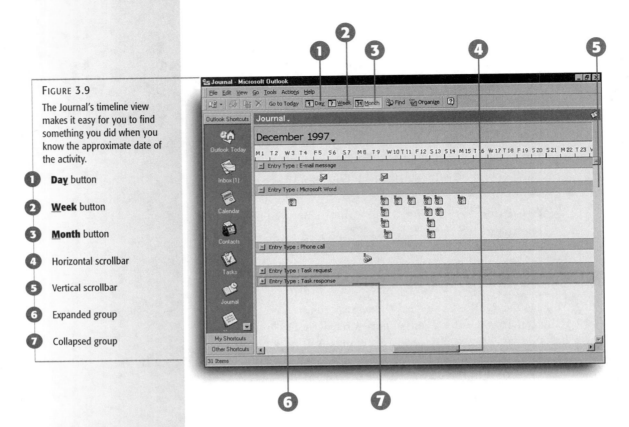

Selecting the Activities That Outlook Records Automatically

To select the activities you want Outlook to record automatically, open the **Tools** menu, choose **Options**, and then choose the **Preferences** tab of the Options dialog box. Choose **Journal Options** to display the Journal Options dialog box shown in Figure 3.10.

The **Automatically record these items** box displays a list of Outlook activities that involve contacts. Check those activities you want Outlook to record.

The **For these contacts** box displays a list of your contacts. Check those contacts for which you want Outlook to record the checked activities in the left box.

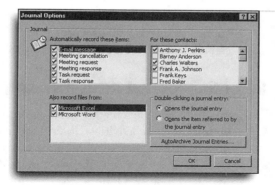

FIGURE 3.10
Use this dialog box to select the activities you want Outlook to record automatically.

The **Also record files from** box contains a list of Office applications and other compatible applications installed on your computer. After you check an application, Outlook will automatically record each time you work with one of that application's files.

Click **OK** twice to close the dialog box. After you've selected what you want Outlook to record, those items are recorded behind the scenes while you work, even while Outlook isn't running.

Recording a Phone Call

To record a phone call, first select a contact in the Contacts Information viewer. Then open the **Actions** menu, choose **Call Contact**, and select a phone number. Outlook displays the New Call dialog box shown in Figure 3.11.

FIGURE 3.11
Click **Start Call** in this dialog box to place a phone call.

If, before starting the call, you check **Create new Journal Entry when starting new call**, Outlook automatically creates a Journal item that records the date and time you placed the call,

What about calls you receive?

As just described, Outlook can automatically create a Journal item for phone calls you make. However, it can't automatically create a Journal item for phone calls you receive. You have to make these records manually, as described in the next section. Perhaps a future version of Outlook will make use of Caller ID to Journal incoming phone calls.

as well as the call's duration. This Journal item doesn't, of course, create an audio recording of the conversation, but you can make notes about the conversation within the Journal item.

Recording Journal Items Manually

You can manually create Journal items that keep records of all your significant activities. To create a manual Journal item for a phone call you receive, choose the **Journal** shortcut in the Outlook Bar, then click the New Journal button [icon] in the Standard toolbar. Outlook displays the Journal Entry form after information has been entered into it, shown in Figure 3.12.

FIGURE 3.12

Use this form to create a record of an activity.

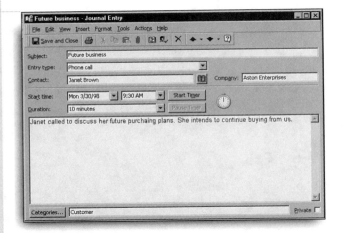

Enter information into the various boxes on the form. In addition to providing information in the named boxes, you can enter miscellaneous information in the large text box in the lower part of the form.

Choose **Save and Close** in the form's Standard toolbar to close the form.

After you've created a Journal item in this way, you can see that item in the Journal Information viewer.

Saving Miscellaneous Information

While you're working at your computer, something might happen that you want to make a note about. For example, you may be given a phone number you want to add to your list of contacts. If it's not convenient to enter it into your list of contacts at that time, you can make a note of it, and subsequently move the number into the appropriate contact item.

One important advantage of using Outlook for saving notes is that you're not likely to lose them, as you might if you just jot a note on a scrap of paper.

Saving a Note

You can use Outlook's notes to temporarily save snippets of information. Subsequently, you can move the information in notes to other Outlook folders or Windows files.

Saving a note

1. Choose the **Notes** shortcut in the Outlook Bar. Outlook displays the Notes Information viewer with any existing notes shown as icons.

2. Choose New Note in the Standard toolbar. Outlook displays a small, yellow note page with the current date and time at the bottom, as shown in Figure 3.13.

3. Type whatever you want on the note. The first line of what you type becomes the title of the note. You can type as much information as you like—the note automatically scrolls as you type.

4. When you've finished, click outside the area of the note to save it. The note is displayed in the Notes Information viewer as an icon with the first line of what you type as its title.

Using Information in a Note

You can easily copy the information from a note into an Outlook item or into an Office document.

FIGURE 3.13

A phone number has been
entered in this note.

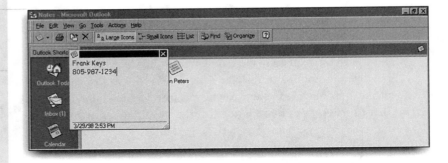

One way you copy a phone number you saved as a note into an
Outlook contact item is described in the following steps.

Moving information from a note into a contact item

1. Double-click the note in the Notes Information viewer,
   select the text you want to copy, then press Ctrl+C to copy
   the note into the Clipboard.

2. Choose the **Contacts** shortcut in the Outlook Bar to open
   the Contacts Information viewer. Then double-click the
   contact into which you want to add the phone number to
   display the Contact form with the current information about
   the selected contact displayed.

3. Place the insertion point in the large text box that occupies
   the lower part of the form, then press Ctrl+V to paste the
   text you selected in the note into that box.

4. Select the phone number in the note, then drag the phone
   number into the appropriate phone number box on the
   form.

It's even easier to copy the note into an Office document. For
example, to copy the note into a Word document:

1. Double-click the note in the Notes Information viewer,
   select the text you want to copy, then press Ctrl+C to copy
   the note into the Clipboard.

2. Open the Word document into which you want to copy the
   note.

3. Place the insertion point where you want to copy the information in the note and press Ctrl+V.

SEE ALSO

➤ *To delete a note, see "Deleting a Note," page 485.*

Finding Information

With an Information viewer open, you can choose the **Find** button in the Standard toolbar to find information in the items displayed in that viewer. For example, if you have the Inbox Information viewer displayed, choose **Find** to display the Find messages in Inbox pane at the top of the Information viewer, as shown in Figure 3.14.

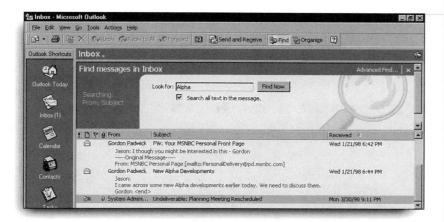

FIGURE 3.14

Enter the word or phrase you want to find in the text box.

If you want to include the text of messages in the search, check **Search all text in the message**. If you don't check this box, Outlook searches only the subjects of messages. Then click **Find Now**. Outlook searches through all the messages in your Inbox and, if it finds messages that contain what you're looking for, displays a list of those messages. After you finish using Find, choose the Close (**X**) button at the top-right of the pane to close it.

If this simple approach to searching doesn't provide what you need, click **Advanced Find** at the top right of the Find in box to display a dialog box in which you can develop more sophisticated searches.

SEE ALSO

➤ *For more detailed information about using Outlook to find information, see Chapter 13, "Finding Information."*

Organizing Information

Two principal ways exist in which you can organize Outlook items:

- By saving items in specific folders
- By assigning one or more categories to items

I suggest that when you start using Outlook, you rely on categories to organize your items. Later, if you find that some folders become inconveniently large, you should consider creating special folders for specific types of items. At that time, you'll have a good basis for deciding what folders you need.

Organizing Information in Folders

By default, Outlook saves each type of item in a separate folder. Outlook saves messages you receive in your Inbox folder, messages you've sent in your Sent Items folder, appointments, meetings, and events in your Calendar folder, and so on.

You can create your own folders so you can organize items more specifically. For example, you can create folders for messages that relate to certain subjects. You might want to create folders for messages from a specific person or about a certain project or subject.

After you've created sender- or subject-related folders for messages, you can define *Rules* that tell Outlook to put specific types of messages in certain folders.

Creating a new folder

1. Choose the **Inbox** shortcut in the Outlook Bar.

2. Open the **File** menu, choose **Folder**; choose **New Folder** to display the dialog box shown in Figure 3.15.

FIGURE 3.15
Use this dialog box to specify
the folder you want to create.

3. Enter a name for the new folder in the **Name** box.

4. Because you have previously selected the Inbox Information viewer, Outlook proposes to create a folder that contains Mail Items, as displayed in the **Folder contains** box.

5. Also because you have previously selected the Inbox Information viewer, Outlook proposes to place the new folder as a subfolder of your Inbox, as displayed in the **Select where to place the folder** list.

6. Click **OK** to create the new folder. Outlook asks whether you want to create a shortcut to the new folder in the Outlook Bar. Click **No**. The dialog box closes.

Now you have a folder ready to receive messages from a specific person and you're ready to move existing messages into that folder.

Moving existing messages to another folder

1. With the Inbox Information viewer displayed, select all existing messages from the contact whose messages you want to place in the new folder. To do so, hold down Ctrl while you click each message.

2. Choose **Organize** in the Standard toolbar to display the Ways to Organize Inbox pane at the top of the Inbox Information viewer, as shown in Figure 3.16.

Using rules to move mail messages into specific folders

After you've created a folder, you're also set to create a rule (set of instructions) that Outlook will use to automatically place messages from that person in the new folder. See Chapter 21, "Organizing Your E-mail with the Rules Wizard" for more information about using Outlook rules.

FIGURE 3.16

In this pane, you can choose to move existing messages from the contact into the new folder and also tell Outlook to place future messages from the contact in that folder.

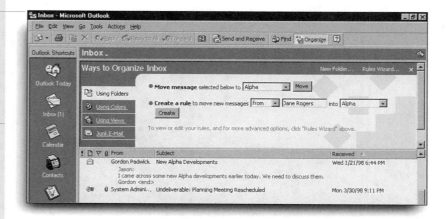

3. In the first line of the Organize pane, open the **Move message selected below to** drop-down list and select the folder into which you want to move the messages you selected in step 1.

The drop-down list of folders doesn't necessarily show all your folders. You can select **Other folder** at the bottom of the list to display the Select Folder dialog box in which you can select from all your folders.

4. Click **Move** to move the selected messages into that folder. Choose the Close (**X**) button at the top-right of the pane to close it.

You can also create a rule (set of instructions) that Outlook will use in the future to place mail you receive from a specific person in the new folder, but we'll postpone dealing with that subject until later in this book.

To see your new folder structure, choose the **View** menu and select **Folder List**. Now you'll see the new folder as a subfolder under Inbox. Select the new folder to see the e-mail items you just moved into it.

SEE ALSO

➤ *For detailed information about rules, see page 340.*

Organizing Information by Categories

You've probably noticed that the forms you use to create Outlook items, such as calendar items, tasks, and contacts, all have a text box labeled **Categories** at the bottom. You can use this box in two ways:

- Enter one or more category names in the **Categories** box, separating one name from the next with a comma.

- Choose the **<u>C</u>ategories** button, and select from a list of available categories.

After you've assigned categories to items, you can display views in which items are grouped by category. For example, to display your contacts grouped by category:

Displaying contacts grouped by category

1. Click the **Contacts** shortcut in the Outlook Bar to display the Contacts Information viewer.

2. Open the **<u>V</u>iew** menu, choose **Current View**, and then choose **By Category** to display the By Category view of your contacts, similar to that shown in Figure 3.17.

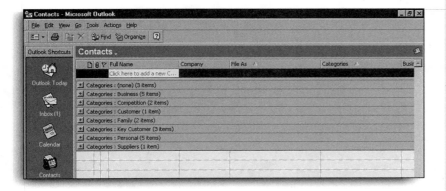

3. To see the contacts within a category, click the **+** at the left of a category name to expand that category. Figure 3.18 shows a typical expanded category.

Categories for e-mail messages

When you create an e-mail message, choose **Options** in the message form's toolbar to display a dialog box in which you can enter categories.

FIGURE 3.17
The By Category view of contacts initially shows just the names of category groups.

FIGURE 3.18

FIGURE 3.18

An expanded category group shows all the contacts to which that category has been assigned with the information in table format.

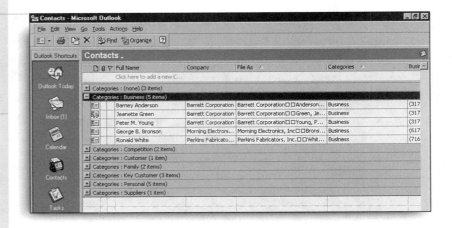

SEE ALSO

➤ *For detailed information about categories, see page 152.*

Using the Outlook Bar

Shortcuts give quick access to Outlook's principal folders

Access your computer environment by using shortcuts

Shortcuts can take you to Public Folders

The Original Outlook Bar

When you open Outlook 98 Messaging and Collaboration Client, you see the Outlook Bar at the left side of the Outlook window as shown in Figure 4.1. While you're using Outlook, the Outlook Bar is always in that position, unless you choose to hide it.

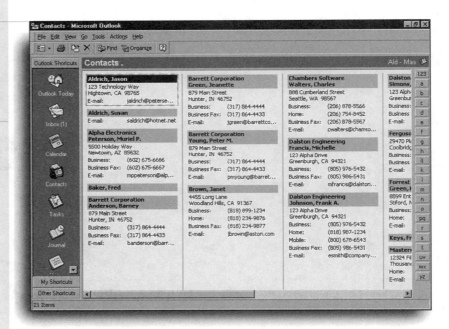

What is a shortcut?

Shortcuts are icons you can click to take you immediately into a specific parts of your computing environment. They're like the shortcuts on your Windows desktop. This chapter focuses on Outlook's shortcuts.

Unread items

The numbers in brackets at the right of some shortcuts represent the number of unread items in the folder to which that shortcut gives access.

The Outlook Bar consists of three sections, each of which contains shortcut icons that represent certain parts of your computing environment. The three sections are named **Outlook Shortcuts**, **My Shortcuts**, and **Other Shortcuts**—names that are somewhat lacking in meaning—don't worry about that, you can easily rename the sections.

Outlook initially displays those shortcuts in the **Outlook Shortcuts** section of the Outlook Bar. A button at the top of this section contains the name of the section. You don't normally see all the shortcuts in this section. Click the small arrow near the bottom of the section to display more shortcuts. After you do so, a small arrow appears near the top of the Outlook Bar section; click that button to scroll up the bar.

Two buttons at the bottom of the Outlook Shortcuts section of the Outlook Bar provide access to the other sections. Choose **My Shortcuts** or **Other Shortcuts** to display the shortcuts in those sections.

SEE ALSO

➤ *To modify the default Outlook Bar, see page 560.*

➤ *To make changes to the appearance of the Outlook Bar and to the groups of shortcuts, see page 561.*

Using Shortcuts in the Outlook Shortcuts Section of the Outlook Bar

These shortcuts in the Outlook Shortcuts section of the Outlook Bar give you quick access to most of the information within your Outlook environment:

- *Outlook Today.* A summary of your current commitments and plans
- *Inbox.* Messages you've received that Outlook has saved in your Inbox folder
- *Calendar.* A calendar that displays your appointments, events, and meetings
- *Contacts.* Information about people and organizations
- *Tasks.* Whatever is on your to-do list
- *Journal.* Outlook's record of your activities
- *Notes.* Miscellaneous information you've saved
- *Deleted Items.* Items you've deleted from Outlook's folders, but are still saved

Click any of the shortcuts in the **Outlook Shortcuts** section of the Outlook Bar to display the information in the corresponding Outlook folder.

SEE ALSO

➤ *For an introduction to using the shortcuts in the Outlook Shortcuts section of the Outlook Bar, see page 66.*

Using Shortcuts in the My Shortcuts Section of the Outlook Bar

Choose the **My Shortcuts** button near the bottom of the **Outlook Shortcuts** section of the Outlook Bar to display the three shortcuts in the **My Shortcuts** section. These three short-cuts—**Drafts**, **Outbox**, and **Sent Items**—provide access to folders with the same names as the shortcuts.

Other Shortcuts

The shortcuts in the **Other Shortcuts** section of the Outlook Bar vary, depending on your computer's operating system and the information services in your profile.

SEE ALSO

➤ *To add and delete shortcuts see page 565.*

Using the My Computer Shortcut

Print a list of folders and files

You can print a list of folders and files, something you can't do from Windows.

A **My Computer** shortcut is always at the top of the **Other Shortcuts** section unless, of course, you delete it. After you click this shortcut, you see information that's somewhat similar to what you see when you choose **My Computer** on the Windows desktop.

At first, you see a list of your computer's disk drives, as shown in Figure 4.2.

FIGURE 4.2

The My Computer Information viewer initially shows a list of your disk drives.

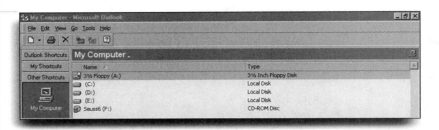

Like the information you see when you choose **My Computer** from the Windows desktop, this Information viewer includes symbols at the left to identify each item displayed. Unlike the

Windows desktop, this Information viewer has a "Type" column that describes each item.

You can right-click the name of any disk to display its context menu.

The most useful menu item in this context menu is **Properties**. Choose **Properties** to display the two-tabbed Properties dialog box. The **General** tab displays the capacity of the disk.

The **Tools** tab offers you three tools:

- *Error-Checking*. Use this tool to check the disk for errors.
- *Backup*. Use this tool to create backup copies of files on the disk.
- *Defragmentation*. Use this tool to defragment the disk.

You can double-click the name of a disk to display a list of folders and files on that disk, as shown in Figure 4.3.

Must have Windows utilities installed

These three tools are only available if the appropriate Windows utilities are installed on your computer.

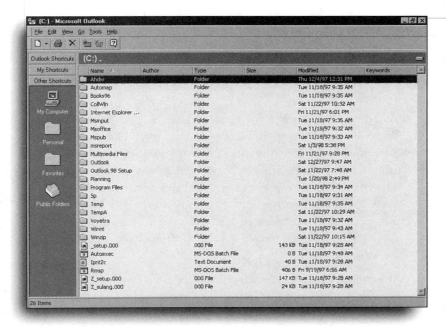

FIGURE 4.3

This Information viewer displays more information about folders and files than the corresponding display you see when you choose **My Computer** on the Windows desktop.

The list is initially displayed with folders in alphabetical order, followed by files in alphabetical order. This order is indicated by the up-pointing arrow (for ascending order) by the side of "Name" in the column titles. To reverse the order, click **Name**; now the folders and files are in reverse alphabetical order and there's a down-pointing arrow (for descending order) by the side of "Name."

You can arrange the list in ascending or descending order based on the information in any column. For example, to arrange the list in date order, click **Modified** in the column titles. Click once to arrange folders and files in ascending date order, with the earliest ones at the top of the list; click a second time to arrange the folders and files in descending date order, with the most recent ones at the top of the list.

With this list displayed, you can

- Right-click the name of any file or folder to display a context menu that provides access to the file or folder.
- Double-click the name of a folder to display the folders and files it contains.
- Double-click the name of an executable file to run it.
- Double-click the name of a file that contains data (text or graphics) to open the application associated with that file to display the text or graphics.

When you double-click the name of a file that can be displayed, Windows starts the application associated with that type of file (identified by its filename extension). If you want to display a file using a different application, click the name of the file to select it, then hold down the Shift key while you right-click the filename to display a context menu. Choose **Open With** in the context menu to display a list of applications, and then choose the application you want to use. The application starts and displays the selected file.

Although it's easy to progress through the hierarchy of folders on a disk, it may not be obvious how you step back up through the hierarchy. You must have the Information viewer's Advanced toolbar displayed. Open the **View** menu, choose **Toolbars**, and then choose **Advanced** to display the Advanced toolbar, as shown in Figure 4.4.

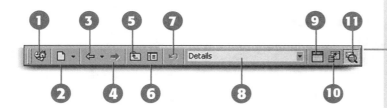

To move up one level in the hierarchy of folders, click the **Up One Level** button in the Advanced toolbar. You can also return to the top level by clicking the **My Computer** shortcut in the Outlook Bar.

Have you ever wanted to print the list of folders and files displayed by My Computer or Windows Explorer? Windows by itself doesn't let you do that, but Outlook does. Click the **My Computer** shortcut in the Outlook Bar and navigate to the folder you want to print. If the Information viewer's Standard toolbar is not displayed, open the **View** menu, choose **Toolbars**, and then choose **Standard** to display the Standard toolbar shown in Figure 4.5.

Click the Print button in the Standard toolbar to print the displayed list of folders and files.

Using Personal and My Documents Shortcuts

If you're running Outlook or **My Documents** under Windows NT, you'll have a Personal shortcut in the **Other Shortcuts** section of the Outlook Bar; if you're running Outlook under Windows 95, you'll have a **My Documents** shortcut. These shortcuts give you direct access to a folder that contains documents you've saved in the default folder.

When you're working with an Office application under Windows NT or Windows 95, the operating system proposes to save your document in a default folder. Windows NT proposes to save the document in your Personal Folder; Windows 95 proposes to save the document in your My Documents folder. You can choose to save your document in the default folder or any other folder.

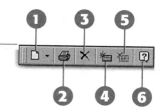

FIGURE 4.5

The Information viewer's Standard toolbar contains buttons that aren't in the Advanced toolbar.

1 New Office Document

2 Print

3 Delete

4 Map Network Drive

5 Disconnect Network Drive

6 Office Assistant

If you do choose to save your documents in the default folder, you'll see those documents listed when you choose the **Personal** or **My Documents** shortcut in the Outlook Bar. In many cases, you'll probably choose to save your documents in project-specific folders, in which case you won't see those documents listed when you choose **Personal** or **My Documents** in the Outlook Bar.

SEE ALSO

➤ *For information about adding a shortcut that gives you access to specific folders, see "Adding an Icon to an Outlook Bar Group" on page 566.*

Using the Favorites Shortcut

Whether you're running Outlook under Windows NT or Windows 95, the **Other Shortcuts** section of the Outlook Bar contains the **Favorites** shortcut. You can use this shortcut to get quick access to folders, files, and *uniform resource locators (URLs)*.

When you click **Favorites**, you see an Information viewer that contains folders and shortcuts in your Favorites folder. You can double-click a folder to open it, or double-click a shortcut to do whatever that shortcut does.

Several ways exist to place items into your Favorites folder. While you're using Internet Explorer, for example, you can save a Web site's URL as a Favorite.

Saving a Web URL as a Favorite

1. Using Internet Explorer, access the site you want to save as a Favorite.

2. In the Internet Explorer menu bar, open the **Favorites** menu and choose **Add to Favorites** to display the Add Favorite dialog box shown in Figure 4.6.

FIGURE 4.6
This dialog box offers you a choice of whether you want to be notified when there are changes to the site.

3. Accept the default choice in this box, or choose one of the alternatives if you prefer.

4. Choose **OK** to save the site's URL as one of your Favorites.

The next time you click **Favorites** in the Outlook Bar, you'll see the URL you just added in your list of Favorites, as shown in Figure 4.7.

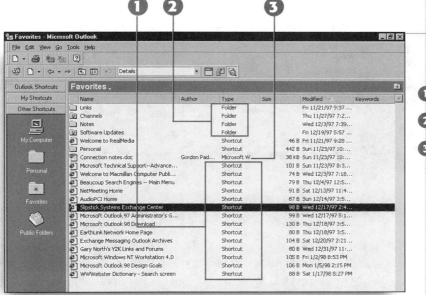

FIGURE 4.7
Your Favorites now contains the URL you just added.

❶ Files

❷ Folders

❸ URL

You can double-click this (or any other) URL in your list of Favorites to open Internet Explorer and go immediately to that site.

One way you can add a folder or file to your list of Favorites is given in the following set of steps.

Adding a file or folder to your Favorites

1. Display Outlook and Windows Explorer side by side on your screen. You only need to be able to see the Outlook Bar in the Outlook window, as shown in Figure 4.8.

FIGURE 4.8

In the Outlook window, display the **Other Shortcuts** section of the Outlook Bar.

Creating a shortcut or copying a file

By following the previous steps, you place a shortcut to the folder or file in your Favorites, leaving the folder or file in its original place. You can also move the file or folder into your Favorites folder by pressing Shift instead of Ctrl while you drag; you will rarely, if ever, want to do that.

2. In the Windows Explorer window, navigate to the folder or file you want to copy to your Favorites.

3. Hold down the Ctrl key while you drag the folder or file from the Windows Explorer window to the **Favorites** short-cut in the Outlook window. Release the mouse button and then release the Ctrl key. A context menu appears.

4. If you are satisfied with the folder or file you selected, choose **C**opy Here. Otherwise, choose **Cancel**.

You can drag as many folders or files as you like into your Favorites folder in this way. When you've finished, close

Windows Explorer and then maximize Outlook. Now you'll see the new shortcuts in your Favorites. Double-click a shortcut to a folder to open that folder and see its contents; double-click a shortcut to a file to open or run the file.

To delete a shortcut from your Favorites, select that shortcut, and then click the Delete button ☒ in the Standard toolbar.

Where deleted shortcuts go

Outlook moves shortcuts you delete into your Recycled folder, not into Outlook's Deleted Items folder.

Using the Public Folders Shortcut

If you have the Exchange Server information service in your profile, you probably have a **Public Folders** shortcut in the **Other Shortcuts** section of the Outlook Bar. Click the **Public Folders** shortcut to display the Public Folders Information viewer. Open the V**iew** menu and choose **Folder List** to see your folders.

When you first open the Public Folders Information viewer, you may see a message telling you that the folder contains only subfolders. If this happens, click **Public Folders** in the viewer's banner to display a list of folders. If necessary, expand the Public Folders folder to see the folders it contains—Favorites and All Public Folders. Expand All Public Folders to display a list similar to that in Figure 4.9.

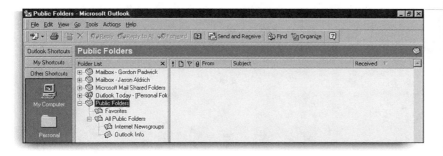

FIGURE 4.9

This is a typical list of Public Folders on your Exchange Server.

You can click the name of any Public Folder in the list and work with it.

SEE ALSO

➤ *For additional information about Public Folders, see Chapter 23, "Sharing Information with Public Folders and Newsgroups."*

Working with Outlook

Controlling How Outlook Starts

When to use Outlook and when to use Outlook Express

Starting Outlook by clicking a desktop icon

Starting Outlook automatically when you start your computer

Optimizing the way Outlook starts

Setting up Windows for Outlook

Choosing Whether to Use Outlook or Outlook Express

If you've just installed Outlook 98 Messaging and Collaboration Client, you'll have an icon named **Microsoft Outlook** and another named **Outlook Express** on your Windows desktop. You can click either icon according to the application you want to start.

Outlook gives you access to a full range of messaging and information management capabilities; Outlook Express provides the capability to send and receive Internet e-mail messages, to interact with newsgroups on the Internet, and to participate in NetMeetings.

Some of the functionality you expect from a full-featured communications application doesn't exist within Outlook, but does exist within Outlook Express or Internet Explorer. That's of no concern because you get Outlook Express with Internet Explorer 4.0, and the Outlook installation process automatically installs Internet Explorer on your computer if you don't already have it.

Some of the points to bear in mind when you choose whether to open Outlook or Outlook Express are

- Outlook Express is a simpler application to use and requires far less of your computer resources than Outlook.
- From Outlook Express you can't switch into Outlook. In contrast, from within Outlook you can call on Outlook Express's newsgroup capabilities.
- Although you can use both Outlook and Outlook Express to send and receive Internet e-mail, each application stores messages in different folders.

Unless you have limited computer resources, I recommend that you normally start Outlook and let Outlook call on Outlook Express whenever you want to access newsgroups. That way, you'll use Outlook for your e-mail and personal information.

Starting Outlook from the Desktop Icon

After you've sorted a few things out (as described in this chapter), you can just click the **Microsoft Outlook** icon on the Windows desktop to start Outlook. Within a couple of seconds, the Outlook Today window is displayed. However, this probably won't happen the first time you try to run Outlook.

When you first start Outlook, you'll probably see a Choose Profile dialog box similar to that shown in Figure 5.1.

FIGURE 5.1

The Choose Profile dialog box opens allowing you to select the desired profile.

What you do at this point depends on whether you have previously used Outlook 97 or Windows Messaging (previously known as Microsoft Mail) on the same computer that you're now using for Outlook 98. If you have, you already have one or more profiles tailored to your needs. Open the drop-down **Profile Name** list in the Choose Profile dialog box, choose the profile you normally use, and click **OK** to let the startup process continue.

On the other hand, if you haven't previously used Outlook 97 or Windows Messaging, the only profile available is the one named Microsoft Outlook.

If your computer isn't connected to a network on which Exchange Server is running, you'll see a message telling you that Your Microsoft Exchange Server is unavailable. Choose **Work Offline** to continue the startup process.

After you have Outlook running, you can specify which profile Outlook should automatically select each time it starts, and whether the Choose Profile dialog box should appear.

Ask your LAN administrator for your profile

If you work in an organization that has a *local area network (LAN)*, your LAN administrator can probably provide you with the profile you need. Otherwise you'll have to refer to Chapter 6, "Creating a Profile," to find out how to create your own profile.

Setting profile options

1. Open the **Tools** menu and choose **Options** to open the Options dialog box (see Figure 5.2).

FIGURE 5.2

By default, Outlook proposes to prompt you for a profile each time it starts.

2. Select the **Mail Services** tab.

3. To have Outlook automatically select a specific profile and start without prompting you for a profile name, choose **Always use this profile**. Then open the drop-down list of profile names, and select the one you want Outlook to use.

4. Click **OK** to close the dialog box.

The next time you start Outlook, it will start using the profile you just selected without asking you to choose a profile. You can, of course, go back to the Options dialog box at any time to select a different profile.

SEE ALSO

➤ *For detailed information about profiles, see Chapter 6, "Creating a Profile."*

Starting Outlook Automatically When You Turn on Your Computer

After you start using Outlook, you'll probably get into the habit of opening Outlook at the beginning of each day. It's convenient, then, for Outlook to open automatically.

Setting Outlook to open on startup

1. If Outlook is running, open the **File** menu and choose **Exit and Log Off** to close Outlook.

2. Choose **Start** on the Windows taskbar, choose **Settings**, and then choose **Taskbar & Start Menu** to open the Taskbar Properties dialog box.

3. Choose the **Start Menu Programs** tab and then choose **Add** to display the Create Shortcut dialog box.

4. Choose **Browse** to display the Browse dialog box.

5. In the **Look in** drop-down list, select the disk drive (probably C:) that contains Outlook.

6. Navigate to the folder that contains Outlook (probably Msoffice\Office). This folder is similar to that shown in Figure 5.3.

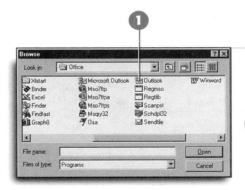

FIGURE 5.3

Make sure to find the file named Outlook or Outlook.exe.

❶ Outlook file

7. Double-click Outlook.exe or Outlook to return to the Create Shortcut dialog box shown in Figure 5.4.

8. Choose **Next** to display the Select Program Folder dialog box shown in Figure 5.5.

9. Select the Startup folder (make sure you don't select Start Menu) and click **Next** to display the Select a Title for the Program dialog box.

10. Enter a name, such as Outlook Startup, for the shortcut and then choose **Finish** to return to the Taskbar Properties dialog box. Choose **OK** to close the dialog box.

Filename extension

Depending on how your computer is set up, executable files such as Outlook.exe may be displayed with or without the filename extension.

FIGURE 5.4

The **Command line** box contains the complete path and filename of the file that runs to start Outlook.

FIGURE 5.5

The folder named Startup contains applications that run automatically when Windows starts.

1 Startup folder

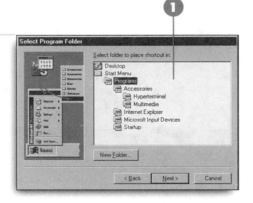

The next time you start Windows, Outlook will be opened immediately.

Choosing an Information Viewer to Display When Outlook Starts

By default, Outlook displays the Outlook Today window when it starts. You can choose to display one of Outlook's Information viewers instead, and you can make other choices about what happens when Outlook starts.

Selecting a default Information viewer

1. Start Outlook and then open the **Tools** menu, choose **Options**, and select the Other tab. Then choose **Advanced Options** to display the Advanced Options dialog box shown in Figure 5.6.

FIGURE 5.6
You can use this dialog box to choose what Outlook displays when it opens.

2. Open the **Startup in this folder** drop-down list and select the Outlook folder whose contents you want Outlook to initially display.

3. Click **OK** twice to close the dialog boxes.

After you've done this, when Outlook starts, it will display the Information viewer you selected. To return to displaying Outlook Today at startup, you can repeat the preceding three steps.

Displaying Outlook Today when Outlook starts

1. Click the **Outlook Today** shortcut in the Outlook Bar to display the Outlook Today window.

2. Choose **Options** at the top of the Outlook Today window to display the Outlook Today Options window.

3. Check the box labeled **When starting, go directly to Outlook Today**.

4. Choose **Back to Outlook Today** at the top of the window to return to the Outlook Today window.

Making Other Startup Choices

Whether you start Outlook by clicking its icon on your Windows desktop, or have Outlook start automatically when you start Windows, Windows executes a command line to run the Outlook.exe program file. You saw an example of such a command line earlier in Figure 5.4.

To make Outlook behave in various ways when it starts, you have to modify the properties of an Outlook shortcut. One of these properties is the command line. By modifying shortcut properties you can

- Make Outlook always open in a maximized window.
- Always have the opportunity to choose a profile before Outlook opens.
- Make Outlook always open with a specific profile selected.

Before continuing, you must have a clear understanding of the icons on your Windows desktop—not all of them are shortcuts. The next section gives you more information on creating shortcuts.

Creating Shortcuts

We often think of all the icons on the Windows desktop as shortcuts because all of them seem to act as shortcuts. In fact, some of these icons represent programs or files themselves, although others represent shortcuts to those programs or files. Each icon that is truly a shortcut has a small square containing an up-and-to-the-right-pointing arrow in its bottom-left corner. Look closely at your desktop—you'll probably see that the Microsoft Outlook icon isn't a shortcut, whereas the Outlook Express icon is a shortcut.

Normally, whether an icon on your desktop is or isn't a shortcut is not a matter of concern. You just double-click an icon to start an application or open a file. When you want to work with Outlook command line options, however, you have to be working with an Outlook shortcut, not with an icon that represents Outlook itself.

Because the Outlook installation process creates an icon on your desktop, rather than a shortcut, you have to create the shortcut yourself.

Creating an Outlook startup shortcut

1. From the Windows desktop, open Windows Explorer and navigate to the folder that contains Outlook.exe (probably C:\Msoffice\Office).

2. Locate **Outlook.exe** (according to your setup, you may not see the filename extension—the file you're looking for in that case is named Outlook and its type is Application).

3. Select **Outlook.exe** (or **Outlook**), then open the **File** menu and choose **Create Shortcut**. An item named **Shortcut to Outlook.exe** appears at the bottom of the list of files in the folder.

4. Drag **Shortcut to Outlook.exe** from Windows Explorer onto your desktop to create an icon on the desktop. This icon is a shortcut.

5. Close Windows Explorer and place the new icon wherever you want on the desktop.

6. While the shortcut is still open on your desktop, you may want to change its name from Shortcut to Outlook.exe to something more specific. Right-click the icon to display its context menu, and then choose **Rename**. Now you can edit the displayed name.

7. Click any unoccupied space on your desktop to close the shortcut.

Now you have an Outlook shortcut icon you can modify to contain command line switches.

Modifying Your Outlook Shortcut

To modify an existing Outlook shortcut, close Outlook and then right-click a Microsoft Outlook shortcut (not an icon that directly represents Outlook) on your Windows desktop to display the shortcut's context menu. Choose **Properties** in that menu to display the Shortcut to Outlook Properties dialog box shown in Figure 5.7.

FIGURE 5.7

You can control how Outlook
starts by making choices in
this dialog box.

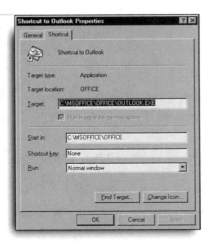

To choose several ways for Outlook to open, create several
Outlook shortcuts on your Windows desktop and set different
properties for each.

To create a copy of the Microsoft Outlook shortcut, right-click
the shortcut and choose **Copy** from the context menu. Then
right-click an empty space on the Windows desktop and choose
Paste Shortcut from the context menu.

If you always want Outlook to be maximized when it starts, open
the **Run** drop-down list box near the bottom of the Shortcut to
Outlook Properties dialog box, and select **Maximized**.

You can make other changes to the way Outlook starts by
appending a switch to the text in the **Target** box. By default, the
text in this box contains the complete path of the program that
starts Outlook—something like this:

```
C:\MSOFFICE\OFFICE\OUTLOOK.EXE
```

You can add switches to this text. For example, if you want
Outlook to open without displaying the Outlook Bar, place the
insertion point at the right end of the text in the **Target** box,
press the Spacebar once, and then type /folder. Now the command line in the **Run** box looks something like this:

```
C:\MSOFFICE\OFFICE\OUTLOOK.EXE /folder
```

Subsequently, when you start Outlook, it's displayed without the Outlook Bar—this might be the way you'd like to initially see Outlook Today.

Perhaps you normally run Outlook under one profile but occasionally want to use a different profile. As explained earlier in the "Starting Outlook from the Desktop Icon" section, you can open the **Tools** menu, choose **Options**, and then select the **Mail Services** tab. In the **Mail Services** tab you can select a profile that Outlook will use when you click the normal Microsoft Outlook icon on the Windows desktop. That solves half of the problem.

You can create an Outlook shortcut on your desktop and modify its properties so when you double-click that shortcut, you are offered a choice of profiles, even though Outlook's options are set for it to open without showing that list.

Using a switch to direct Outlook to open the Choose Profile dialog box

1. Create an Outlook shortcut on your Windows desktop, as explained earlier in this section.

2. Right-click that shortcut to display its context menu, then choose **Properties** to display the Shortcut to Outlook Properties dialog box. Select the **Shortcut** tab, shown previously in Figure 5.7.

3. Append a space and then the switch /profiles to the command line in the **Run** box then click **OK** to close the dialog box.

In addition to the two switches /folder and /profiles described in the preceding examples, there are several others you should know about. Table 5.1 contains a complete list of Outlook's command line switches.

Displaying the Outlook Bar if it's missing

After you've opened Outlook without the Outlook Bar displayed, you can open the **View** menu and choose **Outlook Bar** to display the Outlook Bar.

TABLE 5.1 **Outlook command line switches**

Command Line Switch	Purpose
/a "filename"	Open the Outlook Message form with the specified file as an attachment
/c.ipm.activity	Open the Outlook Journal Entry form

continues…

More than one Outlook shortcut on your desktop

If you frequently open Outlook and go immediately to a particular folder or form, consider creating a shortcut on your Windows desktop for that purpose. You can create as many shortcuts as you need.

TABLE 5.1 Continued

Command Line Switch	Purpose
/c ipm.appointment	Open the Outlook Appointment form
/c ipm contact	Open the Outlook Contact form
/c ipm.note	Open the Outlook Message form
/c ipm.post	Open the Outlook Discussion form
/c ipm.stickynote	Open the Outlook Note form
/c ipm.task	Open the Outlook Task form
/c "message class"	Create an item of the specified message class
/CleanFreeBusy	Clean and regenerate free/busy information
/CleanReminders	Clean and regenerate reminders
/CleanSchedPlus	Delete all Schedule+ data from the server and allow the free/busy information in the Outlook calendar to be used by Schedule+ users
/CleanViews	Restores default views
/Folder	Hide the Outlook Bar
/Profiles	Offer a choice of profiles at startup (regardless of the setting in the Options dialog box)
/Profile "profilename"	Open using the specified profile (regardless of the setting in the Options dialog box)
/ResetFolders	Restores missing folders for the default delivery location
/ResetOutlookBar	Rebuild the Outlook Bar
/select "folder name"	Open with the contents of the specified folder displayed

You can append more than one switch to a command line.

Having Two or More Outlook Windows Visible

You may be one of those fortunate people who have large monitors—17 inches or more. If that's the case, you can often speed your work by having two or more Outlook Windows visible at the same time. For example, it's often convenient to display your Inbox and Calendar simultaneously.

Displaying your Inbox and Calendar simultaneously

1. Open Outlook as you normally do and click **Inbox** in the Outlook Bar to display your Inbox Information viewer.

2. If your Outlook window is maximized, click the **Maximize/Restore** button in the title bar and drag the borders of the window so it occupies about a quarter of your screen—make sure the Outlook Bar is visible.

3. Right-click **Calendar** in the Outlook Bar to display the context menu.

4. Choose **Open in New Window** to display the Calendar Information box in a separate window.

5. If the new window is maximized, click the **Maximize/Restore** button in its title bar. Then position and size the window so that it occupies the remainder of the screen, as shown in Figure 5.8.

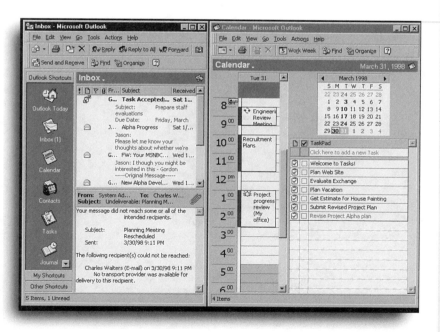

FIGURE 5.8

With two Outlook windows displayed, click either window to activate it. Alternatively, press Alt+Tab to switch from one window to the next.

Viewing two profiles at once

I've been asked if it's possible to open two instances of Outlook, using different profiles, to see two people's calendars, messages, or whatever, side by side on the screen. It doesn't seem to be possible. How about it, Outlook team at Microsoft?

Now you can refer to your calendar while you read messages you've received. Instead of having the windows side by side on your screen, you can maximize them and then press Alt+Tab to bring each window up in turn.

Displaying or Hiding the Office Assistant

By default, the Office Assistant appears whenever you start Outlook. After you've started Windows a few times, you'll become weary of having to close the Office Assistant so you can get on with your work (even though all you have to do to close the Office Assistant is press Enter).

Hiding the Office Assistant

1. In the Welcome to Microsoft Office! balloon, remove the check mark from **Show these choices at startup**.

2. Right-click the Office Assistant's title bar to display its context menu.

3. Choose **Options** in the context menu to display the Office Assistant dialog box. Selection the **Options** tab shown in Figure 5.9.

FIGURE 5.9

The choices you make in this dialog box control when the Office Assistant is displayed.

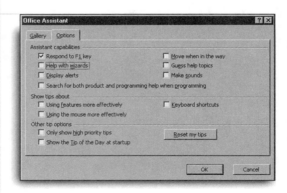

4. Remove the check marks from all the check boxes except **Respond to F1 key**; then click **OK**.

Subsequently, when you start Outlook you won't see the Office Assistant. You can call up the Office Assistant whenever you want either by pressing F1 or by opening the **Help** menu and choosing **Microsoft Outlook Help**.

Starting Outlook Express

Double-click the **Outlook Express** shortcut on the Windows desktop to start Outlook Express. Almost immediately you see the Outlook Express window, as shown in Figure 5.10.

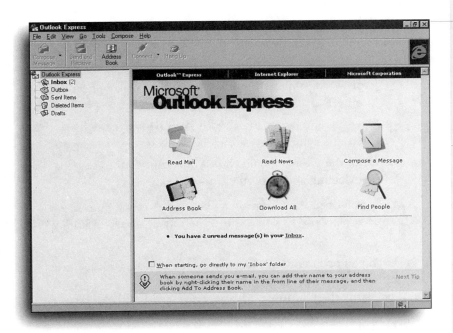

FIGURE 5.10

The Outlook Express window consists of a pane that lists the available folders and a pane that provides access to various things you can do. You might also see the Outlook Bar at the left.

This book is primarily about Outlook, rather than Outlook Express, so we won't go into details about using Outlook Express as a separate application.

Notice, however, that the Outlook Express toolbar contains buttons named **Compose Message**, and **Send and Receive**. Also notice that the list of folders contains Inbox, Outbox, Sent Items, and Drafts. You can use Outlook Express to send and receive Internet e-mail messages but, if you do, these messages are kept in separate folders from those you send and receive

Using Outlook or Outlook Express for e-mail

You should decide to use either Outlook or Outlook Express for your Internet e-mail. If you use Outlook for other types of e-mail, you should also use Outlook for Internet e-mail.

using Outlook. Although Outlook Express contains folders that have the same names as those in Outlook, they are not the same folders.

Accessing Outlook Express from Outlook

When you're working in Outlook and decide to use a capability that's in Outlook Express or Internet Explorer, Outlook automatically opens Outlook Express or Internet Explorer to provide that capability.

For example, in Outlook you can

- Open the **Go** menu and choose **News** to access Outlook Express's capability of interacting with newsgroups on the Internet.
- Open the **Go** menu and choose **Web Browser** to open Internet Explorer so you can access Web sites.
- Open the **Go** menu and choose **Internet Call** to call up NetMeeting and start an electronic conference.

When you open the **Go** menu and choose **News**, Outlook Express opens and its window is displayed, as shown in Figure 5.11.

When you open Outlook Express from Outlook, you can't use Outlook Express to send and receive Internet e-mail messages. That's why the **Compose Message** and **Send and Receive** buttons in the toolbar are dimmed and the Inbox folder is not listed; also, the Read Mail, Address Book, and Compose a Message buttons are missing. You can, however, use Outlook Express to send messages to, and receive messages from, newsgroups.

After you've finished using Outlook Express, open the **File** menu and choose **Exit** to close Outlook Express and return to Outlook.

SEE ALSO

➤ *For information about accessing newsgroups see Chapter 23, "Sharing Information with Public Folders and Newsgroups."*

FIGURE 5.11
Notice the differences between this Outlook Express window and that shown previously in Figure 5.10.

Choosing Windows Settings

To use Outlook properly, you should make sure that certain Windows settings are set correctly. To work with Outlook, you need to choose an appropriate resolution for your monitor. Outlook relies on your computer's internal clock, so you must make sure the clock is set correctly. You should also make sure that Regional Settings is correct.

Setting Your Monitor Resolution

Outlook's Information viewers can contain a lot of information. To show as much information as possible, you should set the resolution of your monitor so you can see as much as you want to but not, of course, to the extent that the text is difficult to read.

If you have a 15-inch or 17-inch monitor, you'll probably be comfortable using a resolution of 800×600 pixels. If you have a larger monitor, 1024×768 pixels might be better. If you're on the

Learn more about advanced Windows 95 settings

For detailed information on Windows settings, refer to a book such as *Using Windows 95* or *Using Windows NT Workstation 4.0*, both published by Que.

Maximum resolution depends on your hardware and software

The maximum resolution you can use depends on the capabilities of your graphics card, graphics driver, and monitor.

road with a laptop, you'll probably prefer the standard VGA resolution of 640×480 pixels.

Adjusting your monitor resolution

1. With the Windows desktop displayed, choose **Start** on the Windows desktop, **Settings**, and then **Control Panel**.

2. On the Control Panel, double-click **Display** to open the Display Properties dialog box. Choose the **Settings** tab.

3. In the **Desktop Area** section of the dialog box, drag the slider to the right to increase the resolution or to the left to decrease it.

4. Choose **Test** to check whether your monitor can display the resolution you've selected.

5. You'll see a message asking you to confirm whether you saw the test bitmap correctly. Click **Yes** or **No**.

6. If you clicked **No**, you'll have to go back to your previous resolution. If you clicked **Yes**, click **OK** to accept the new resolution; you might see a message telling you to restart Windows.

Making Sure Your Computer's Clock Is Correct

Much of what you do in Outlook involves dates and times. When you click **Calendar** in the Outlook Bar, Outlook displays your commitments for today; when you send an e-mail message, Outlook marks that message with the current date and time; when Outlook creates a Journal item, Outlook records the item with the date it was created.

All this depends on your computer knowing the current date and time. As you probably know, your computer keeps track of the date and time, but it's not a Rolex watch. From time-to-time you should check to make sure your computer knows the current date and time and, if necessary, make corrections.

Setting your computer's clock

1. With the Windows desktop displayed, choose **Start** in the Windows taskbar, then **Settings**, and **Control Panel**.

2. In the Control Panel, double-click **Date/Time** to display the Date/Time Properties dialog box that displays the current date and time.

3. As necessary, correct the displayed date and time; then click **OK**.

Checking Your Computer's Regional Settings

Outlook uses your computer's regional settings to automatically provide a country name when you create a new contact—you can, of course, provide a different country name for foreign contacts.

Checking regional settings

1. With the Windows desktop displayed, choose **Start** in the Windows taskbar, then **Settings**, and **Control Panel**.

2. In the Control Panel, double-click **Regional Settings** to display the Regional Settings Properties dialog box.

3. If the region displayed is not correct, open the drop-down list of regions and choose the appropriate one; then click **OK**.

Creating a Profile

No profiles in Outlook with Internet Only Support

If you've installed Outlook with Internet Only Support, you will notice that profiles are not used. You'll only need to know about profiles if you've installed Outlook with Corporate/Workgroup Support.

Windows default profiles

The process of installing Windows 95 or Windows NT on a computer creates a profile that controls how messages are delivered to and from a Windows Messaging (previously called Exchange) mailbox. After installing Outlook, you have a profile that has more extensive control over your messaging environment.

What Is a Profile?

A *profile* is information that defines how Outlook 98 Messaging and Collaboration Client works. A profile contains the following:

- *Information Services*. A list of information services and the properties of each of those services.
- *Delivery*. The location to which new e-mail should be delivered, and the order in which information services processes the mail you send.
- *Addressing*. The default Address Book to use when addressing e-mail and the order in which address books should be searched to verify recipients' names.

Each computer on which Outlook is installed has one or more profiles.

Why would a computer have more than one profile? Suppose you have a laptop. Most of the time you use the laptop in your office and have it connected to your LAN. You take your laptop with you when you travel—it's not connected to anything when you use it on a plane; it may be connected to your LAN by way of a dial-up connection when you're in your hotel room. You need three profiles:

- One to use when you're in your office
- Another to use while you're flying
- Yet another to use in your hotel room

Or suppose you share a desktop computer with other people. Each person requires a separate profile in order to keep information separate from other users' information.

The following pages of this chapter will help you understand more about profiles and their contents.

Viewing and Modifying a Profile from the Windows Desktop

After you install Outlook 98 on your computer, you have a profile named Microsoft Outlook. You can examine and modify a profile either from the Windows desktop or from within Outlook. This section deals with viewing and modifying profiles from the Windows desktop.

If you've not previously used Outlook 97 on your computer, you'll have the default Microsoft Outlook profile; if you have previously used Outlook 97 and modified the Microsoft Outlook profile, then you'll have that modified profile. The following paragraphs assume that you haven't modified the Microsoft Outlook profile.

Viewing a Profile from the Windows Desktop

1. From the Windows desktop, choose **Start** to display the **Start** menu. In that menu, choose **Settings** and then choose **Control Panel** to display the Control Panel.

2. In the Control Panel, double-click **Mail**. You'll see a Properties dialog box that contains information about your current default profile.

3. Choose **Show Profiles** to display a list of profiles available on your computer.

4. Select **Microsoft Outlook** and choose **Properties** to display the properties of the Microsoft Outlook profile, as shown in Figure 6.1.

The Microsoft Outlook Properties dialog box opens with the **Services** tab selected. This tab shows you the services available in the Microsoft Outlook profile. Each service provides a way for Outlook to handle information:

- The Microsoft *Exchange Server* information service provides a way for Outlook to call on Exchange Server for information.

- The Outlook *Address Book* information service gives Outlook access to information in your Outlook address book.

- The *Personal Folders* information service lets Outlook save and retrieve information from your personal folders.

FIGURE 6.1

The Microsoft Outlook profile contains certain information services.

SEE ALSO

➤ *To learn more about Exchange Server, see Chapter 22, "Using Outlook as an Exchange Server Client."*

➤ *To learn more about the Outlook Address Book, see "Creating an Outlook Address Book" on page 262.*

➤ *To learn more about Personal Folders, see "Using Personal Folders File" on page 201.*

Adding an Information Service

You can add more *information services* to the Microsoft Outlook Profile by choosing **Add**. After you do so, you'll see several more information services that are supplied with Outlook. Even more information services are available from Microsoft and other suppliers.

You can easily add any of the information services supplied with Outlook to a profile. For example, to add the Personal Address Book information service, select it, and then choose **OK**. A dialog box appears telling you that the information service will be named Personal Address Book and it will save information in a file named Mailbox.pab. Choose **OK** to add the new information service to your profile. As soon as you do, you'll see the new information service listed in the **Services** tab of the Microsoft Outlook Properties dialog box.

A new information service may not be available immediately

Some information services are immediately added to a profile, as described previously. In the case of other information services, you have to close and reopen Outlook to be able to use the new service.

SEE ALSO
➤ *To learn about the Personal Address Book information service, see Chapter 16, "Creating a Personal Address Book."*

Deleting an Information Service

You can delete an information service from a profile by selecting that service and then choosing **Remove**. If you don't have access to Microsoft Exchange Server, for example, you should remove that service from the list.

Modifying an Information Service

To find out about, and modify, how an information service works, select that service and then choose **Properties** to display a dialog box as shown in Figure 6.2.

FIGURE 6.2
The properties for the Microsoft Exchange Server information service are shown in this dialog box's four tabs.

You can enter information into the **General** tab shown here, as well as the other three tabs, to tailor the information service to suit your requirements.

Each information service has different properties. Rather than attempt to cover all the information services Outlook can use in this chapter, the properties of individual information services are described in Chapter 7, "Setting Up Information Services" and also in the chapters that deal with each of those services.

SEE ALSO
➤ *For detailed information about the Microsoft Exchange Server information service properties, see page 130 and page 358.*

What does delivering mean?

In Outlook's terminology, "delivering" refers to both sending and receiving e-mail. Mail you send is delivered from you; mail you receive is delivered to you.

Delivering E-mail

As you've already seen, the Services dialog box has three tabs: the **Services** tab is where you define the information services available in a profile. The other two tabs—**Delivery** and **Addressing**—are where you define how your e-mail messages are to be delivered and addressed.

Choose the **Delivery** tab to display a dialog box similar to that shown in Figure 6.3.

FIGURE 6.3

Use this dialog box to specify where e-mail messages you receive should be saved and how Outlook should send e-mail messages you create.

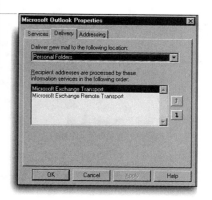

The **Deliver new mail to the following location** list box allows you to specify where you want to save the e-mail messages you receive. If you have the Microsoft Exchange Server and Personal Folders information services in the profile you're using, you can choose between saving messages you receive in your personal folders (that is, in a file on your local hard disk) or in your Exchange Server mailbox.

Many people prefer to save their e-mail messages in their Personal Folders file. I recommend that you choose Personal Folders as the place to save the e-mail messages you receive.

To choose where your incoming mail is to be saved, open the **Deliver new mail to the following location** drop-down list box on the Delivery tab, and select from the listed locations.

The lower part of the Delivery tab deals with how your computer sends e-mail messages. As you know, you can use Outlook to send messages by way of various messaging systems.

Saving e-mail when you're traveling

If you travel with a laptop computer, you should save your incoming messages on your e-mail server so you can easily access them from a remote location. Also, if you're using a PC that doesn't have a local hard drive, you'll have no option but to save your messages on the mail server.

In most cases, Outlook automatically sends messages by way of the appropriate messaging system. One exception to this, however, occurs when you have the Internet E-mail and Microsoft Exchange Server information services in your profile, and you send a message to an Internet e-mail address. Outlook can handle this message either by directly accessing an Internet e-mail server from your workstation or by requesting Exchange Server to access an Internet e-mail server.

Outlook chooses which way to handle Internet e-mail messages according to the order those services are listed in the **Delivery** tab of the Services dialog box. If Internet E-mail comes first, Outlook attempts to send your Internet e-mail messages directly to your Internet e-mail server. If Microsoft Exchange Transport comes first, Outlook calls on Exchange Server to handle your Internet e-mail messages.

To set the order of priority in which Outlook attempts to send e-mail messages, adjust the order of the information services in the lower box on the **Delivery** tab. You can do this by selecting a service and then clicking one of the arrow buttons at the right side of the tab. For example, you might have two ways of sending Internet e-mail messages, by way of Exchange Server on your LAN or by a dial-up connection from your connection. By placing Microsoft Exchange Transport above Internet E-mail, Outlook will attempt to send your messages by way of Exchange Server, but, if that's not available, it will send them by way of your dial-up connection.

SEE ALSO

➤ *To learn more about saving your messages in an Exchange Server postoffice, see page 361.*

Addressing E-mail

The **Addressing** tab of the Services dialog box, shown in Figure 6.4, defines various aspects of addressing and sending e-mail messages.

The easiest way to address an e-mail message is to open one of your address lists and select a recipient. When you choose the **To** button on the Message form, Outlook automatically opens

Make sure your e-mail was actually sent

Unfortunately, Outlook isn't always smart enough to try one way of handling Internet e-mail and, if that fails, try an alternative way. If you send e-mail by way of the Internet, after you've sent the mail, look in your Sent Items folder to make sure the e-mail was sent.

your default address list. If the name you want isn't in that list, you can open a list of address lists and select one of them.

In the **Addressing** tab of the Services dialog box, you can choose which of your address lists is the default. You should, of course, select the one that contains the people you most often send messages to.

To select a default address list, open the **Show this address list first** drop-down list at the top of the tab to see a list of address lists. Then select the appropriate one.

The second box in the **Addressing** tab is where you might expect to be able to choose the address list in which Outlook will store new names you save. Although the tab has a drop-down list box, the only address lists available are your Personal Address Book and the CompuServe Address Book. These are, of course, only available if your profiles contain the Personal Address Book and CompuServe information services.

When you send an e-mail message, or when you choose **Check Names** on the Message form, Outlook compares recipients' names with names in your address lists. The **When sending mail, check names using these address lists in the following order** list near the bottom of the **Addressing** tab shows the order in which Outlook searches your address lists. You can choose **Add** to add address lists to the list of those to be searched, or you can choose **Remove** to remove address lists from those to be searched.

SEE ALSO
➤ *To learn how to use address lists, see Chapter 15, "Creating a Contact List and Outlook Address Book."*

Creating a Profile

The preceding pages of this chapter have given you an overall idea of what's in the Microsoft Outlook profile and how to modify those contents. Now we'll look at how you go about creating a new profile that suits your personal needs.

Create a new profile

1. From the Windows desktop, choose **Start** to display the **Start** menu. In that menu choose, **Settings** and then choose **Control Panel** to display the Control Panel.

2. In the Control Panel, double-click **Mail** to display your default Properties dialog box.

3. Choose **Show Profiles** to display a list of the profiles already on your computer.

4. Choose **Add** to display the first Microsoft Outlook Setup Wizard window, shown in Figure 6.5.

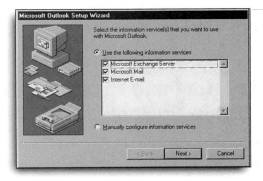

FIGURE 6.5

The wizard proposes to create a new profile that contains three information services.

5. If you want to create a new profile that contains the three information services listed, choose **Next**. Otherwise, choose the option button labeled **Manually configure information services**. The following steps assume you want to create a profile that contains the proposed information services.

6. After choosing **Next**, you see the window shown in Figure 6.6 in which you can give the new profile a name.

FIGURE 6.6

This window proposes a name for the new profile.

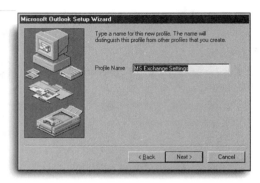

7. Replace the proposed name with whatever name you want to use for the profile. If it's to be your personal profile, you could use your own name as the profile name. Click **Next** to access the first of a series of windows in which you supply information required by each of the information services.

After you've provided all the information required for the new profile, that profile is available for you to use.

SEE ALSO

➤ *To create a profile that contains your choice of information services, see page 109.*

➤ *For detailed information about each information service, see page 112.*

Creating and Accessing Profiles from Within Outlook

The preceding pages of this chapter talked about accessing profiles from the Windows desktop. You can also access profiles from within Outlook.

When you double-click the **Microsoft Outlook** icon on the Windows desktop, either:

- Outlook immediately opens using your default profile.

- A dialog box is displayed in which you can choose which profile to use and in which you can choose to create a new profile.

If Outlook opens without offering you a choice of profiles, you must change Outlook's options to have this choice.

Showing a choice of options when Outlook starts

1. With Outlook open, choose **Tools** in the menu bar, and then choose **Options** to display the Options dialog box. Select the **Mail Services** tab.

2. In the **Startup settings** section, choose **Prompt for a profile to be Used**, then choose **OK**.

3. Choose **File** in the menu bar and then choose **Exit and Log Off** to close Outlook.

4. Double-click the **Microsoft Outlook** icon on the Windows desktop to restart Outlook.

Now you see the Choose Profile dialog box, shown in Figure 6.7.

FIGURE 6.7
This dialog box offers you a choice of profiles.

In this dialog box, open the **Profile Name** drop-down list to choose an existing profile, or you can choose **New** to display the first Microsoft Outlook Setup Wizard window and proceed to create a new profile.

Setting Up
Information Services

What Is an Information Service?

The way Outlook 98 Messaging and Collaboration Client works depends on profiles that contain one or more information services. Each information service determines how Outlook handles specific types of information. In this chapter, you learn how to set up information services to suit your needs.

Outlook is a multipurpose application that handles items of information in various ways. These items include

- E-mail and fax messages
- Time-related information about appointments, events, and meetings
- Information about people and organizations
- Tasks on your to-do list and tasks you have asked other people to do
- A record of what you've done
- Miscellaneous notes

This chapter is only applicable to Outlook with Corporate/ Workgroup Support

Outlook with Internet Only Support provides access to Internet e-mail and personal folders. Therefore, the information in this chapter pertains only to those who have installed Outlook with Corporate/Workgroup Support.

In addition, Outlook provides access to your entire computing environment—not only your own computer, but also networks to which you can connect, including the Internet.

To have access to all this information, you must have a profile that contains information services. Each information service gives Outlook the capability to use a specific information source. These information sources include

- A postoffice to which you can send e-mail and from which you can receive e-mail
- Address Books that contain information about your contacts
- Personal Folder files that contain such information as your personal calendar, your to-do list, and your Journal of activities

This chapter leads you through the process of creating a profile that contains many information services. You should, of course, only include in your own profile those services you intend to use.

As described in Chapter 6, "Creating a Profile," you can create a new profile either from the Windows desktop or from within Outlook. We'll use the Windows desktop here.

Creating a new profile

1. From the Windows desktop, choose **Start** to display the **Start** menu. Then choose **Settings** and **Control Panel** to display the Control Panel.

2. In the Control Panel, double-click **Mail** to display your default Properties dialog box.

3. Choose **Show Profiles** to display a list of profiles currently available on your computer.

4. Choose **Add** to display the first Microsoft Outlook Setup Wizard window, in which you begin to create a new profile (see Figure 7.1).

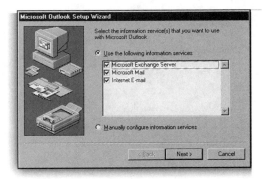

FIGURE 7.1
This wizard window proposes that you create a profile that contains certain information services.

5. Instead of accepting the information services the wizard proposes, choose **Manually configure information services** and then choose **Next**.

6. In the second wizard window, enter a name for your new profile. If this profile is to be your personal Profile, enter your own name. Then choose **Next** to display a Properties dialog box in which you can add information services (see Figure 7.2).

Begin modifying your new profile by adding the Personal Folders information service.

FIGURE 7.2

The Properties dialog box is initially displayed with no information services listed.

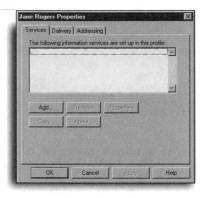

SEE ALSO

➤ *To learn more about profiles, see Chapter 6, "Creating a Profile."*

The Personal Folders Information Service

Which folder to use?

By default, Outlook proposes to place your Personal Folders file in your Windows (if you're using Windows 95) or WINNT (if you're using Windows NT) folder. I suggest you create an Outlook folder and use that instead.

The Personal Folders information service manages Outlook information that you save. When you add this service to a profile, you create a Personal Folders file that contains a set of folders. Outlook saves each type of item in a separate folder—calendar items in the Calendar folder, contact items in the Contact folder, and so on.

Before you begin, display the profile's Properties dialog box.

Adding the Personal Folders information service

1. Choose **Add** to display the Add Service to Profile dialog box, as shown in Figure 7.3.

FIGURE 7.3

The Add Service to Profile dialog box lists the information services available to be added to a profile.

2. Select **Personal Folders** and then choose **OK** to add the Personal Folders information service to the new profile. The Create/Open Personal Folders File appears as shown in Figure 7.4.

FIGURE 7.4

This dialog box proposes to create a file for your Personal Folders in your Windows folder.

3. In this dialog box, navigate to the folder in which you want to create your Personal Folders file. In the **File name** box, replace *.pst with the actual name (such as your initials) you want to give to your Personal Folders file. You don't need to provide the filename extension—Outlook provides the extension automatically. Whatever you do, don't provide a filename extension other than .pst—Outlook doesn't like that! Choose **Open** after you've provided a filename. At this stage you see a dialog box similar to that in Figure 7.5.

FIGURE 7.5

You can use the Create Microsoft Personal Folders dialog box to customize your Personal Folders file.

Encrypting your data

If you choose **No Encryption** in the Create Microsoft Personal Folders dialog box, your data is not encrypted. If you choose **Compressible Encryption**, your data is compressed only if you have a compression program installed on your computer. If you choose **Best Encryption**, your data is also compressed only if you have a compression program installed on your computer; the data is better encrypted, but less compressed, than when you choose **Compressible Encryption**.

4. You can replace the default name "Personal Folders" with another name, you can choose a level of encryption, and you can provide password-protected access to the information you subsequently save in your Personal Folders. After you've made your choices in this dialog box, choose **OK** to return to the Properties dialog box in which the new information service is listed.

After you've created a Personal Folders information service, you can change some of its properties. Select the information service in the list of information services (if it's the only information service in the profile, it's already selected), and then choose **Properties** to display the dialog box shown in Figure 7.6.

FIGURE 7.6

You can use this dialog box to change the name of the information service, to provide (or change) its password, and to compact the data it contains.

While you're working with Outlook, you create various items of information in your Personal Folders folder. Over time, this folder can become quite large. Although you can delete items, Outlook doesn't automatically recover the space those items occupied on your disk. One of the ways you can recover the space previously occupied by deleted items is to choose **Compact Now** in the Personal Folders dialog box shown earlier in Figure 7.6.

Check the **Allow upgrade to large tables** check box if you anticipate saving a lot of information in your Personal Folders file. With this check box unchecked, you can have approximately 16,000 folders in your Personal Folders file and approximately 16,000 items in each folder. If you check the check box, you can have approximately 64,000 folders in your Personal Folders file and 64,000 items in each folder.

You can use the **Comment** box at the bottom of the dialog box to add any descriptive text or notes about the Personal Folder. Whatever you enter here has no effect on Outlook's operation.

After you've finished working with this dialog box, choose **OK** to return to the Properties dialog box.

SEE ALSO

➤ *For more information about encryption, see "Specifying Security Options" on page 549.*

The Outlook Address Book Information Service

The Outlook Address Book information service lets you use e-mail addresses in your Contacts folder for addressing e-mail messages, and also fax numbers for sending faxes. After you add this service to your profile, you have an Outlook Address Book that contains the names of all the contacts for whom you entered an e-mail address or a fax number.

Adding the Outlook Address Book information service to a profile

1. With the profile's Properties dialog box displayed, choose **Add** to display the Add Services to Profile dialog box.

2. Select **Outlook Address Book**, and choose **OK**. The Properties dialog box now contains Outlook Address Book in its list of services.

3. With Outlook Address Book selected, choose **Properties**. You'll see a message telling you how to designate a Contacts folder as an Outlook Address Book. You must follow the instructions in this box before your contacts are available in the Outlook Address Book.

As you see, you must open Outlook before you can continue setting up the Outlook Address Book. Although you can add more information services without opening Outlook, as you have to open Outlook at this time anyway, the remaining pages of this chapter show how you can add information services to a profile within Outlook.

Adding information services to your profile while working in Outlook

1. Close the Microsoft Outlook Address Book dialog box, and choose **OK** to close the profile's Property dialog box. Then choose **Finish** to close the setup wizard, and choose **Close** to close the Mail dialog box.

2. Close the Control Panel.

3. Double-click the **Microsoft Outlook** icon on the Windows desktop to start opening Outlook.

4. When the Choose Profile dialog box appears, open the drop-down list of profiles and select the one you're in the process of creating. Choose **OK** to continue opening Outlook.

5. Open the **View** menu and choose **Folder List** to display a list of folders accessible to the profile you're creating.

6. Right-click **Contacts** in the list of folders to display a context menu. Choose **Properties** in that menu to display the Contacts Properties dialog box.

7. Select the **Outlook Address Book** tab shown in Figure 7.7.

How do you choose a profile?

If Outlook opens without displaying the Choose Profile dialog box, open the **Tools** menu, choose **Options**, and then choose the **Mail Services** tab of the Options dialog box. Choose **Prompt for a profile to be used**, and then choose **OK**. Open the **File** menu and choose **Exit and Log Off** to close Outlook. Double-click the **Microsoft Outlook** icon on the Windows desktop. This time, you'll see the Choose Profile dialog box.

FIGURE 7.7

Make sure **Show this folder as an e-mail Address Book** is checked.

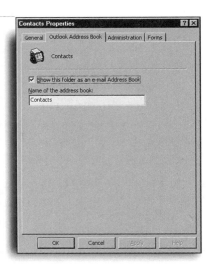

8. Outlook normally proposes to name the Address Book Contacts. You can replace this name with something else if you prefer.

9. Choose **OK** to close the dialog box.

Now you can use e-mail addresses for your contacts to address e-mail messages, and fax numbers to send faxes.

Confirming that your Outlook Address Book contains items in your Contacts folder

1. Open the **Tools** menu and choose **Services** to display the Services dialog box.

2. In the Services dialog box, select **Outlook Address Book.**

3. Choose **Properties** to display the Microsoft Address Book Properties dialog box, in which Contacts: Personal Folders is now listed as an Outlook Address Book.

After adding the Outlook Address Book information service to your profile and setting the properties of your Contacts folder so it can be shown as an e-mail Address Book, you can use e-mail addresses in your Contacts folder for addressing e-mail and fax numbers for sending faxes.

The Internet E-mail Information Service

To use Outlook to send and receive e-mail messages, you must have a physical connection to other computers, and your computer must be set up to communicate with those computers. The physical connection is either a network adapter—sometimes known as a *network interface card* (NIC)—that provides a connection to a LAN, or a modem that provides a dial-up connection to a server.

When computers communicate, they use a set of rules known as a *protocol*. The protocol used for communication by way of the Internet goes by the name of *TCP/IP*. You don't need to understand TCP/IP to use the Internet; you just have to make sure the TCP/IP protocol is properly installed on your computer.

What is a network adapter?

A network adapter is a module that's plugged into a desktop computer or can be attached to a laptop. The adapter enables your computer to send information to, and receive information from, a LAN.

For information about installing the TCP/IP protocol and connecting to the Internet under Windows 95, see the Windows 95 Help topic **Connecting to the Internet**. In that topic, choose **How to connect to the Internet Using Dial-Up Networking**. If you're using Windows NT, refer to the Windows NT Help topic **Connecting to the Internet**.

These Help topics provide all you need to know about installing the TCP/IP protocol and setting up Dial-Up Networking.

To use Outlook for Internet e-mail, you must add the Internet e-mail information service to your profile. You can do this either from the Windows desktop or from within Outlook. The following information assumes you are working within Outlook.

Add the Internet e-mail information service

1. Open the **Tools** menu and choose **Services** to display the Services dialog box.

2. Choose **Add** to display the Add Service to Profile dialog box.

3. Select **Internet E-mail** in the list of services and choose **OK** to display the Mail Account Properties dialog box.

Setting the General Properties

Use the five text boxes in the **General** tab of the Properties dialog box to provide a name for your e-mail account, to identify yourself and your organization, and to provide your e-mail address.

Enter information in the General tab

1. For **Mail Account**, enter whatever name you prefer, such as the name of your Internet e-mail server. The name you enter here identifies your e-mail account only on your own computer.

2. For **Name**, enter your own name. When you send e-mail messages, this name (together with your e-mail address) appears in the **From** box in your messages.

3. For **O**__**rganization**__, enter the name of your organization, company, or group.

4. For **E-m**__**ail address**__, enter the address people should use when sending e-mail to you.

5. Normally you would leave the **Repl**__**y**__ **address** box empty. If you want to have replies to your messages sent to an address other than your e-mail address, enter that address here.

Figure 7.8 shows the **General** tab with typical entries.

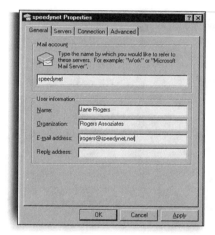

FIGURE 7.8
This example shows a completed **General** tab.

Setting the Server's Properties

Your computer sends Internet e-mail messages to, and receives Internet e-mail messages from, a mail server. Most likely you use the same server for outgoing and incoming e-mail, but Outlook enables you to use different servers. You identify the outgoing and incoming mail servers in the **Servers** tab, and also provide information to those servers.

Enter information in the Servers tab

1. For **O**__**u**__**tgoing mail (SMTP)**, enter the name of the SMTP server to which you want to send outgoing e-mail.

2. For **I**__**ncoming mail (POP3)**, enter the name of the POP3 server from which you want to receive incoming e-mail.

Getting names for your SMTP and POP3 servers

You can obtain the names of the SMTP and POP3 servers from your Internet service provider. These abbreviations refer to the protocols used for e-mail messages.

Secure password authentication

If your server requires secure password authentication, your server
administrator will probably give you
an account name and password to
use when you log on.

3. By default, Outlook proposes that you'll log on using an
account name and password. If this is the case, make sure
Log on using is selected, then enter your **Account name**
and **Password** in the two boxes. If your server requires
secure password authentication for you to receive e-mail,
choose **Log on using Secure Password Authentication**.

4. If your server requires secure authentication for you to send
e-mail messages, check the box labeled **My server requires
authentication**, then choose **Settings** to display a dialog
box in which you can specify your account name and password.

Figure 7.9 shows the **Servers** tab with typical entries.

FIGURE 7.9

This example shows a com-
pleted **Servers** tab.

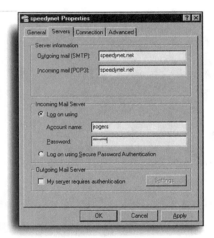

Setting the Connection Properties

Use the **Connection** tab to specify how your computer is connected to your mail server.

Enter information in the Connection tab

1. In the **Connection** section, choose the appropriate option
button according to how you will be connecting to the
Internet e-mail server.

2. If you chose to connect by using a phone line, the **Modem** section of the dialog box becomes active. If you've already set up a dial-up connection, you can choose it by opening the **U̲se the following Dial-Up Networking connection** drop-down list and selecting the appropriate connection. You can select an existing dial-up connection and then choose **Properties** to modify its configuration. You can also choose **Ad̲d** to create a new dial-up connection.

Figure 7.10 shows the **Connection** tab with typical entries.

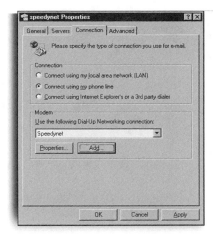

FIGURE 7.10

This example shows a completed **Connection** tab.

Setting the Advanced Properties

The preset properties in the **Advanced** tab, shown in Figure 7.11, are usually satisfactory. Don't change the settings in the **Server port numbers** section at the top of the tab unless you're instructed to do so by your server's administrator.

Your Internet e-mail provider may enable you to leave a copy of messages you've received on the server after you've read them. If that's the case, you can check the box labeled **Leave a copy of messages on server**. Then you can specify the number of days the messages will be kept on the server. The size of messages (including attachments) you can save and the length of time you can save them may be limited.

Are you being disconnected?

If after starting to use the Internet you find that you become disconnected before you're able to send or receive messages, drag the slider in the **Server t̲imeouts** section to the right. That might solve the problem.

Keeping received messages on the server

If you read your e-mail at a computer other than the one you normally use, it's convenient to leave messages on the server so you can subsequently save them on your principal computer.

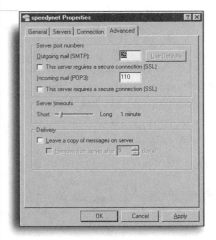

FIGURE 7.11

The default settings in the **Advanced** tab are usually okay as they are.

If your provider does not enable you to save messages on the server and you attempt to do so, a message box warns you that messages will not be saved.

After you've set all the necessary properties for the Internet e-mail information service, choose **OK** to close the Properties dialog box. Outlook displays a message telling you that you must close Outlook and then restart it before you can begin to use the information service.

SEE ALSO

➤ *To learn all the details about sending and receiving e-mail messages, see Chapter 18, "Sending an E-mail Message" and Chapter 19, "Receiving an E-mail Message."*

The Microsoft Mail Information Service

If you share information with other computers by way of a peer-to-peer network or small LAN, you may use Microsoft Mail to exchange e-mail messages. To use Microsoft Mail, you must add the Microsoft Mail information service to your profile. Also, of course, you must have a network adapter installed in your computer with cabling to the other computers in the network.

Add the Microsoft Mail information service to your profile

1. Open the **Tools** menu and choose **Services** to display the Services dialog box.

2. Choose **A**d**d** to display the Add Service to Profile dialog box.

3. Select **Microsoft Mail** in the list of services and choose **OK** to display the Microsoft Mail dialog box shown later in Figure 7.12.

SEE ALSO

➤ *To learn all the details about sending and receiving e-mail messages, see Chapter 18, "Sending an E-mail Message" and Chapter 19, "Receiving an E-mail Message."*

Setting the Connection Properties

Microsoft Mail uses a postoffice located in a shared folder on the network to maintain information about users and to distribute e-mail. The postoffice must be created before you can set up Microsoft Mail.

Enter the full path to your postoffice in the text box. If you don't know the location of the postoffice, either ask your network administrator or choose **Browse** to search for it. The postoffice is normally, but not necessarily, in a folder named \Postoffice\ wgpo0000\.

You can choose among four option buttons to determine if and how Outlook connects to the Microsoft Mail postoffice when you open Outlook—usually the first is satisfactory. After you choose **Automatically **s**ense LAN or Remote**, Outlook automatically determines whether the computer is connected to the postoffice by way of a LAN or a dial-up connection; if no connection is available, a dialog box offers you the choice of working offline. If you want to disable use of Microsoft mail without removing the Microsoft Mail information service from your profile, choose the last option, **Offline**.

Figure 7.12 shows the **Connection** tab with typical settings.

To learn more about the Microsoft Mail postoffice, refer to Chapter 31 in *Platinum Edition Using Windows 95* published by Que. Also, see *Special Edition Using Windows NT Workstation 4.0* for Microsoft Mail postoffice and Windows NT.

FIGURE 7.12

The typical settings in the Connection tab are shown here.

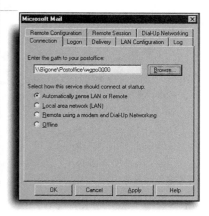

Setting the Logon Properties

Use the text boxes in the **Logon** tab of the Microsoft Mail dialog box to provide your account name and password for Microsoft Mail.

You should normally check the box labeled **When logging on, automatically enter password**. By doing so, you save your Microsoft Mail password in your profile so you don't have to provide it each time you start Outlook.

You can change your Microsoft Mail password by choosing **Change Mailbox Password**. This opens a dialog box in which you identify yourself by entering your current password and then replacing that password with a new one.

Figure 7.13 shows the **Logon** tab with typical settings.

Setting the Delivery Properties

In the **Delivery** tab of the Microsoft Mail dialog box, the two check boxes near the top should be checked to enable delivery of incoming and outgoing mail.

By default, Outlook sends all types of mail to the Microsoft Mail postoffice. If you want to send some types of mail (such as faxes) by way of a different information service, however, you can choose **Address Types** to display the Address Types dialog box that lists the types of mail available in your profile. Uncheck

Sending e-mail to a Microsoft Mail postoffice

If you have the Microsoft Mail information service in your profile, revisit the Address Types dialog box each time you add a new service to make sure only the appropriate types of mail are sent to the Microsoft Mail postoffice.

those types you don't want to go to the Microsoft Mail postoffice.

FIGURE 7.13
These are the typical settings in the **Logon** tab.

By default, Outlook attempts to send new e-mail to, and receive e-mail from, the Microsoft Mail postoffice every ten minutes. You can change this number to whatever you prefer.

Check the **Immediate notification** check box if you want to have immediate notification when e-mail arrives on your computer and you want the recipients of messages you send to be notified immediately when mail you send arrives on their computers. You must have NetBIOS installed on the network to use this capability.

To learn more about NetBIOS, refer to the "Network basic input/output system (NetBIOS)" topic in Windows NT Help. Windows 95 Help does not have a corresponding topic.

To find out whether you have NetBIOS installed, go to the Windows desktop and choose **Start** to open the **Start** menu. Move the pointer onto **Settings** and choose **Control Panel**. In the Control Panel, double-click **Network** to display the Network dialog box; choose the **Services** tab. You'll see NetBIOS Interface listed if you have NetBIOS installed.

The bottom check box labeled **Display Global Address List only** appears to have no effect when you're using Outlook.

Figure 7.14 shows the **Delivery** tab with typical settings.

FIGURE 7.14

The typical settings in the **Delivery** tab are shown here.

Setting the LAN Configuration Properties

The settings in this tab apply only when your computer is connected to the Microsoft Mail postoffice by way of a LAN. You can use these settings to speed up transferring mail and to minimize LAN traffic.

If you prefer to receive only message headers rather than complete messages, check **Use Remote Mail**. Subsequently, you can open the **Tools** menu and choose **Remote Mail** to receive specific messages in full.

Also, instead of accessing the Address Book on the postoffice, you can minimize connection time by choosing **Use local copy** to use a copy of the Address Book stored on your computer.

You may be able to speed up mail delivery by choosing to use the external delivery agent. The external delivery agent (External.exe) must always be running on the server. Consult with your LAN administrator before checking **Use external delivery agent**.

Figure 7.15 shows the **LAN Configuration** tab with typical settings for a slow LAN.

Setting the Log Properties

After you check **Maintain a log of session events**, Windows keeps a log of the important Microsoft Mail events. This log is a text file with either the default name or a name you specify. You can open this log in Windows Notepad or another text editor to see the history of your connections to the Microsoft Mail post-office. The events this log records include

- Each time you connect to the postoffice
- The connection speed (number of bytes per second)
- The number of mail items you send and receive in each session
- Any errors that occurred when you attempted to connect to the postoffice or when you attempted to send or receive mail

FIGURE 7.15
The typical settings in the **LAN Configuration** tab are shown here.

If you experience problems with Microsoft Mail, this log can often provide useful information about what's going wrong.

You can save the log in the default file Outlook proposes, or in any other file you specify.

Figure 7.16 shows the **Log** tab with typical settings.

Setting the Remote Configuration Properties

The settings in this tab apply only when your computer has a dial-up connection to the Microsoft Mail postoffice. The settings available are identical to those in the **LAN Configuration** tab described previously.

FIGURE 7.16

The typical settings in the **Log** tab are shown here.

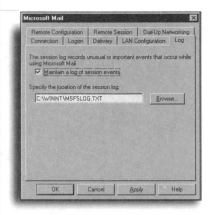

FIGURE 7.16

The typical settings in the **Log** tab are shown here.

SEE ALSO

➤ *To learn more about using remote mail, see Chapter 32, "Working Remotely."*

Setting the Remote Session Properties

The settings in this tab apply only when your computer has a dial-up connection to the Microsoft Mail postoffice.

To connect automatically by way of a dial-up connection to the Microsoft Mail postoffice when Outlook starts, check the **When this service is started** check box.

You can check any combination of the lower three check boxes to control when the dial-up connection ends. By choosing the appropriate check boxes, you can avoid incurring unnecessarily high telephone charges.

To schedule regular automatic dial-up connection, choose **Schedule Mail Delivery**. A dialog box displays the delivery schedule in place. You can choose **Delete** to delete any existing schedule, and you can choose **Add** to add a new schedule.

Figure 7.17 shows the **Remote Session** tab with typical settings.

Setting the Dial-Up Networking Properties

The settings in this tab apply only when your computer has a dial-up connection to the Microsoft Mail postoffice.

FIGURE 7.17
The typical settings in the **Remote Session** tab are shown here.

In this tab, open the **Use the following Dial-Up networking connection** drop-down list box and select the Dial-Up Networking connection you want to use. Choose **Add Entry** to create a new dial-up connection. Choose **Edit Entry** to make changes to an existing dial-up connection.

Figure 7.18 shows the **Dial-Up Networking** tab with typical settings.

In the center section of the tab, set the number of times you want Dial-Up Networking to retry establishing a connection and the interval between those tries.

In the bottom part of the tab, choose an option button according to how you want to be notified about the success or failure of a connection.

Connecting to a Microsoft Mail Remote Server

To connect to a Microsoft Mail remote server, you must use Dial-Up Networking to connect to the network on which your Microsoft Mail shared directory is accessible.

FIGURE 7.18
The typical settings in the **Dial-Up Networking** tab are shown here.

After you've finished working with Microsoft Mail settings, choose **OK** to close the dialog box. You must close and restart Outlook before you can begin to use Microsoft Mail.

To learn about Dial-Up Networking, refer to the "Accessories: Using Dial-Up Networking to connect to a computer or network" topic in Windows 95 Help or to the "Using Dial-Up Networking to connect to a remote computer or network" topic in Windows NT Help.

The Microsoft Exchange Server Information Service

What is Microsoft Exchange?

Like many people, you may be somewhat confused about Microsoft Exchange. You probably first heard about Microsoft Exchange when you started working with Windows 95. Microsoft included an application named Microsoft Exchange with Windows 95, but this wasn't the Exchange Server—it was an e-mail client you could install on your own computer and use to send and receive e-mail. To avoid confusion between that client application and Exchange Server, Microsoft has renamed the original Exchange client—it's now known as Windows Messaging.

Exchange Server runs only under Windows NT Server. It provides enterprise-wide e-mail and information-sharing capabilities.

Microsoft Exchange Server is becoming an increasingly popular e-mail server that offers such additional facilities as shared folders and shared calendars. To use Exchange Server facilities, your computer must be connected to a LAN based on Windows NT Server. The LAN must include one or more computers with Windows NT Server installed that act as domain controllers. These computers, or others that are e-mail servers, must have Exchange Server installed.

Outlook is the principal client for Exchange Server. To access Exchange Server facilities, you must have the Microsoft Exchange Server information service in your profile.

Add the Microsoft Exchange Server information service to your profile

1. Open the **Tools** menu and choose **Services** to display the Services dialog box.

2. Choose **Add** to display the Add Service to Profile dialog box.

3. Select **Microsoft Exchange Server** in the list of services and choose **OK** to display the Microsoft Exchange Server dialog box shown in Figure 7.19.

SEE ALSO

➤ *To learn all the details about sending and receiving e-mail messages, see Chapter 18, "Sending an E-mail Message," and Chapter 19, "Receiving an E-mail Message."*

➤ *For information about how you can use Outlook to access many of the facilities available in Exchange Server, see Chapter 22, "Using Outlook as an Exchange Server Client."*

Setting the General Properties

Use the **General** tab of the Microsoft Exchange Server dialog box to identify your Exchange Server.

Enter settings in the General tab

1. In the **Microsoft E̲xchange server** box, enter the name of your Microsoft Exchange server. Your LAN administrator can provide this name if you don't already know it.

2. In the **Mail̲box** box, enter the name of the mailbox the Exchange Server administrator has provided for you. After you enter your mailbox name, you can choose **Chec̲k Name** to verify you've entered a name Exchange Server recognizes.

3. In the **When starting** section of the tab, choose what you want to happen when Outlook starts. In most cases, choose **Automatically d̲etect connection state**. If you're creating a profile for use when you're working remotely or offline, choose **M̲anually control connection state**, then choose **C̲onnect with the network** or **Work o̲ffline and use dial-up networking**.

4. Leave the default number of seconds in the **Seconds Until Server Connection T̲imeout** unchanged unless, for some reason, ten seconds isn't long enough to establish a server connection.

Figure 7.19 shows the **General** tab settings.

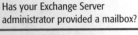

Has your Exchange Server administrator provided a mailbox?

When you choose **Check Name**, Outlook queries Exchange Server to verify that the name is valid. If the Exchange Server administrator has created a mailbox for you, the name in the **Mailbox** box becomes underscored and the **Check Name** button becomes disabled.

If Exchange Server doesn't recognize your name, a message from Exchange Server tells you that `the name could not be matched to a name in the address list`. In that case, you must ask the Exchange Server administrator to create a mailbox for you.

FIGURE 7.19

The settings for the **General** tab are shown here; note that **Seconds Until Server Connection Timeout** has been altered to allow more time to connect to the server.

Setting the Advanced Properties

You can make several choices in the Advanced tab.

Choosing Advanced properties

1. If you have delegate access permission to mailboxes other than your own, choose **A̲dd** to display a dialog box in which you can enter the names of those mailboxes. Subsequently, when you open Outlook, you'll have access to those mailboxes. Choose **R̲emove** to remove the names of mailboxes to which you no longer have delegate access permission.

2. In the **Encrypt information** section of the tab, check the appropriate boxes if you want to encrypt information.

3. Open the **Logon network security** drop-down list and select the security you want to use.

4. Choose **Offline F̲older File Settings** to open a dialog box in which you can select encryption settings for your offline folder file.

Figure 7.20 shows typical settings for the **Advanced** tab. In this case, no delegate access permissions are shown.

FIGURE 7.20

The typical settings in the **Advanced** tab are shown here.

SEE ALSO

➤ *To learn more about having delegate access to mailboxes, see "Granting Delegate Access to Your Mail" on page 361.*

➤ *To learn more about offline folders, see "Making a Public Folder Available Offline" on page 379.*

Setting the Dial-Up Network Properties

This tab is where you can specify a Dial-Up Networking connection you plan to use to access Exchange Server.

Choose Dial-Up Networking properties

1. To establish a dial-up connection, open the drop-down list of dial-up connections and select the one you want to use. You can choose **New** to create a new dial-up connection, **Properties** to change the properties of an existing dial-up connection, or **Location** to identify the location from which you want to make the dial-up connection.

2. Enter your **User name**, **Password**, and your network **Domain** in the appropriate boxes.

3. If you're already connected to the network, choose **Do not dial, use existing connection**.

Figure 7.21 shows typical settings for the **Advanced** tab.

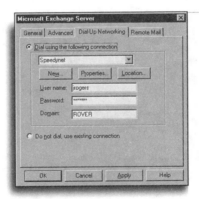

FIGURE 7.21

The typical settings in the **Dial-Up Networking** tab are shown here.

Setting the Remote Mail Properties

The settings in this tab determine how you make a remote connection to the Exchange Server.

Establishing a remote connection to an Exchange Server

1. Select **Process marked items** if you want to work with the items you've marked in Remote Mail.

2. Select **Retrieve items that meet the following conditions** if you want to select only certain items. After you select this, choose **Filter** to display a dialog box in which you can specify a message sender or a message subject (and more advanced criteria).

3. Check **Disconnect after connection is finished** (the default) if you want to automatically disconnect from the dial-up connection after all messages have been transmitted.

4. Choose **Schedule** to open a dialog box in which you can specify the time or interval at which you want Outlook to automatically make a dial-up connection to Exchange Server. After you create a schedule, you can choose to process marked items or retrieve items that satisfy certain conditions.

Figure 7.22 shows typical settings for the **Remote Mail** tab.

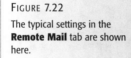

Filtering messages

If you choose **Retrieve items that meet the following conditions**, you can then choose **Filter** to open a dialog box in which you can specify the mail items you want to retrieve.

FIGURE 7.22

The typical settings in the **Remote Mail** tab are shown here.

After you've finished working with Exchange Server settings, choose **OK** to close the dialog box.

SEE ALSO

➤ *To learn more about remote connections, see Chapter 32, "Working Remotely."*

The Personal Address Book Information Service

You may wonder why Outlook provides so many lists of addresses. As you've already seen, an Outlook Address Book provides access to all the people in your Contacts folder for whom you've noted e-mail or fax addresses. In addition, you can access address lists (known as *Global Address Lists*) maintained in the mail servers you use. So why do you need yet another Address Book?

You really don't need a Personal Address Book, but having one is often quite convenient for three reasons:

- You can copy information about people with whom you have frequent contact into your Personal Address Book. By doing so, you have all these people in one place and can save time when addressing messages.

- A Personal Address Book is a convenient place to keep information about personal friends and contacts.

- It's easy to create and maintain distribution lists consisting of names in your Personal Address Book and other Address Books.

Add the Personal Address Book information service to your profile

1. Open the **Tools** menu and choose **Services** to display the Services dialog box.

2. Choose **Add** to display the Add Service to Profile dialog box.

3. Select **Personal Address Book** in the list of services and choose **OK** to display the Personal Address Book dialog box shown in Figure 7.23.

SEE ALSO
➤ *For detailed information about Personal Address Books, see Chapter 16, "Creating a Personal Address Book."*

FIGURE 7.23
Use the two tabs in this dialog
box to set up your Personal
Address Book.

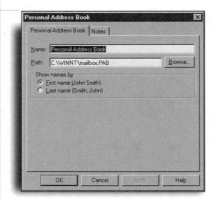

Setting the Personal Address Book Properties

Use the **Personal Address Book** tab to name your Personal
Address Book and to specify the order in which you want names
to be listed.

Choose Personal Address Book properties

1. In the **Name** box, Outlook proposes to call the service
   Personal Address Book. You can accept this name, or replace
   it with another name.

2. In the **Path** box, Outlook proposes to save your Personal
   Address Book information in a file named Mailbox.PAB. You
   can accept this name, or replace it with another name.

3. Select whether you want names in your Personal Address
   Book to be alphabetized by first name or last name.

Setting the Notes Properties

The **Notes** tab contains a text box in which you can enter information about your Personal Address Book.

After you've finished working with Personal Address Book settings, choose **OK** to return to the Services dialog box. You must
close and restart Outlook before you can begin to use your
Personal Address Book.

**Keeping your Personal Address
Book personal**

If you share a computer with other
people, you should change the
name of your Personal Address
Book to something other than
Mailbox.PAB. If you don't, you could
find yourself sharing that file with
other users who create a Personal
Address Book. To avoid using too
many different names, you could
give your Personal Address Book
the same name as your e-mail login
name.

Other Information Services

Various other information services are available, some provided by Microsoft and some provided by other companies. These information services include

- The Microsoft Fax information service that enables you to use Outlook to send and receive faxes
- The Lotus cc:Mail information service you can use to send and receive e-mail by way of a cc:Mail server
- The CompuServe Mail information service you can use to send and receive e-mail by way of CompuServe
- The AOL Mail information service you can use to send and receive e-mail by way of America Online

At the time this chapter was written, Microsoft and Lotus were jointly developing an information service that is intended to let Outlook be used as a client for Lotus Notes.

Among other recent developments are information services such as MobileCHOICE Messenger from Ikon Technology Services that enables Outlook to send messages to numeric and alphanumeric pagers.

For up-to-date information about information services and other add-ons available for Outlook from Microsoft, go to the Internet site at the following address:

`http://www.microsoft.com/Outlook/`

For information about information services and other add-ons available from companies other than Microsoft, go to the Internet site at this address:

`http://support.microsoft.com/support/kb/articles/`
`➥q172/8/42.asp`

SEE ALSO
➤ *To learn more about MobileCHOICE Messenger, see Chapter 25, "Sending Messages to Pagers."*

Creating Outlook Items

What Is an Outlook Item?

The preceding chapters have often referred to Outlook 98 Messaging and Collaboration Client *items* without being specific as to what an Outlook item is. It's time to get a clear understanding of Outlook items.

Specifically, in Outlook, an item is a unit of information. Outlook deals with information—not information in general, but information about contacts, appointments, messages, tasks, and so on. Let's consider contacts as an example. Each contact is an Outlook item; that item contains specific fields of information such as First Name, Middle Name, Last Name, Organization, Home Street, Home City, Home State/Province, Home Zip/Postal Code, Home Country/Region, and many more. In fact, Outlook has 130 fields of information for each contact. Not surprisingly, you'll rarely supply information for more than a few of these fields for each contact.

Each contact, then, is an item of information. That item consists of 130 fields. Whether you supply information for a few or many of these fields, the item occupies the same space on your disk.

The other types of items Outlook deals with—appointments, messages, tasks, and so on—are similar. Each type of item has a specific number of information fields.

Outlook saves items in what it calls *folders*, using a separate folder for each type of item. When you see the word "folder," you probably think of what you used to call directories and subdirectories—regions on your hard disk that contained files. Outlook uses the word "folder" in a more fundamental sense: An Outlook folder is an information container.

When working with Outlook, you normally have a file named Personal Folders. This is a file in the conventional sense; you can use Windows Explorer to see what's on your hard disk and see one or more files that have .pst as their filename extension—Outlook's Personal Folders files.

Your Personal Folders file contains several folders. Each of these folders contains Outlook items of a specific type. One folder

What about attachments to items?

You can attach extra information to any item. The space required by *attachments* is in addition to the space ordinarily occupied by items.

exists for contacts, one for calendar items, one for messages you've received, and so on. Although Outlook refers to these as folders, you can't use Windows Explorer to see them. You can, of course, access them from within Outlook.

SEE ALSO

➤ *To learn more about your Personal Folders, see Chapter 12, "Creating and Using Folders."*

Using a Form to Create a New Item

You can create Outlook items in two ways:

- Import data from another file, such as from a database, spreadsheet, or some other structured source such as a Word table.

- Enter data into an Outlook form.

In this section, we deal with creating Outlook items from scratch—by entering information into Outlook forms.

Outlook has separate forms to use for entering each type of item. Although each of the forms is somewhat different, the general technique for entering information into forms is similar. We'll use the New Appointment form as an example. After you understand how to enter an appointment item, you'll understand how to enter other types of items.

Start by selecting the Information viewer that displays the type of item you want to create. In this case, you're going to create an appointment item that's displayed in the Calendar Information viewer; click **Calendar** in the Outlook Bar to display the Calendar Information viewer. With the Calendar Information viewer displayed, choose the New Appointment button 🖼️▾ in the Standard toolbar to display the Untitled – Appointment form shown in Figure 8.1. This form is much like the dialog boxes you use in other Office applications.

Let's take a careful look at this form to make sure we understand everything it contains.

Outlook is similar to a database application

If you're familiar with databases, it might help to think of Outlook as a database application. You can use Outlook's forms to enter information into the database; you can use Outlook's Information viewers as reports of what's in the database.

Also, think of Outlook's folders as database tables. The Contacts folder is really a table that contains the fields of information about contact items.

A form, a window, a dialog box

Let's get some terminology straight. In Outlook, a *form* is a window used to display and collect information. The form you see in Figure 8.1 supplies information to Outlook about appointments. You could call this window a dialog box; however, that term is more often used to refer to a window in which you make choices about how an application works.

FIGURE 8.1

The Appointment form contains fields in which you provide information about a new appointment.

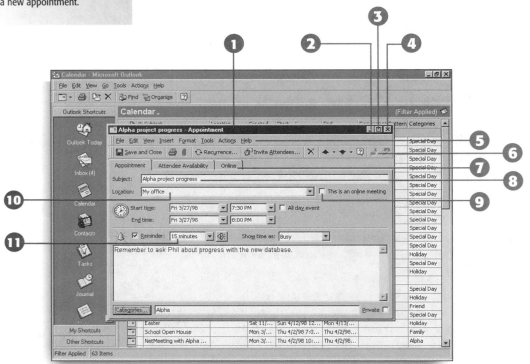

1 Title bar

2 Minimize button

3 Maximize/Restore button

4 Close button

5 Menu bar

6 Toolbar

7 Tabs

8 Text field

9 Check box

10 Drop-down list

11 Default information

SEE ALSO

➤ *To learn more about working with appointments in Outlook, see Chapter 26, "Planning Your Time."*

Understanding the Title Bar

In common with other windows, dialog boxes, and forms, the form you're now dealing with has a title bar. The main point to notice about the title bar is that it contains the name of the form at the left, and the usual Minimize, Maximize/Restore, and Close buttons at the right. The menu bar contains the same menu names as those in the Information viewer, although many of the items in each of the menus are different. While you're working with a form, make sure you choose the form's menus, not the underlying Information viewer's menus.

A form's toolbars contain buttons appropriate for that form. Initially the form's Standard toolbar is displayed. In the Appointment form's menu bar, you can open the **View** menu, choose **Toolbars**, and then choose **Formatting** to display the Formatting toolbar. You can also choose **Customize** to customize the menu bar and toolbars.

The Appointment form, in common with many other Outlook forms, consists of several tabs. In this form, the **Appointment** tab is initially displayed. You can choose the **Meeting Planner** or **Online** tabs to enter information relevant to those activities.

The Information bar (immediately under the tabs) provides hints about the information you've provided on the form (or information Outlook has provided by default). When you begin to create an appointment, Outlook assumes that appointment is for the first half-hour of your working day. If the current time is after that, the Information bar warns you This appointment occurs in the past. Subsequently, after you change the appointment time to the future, that warning disappears. If the appointment you create conflicts with an already-existing appointment, the Information bar alerts you to that as well.

The Information bar isn't always displayed

The Information bar only appears when there's information to display in it. At other times, you won't see an Information bar on your forms.

SEE ALSO

➤ *For information about customizing the menu bar and toolbars, see Chapter 34, "Customizing the Outlook Bar."*

Entering Information in the Subject Text Box

The subject of a form becomes part of its title

After you've entered a subject for an appointment, the text in the form's title bar changes from Untitled to the subject of the appointment.

The **Subject** text box is similar to text boxes in other forms. Use this box to provide a description of your meeting. To enter information into the **Subject** box, click in the box to place the insertion point in it, then start typing. In this box, you can type as many as 255 characters. If you enter more characters than will fit into the width of box, the box expands vertically to provide more space for your text. If you try to type more characters than allowed, Outlook won't accept them. After you've completed typing what you want to put in the box, press Tab or Enter to move to the next box in the form.

Selecting Information from a List

The **Location** box is a little different from the **Subject** box—notice the arrow at the right end of the box. As for the **Location** box, you can enter the location for the appointment—My Office, Conference Room, or whatever. Outlook remembers each location you enter. You can see all the locations you've entered for previous appointments by clicking the arrow at the right end of the **Location** box. Instead of entering the location again, just select one of the locations in the list.

Marking Check Boxes

Option buttons

Some forms, but not the Appointments form, contain groups of option buttons. You can choose one option button in a group.

The Appointments form, like other Outlook forms, contains check boxes you can use to mark things true or false (yes or no). On the Appointments form, the **This is an online meeting** check box is empty by default, indicating the appointment is not an online meeting. If the appointment is an online meeting, click the check box. After you do so, a check mark appears in the box. Click again if you want to remove the check mark.

Specifying Dates and Times

In Outlook's terminology, an appointment starts at a specific time on a certain date and ends at a specific time on a certain date. By default, the Appointments form initially shows the start and end date as the current date, the start time at the beginning of your work day, and the end time 30 minutes later.

Whenever Outlook asks you for a date, such as the start or end date for an appointment, you can either select a date or enter a date. To select a date, click the arrow at the right end of the date field to display the current month's calendar, as shown in Figure 8.2.

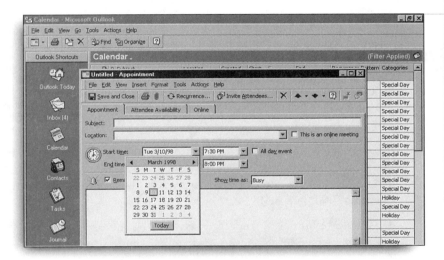

FIGURE 8.2
Outlook displays the current month's calendar.

If the date you want is within the current month, just click that day in the calendar. If the date you want is in another month, click the arrow in the month's title bar to display another month, and then click the appropriate day in that month. In either case, the calendar disappears and the date you selected is displayed in the date box on the form.

Instead of selecting a date from a calendar, you can enter a date in any of the formats Windows recognizes. To do so, select the default date in the start date box, and then type a date, such as

1/1/98

Yet another alternative is to describe the date. You can type such words and phrases as: "tomorrow," "next Wednesday," "second day of next week," "New Year's," and "two months from now."

Outlook displays selected dates

When you select dates in the Calendar form in this way, the dates you select appear in the start date and end date boxes.

Other ways to enter dates in Outlook

For more examples of the ways you can describe dates, refer to the Outlook Help topic "What you can enter in date and time fields."

You can select most holidays and other special days that occur on the same date every year by entering the name of the day (such as Independence Day and Valentine's Day). You can't select days that don't occur on the same date every year in this way.

Although most appointments start and end on the same day, Outlook doesn't object if you enter an end date on a day subsequent to the start date. Outlook does not accept an appointment in which the end date occurs before the start date.

You can provide the start and end times for an appointment by selecting from a list or by entering a time. To provide a start time by selecting from a list, open the drop-down list of times by clicking the arrow at the right end of the **Start time** box. By default, Outlook provides a list of times at half-hour intervals. Select any time in the list as the start time. You can provide the end time for an appointment in a similar way.

Instead of selecting a time from a list, you can enter a time using the Windows standard 12-hour or 24-hour formats. For example, if your meeting starts at three o'clock in the afternoon, you can enter 3:00 p.m. or 15:00.

As is the case for dates, you can describe times. For example, you can enter noon, midnight, three o'clock p.m. and eight-thirty am.

Providing Additional Information

The Notes box

The box on the appointment form (and other forms) isn't named. In this book, the box is referred to as the **Notes** box.

The lower part of the Appointment form (as well as forms you use to create other types of items) contains a large, unnamed text box in which you can provide whatever additional information is appropriate. Just place the insertion point in this box and start typing.

Unlike all the other boxes on a form, there's no specific limit to the amount of information you can enter into the **Notes** box. In some cases you'll leave it empty and in other cases you'll enter either a few words of explanation or a lot of information.

As stated previously, you can type whatever text you want into the **Notes** box. You can also drag files into it. For example, suppose you want a picture of the person with whom you have an appointment, and that picture is available as a graphics file. Just drag the graphics file into the **Notes** box. After you've done so, the **Notes** box contains an icon that represents the graphics file. You can subsequently double-click the icon to open the graphics file and see the picture.

SEE ALSO

➤ *To attach a photograph to a contact item, see "Adding Notes and Attachments" on page 254.*

Assigning Categories to an Item

At the bottom of the Appointment form (as well as other forms you use to create Outlook items), you'll see a box labeled **Categories**. You can use this box to assign one or more categories to each item.

Why would you want to assign categories to items? The quick answer to this question is that categories are the key to keeping your Outlook items organized.

In this chapter, we're using appointments as an example of Outlook items. During a year, you probably have many types of appointments: appointments relating to specific business matters, and other appointments relating to specific personal matters. If you assign an appropriate category to each appointment, you can subsequently find records of your appointments easily.

You can assign categories to an item in three ways:

- Enter one or more category names in the **Categories** box. Separate one category name from the next with a comma or semicolon.

- Choose the **Categories** button and Outlook displays a list of categories, as shown in Figure 8.3. Select one or more of the listed categories. The selected category names appear in the box at the top of the dialog box. After you've selected the appropriate category names, choose **OK** to show those categories in the **Categories** box on the form.

- Choose the **Categories** button and if the categories you want aren't in the list of categories, enter a new category name in the **Item(s) belong to these categories** box.

The Notes box adds to the size of your folder

The **Notes** box provides unlimited flexibility in what you can save as part of an Outlook item. However, everything you save in this box adds to the size of the folder in which you save items. You should use the **Notes** box wisely.

What if the Categories box isn't there?

If you don't see the **Categories** box on your form, you need to enlarge the form (except in the case of the Message form). Point onto the lower border of the form (the pointer becomes a two-headed arrow). Press the mouse button and drag down to enlarge the form.

To see the **Categories** box for a Message form, choose **Options** in the form's Standard toolbar to display the Message Options dialog box that contains the **Categories** box.

Choose **Add to list** to save these categories in the list of **Available categories**, then choose **OK** to show those categories in the **Categories** box on the form.

FIGURE 8.3

You can select categories for an item from this predefined list, or you can define your own categories.

SEE ALSO

➤ *To learn more about using categories, see Chapter 9, "Creating and Using Category Lists."*

Saving an Item

After you've created an item by entering or selecting information in the item's form, such as the Appointment form, you must save the item. The usual way to do that is to choose **Save and Close** in the form's toolbar. Outlook saves the item in the appropriate folder—the Calendar folder in the case of an appointment item—and closes the form.

Editing an Item

You may want to make changes to an item after you've saved it. One way to do so is to open the item to display its information in a form, and then change the information in that form.

To edit information in the Appointment form

1. Display an appointment in the Calendar Information viewer.

2. Double-click the appointment in the **Appointment** area to display the details of the appointment in an Appointment form.

3. Make whatever changes you want in the form, then choose **Save and Close** to save the changed appointment.

You can make changes to specific types of Outlook items in other ways too. Other methods are described in the chapters that deal with those specific items.

Deleting an Item

At times you'll want to delete an item you previously created. For example, you might create an appointment item and subsequently cancel that appointment. You can delete an item from the Information viewer in which it's displayed, and from the form that shows the details of the item.

Deleting an Item from an Information Viewer

When you delete an item, Outlook moves the item from its original folder to your Deleted Items folder. If you delete an item by mistake, you can subsequently move it from the Deleted Items folder back into its original folder. To permanently delete an item, you must delete it from the Deleted Items folder.

To delete an item

1. Click **Calendar** in the Outlook Bar to display the Calendar Information viewer.

2. Using the Date Navigator, display a day on which there is a calendar item you want to delete.

3. Select the item you want to delete.

4. Choose the Delete button ☒ in the Standard toolbar.

Outlook immediately moves the item from your Calendar folder to your Deleted Items folder. You no longer see the item in your calendar. However, the item is still available (and still occupies space on your disk).

Use the Shortcut menu to delete items

Another way to delete an item is to right-click the item and choose **Delete** from the menu that appears.

Deleting Items from a Form

If you have an item displayed in a form, you can delete that item by choosing the Delete button ☒ in the form's toolbar. Outlook moves the item from the form to your Deleted Items folder.

Creating and Using Category Lists

Understanding Categories

Categories are key to keeping your information organized and easy to find. If you discipline yourself to assign categories to all your Outlook 98 Messaging and Collaboration Client items, you'll be amazed at how organized you are. On the other hand, if you ignore categories, you'll have the electronic equivalent of piles of paper on your desk.

A *category* is an identifying word or short phrase you can assign to items, such as mail messages, calendar activities, and so on. If you make a practice of consistently assigning categories to items, you can easily find items you're looking for and you can display related items together.

Suppose that you have a project named Alpha. You can create a category named Alpha and assign that category to every Outlook item—appointments, meetings, contacts, messages, and tasks—that have anything to do with the project. Then you can easily use Outlook to find all items related to project Alpha. Some of your items might relate to several projects. No problem! You can assign as many categories as you like to an item.

Outlook considers every piece of information to be an *item*. Each mail message, calendar activity, task, and so on is an item. You can assign one or more categories to each item either by

- Entering the category in a form's **Categories** box.
- Selecting from a master list of categories, which is explained in the next section.

SEE ALSO

➤ *To learn more about working with Outlook Items, see Chapter 8, "Creating Outlook Items."*

➤ *For more information on adding categories to the Master Category List, see "Adding Categories On-the-fly" on page 156.*

Using a Master Category List

Outlook is supplied with an initial category list. You can see this list in two ways:

It's best to select from a Master Category List

You should normally select from a Master Category List to ensure that you use consistent category names. If the Master Category List doesn't contain the categories you need, you can add more categories.

- Open an Information viewer that displays items in one of Outlook's folders (such as the Inbox Information viewer). Then open the **Edit** menu and choose **Categories**.

- Open one of the forms in which you create a new item (such as the Appointment form) and choose the **Categories** button.

In either case, you'll see a list of categories, as shown in Figure 9.1.

FIGURE 9.1

The default Outlook 98 Master Category List includes a variety of predefined categories.

SEE ALSO

➤ *For basic information about how you assign a category to an item, see "Assigning Categories to an Item" on page 147.*

Understanding How Outlook Saves Master Category Lists

Before going any further, you need to understand that Outlook maintains at least two Master Category Lists.

The process of installing Outlook writes the original Master Category List into the Windows *Registry*—a database that contains information about the settings for Windows itself and the applications that run under Windows.

The information in a user profile is also maintained in the Registry; each user's profile contains a copy of the Master Category List. When a user makes changes to the Master

Category List, only the copy of the Master Category List in that user's profile is changed. That's why each user can have a different Master Category List.

A user can restore the categories in that user's own profile by choosing **Reset** in the Master Category List dialog box. This deletes all the categories in that user's Master Category List and then copies the default categories into it.

Customizing Your Master Category List

More than likely, the Master Category List supplied with Outlook won't suit your personal needs. Fortunately, it's easy to delete those categories you don't expect to use and add those you will use.

Planning Your Master Category List

It's worth taking the time to give some serious thought to planning your categories, just as you would before setting up a file system for paper documents. You'll probably want to have categories for business and personal items. Categories you might need for business items include

- Separate categories for each project you're involved with
- Separate categories for each type of business contact
- Separate categories for each of your organization's departments

Categories you might need for personal items include

- Separate categories for each type of personal contact (family, friend, medical, finance, legal, and so on)
- Separate categories for each of your interests and hobbies
- Separate categories for each type of family activity

These are just suggestions to start you thinking. When planning your categories, remember that you can assign several categories to each item. When you assign several categories to one item, Outlook saves the item only once. When you display items

Think ahead when creating a category list

Try to make your list of categories fairly complete. Although you may add categories at any time, doing so may make it necessary to change the categories you've already assigned to items—a time-consuming process.

sorted by category, however, you'll see the item listed several times, once under each category assigned to the item.

SEE ALSO
➤ *To learn about displaying items sorted by category, see "Grouping Items in Table Views" on page 168.*

Adding and Deleting Categories in Your Master Category List

After you have a reasonably complete list of your personal categories, display the Categories dialog box shown previously in Figure 9.1. Then choose **Master Category List** to display the dialog box shown in Figure 9.2.

FIGURE 9.2
Use this dialog box to delete existing categories and to add new ones.

Deleting a category from your Master Category List

1. Select the category you want to delete. As soon as you select an item, the **Delete** button becomes enabled.

2. Choose **Delete**. The selected item is immediately deleted from your personal Master Category List.

Add a category to your personal Master Category List

1. Place the insertion point in the **New Category** text box.

2. Type a word or short phrase to name the new category. As soon as you type the first character, the **Add** button becomes enabled.

3. Choose **Add**. The new category immediately appears in the Master Category List in its correct alphabetical position.

Deleting several categories simultaneously

You can select several categories and delete them all at the same time. To select several categories, select one category, then hold down the Ctrl key while you select other categories. To select consecutive categories, select the first category, then hold down the Shift key while you select the last category.

4. Repeat the three steps to add as many new categories as you need.

5. When you've finished deleting and adding categories, choose **OK** to close the Master Category List dialog box. Now you can use your new Master Category List to assign categories to items.

Adding Categories On-the-fly

Sometimes you won't be able to find the category you want to assign to an item in your Master Category List. You can, of course, use the method described in the previous section to add a new category to your Master Category List, but there's an even faster way to add a new category.

Add a category on-the-fly

1. Display the Categories dialog box shown previously in Figure 9.1.

2. Enter the name of the new category in the **Item(s) belong to these categories** box, as shown in Figure 9.3.

FIGURE 9.3

Enter a new category directly into the Categories dialog box.

3. Choose **Add to List** to add the new category to your Master Category List. The new category immediately appears in the list of **Available Categories.** It's automatically checked to indicate it will be assigned to the Outlook item you're creating.

4. Choose **OK** to assign the category to the Outlook item.

The next time you open your Master Category List (as described earlier in this chapter) you'll find the new category is included.

Understanding How Categories Are Assigned to Items

As explained in Chapter 8, "Creating Outlook Items," each item consists of many predefined fields. All Outlook items contain a **Category** field. When you assign a category to an item, the name of the category is copied into the item's **Category** field.

After you've assigned a category to an item, it doesn't matter whether that category still exists in your Master Category List. By deleting a category from your Master Category List, you don't delete that category from the items to which you previously assigned it.

I recommend that you assign categories to items by choosing categories from your Master Category List, not by typing category names into a form's **Categories** box. If you insist on doing so, however, nothing prevents you from just entering category names into the **Categories** box on a form.

The problem that arises when you do this is that you won't always enter category names consistently. If you use the singular form of the name one time and the plural form another, Outlook will see two category names. Even the slightest difference between one category name and another results in separate categories. Avoid this potential problem by always choosing categories from your Master Category List.

Items in your Outlook folders have categories assigned to them in yet another way when you receive Outlook items from other people. If someone creates an e-mail message, assigns categories to it, and sends it to you, the item in your Inbox folder has those categories assigned to it, whether or not those categories are in your Master Category List.

Of course, you have no control over the categories assigned to Outlook items by people outside your own organization. When you receive those messages, however, you can change the assigned categories to those in your own Master Category List. By doing so, Outlook items you receive are organized in a way that is consistent with the organization of items your create.

Determining and Changing Categories

You can find out what categories are assigned to any item and, if necessary, change those categories. In this section, you'll find out how you can look at categories assigned to a message you've received. Remember, of course, that categories can be assigned to any Outlook item, including e-mail messages, calendar items, and so on.

View categories assigned to an item

1. Double-click the message to display it in the Message form.

2. Open the form's **View** menu and choose **Options**. The Message Options dialog box contains a **Categories** box in which the assigned categories are listed.

You can delete the assigned categories and then select new categories by choosing the **Categories** button.

Within your own group, it's preferable that everyone has the same Master Category List. Refer to the next section for information about sharing Master Category Lists.

Sharing Your Master Category List

The "Understanding How Outlook Saves Master Category Lists" section earlier in this chapter explained that Outlook keeps your personal Master Category List in the Windows Registry.

Saving Your Master Category List

After customizing your Master Category List, close or minimize Outlook, then proceed as follows.

Changing categories assigned to items

You can use the method described in this section to change the categories assigned to any item, not just to categories assigned to messages you receive.

Sharing your Master Category List

If you want to share your Master Category List with someone else, you must copy part of the Registry on one computer and then copy that part into the Registry on the other computer (described later in this section). This also works well if you want to copy the Master Category List you use at home onto the computer you use in your office.

Be careful when working with the Registry

Don't mess with the Registry unless you know what you're doing. Windows 95 and Windows NT, together with the applications that run under them, depend on the information in the Registry. Any mistake you make while working with the Registry could make Windows or an application unusable.

If you are familiar with the Registry, or enjoy sky-diving, bungee-jumping, and other life-threatening activities, use the information that follows. Otherwise, leave well alone.

Copy your Master Category List to a folder

1. In the Windows taskbar, choose **Start** to display the **Start** menu.

2. In the **Start** menu, choose **Run** to display the Run dialog box. Enter regedit in the **Open** box, as shown in Figure 9.4. Regedit is the name of the Registry editor application you can use to gain access to the information in the Registry database.

FIGURE 9.4

Run regedit to access the Registry.

3. Choose **OK** to display the top-level Registry keys, as shown in Figure 9.5.

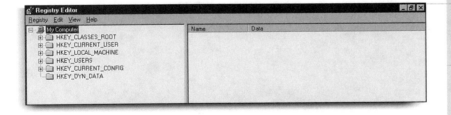

FIGURE 9.5

The Registry editor displays a list of Registry keys.

The Registry editor displays information in the Registry in much the same way that Windows Explorer displays information on a disk. Initially, the Registry editor shows the top-level keys, just as Windows Explorer shows top-level folders. You navigate through the Registry by clicking the **+** beside a top-level key name to expand that key so you can see the subkeys it contains. Continuing in this way, you can drill down to see the lowest-level keys.

In this case, the Registry key you're interested in is HKEY_CURRENT_USER.

Back up your Registry first

Before working with your Registry, you should back up the Registry file. That way, if you make mistakes, you can restore the Registry to its original state with your backup copy. For more information on performing a Registry backup with Windows 95, please see *Platinum Edition Using Windows 95* (published by Que).

Locate your Master Category List

1. Click the **+** at the left of HKEY_CURRENT_USER to display its subkeys, one of which is named Software.

2. Click the **+** at the left of Software to display its subkeys, one of which is Microsoft.

3. Click the **+** at the left of Microsoft to display its subkeys, one of which is Office. Microsoft usually has many subkeys, so you'll probably have to scroll down to see the Office subkey.

4. Click the **+** at the left of Office to display its subkeys, one of which is 8.0 (that's the internal number for Office 97). You've probably installed Outlook 98 as a component of Office 97.

5. Click the **+** at the left of 8.0 to display its subkeys, one of which is Outlook.

6. Click the **+** at the left of Outlook to display its subkeys, one of which is Categories, as shown in Figure 9.6.

FIGURE 9.6

One of Outlook's subkeys is Categories. This display shows Categories selected.

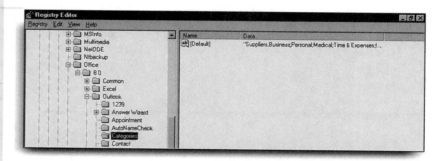

Categories is the subkey you're seeking. As you see, no **+** is beside this key, so you know it's a lowest-level key. Select Categories to see what the key contains. The right pane of the Registry editor shows the beginning of the list of categories in that key—your Master Category List—each one separated from the next by a semicolon as shown previously in Figure 9.6.

Having found the key that contains your Master Category List, you can save that key to a file.

Save your Master Category List

1. With the Categories key selected, open the **Registry** menu and choose **Export Registry File** to display the Export Registry File dialog box.

2. In the Export Registry File dialog box, navigate to the drive and folder in which you want to save the Categories subkey. If you're planning to copy the Master Category List to another computer, save the list in a folder to which that computer has access or, possibly, to a floppy disk.

3. In the **File Name** box, enter a name for the file (such as MCL).

4. Choose **Save** to save the file.

5. Open the **Registry** menu and choose **Exit** to close the Registry Editor.

You can open Windows Explorer to find the file you saved listed as MCL.reg.

To learn more about working with the Windows Registry, refer to Chapter 14, "Introduction to REGEDIT" in *Platinum Edition Using Windows 95* (published by Que).

Copying Your Master Category List to Another Computer

Copy your Master Category List to another computer

1. On the other computer, choose **Start** in the Windows taskbar. Then, in the **Start** menu, choose **Run**.

2. In the Run dialog box, enter regedit in the **Open** box and choose **OK** to start the Registry editor.

3. Open the **Registry** menu and choose **Import Registry File** to display the Import Registry File dialog box.

4. Navigate to the folder in which you saved the Master Category List.

5. Select the Master Category List file, such as MCL.reg, and choose **Open**. A message box appears telling you that information in the file has been successfully transferred into the Registry.

If you administer a workgroup or LAN, consider using this procedure to copy a standard Master Category List to everyone's computer.

Viewing Outlook Items

Understanding Outlook's Views

Outlook uses *views* to control how Information viewers display items in a folder. You can choose among several views supplied with Outlook, modify these views to suit your own requirements, and create your own views.

You can also control how Outlook displays information from your Tasks folder in the TaskPad that appears in the Calendar's Day, Work Week, Week, and Month views. Outlook's Information viewers display items—Calendar items, Journal items, e-mail messages, notes, and tasks—in various views, each view containing fields of information in a specific structure.

Each of these items contains various fields of information. For example, some of the fields in a Contact item contain information about contacts such as names, addresses, phone numbers, and e-mail addresses.

A view displays or prints information about one type of item. Each view contains certain fields, arranges items in a specific order, and has a specific structure. The Address Cards view of Contact items, for example, contains fields of basic information about each of your contacts, and arranges those contacts in a specific order (such as in alphabetical order by the File As name). This view displays or prints the view in a card structure (similar to a conventional file card).

Views can have the five structures listed in Table 10.1.

TABLE 10.1 **Outlook's view structures**

Structure	Description	Best Used For...
Card	Items are shown in the form of cards. An index at the right provides quick access to cards.	Contacts
Day/Week/Month	Items are arranged in a calendar format.	Appointments, meetings, and tasks
Icon	Items and files are represented by icons.	Notes and files
Table	Items are displayed as rows of a table with each column containing one field.	Messages and tasks

Structure	Description	Best Used For...
Timeline	Items are displayed as icons in chronological order.	Journal items, appointments, meetings, tasks, and messages

Outlook's built-in views use structures that are usually best-suited for each type of item. When you create your own views, you can choose whichever structures you prefer.

The remainder of this chapter focuses mainly on views of Calendar items. However, you can apply this information to views of other types of items.

SEE ALSO

➤ *See Chapter 11, "Printing Outlook Items," for more information on preparing your Outlook Items to be printed.*

Working with Views

Each Information viewer contains **View** menu on its menu bar. You can use this menu to select the view you want to see in the Information viewer.

Selecting a view

1. Click the **Calendar** shortcut in the Outlook Bar to display the Calendar Information viewer.

2. Open the **View** menu and choose **Current View** to display the list of available views shown in Figure 10.1.

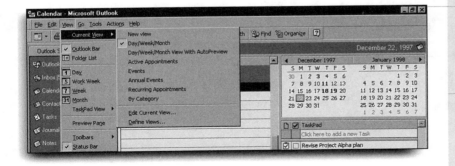

FIGURE 10.1

The currently selected view is checked in this list. Select the name of the view you want to use.

Selecting views from the Advanced toolbar

1. If you only have the Standard toolbar displayed, open the **View** menu in the menu bar and choose **Toolbars**.

2. Choose **Advanced** in the list of toolbars. The menu disappears and you now have two toolbars at the top of the Information viewer, as shown in Figure 10.2.

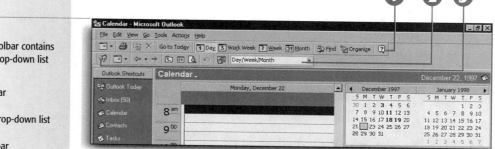

FIGURE 10.2

The Advanced toolbar contains a current view drop-down list box.

1 Standard toolbar

2 Current view drop-down list

3 Advanced toolbar

3. Choose the arrow button at the right end of the current view drop-down list in the Advanced toolbar to display a list of available views, as shown in Figure 10.3.

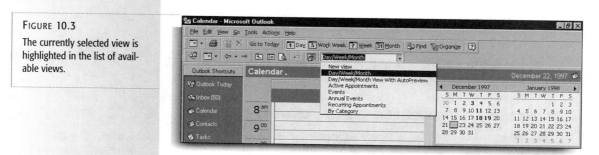

FIGURE 10.3

The currently selected view is highlighted in the list of available views.

4. Select the name of the view you want to see. When you do so, the list disappears and the Information viewer displays the view you just selected.

Understanding What's in a View

While the names of Outlook views are fairly self-explanatory, they don't always tell you the whole story. You can find out more about a view from a view's *banner* and from the Define Views dialog box.

The view's banner (across the top of the Information viewer) shows you whether all items or just selected items are displayed in the current view. With the Calendar Information viewer displayed, choose the **Active Appointments** view. At the right end of the view's banner you'll see the words Filter Applied. This tells you that the view you're seeing filters items—it shows only items that satisfy certain conditions. If these words don't appear in the banner, the view contains all items.

The Define Views dialog box shows you what fields are included in the view. For example, to find out what fields are included in the Calendar's Active Appointments view, select that view, open the **View** menu, choose **Current View**, and then choose **Define Views** to display the Define Views for "Calendar" dialog box. The bottom section of the dialog box contains a description of the view, as shown in Figure 10.4.

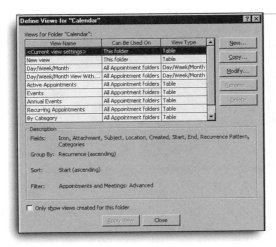

FIGURE 10.4

The **Description** section of the Define Views dialog box contains a complete description of the selected view. After you've examined a view in this way, choose **Close**.

Choosing which views are viewable

The **Only show views created for this folder** check box determines whether the views supplied with Outlook are listed when you select **Current View** (in the **View** menu or in the Advanced toolbar). When this check box is unchecked (the default) all views are listed; when it's checked, only the views you've created are listed (this has no effect on the views listed in the Define Views dialog box). You see the effect of checking or unchecking this box after you close the Define Views dialog box.

Grouping items is one way to find items quickly

By grouping items in a table view, you can easily find specific items. For example, you can easily find e-mail from a specific person by grouping message items in your Inbox based on the **From** field.

Here you can see a complete list of the fields included in the view, together with other information, including sort information, grouping options, and filters—all described in detail later in this chapter. While you have this list displayed, you can select any other views available for calendar items to see what fields they contain.

When you've finished examining this dialog box, choose **Close**.

Grouping Items in Table Views

While a primary view for each type of Outlook item (Day/Week/Month for Calendar items, Address Cards for Contact items, and so on) exists, you can also display all types of items in table views. In table views (also in timeline views), you can group items on the basis of one or more fields. Many of Outlook's standard views group items in this way.

Examining and modifying how table view items are grouped

1. Display a table or timeline view, such as Calendar's Active Appointments view. Open the **View** menu, choose **Current View**, and then choose **Edit Current View** to display the View Summary dialog box shown in Figure 10.5.

FIGURE 10.5

Use the View Summary dialog box to examine and modify the current view.

2. Choose **Group By** to display the Group By dialog box, shown in Figure 10.6.

FIGURE 10.6

This Group By dialog box defines two levels of grouping.

3. To define or change the first grouping level, open the drop-down list in the **Group Items by** section at the top of the dialog box and select the field by which you want to group items. Choose **Ascending** or **Descending** grouping order. Leave **Show field in view** unchecked.

4. Define or change the next levels of grouping in the same way as the first.

5. Open the **Expand/collapse defaults** drop-down list at the bottom of the dialog box and select how you want Outlook to display groups. You can select **All expanded**, **All collapsed**, or **As last viewed**.

6. Choose **Cancel** if you've just been looking at grouping and don't want to save any changes, or choose **OK** to save changes and close the dialog box and return to the View Summary dialog box that now contains a description of the grouping you've selected. Choose **OK** to close the View Summary dialog box.

Outlook displays grouped views in sections within an Information viewer, each section being headed with the group name, as shown in Figure 10.7. Each group can be

- *Expanded*. All items in the group are displayed. In this case, a small square at the left end of the group name contains a minus sign (choose the minus sign to collapse a group).

What are the expand/collapse defaults?

All expanded means that all items in the view are shown. **All collapsed** means that the view displays only the group headings. **As last viewed** is usually the most useful.

Grouping on fields not in a view

You are not limited to grouping on the fields a view contains. For example, you could choose to group items in the Active Appointments view by the Created field (the field that contains the date and time on which you created items), even though that view doesn't include the Created field. You can open the **Select available fields from** list at the bottom of the dialog box to have access to more than just frequently used fields.

Canceling grouping

To remove grouping from a view, choose **Clear All** in the Group By dialog box.

Another way to expand and collapse groups

You can also choose **View** and then select **Expand/Collapse Groups** to expand or collapse a selected group or all groups. These options only appear in the View menu when the selected Outlook Bar item contains grouped items.

- *Collapsed*. All items in the group are hidden. In this case, a small square at the left end of the group name contains a plus sign (choose the plus sign to expand the group).

Another way to group items in a table view is to choose the Group By box button 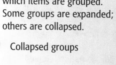 in the Advanced toolbar. Outlook then inserts the Group By box between the banner and the column headings, as shown in Figure 10.8. You can drag field names from the column headings into the Group By box to visually create groups in a table view.

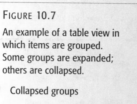

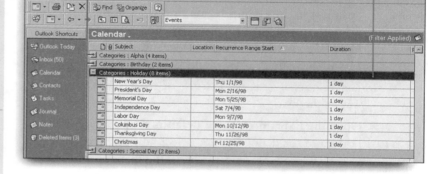

FIGURE 10.7

An example of a table view in which items are grouped. Some groups are expanded; others are collapsed.

1 Collapsed groups

2 Expanded group

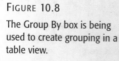

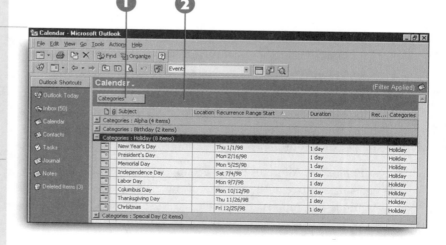

FIGURE 10.8

The Group By box is being used to create grouping in a table view.

1 Field name dragged into Group By box

2 Group By box

To remove the Group By box from a view, choose the Group By box button 🔲 in the Advanced toolbar. Any grouping changes you made in the Group By box are retained in the view.

To remove the grouping you created by dragging a field name into the Group By box, drag the field name from the Group By box back into its original position in the table title row.

When grouped items are displayed in a table or timeline view, you can easily expand or collapse groups. In the **View** menu, point to **Expand/Collapse Groups**. Then choose

- **Collapse This Group** to collapse a selected group.
- **Expand This Group** to expand a selected group.
- **Collapse All** to collapse all groups.
- **Expand All** to expand all groups.

Use the Group By box

Whereas you can set up groups based on any field (including fields not shown in a view) you can only group by fields included in a view when you use the Group By box.

Controlling How a View Is Displayed

You can modify how a view appears on your screen in various ways. You can

- Change the width of columns.
- Change the order in which columns of a table view are displayed across the screen.
- Select the column that determines the order of rows.
- Change the fonts used in views.
- Add and delete fields included in a view.

Changing Column Width in a Table View

When you first choose a table view, such as the Active Appointments view of calendar items, the width of each column is intended to be suitable for the information displayed in that column. You can easily change the width of individual columns.

One way to change the width of a column is by dragging. Place the mouse pointer on the vertical dividing line in the table's title row at the right side of a column (when the pointer is in the correct place, its shape changes to two vertical lines with arrows pointing to the left and right). Press the mouse button and drag to the right to make the column wider or drag to the left to make the column narrower.

You can also adjust the width of a column so it is just wide enough for the biggest information entry in that column. To do so, double-click the column dividing line in the title row.

By default, the horizontal space available to display columns is limited to the width of the window. Consequently, when you make one column wider, Outlook automatically makes other columns narrower. You can change this default so you can display columns of any width and use a horizontal scrollbar to display hidden columns.

Change to a scrollable window

1. Display an Information viewer and select a table view.

2. Open the **View** menu, move the pointer onto **Current View**, and choose **Edit Current View** to display the View Summary dialog box.

3. Choose **Other Settings** to display the Other Settings dialog box shown in Figure 10.9.

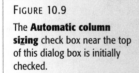

FIGURE 10.9

The **Automatic column sizing** check box near the top of this dialog box is initially checked.

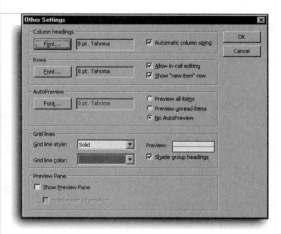

4. Uncheck the **Automatic column sizing** check box, and then choose **OK** twice to close the dialog boxes.

Now you can increase the width of certain columns without the width of other columns being automatically decreased. You can use the horizontal scrollbar at the bottom of the Information viewer, shown in Figure 10.10, to scroll to hidden columns.

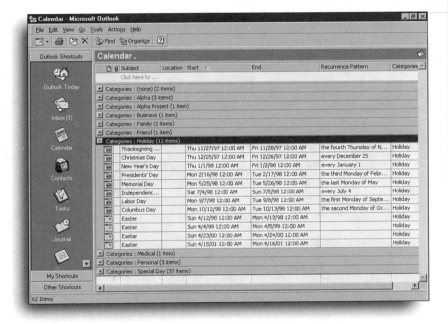

FIGURE 10.10

The table view now has a horizontal scrollbar.

Specifying the Exact Width of a Column

Specify exact column widths

1. Point into the title of a column and right-click to display the context menu shown in Figure 10.11.

FIGURE 10.11

The context menu contains items you can choose to control the appearance of a table view.

2. Choose **For_mat Columns** to display the dialog box shown in Figure 10.12.

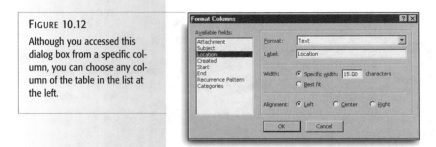

3. In the **Width** section of the dialog box, choose either **Specific _width** and then enter the width in terms of the number of characters, or choose **Best fit**. Notice that you can also use this dialog box to specify how information is aligned in the selected column. Choose **OK** to close the dialog box and apply your choices.

Changing the Width of Cards in a Card View

The card view, often used to display contact information, displays two, three, or four cards side-by-side in the Information viewer (the number depends on the resolution of your monitor). The default width of cards may be insufficient to show all the information on the cards. In particular, e-mail addresses may be truncated.

You can easily make all cards wider. Point onto the vertical line that separates one column of cards from the next. Press the mouse button and drag to the right to make the column wider. By dragging one line, all columns of cards become wider.

Changing Column Order in a Table View

You can change the order in which columns appear across the width of an Information viewer that's displaying a table view by dragging.

Changing the column order in the Information viewer

1. Place the mouse pointer within the title of the column you want to move.

2. Press the mouse button and hold it down.

3. Drag to the left or right. After you drag a little way, the title you're dragging breaks free from its original position. Continue dragging until red arrows appear above and below the place in the title row to which you want to move the column.

4. Release the mouse button. The title you dragged and, of course, the information in the rows under it move to the new position.

Controlling Row Order in a Table View

When you first display a table view, the rows appear in the order in which items were created. You can change this order by selecting a column and using the information in that column to arrange items in ascending or descending order. Columns containing alphanumeric information are arranged in alphabetical order, those containing numeric information in numeric order, and those containing dates in date order.

Set the row order in table view

1. Click the title of the column you want to use as the basis of row order. The table is immediately redisplayed in ascending order based on the information in the selected column. A small up-pointing arrow at the right of the column's title lets you know that the information order is based on that column.

2. Click the title of the same column again. The table is immediately redisplayed in descending order. A small down-pointing arrow appears at the right of the column's title.

You can also choose sort-order from the context menu shown previously in Figure 10.11. Choose **Sort Ascending** or **Sort Descending** in this menu.

> **Another way to change the column order**
>
> You can also use the Show Fields dialog box to change the order of columns. Refer to "Deleting a Field from a View" later in this chapter for information about this dialog box.

Changing the Fonts Used in a View

Outlook uses default fonts in all the preset views. You can easily change these fonts.

As an example of changing default fonts, choose **Calendar** in the Outlook Bar and display one of the Day/Week/Month views. Open the **View** menu, choose **Current View**, and then select **Edit Current View** to display the View Summary dialog box. In this dialog box, choose **Format** to display the dialog box shown in Figure 10.13.

FIGURE 10.13

Use this dialog box to choose the fonts used in the Day, Week, and Month views of the calendar.

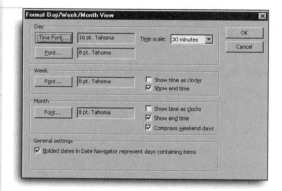

To change the font used to display information in the Day view, choose **Font** to display the standard Windows Font dialog box in which you can select a font name, style, and size. Change the fonts used in the Week and Calendar views by choosing the appropriate **Font** button.

Besides choosing fonts, you can use this dialog box to choose:

- The time increments displayed in the Day view's Appointment Area (instead of the default of 30 minutes).
- To display times in the Week and Month view as clocks (to save space).
- To display weekend days compressed (with Saturday and Sunday at half size) in the Month view.
- To use bolded numbers in the Date Navigator for days on which you have appointments or meetings scheduled.

You can use a similar method to change the fonts and some other features of each of Outlook's views.

Changing the Fields in a View

You can delete fields from any view and also add fields to any view. For example, the Address Cards view of contacts doesn't display the Spouse Name field. You can add that field to the view so the name of a contact's spouse is shown in the Address Cards view. Later, if you decide you don't want the Spouse Name, or any other field, in the view, you can remove that field.

Deleting a Field from a View

To delete a field from a table view, right-click the field's name to display its context menu (shown previously in Figure 10.11). Choose **Remove This Column** to delete the field. Deleting a field from other views takes a little more work.

Delete a field from any view

1. Select the view from which you want to delete a field.

2. Choose **View** in the menu bar, move the pointer onto **Current View**, and choose **Edit Current View** to display the View Summary dialog box.

3. In the View Summary dialog box, choose **Fields** to display the dialog box shown in Figure 10.14.

4. Select the field you want to remove from those in the list at the right, then choose **Remove**.

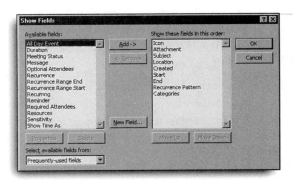

FIGURE 10.14
This dialog box shows the fields in the current view listed at the right.

You can also use the Show Fields dialog box to change the order of fields in a view. Select the field you want to move, then choose **Move Up** or **Move Down**.

Adding a Field to a View

What is the Created field in an item?

Outlook uses the Created field to keep a record of when each item was created. None of the standard views contains this field, but you can add it to them.

This section uses the Active Appointments view of Calendar items as an example of adding a field to a view. Display the Calendar Information viewer and select the Active Appointments view. This is a table view that contains the following fields (listed in order from left to right in the view):

- *Icon*. Identifies the type of item.
- *Attachment*. Indicates the presence of attachments.
- *Subject*. The subject of the activity.
- *Location*. The location of the activity.
- *Start*. The starting date and time.
- *End*. The ending date and time.
- *Recurrence Pattern*. For recurring activities.
- *Categories*. Categories assigned.

Notice that the view's banner contains "Filter Applied" indicating that the view doesn't display all the items in the Calendar folder.

Adding fields to a view

1. Choose **View** in the menu bar, move the pointer onto **Current View**, and choose **Edit Current View** to display the View Summary dialog box.

2. In the View Summary dialog box, choose **Fields** to display the View Summary dialog box shown previously in Figure 10.5. The list at the left shows some of the fields you can add to the view.

3. In the **Available fields** list, select the field you want to add to the view (such as Created), then choose **Add**. This results in the selected field moving from the left list to the bottom of the right list.

4. Choose **Move Up** as many times as necessary to move the added field into the appropriate position in the list.

5. Choose **OK** to return to the View Summary dialog box in which the description now contains the added field in the list of fields.

6. Choose **OK** to close and redisplay the Information viewer with the added field incorporated. From now on, the Active Appointments view contains the additional field.

More fields are available

The list at the left initially contains only frequently used fields. To display more fields, open the **Select available fields from** drop-down list and choose among the many available categories of fields.

Creating a New View

You can create a new view based on an existing view, or you can create a new view from scratch. Some of the views I've created and find useful are

- *Inbox and Sent Items Information viewers*. Views that contain e-mail items received and sent last month and this month.

- *Calendar Information viewer*. View that lists events to which I've assigned the category "Birthday."

- *Contacts Information viewer*. Views that list contacts to which certain categories (such as Family, Medical, and Que are assigned).

- *Tasks Information viewer*. Views that list tasks associated with specific projects.

I've created all these views that filter items by date or category, and saved each new view with an appropriate name. Each of these views simplifies finding what I'm looking for and saves time.

Creating a new view from scratch

1. Display the Calendar Information viewer (or the viewer for which you want to create a new view) choose **View** in the menu bar, move the pointer onto **Current View**, and select **Define Views**.

2. Choose **New** to display the Create a New View dialog box shown in Figure 10.15.

FIGURE 10.15

Use this dialog box to begin creating a new view.

3. Enter a name for the new view in the **Name of new view** box, and choose one of the view types in the **Type of view** list.

4. Select one of the option buttons in the bottom section of the dialog box. The default **This folder, visible to everyone** is usually appropriate.

5. Choose **OK** to display the View Summary dialog box, and choose **Fields** to display the Show Fields dialog box (shown previously in Figure 10.12). The box on the right lists the fields in the view that was displayed before you started creating the new view.

6. One at a time, select any of the fields listed in the right box that you don't want in the new view and choose **Remove**. One at a time, select fields in the left box and choose **Add** to move those fields into the new view.

7. Choose **OK** to return to the Define View Summary dialog box. Choose **Format** to display the dialog box in which you can select fonts and, in the case of a table view, how you want grid lines to appear.

8. Choose **OK** to return to the View Summary dialog box, then choose **OK** to return to the Define Views dialog box in which the new view is now listed.

9. Choose **Apply View** to display the Calendar Information viewer with the new view selected.

Filtering a View

Filtering means using one or more conditions so a view contains only certain items. For example, the Calendar's Active Events view is filtered so it shows only those events scheduled for today or later. Outlook alerts you to the fact that a view is filtered by displaying "Filter Applied" in the view's banner.

Change the filter in any view

1. Display the view, choose **View** in the menu bar, move the pointer to **Current View**, and select **Edit Current View** to display the View Summary dialog box. Choose **Filter** to display the dialog box shown in Figure 10.16.

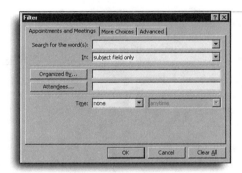

Tab names depend on the type of item

The name of the left tab and some of its contents are different if you started with other than the Calendar Information viewer.

FIGURE 10.16
Use this dialog box to define how you want to filter the view. Initially, the **Appointments and Meetings** tab is selected.

2. Choose **Clear All** to remove all filter conditions that may already exist in any of the three tabs.

3. Enter or change the contents of the boxes in this tab as appropriate. For example, if you want the view to display only appointments and meetings for which a certain phrase appears in the **Subject** box, enter that word or phrase in the **Search for the word(s)** box.

4. If you want to have only meetings organized by, or attended by specific people, enter those names in the **Organized By** and **Attendees** boxes.

5. If you want to have only appointments or meetings that have a relationship to time, open the drop-down **Time** list and choose among **None**, **Starts**, **Ends**, **Created**, and **Modified**.

Filter conditions are additive

All the conditions you specify in the three tabs of the Filter dialog box must be satisfied for an item to be displayed in a view.

After you choose any of these other than None, open the drop-down list on the right to choose from a list of available conditions.

6. Select the **More Choices** tab as shown in Figure 10.17.

FIGURE 10.17

Choose those specific categories you want to include in the view (those you don't name are filtered out of the view), and also check appropriate conditions.

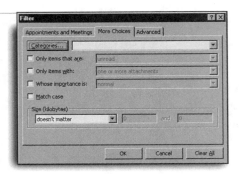

7. Choose the appropriate conditions, and then select the **Advanced** tab shown in Figure 10.18.

FIGURE 10.18

This tab lets you define specific criteria, such as the one for Active Appointments shown here.

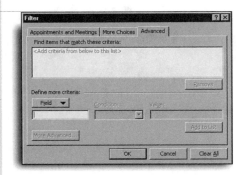

8. In the lower part of this tab, choose **Field** to display a list of field types. Move the pointer onto the type of field you want to use; Outlook displays a list of fields. Select a field; the list of fields disappears and the selected field name appears under the **Field** button.

9. Open the **Condition** drop-down list, then select one of the available conditions. If it's appropriate for the selected condition, enter a value in the **Value** box.

10. Choose **Add to List** to add the condition into the **Find items that match these criteria** list in the upper part of the tab.

11. Repeat steps 7, 8, and 9 to define more conditions.

12. Choose **Cancel** if you've only been looking at a filter, or choose **OK** if you've created or changed a filter and want to save the view with the filter.

Deleting or Resetting a View

You can delete a view you've created, but not one of Outlook's built-in views. If you've modified one of Outlook's built-in views, you can reset it to the original version.

Deleting or resetting a view

1. With an Information viewer displayed, choose **View** in the menu bar, move the pointer to **Current View**, and select **Define Views**.

2. Select the view you want to delete or reset. If the view you select is the one you created, the fifth button near the right edge of the Define Views dialog box is named **Delete**; if the view is one of Outlook's built-in views, the button is named **Reset**.

3. Choose **Delete** or **Reset** to delete or reset the view. Outlook asks you to confirm that you want to delete or reset the view. Choose **OK** to continue. Choose **Apply View** to return to the Information viewer.

Changing the TaskPad View

The Day/Week/Month view of Calendar items contains the TaskPad that provides a summary of items in your Tasks folder. You can choose various TaskPad views in much the same way as you choose Information viewer views.

Display the Calendar Information viewer and select the Day view.

Selecting a TaskPad view

1. Choose **View** in the menu bar and right-click within the TaskPad to display the context menu shown in Figure 10.19.

2. Move the pointer onto **TaskPad View** to display the list of views shown in Figure 10.20. The currently selected TaskPad view is checked.

3. Select the TaskPad view you want to display. The TaskPad immediately displays your tasks according to the conditions specified in the new view.

Creating or modifying a TaskPad view

1. Right-click the TaskPad to display the context menu previously shown in Figure 10.19.

2. Choose **TaskPad Settings** to display the context menu shown in Figure 10.21.

Choose the items in this menu to work with the Taskpad view in similar ways to those previously described in this chapter for Information viewer views:

- **Show Fields**. Delete fields from, or add fields to, the TaskPad. Also change the order of fields in the TaskPad.

- **Group By**. Group tasks in the TaskPad. For example, if you create categories with project names, you can group tasks by categories so the tasks in each project are displayed in a group.

- **Sort**. Sort tasks according to the information in specific fields.

- **Format View**. Select the fonts to be used for column headings and rows in the TaskPad. Also select how you want grid lines to be displayed.

Printing Outlook Items

Printing lists of Outlook items

Printing details of individual items

Printing Address Books

Printing e-mail messages

Printing calendars

Having a printer available

This chapter assumes your computer is already set up to print to a local or network printer.

Printing from Table Views

As you learned in Chapter 10, "Viewing Outlook Items," you can select a table view to see the contents of any Outlook 98 Messaging and Collaboration Client folder. When you have a table view selected, you can print

- The entire contents of the table
- The information in selected items in the table

Printing the Entire Contents of a Table

As a first example of printing the entire contents of a table, click **Calendar** in the Outlook Bar and select the **Active Appointments** view.

Although the information on the next few pages relates directly to printing a table from a table view of a folder's contents, much of it applies to printing individual items in a table, and to printing from other views of Outlook items.

Print the contents of a table

1. Open the **File** menu and choose **Print** to display the Print dialog box shown in Figure 11.1.

FIGURE 11.1

The Print dialog box is similar to the corresponding dialog boxes you see in other Office 97 applications.

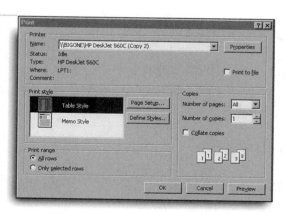

2. In the **Print style** section of the dialog box, choose **Table Style**.

3. Choose **Pre<u>v</u>iew** to display a preview of what Outlook proposes to print, as shown in Figure 11.2.

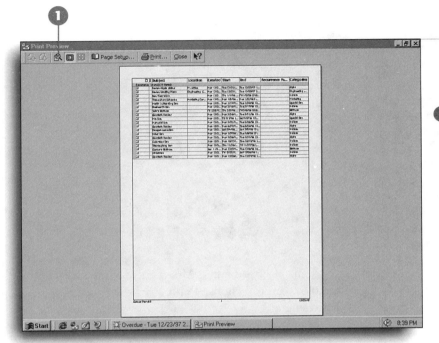

FIGURE 11.2
To see a full-size preview, click
the Actual Size button in the
toolbar.

① Actual Size button

4. Click **Print** in the toolbar to return to the Print dialog box.

5. If you're satisfied with the preview, choose **OK** to print the table. Otherwise, modify the page setup, as described in the next section.

SEE ALSO
➤ *For information about how to display the Appointments view, see "Working with Views" on page 165.*

Setting Up the Page to Be Printed

Before or after you've previewed the page to be printed, you can change the appearance of the page. Because the process for setting up print options in Outlook is similar to that of any other Office application, it's not extensively covered here.

Magnifying the page

Point onto the page and click the mouse button to display the page enlarged to the size at which it can be printed. Click the mouse button again to go back to the original size.

Choose **Page Setup** to display the dialog box shown in Figure
11.3. You can also display this dialog box from the **File** menu
and from the Print Preview window.

FIGURE 11.3

Use the three tabs in this dialog box to control the appearance of the printed page.

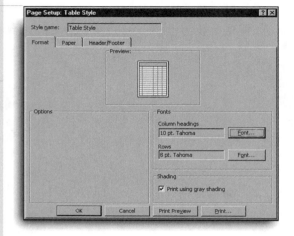

Select the tabs one after the other. After you've made a change
in any of the tabs, you can choose **Print Preview** to see the
effect of that change:

- *Format*. Select fonts to use in the column headings and in
  the rows. Also select whether or not you want shading in the
  printed pages.

- *Paper*. Select the size of the sheets of paper you'll be printing on, the paper source (if your printer has more than one
  paper source), and the page margins. Also select how you
  want each page of your table to be arranged on the sheets of
  paper (you can select arrangements that allow the printed
  sheets to be folded in various ways). Select **Portrait** or
  Landscape in this tab.

- *Header/Footer*. Enter text to be printed in the header and
  footer of each printed page. You can also specify fields that
  automatically print page numbers, the date and time, and the
  user's name in the header or footer.

Specifying a Printer

If you have access to more than one printer, open the **Name** drop-down list in the **Printer** section of the Print dialog box to select a printer. After selecting a printer, you can choose **Properties** to open the properties dialog box appropriate for that printer. The available properties are different for each type of printer. In some cases, you may be able to select such properties as

- Print quality
- Color or grayscale
- How graphics are rendered

Defining Print Styles

When you first display the Print dialog box (refer to Figure 11.1), two print styles are available: **Table Style** and **Memo Style**. After selecting one of these styles, you can choose **Page Setup** to modify the details of that style (as described in "Setting Up the Page to Be Printed" earlier in this chapter). Outlook saves all the setup changes you make as part of the selected style.

What if you want two or more versions of the same style? For example, you may want to print your active appointments first in a format suitable for pinning on the wall, and secondly in a format that fits into your Day Timer. That's where defining print styles comes in.

Defining a print style

1. Choose **Define Styles** in the Print dialog box to display the dialog box shown in Figure 11.4.

FIGURE 11.4

The Define Print Styles dialog box lists the styles available for the view you previously selected.

2. Select an existing style as the basis for a new style. For example, select **Table Style**. Then choose **C**opy. Outlook displays a dialog box named Page Setup: Copy of Table Style. This dialog box is almost the same as the Page Setup dialog box shown previously in Figure 11.3.

3. Use the three tabs in this dialog box to set up the new style.

4. Enter a name for the new style in the **Style name** box. For example, if you're creating a style for Day Timer pages, you could call the style Day Timer.

5. Choose **OK** to save the new style and return to the Define Print Styles dialog box where you'll see Day Timer listed as a style.

6. Choose **Close** to close the Define Print Styles dialog box and return to the Print dialog box.

The **Print Style** section of the Print dialog box now contains the name of the new style. Because more style names are available than can fit into the available space, use the scrollbar to scroll through the style names.

You can create as many styles as you like for each type of view in this way.

Printing Individual Items from a Table

Print individual items from a table view

1. In the table view, select the item or items you want to print, such as one or more appointments in the Active Appointments view of your Calendar folder.

2. Open the **File** menu and choose **Print** to display the Print dialog box shown previously in Figure 11.1.

3. In the **Print Style** section of the Print dialog box, select **Memo Style**.

4. In the **Print range** section at the bottom left of the dialog box, choose **Only selected rows**.

5. Choose **Preview** to see what the items will look like when printed.

Editing and deleting existing styles

You can also use the Define Print Styles dialog box to edit existing styles and to delete styles.

Selecting individual items to print

To select multiple, noncontinuous items, click one item to select it, and then hold down the Ctrl key while you click additional items. To select several consecutive items, select the first item, and then hold down the Shift key while you select the last item.

6. If necessary, click the **Page Se_t_up** button to open the Page Setup dialog box to make changes to the appearance of the printed items.

7. Choose **OK** to print the items.

Printing E-mail Messages

You can print your e-mail messages if desired. One way to do this is to select the messages you want to print from a table view.

When you click **Inbox**, **Outbox**, or **Sent Items** in the Outlook Bar, you normally see your messages in a message view. The message view is a table view, even though it might not look like it because it doesn't have gridlines.

You can select one or more messages, just as you can select other items in a table view, and then print them.

Printing Your To-Do List

The tasks you've assigned to yourself and others are in your Tasks folder. Click **Tasks** in the Outlook Bar to display an Information viewer that shows your tasks. With the exception of Task Timeline, all the default views for tasks are tables.

Select one of the table views of tasks. Now you can print the tasks in the selected table.

Printing from Other Views

As explained in Chapter 10, Outlook has five view structures: card, day/week/month, icon, table, and timeline. The preceding pages of this chapter have focused on printing from table views. Outlook can also print from card, day/week/month, and icon views, but not from timeline views. You can print your Address Book from a card view of your contacts folder, and you can print your calendar from a day/week/month view of your calendar folder. Although you can print from an icon view, I haven't come across a useful reason to print from this view.

Printing E-mail Messages

You can print e-mail messages you've received or sent in several ways.

Printing an e-mail message

1. Click **Inbox** in the Outlook Bar to display a list of messages you've received, or click **Sent Items** to display a list of messages you've sent.

2. Select one or more messages you've received or sent.

3. Choose the Print button 🖨 in the Standard toolbar to print the selected messages.

Printing Your Address Book in Card View

You can print your Address Book in several formats, those supplied with Outlook and others you create for yourself.

Whereas Outlook offers only two print styles for table views, it offers five predefined styles for printing from the card view:

- Card Style
- Small Booklet Style
- Medium Booklet Style
- Memo Style
- Phone Directory Style

Rather than attempt to explain how each of these print styles prints your contact information, I suggest you select each style in turn and then choose **Preview** to see what it looks like.

Printing your Address Book from a card view

1. Click **Contacts** in the Outlook Bar to display the Contacts Information viewer.

2. Select the **Address Cards** view of contacts to display your contact information in card format.

3. Open the **File** menu and choose **Print** to display the Print dialog box shown in Figure 11.5.

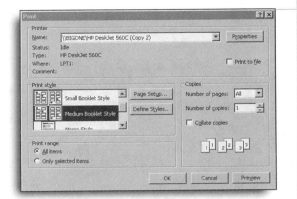

FIGURE 11.5
The **Print style** section of this dialog box contains several predefined print styles for contact items.

4. Scroll in the **Print style** list to locate the style you want to use and select that style.

5. Choose **OK** to print your address cards.

Remember, if the predefined styles don't offer exactly what you need, you can create your own.

Printing Your Calendar in Day/Week/Month View

Outlook also has predefined styles you can use to print your calendar. The five styles are

- Daily Style
- Weekly Style
- Monthly Style
- Tri-fold Style
- Calendar Details Style

I suggest you select each style in turn and then choose **Preview** to see what it looks like. If the predefined styles don't offer exactly what you need, you can create your own.

Printing your calendar

1. Click **Calendar** in the Outlook Bar to display the Calendar Information viewer.

2. Select a **Day/Week/Month** view of calendar items to display your calendar information in day/week/month format.

   3. Open the **File** menu and choose **Print** to display the Print
   dialog box shown in Figure 11.6.

FIGURE 11.6

The **Print style** section of this
dialog box contains several
predefined print styles for calendar items.

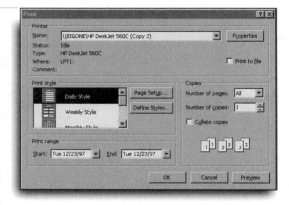

   4. Scroll in the **Print style** list to find the style you want to use
   and select that style.

   5. Choose **OK** to print your calendar.

Printing from Forms

You can print the information about an item from the form you
use to create or edit it. To display an item in a form, double-click
the item in an Information viewer.

Displaying and printing an e-mail message displayed in a form

   1. Click **Inbox** in the Outlook Bar to display a view of the
   items in your Inbox folder.

   2. In any view of the Inbox folder, double-click an item.
   Outlook displays the selected e-mail item in a Message
   form.

   3. Open the form's **File** menu and choose **Print**. Outlook displays the Print dialog box with only the Memo Style print
   style available.

   4. Choose **OK** to print the message.

Creating and Using Folders

What Are Outlook Folders?

**Different folder list for Outlook
with Internet Only Support**

If you've installed Outlook with
Internet Only Support, you'll see
only Personal Folders in your Folder
List. You won't see Public or Shared
Folders.

Folders are containers in which Outlook 98 Messaging and
Collaboration Client keeps items of information. We've talked
about folders in several of the preceding chapters. It's now time
to look at folders in more detail.

To see the Outlook folders available on your computer, open
Outlook, open the **View** menu, and choose **Folder List**. You'll
see a list similar to that shown in Figure 12.1.

FIGURE 12.1

The list of folders available on
your computer may be different from the list shown here,
particularly if you've installed
Outlook with Internet Only
Support.

The list shown in Figure 12.1 contains four top-level folders.
Those you see on your computer are undoubtedly different from
those shown in the figure.

Each of the top-level folders in the list shown in Figure 12.1 is
marked with a symbol that represents a box containing items of
mail. One of these symbols has a small house on top of it; that
symbol indicates your home folder—the folder to which your
mail is delivered and in which you keep your personal information.

The four top-level folders shown in Figure 12.1 are: **Mailbox –
Gordon Padwick, Mailbox – Jason Aldrich, Outlook Today –
[Personal Folders]**, and **Public Folders**. You may have fewer
than four top-level folders, depending on whether you have
access to an Exchange server.

If you don't have access to Exchange Server, you have only one
top-level folder: **Outlook Today – [Personal Folders]**. That's

your Personal Folders file that contains folders in which you save all your Outlook items.

If you do have access to Exchange Server, you have several top-level folders. One folder that is always present provides access to your personal Exchange Server mailbox—that's **Mailbox – Jason Aldrich** in this example (assuming you are Jason Aldrich). If other people have granted you access to their Exchange Server mailboxes, these folders are shown in your list of folders. In the example, Gordon Padwick has granted access to his mailbox, so **Mailbox – Gordon Padwick** is in the top-level list of folders.

If your computer is not connected to a LAN on which Exchange Server is installed, you can save Outlook items only in your Personal Folders file. If you have access to Exchange Server, however, you can choose to save Outlook items either in the Personal Folders file on your own computer or in your Exchange Server mailbox.

Choose where you want to save your Outlook items

1. Open the **Tools** menu and choose **Services** to display the Services dialog box. Choose the **Delivery** tab.

2. Open the **Deliver new mail to the following location** drop-down list. The list contains **[None]**, **Personal Folders**, and (if you have access to Exchange Server) the name of your mailbox on Exchange Server.

3. Select **Mailbox** to have your e-mail delivered to your Exchange Server mailbox or select **Personal Folders** to have your mail delivered to your Personal Folders.

4. Choose **OK** to close the dialog box.

5. Open the **File** menu and choose **Exit and Log off** to exit from Outlook. Restart Outlook.

SEE ALSO
➤ *For more information about using Outlook as an Exchange Server Client, see Chapter 22, "Using Outlook as an Exchange Server Client."*

Mailbox Folders

The folder named Mailbox provides access to the information you've saved in Exchange Server.

Exchange Server also gives you access to Public Folders

If you have Exchange Server, you also have access to some Public Folders, folders that are accessible to everyone who has an account on the Exchange Server on your LAN. The Public Folders top-level folder on your list of folders provides access to these folders.

This folder contains various subfolders in which you can save your Outlook items. The name (Jason Aldrich in this case) is the name assigned by the Exchange Server administrator to your mailbox.

Click the **+** at the left of the folder name to display a list of the subfolders as shown in Figure 12.2.

FIGURE 12.2

This folder contains subfolders for the various types of Outlook items.

Select individual subfolder names to see what each subfolder contains.

The symbol at the left of each folder name indicates the type of item that folder contains. You may see some folder symbols that contain a small square containing a **+** at the bottom-left corner. Folders marked this way (none are shown in Figure 12.2) are *offline folders*.

SEE ALSO

➤ *Learn about offline folders on page 513.*

➤ *Learn about adding the Microsoft Exchange Server information to your profile in Chapter 7, "Setting Up Information Services."*

Microsoft Mail Shared Folders

The Microsoft Mail Shared Folders folder provides access to the mailbox maintained in the Microsoft Mail postoffice. This folder is listed only if you have a LAN connection to a disk on which a Microsoft Mail postoffice is installed, you have an account in that postoffice, and you have the Microsoft Mail information service in your profile.

If you have the Microsoft Mail information service in your profile, you'll also have Personal Folders. All mail you receive from Microsoft Mail is saved in your Personal Folders Inbox folder; all mail you send to Microsoft Mail is saved in your Personal Folders Sent Items folder.

Outlook Today - [Personal Folders]

Personal Folders is a file on a disk that is accessible to your computer, normally one of your computer's hard disks. This file contains folders with the same names as those in the Mailbox folder. You can use these folders to save your Outlook items.

Click the name of the Personal Folders file to display the Outlook Today window. Click the **+** at the left of the folder symbol to display the folders within your Personal Folders file.

Public Folders

Public Folders are maintained by Exchange Server. You have access to these folders only if you have an account on a server on which Exchange Server is installed, you have an account on Exchange Server, and you have the Microsoft Exchange Server information service in your profile. You can use these folders to share information with other users.

In the remainder of this chapter, we'll focus primarily on the Outlook Today [Personal Folders] file and on its folders because they are a fundamental part of Outlook.

You may have more folders

After you install certain Outlook add-ins, Outlook has access to folders in addition to those described here.

Using the Personal Folders File

The section "The Personal Folders Information Service" in Chapter 7, "Setting Up Information Services," explained how to add the Personal Folders information service to your profile and how to give your Personal Folders file a name—it suggested using your initials for the name of the folder. I used my initials for the name of my Personal Folders folder, so now I have a file on my hard drive named gcp.pst.

Naming your personal folders file

You can give your Personal Folders file any name you like. Outlook automatically provides pst as the filename extension.

What the Personal Folders File Contains

A Personal Folders file contains Outlook items in ten folders; one subfolder for Calendar items, one for Contact items, one for Deleted Items, and so on. You can create additional folders.

You can see what's in a folder in two ways:

- Click a shortcut in the Outlook Bar.
- Click a folder name in the Folder List.

For example, to see what's in your Contacts folder, click **Contacts** in the Outlook Bar. You'll immediately see your contacts in the Contacts Information viewer. Alternatively, open the **Folder List** and click **Contacts**.

Creating Folders and Subfolders

The purpose of folders is to organize your Outlook information. In many cases, Outlook's default folders provide an adequate organization for your information, but you may prefer to have a more detailed organizational structure. You can create additional top-level folders, and you can create subfolders under top-level folders. You can also create a hierarchy of subfolders.

Organizing items with categories or folders

I suggest you first try organizing your Outlook items by assigning categories to them. If you find this approach doesn't provide the organization you need, then consider creating and using subfolders.

Before going too far in creating a customized structure of folders and subfolders, however, remember you can assign categories to items. After you've assigned categories, you can display items grouped by categories—you don't need to keep items in separate folders to keep like items together.

The following are a couple examples of how you might find additional folders and subfolders useful:

- *Saving messages by contact*. Instead of saving all your incoming messages in your Inbox folder, and all your outgoing messages in your Sent Items folder, you might like to create a folder for each important contact and save incoming and outgoing messages together in that folder.
- *Saving tasks by project*. Instead of saving all your task items in one folder, you may prefer to create separate subfolders for each project.

The folder structure you create is up to you, just as the folder structure you create on your hard drive is a matter of your preference. You can create additional top-level folders and add subfolders to them; or you can add subfolders to existing folders.

Create a subfolder

1. Display any Information viewer and open the **File** menu. Move the mouse pointer over **Folder** to display the menu shown in Figure 12.3.

FIGURE 12.3

Use the Folder to create subfolders.

2. Choose **New Folder** to display the dialog box shown in Figure 12.4.

FIGURE 12.4

Use this dialog box to name the new folder, define what type of items it will contain, and decide where the folder will be placed.

3. Enter a name for the folder in the **Name** box.

4. Open the **Folder contains** drop-down list and choose one of the six types of Outlook items.

5. In the **Select where to place the folder** list, select the existing folder that the new folder will be subordinate to.

6. Choose **OK** to close the dialog box. A message box asks `Would you like a shortcut to this folder added to your Outlook Bar?`. You should normally answer **No** to this message to avoid cluttering your Outlook Bar. The Folder list now contains the new folder name as shown in Figure 12.5.

FIGURE 12.5

In this case, a subfolder under Tasks has been created.

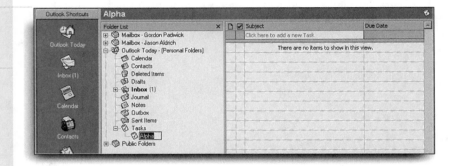

Moving and Copying Items from One Folder to Another

After you've created a new folder, you probably want to move items from an existing folder into the new folder.

Two possible situations for moving and copying are

- The folders from which, and to which, you move or copy the item are of the same type (such as mail item).

- The folders from which you move the item are of a different type from the folder to which you move the item. For example, you may move an item from a folder for mail items to a folder for contact items.

Move an item between like folders by dragging

1. Open the **View** menu and choose **Folder List** to display the **Folder List**.

2. In the **Folder List**, select the folder from which you want to move an item.

3. Select the item you want to move, and then drag it onto the name of the new folder in the **Folder List**.

Recovering a deleted item

If you delete an item by mistake, you can use the methods described here to move the item from the Deleted Items folder back into its original folder.

Move an item between like folders by using menu commands

1. Open the Information viewer that displays the name of the item you want to move.

2. Right-click the item to display the context menu shown in Figure 12.6.

FIGURE 12.6

The context menu contains items appropriate for the type of item you selected.

3. Choose **Move to Folder** to display the dialog box shown in Figure 12.7.

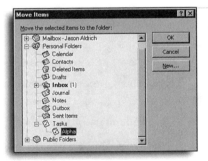

FIGURE 12.7

The Move Items dialog box contains a list of existing folders.

4. Select the folder into which you want to move the selected item, and then choose **OK**.

Now consider moving or copying an item from a folder of one type to a folder of another type. Need an example of why you might want to do that? You can copy an incoming e-mail message from a mail-type folder into a contact folder to automatically add the sender's name and e-mail address to your contacts list.

Move an item between unlike folders

1. Open the **View** menu and choose **Folder List** to display the **Folder List**.

2. In the **Folder List**, select the folder from which you want to move an item.

3. Select the item you want to move, and then hold down the Ctrl key while you drag the item onto the name of the Contacts in the **Folder List**. When you release the mouse button, the Contact form appears with the sender's name and e-mail address in the appropriate boxes. The entire message appears in the form's Notes box; you probably don't want to save the message there, so just delete it.

AutoCreate can save you a lot of time and effort while you're working with Outlook. It's simple to use—all you do is copy an item of one type into a folder of another type, such as an e-mail message into a Contacts folder. The following are some suggestions for using AutoCreate:

- Copy the name and e-mail address of someone who sent you a message into your Contacts folder (described in detail previously).

- After you receive a message asking you to do something, copy the e-mail message into your Tasks folder.

- Make a message public by copying it into a Public Folder.

- Copy information you receive about an event into your Calendar folder.

Many possibilities exist. I suggest you take some time to investigate how you can take advantage of AutoCreate.

Deleting a Folder

The easiest way to delete a folder is to open the **View** menu and choose **Folder List** to display the **Folder List**. Select the folder you want to delete, and then click the Delete button ⊠ in the Standard toolbar.

AutoCreate automatically creates Outlook items

Outlook's capability to create one type of item from another is known as *AutoCreate*.

Deleted items become subfolders–of the Deleted Items folder

When you delete a folder, that folder becomes a subfolder of the Deleted Items folder.

Setting Folder Properties

To set folder properties, right-click an icon in the Outlook Bar or in the Folder List to display the context menu. Choose **Properties** to display the dialog box shown in Figure 12.8.

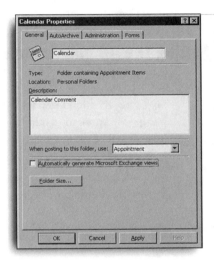

Setting the General Properties

With the **General** tab selected, you can

- Change and expand the **Description** of the selected folder. It's useful to supply a description of a folder you've created and intend to use for a specific purpose.
- Check **Automatically generate Microsoft Exchange views**. Check this option for Public Folders that contain items that might be opened by users of an Exchange client.
- Choose **Folder Size** to see the size of the selected folder and its subfolders.

Setting the AutoArchive Properties

With the **AutoArchive** tab selected, you can

- Choose whether AutoArchive operates on the selected folder.

- If AutoArchive does operate, state the frequency at which AutoArchive should occur.

- Choose whether old items are deleted or saved to a file when AutoArchive occurs.

- If AutoArchive saves items, define the name of the file in which they will be saved.

Setting the Administration Properties

With the **Administration** tab selected, you can

- Choose which view you want to see when the folder first opens. You can display available views in a drop-down list and select one of them.

- Make various choices if the folder is a Public Folder on Exchange Server. These choices don't apply to folders within your Personal Folders file.

SEE ALSO

➤ *To learn how to use Public Folders, see Chapter 23, "Sharing Information with Public Folders and Newsgroups."*

Setting Forms Properties

With the **Forms** tab selected, you can manage the forms available in the selected folder.

Finding Information

Searching for Information

After you've used Outlook 98 Messaging and Collaboration Client for several months, you're likely to have a lot of information stashed away in your folders. Some of it is easy to find, but some is more difficult to find.

It's easy to find the e-mail you've sent. To see all the items listed alphabetically by the name of the person to whom you've sent mail, just open your **Sent Items** folder and click **To**.

What if you want to find e-mail you've sent that made reference to a certain subject? That's not quite so easy, but Outlook has a solution. You can use Outlook's Find feature to locate all sorts of information.

Outlook isn't limited to finding Outlook items; it can also find files anywhere on your computer as well as on other computers to which you have access, much like Windows Explorer.

Finding Outlook Items

Outlook searches only in the selected folder

You must select the folder in which you want to search before you choose **Find**.

As an introduction to using Outlook's Find capability, we'll look at how you can find messages you've received.

To find an e-mail message, display the Inbox Information viewer, then choose the **Find** button in the Standard toolbar (alternatively, open the **Tools** menu and choose **Find**). When you do so, the **Find messages in Inbox** pane appears at the top of the Information viewer, as shown in Figure 13.1.

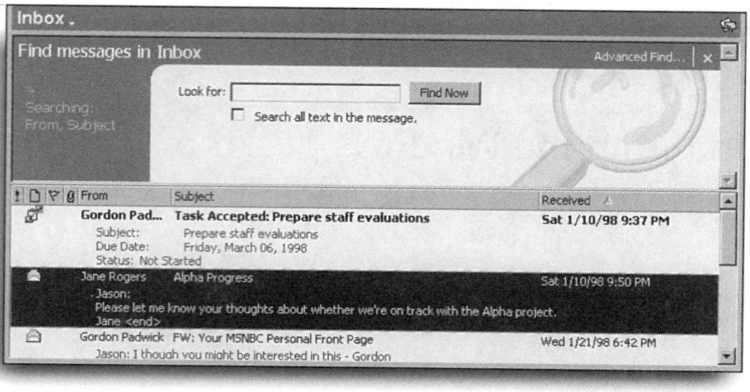

FIGURE 13.1

The Find Messages pane provides an easy way to look for text in a message.

Using the Find Messages function

1. In the **Look for** box, enter the word or phrase you want to find.

2. Leave the **Search all text in the message** check box unchecked if you want to search only the subject of messages. Check this box if you want to search the subject and the entire text of messages.

3. Choose **Find Now** to initiate the search.

If you search only in message subjects, the search is quite fast. Almost immediately, a list of messages with subjects that match your search word or phrase appears in the Information viewer. If you search through the entire text of messages, however, the search takes longer. In either case, if no matches are found, Outlook displays No items found. Also at the completion of the search, two small buttons labeled **Go to Advanced Find** and **Clear Search** appear in the pane.

After making one search, you can choose **Clear Search** to clear the list of found items and also clear the search text. Then you can enter another search word or phrase and begin another search. When you've finished searching, close the pane.

You can use the same technique to search for Outlook items in any folder. For example, to find specific contacts, open the Contacts Information viewer, and choose **Find** to open the Find pane. To find a contact based on the File As text, leave the **Search all text in contact** check box unchecked. To find a contact based on other text in contact items, select the check box— you could do this to find all contacts in a specific city, state, or country.

Using Advanced Find to Find Words and Phrases

Although the Find pane described in the previous section provides an easy way to find certain types of information, it won't always provide what you need. You can't use the Find pane to find Outlook items that contain specific text in certain fields. For

Search results appear in the most recent view

The search results appear in the view you were using when you started the search. For example, if you were using the Last Seven Days view of your Inbox, the search results displayed contain only messages you received in the last seven days. If Outlook doesn't find what you're looking for, you may have to choose a different view and then try **Find** again.

example, you can't find contacts who have a specific telephone area code in this way. Advanced Find can make these sorts of searches, however, and much more.

Accessing Advanced Find

Another way to start Advanced Find

After you've completed a search initiated from the Find pane, Outlook asks you, Did you find it? At this point, you can choose **Go to Advanced Find**.

To access Advanced Find, start by choosing the **Find** button to display the Find pane, as described previously in this chapter. As shown earlier in Figure 13.1, the words **Advanced Find** are at the top-right of the pane. Move the pointer over those words and a button appears. Choose the button to display the Advanced Find dialog box shown in Figure 13.2.

FIGURE 13.2

The Advanced Find dialog box opens with the first tab selected.

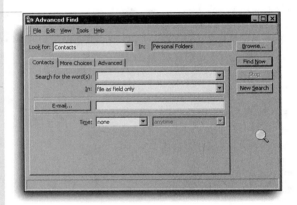

The Advanced Find dialog box contains a three-tabbed section. The name of the first tab corresponds to the name of the Information viewer that was open when you displayed the Find pane. Figure 13.2 shows this tab named **Contacts** because the Contacts Information viewer was open when Advanced Find was chosen. The other two tabs are always named **More Choices** and **Advanced**.

Specifying the Type of Item to Find

Outlook assumes you want to find items of the type contained in the currently open folder and displayed in the current Information viewer. If Outlook is displaying Contact items in your Personal Folders when you start Advanced Find, the first tab within the dialog box named **Contacts**, the **Loo<u>k</u> for** box contains the word **Contacts** and the **In** box contains **Personal Folders**.

If you want to look for a different type of item, open the **Loo<u>k</u> for** drop-down list in which you can select:

Finding all items to which a category is assigned

- Any type of Outlook item
- Appointments and Meetings
- Contacts
- Files
- Files (Outlook/Exchange)
- Journal entries
- Messages
- Notes
- Tasks

Choosing **Any type of Outlook item** can be particularly useful if you want to find all the Outlook items that relate to a particular subject, such as a person or project.

After you've selected a type of item from the list, that item name appears in the **Look for** box, and also as the name for the first tab.

Where to Look for the Item

Outlook items may be in various places. If you haven't changed the default folders, items are usually in one of two places:

- In the folders within your Personal Folders (if you're not using Outlook as a client for Exchange Server)
- In the folders within your Outlook Today mailbox (if you are using Outlook as a client for Exchange Server)

If you have modified the default folder structure, however, the items you want to search for may be in a folder you've created.

When you first open the Advanced Find dialog box, the **I<u>n</u>** box (near the top-right) contains Personal Folders or Mailbox (followed by the name of the Exchange Server mailbox). This means that Outlook is ready to search all the folders within Personal Folders (or Mailbox) for whatever item you specify. After you open the **Look for** drop-down list and select a type of item, Outlook replaces Personal Folders (or Mailbox) with the name of the folder in which the type of item you've selected is normally kept. For example, if you select **Tasks**, Outlook expects to find task items in the Tasks folder.

If the name in the **In** box isn't where you want to search, choose **Browse** to open the dialog box shown in Figure 13.3.

FIGURE 13.3
The Select Folder(s) dialog box lists the available folders.

In this dialog box, expand the appropriate top-level folder if necessary, select the folder in which you want Outlook to search, and choose **OK**. The name of the folder you select appears in the **In** box.

SEE ALSO
➤ *For information about modifying the default folder structure, see "Creating Folders and Subfolders" on page 202.*

Starting Your Search

Suppose you want to search for a contact. You've selected Contacts to look for and you accept Outlook's proposal to search in the contacts folder. Now select the **Contacts** tab.

Setting up your search

1. Enter the word or phrase you want to search for in the **Search for the word(s)** box.

Selecting two or more folders

You can select any number of folders in this way. If you select two or more folders, one folder name is separated from the next in the **In** box by a semicolon.

Using a previous search word or phrase

If you've previously searched for the same word or phrase, you can open the drop-down list and select that word or phrase.

2. If you don't want to search in the field proposed in the **In** box (the one in the **Contacts** tab, not the **In** box at the top of the dialog box), open the **In** drop-down list and select the fields in which you want to search. The selection available varies according to the type of item you're looking for.

In many cases, the information you've entered and selected so far is all that's necessary. Choose **Find Now** to initiate the search. Outlook displays the results of the search at the bottom of the Advanced Find box, as shown in Figure 13.4.

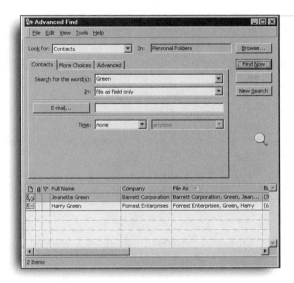

FIGURE 13.4

Outlook displays the result of the search in a table.

You can double-click any item in the search results table to open that item in the Outlook form in which the item was originally created.

Understanding How Outlook Searches

In the preceding pages of this chapter, you've been told to enter the word or phrase you want Outlook to search for. There's more to know than you might expect about how Outlook interprets a word or phrase.

Looking for Several Words

When you enter several words, Outlook searches for those words as a phrase. The entire phrase must exist for Outlook to find it.

Outlook can also search for items that contain one word or another. For example, if you want to search for an item that contains the word "apple" or the word "orange," you enter these words in the **Search for the word(s)** box with a comma or semicolon separating one word from the next. If you enter

```
apple orange
```

Outlook searches for items that contain the phrase "apple orange." If you enter

```
apple,orange
```

or

```
apple;orange
```

Outlook searches for items that contain either "apple" or "orange" or both words.

Instead of single words, you can use phrases. For example, if you enter

```
sweet apples,bitter oranges
```

Outlook searches for items that contain either the phrase "sweet apples," or the phrase "bitter oranges," or both phrases.

Punctuation Marks

If you want to search for a phrase that contains punctuation marks, you must enclose the entire phrase within quotation marks. For example, if you want to search for items that contain the phrase "apple, orange, or banana" enter

```
"apple, orange, or banana"
```

If you omit the quotation marks, Outlook will search for items that contains either "apple," "orange," or "or banana."

Plurals

If you ask Outlook to search for "apple," it finds items that contain "apple" and also items that contain "apples." However, if you ask Outlook to search for "apples" it only finds items that contains "apples"—not items that contain "apple."

Outlook's capability to find plurals when you specify a singular noun extends to nouns that have slightly irregular plural forms. For example, if you specify "box," Outlook finds items that contain "box" and "boxes." Outlook isn't smart enough, however, to find "mice" when you specify "mouse."

Play it safe when looking for plurals

To be on the safe side, if you want Outlook to find singular and plural forms of nouns that have irregular plurals, specify both forms (separated by a comma or semicolon) in the search text.

Finding Items in Other Ways

You can use Advanced Find to find words and phrases in any type of item. You can also look for items based on something other than words or phrases. What you can search for depends on the type of item you're searching.

Finding Calendar Items

If you select Appointments and Meetings in the **Look for** box, the **Appointments and Meetings** tab contains three sections, as shown in Figure 13.5.

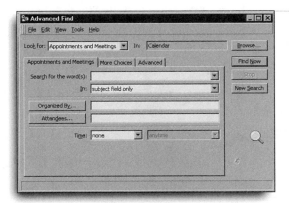

FIGURE 13.5
You can search for meeting organizers, meeting attendees, and time in calendar items.

You can enter search criteria in any one or more of these sections. It's important to understand that all the criteria you enter must be satisfied in order for Outlook to find an item. Suppose, for example, you enter the word "Alpha" in the **Search for the**

words box, and you enter the name of an attendee (such as Jane Rogers) in the **Attendees** box. Outlook then finds those appointments and meetings for which the subject contains the word "Alpha" and the people with whom you had the appointment or attended the meeting includes Jane Rogers.

The top section is where you can enter a word or phrase to search for, as already described.

The second section applies to calendar items that represent meetings. In this section, you can specify one or more people who organized meetings and one or more people who were invited to attend meetings.

The third section applies to all types of calendar items. By default, **none** appears in the **Time** box—time is not used as a basis for finding items. Open the **Time** drop-down list and select among **none**, **starts**, **ends**, **created**, and **modified**. After you select any of these except **none**, the adjacent drop-down list is enabled with **anytime** selected. Open this drop-down list and select among the 12 timeframes. For example, you can direct Outlook to search for items received or created today, tomorrow, in the last seven days, and so on. This feature can help narrow your search, thus helping you find items quickly.

Enter the appropriate search criteria in all three sections of this tab.

SEE ALSO

➤ *For information about using Date fields to select specific dates, see "Using the Advanced Tab" on page 232.*

Finding Contact Items

If you select Contacts in the **Look for** box, the **Contacts** tab contains three sections, as shown in Figure 13.6.

Use the top section of this tab to enter words and phrases to search for, as previously described.

In the second section, you can enter a complete or partial e-mail address. You can use this to find all your contacts who have e-mail addresses on a certain server by entering the name of the server. For example, enter the name of that server (such as hotnet.net) in the **E-mail** box. Outlook will subsequently find all your contacts who have an account on that server.

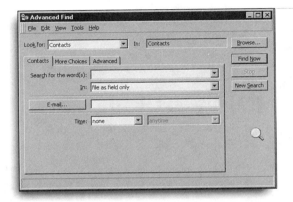

FIGURE 13.6
You can search for e-mail addresses and time in contact items.

The third section is similar to the third section of the **Appointment and Meetings** tab, but with fewer selections.

Finding Journal Items

If you select Journal entries in the **Look for** box, the **Journal Entries** tab contains three sections, as shown in Figure 13.7.

By now you should be getting the picture. You can search each type of Outlook item for words and also define times. In addition, a special search criterion is available for each type of item.

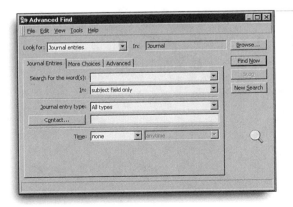

FIGURE 13.7
You can search for specific Journal entry types, contacts, and time in Journal items.

For Journal items, you can open the **Journal entry type** drop-down list and select all types, or a specific type of Journal entry. You can also choose **Contact** to open the Select Names dialog box in which you can select a contact's name (or several contacts' names).

SEE ALSO

➤ *To learn more about searching, see "Using Advanced Find to Find Words and Phrases" on page 211.*

Finding Message Items

If you select **Messages** in the **Look for** box, the **Messages** tab contains three sections, as shown in Figure 13.8.

FIGURE 13.8

You can search for names of message senders and recipients, for your involvement with the message, and for time in message items.

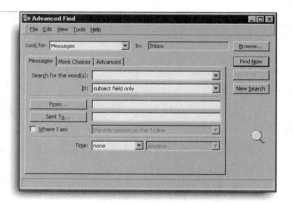

Choose **From** or **Sent To** (or both) to open the Select Names dialog box to select the name or names of people to whom you've sent messages or from whom you've received messages.

If you want to have your involvement in the message as a part of the search criteria, check the **Where I am** box to activate the drop-down list at its right. Open the drop-down list and select from the following:

- The only person on the To line
- On the To line with other people
- In the CC line with other people

Finding Notes Items

If you select **Notes** in the **Look for** box, the **Notes** tab contains two sections, as shown in Figure 13.9. Outlook also gives you the options to search Notes for words or to search based on time constraints.

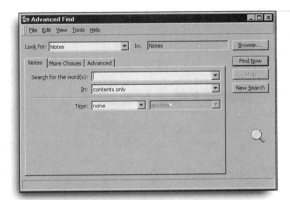

FIGURE 13.9

You can search time in Notes items.

Finding Task Items

If you select **Tasks** in the **Look for** box, the **Tasks** tab contains three sections, as shown in Figure 13.10.

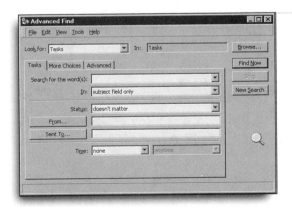

FIGURE 13.10

You can search for status, whom you received tasks from, and whom you sent tasks to in task items.

Open the **Sta<u>tu</u>s** drop-down list and select from the following:

- Doesn't matter
- Not started
- In progress
- Completed

Choose **F<u>r</u>om** or **Sent T<u>o</u>** (or both) to open the Select Names dialog box to select the name or names of people who you've sent tasks to or received tasks from.

Viewing Find Results

Outlook displays the results of a search, whether you start from the Find pane or the Advanced Find dialog box, as a table in a default view. The default view Outlook uses depends on the type of item you're finding. If you're using Advanced Find, you can easily choose a different view of the results of the search.

After you've used Advanced Find to search for items, the items that match your search criteria are displayed in a table at the bottom of the Advanced Find dialog box. To see the items in a different view, open the dialog box's **<u>V</u>iew** menu, choose **Current <u>V</u>iew**, and select the view in which you want to see the search results.

SEE ALSO

➤ *To learn more about using Outlook views, see Chapter 10, "Viewing Outlook Items."*

Saving and Reusing Search Criteria

After you've constructed a set of search criteria (and confirmed that it satisfies your needs) you can save it so it's immediately available to be used again.

Saving your search criteria

1. In the Advanced Find dialog box, open the **<u>F</u>ile** menu and choose **Save <u>S</u>earch** to display the Save Search dialog box.

2. Navigate through your folder structure to find the folder in which you want to save the search or, alternatively, create a new folder.

3. Enter a name for the search file (Outlook provides .oss as the filename extension).

4. Choose **OK** to save the search.

Reusing your search criteria

1. Open the Advanced Find dialog box.

2. Open the **File** menu and choose **Open Search**.

3. Navigate to the folder in which you saved searches and select the one you want to use.

4. Choose **OK** to run the search.

Creating Precise Searches

What you've learned about searching for items so far in this chapter might be all you'll ever need. Chances are, however, that there will be times when you need more. That's when you'll use the **More Choices** and **Advanced** tabs in the Advanced Find dialog box.

Before going any further, you need to understand one thing clearly. You can specify search criteria in any or all the three tabs of the Advanced Find dialog box. When you choose **Find Now**, Outlook looks for items that satisfy all the criteria specified in all three tabs. Although you can only see one tab at a time, Outlook sees all three. If you're not getting the search results you expect, a likely cause is that there are search criteria in one of the tabs you haven't looked at.

I strongly recommend that before you start creating a set of criteria, choose **New Search**. When you do that, all search criteria in all three tabs are cleared. That way you know you're starting from scratch. Now, any criteria set in the tabs you're not looking at can't affect your search.

Refining Your Search

Choose the **More Choices** tab in the Advanced Find dialog box to see the additional criteria you can use to narrow your search (see Figure 13.11).

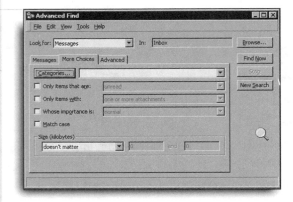

The most useful part of this tab is the **Categories** button. I
can't stress too strongly the benefits of assigning categories to all
your Outlook items. If you want to take advantage of Outlook's
capability to give you control over your personal and business
activities, you must assign one or more categories to every
Outlook item.

Suppose you are involved in a project called Alpha and you create a category named Alpha. Each time you enter an appointment or meeting item related to the project, you assign the
category Alpha to that calendar item; the same goes for every
Alpha-related message you send and receive, contacts involved
with the project, and tasks. Every Outlook item that has to do
with project Alpha has the Alpha category assigned to it.

Now you can easily find every Outlook item that relates to project Alpha.

Using categories to find Outlook Items

1. Open Advanced Find and click the **New Search** button to
make sure no search criteria exist.

2. In the **Look for** list, select **Any type of Outlook item**.

3. Open the **More Choices** tab and choose **Categories**.

4. In the **Available categories** list, choose **Alpha** and then
choose **OK**.

5. Choose **Find Now** to display a list of all Outlook items to
which the category Alpha is assigned.

Choosing more than one category

If you choose more than one category, Outlook finds all the items to
which at least one of the categories
is assigned.

Being able to search by category is a powerful capability, but only if you're meticulous about assigning categories to all Outlook items.

The five other choices you can make in the **More Choices** tab are

- *Only items that are*. Check this and then select either **unread** or **read**.

- *Only items with*. Check this and then select **one or more attachments** or **no attachments**.

- *Whose importance is*. Check this and then select **normal**, **high**, or **low**.

- *Match case*. Check this if you want the search for text specified in the first tab to be matched for case (uppercase or lowercase).

- *Size (kilobytes)*. By default, **doesn't matter** is selected. You can open the drop-down list and then select among **doesn't matter**, **equals (approximately)**, **between**, **less than**, or **greater than**. After you select any of these other than **doesn't matter**, one or both of the boxes on the right become enabled so you can enter the size in kilobytes.

SEE ALSO

➤ *To learn more about assigning categories to items, see Chapter 9, "Creating and Using Category Lists."*

Defining Advanced Search Conditions and Values

Click the **Advanced** tab if you want to get serious about your searches. In this tab, you can define conditions and values for one or more fields in an item. You can create search criteria above and beyond what's available in the other two tabs. You can, for example, use a date field as a criterion to search for items that contain a specific date in a date field.

The top part of this tab contains the **Find items that match these criteria** box. Initially this box tells you **Add criteria from below to this list**, as shown in Figure 13.12.

Suppose you want to search for contacts whose home phone number is within a certain area code.

How you find the size of items

Each type of Outlook item contains a Size field that contains the item's size in kilobytes. The value isn't displayed in any standard view. However, you can add the Size field to a table view. Refer to "Adding a Field to a View" in Chapter 10, "Viewing Outlook Items," for information about how to do so.

FIGURE 13.12

You can be creative in defining searches.

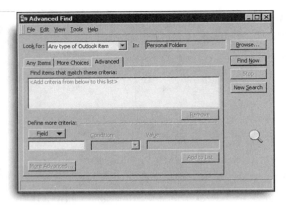

FIGURE 13.12

You can be creative in defining searches.

Searching for Contacts who have a specific area code

1. Open the **Loo<u>k</u> for** drop-down list and choose **Contacts**.

2. Display the **Advanced** tab and choose **F<u>i</u>eld** to display the list of field types, and point to **Phone number fields**. Outlook displays the list of the type of phone number fields shown in Figure 13.13.

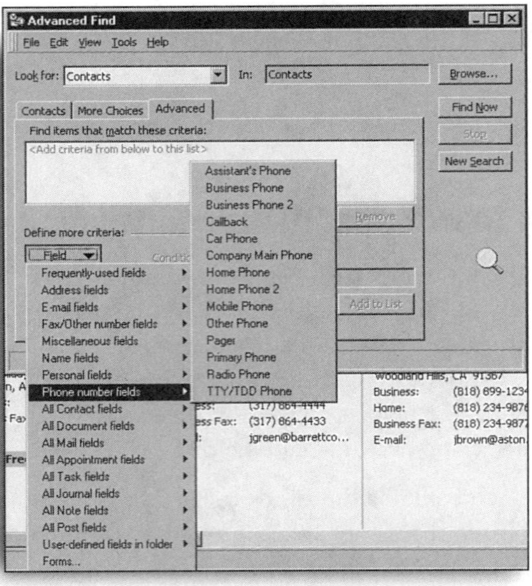

FIGURE 13.13

Outlook displays a list of all phone number fields.

3. Select **Home Phone**. The field you selected appears in the **Field** box. Now the **Condition** box is enabled as shown in Figure 13.14.

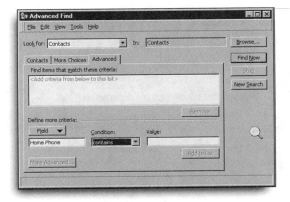

FIGURE 13.14
The **Condition** box initially lists **contains**.

4. You can open the **Condition** drop-down list to select various possible conditions. In this case, **contains** is what you want.

5. In the **Value** box, enter the area code you want to find, such as (818).

6. Choose **Add to List** to add the criteria into the **Find items that match these criteria** box.

7. Choose **Find Now** to start the search.

Outlook searches your Contacts folder and displays all items in which the **Home Phone** field contains the area code you specified.

The preceding example showed only one criterion specified. You can make your search more specific by adding more criteria. For example, you could add a criterion that specifies a certain last name.

Searching for items by multiple criteria

1. Choose **Field**, select **Name fields**, and then select **Last Name**.

2. Enter the last name you want to search for in the **Value** box.

3. Choose **A̲dd to List** to add the second condition into the **Find items that m̲atch these criteria** box. The **Advanced** tab now contains two search criteria, as shown in Figure 13.15.

FIGURE 13.15
This is an example of a search based on two criteria.

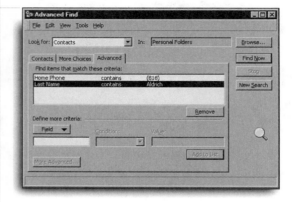

4. Choose **Find N̲ow** to initiate the search.

This search finds only those contacts who have the specified area code and the specified last name.

Finding Files

So far in this chapter we've looked only at finding Outlook items. You can also use Outlook to find files on any disk accessible to your computer.

Specifying Folders

The difference between **Files** and **Files (Outlook/Exchange)**

If you choose **Files (Outlook/Exchange)**, Outlook will look for files within an Outlook folder, such as a Word document in the Inbox folder. Make sure you choose **Files** (not **Files (Outlook/Exchange)**) if you want to find files within the Windows folder structure.

Finding files

1. Start with any Outlook information viewer displayed. Choose **Fi̲nd** and then choose **Advanced Find**.

2. Open the **Loo̲k for** drop-down list and choose **Files** to display the dialog box shown in Figure 13.16. Notice that the first tab is named **Files**.

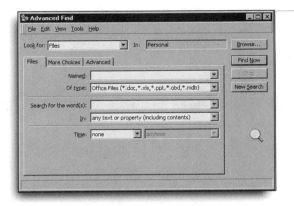

3. If you want to search in a folder other than Personal (or My Documents), choose **Browse** to open the Select Folders dialog box and navigate in it to the folder in which you want to search. Choose **OK** to close the dialog box.

Specifying Filenames and Types

You can specify the file you want to search for by filename and extension.

Outlook initially assumes you want to search for an Office file, so the **Of type** box contains the standard filename extensions for Office files. You can open the drop-down list of types and select from the following:

- *All Files (*.*)*
- *Office Files (*.doc, *.xls, *.ppt, *.obd, *.mdb)*
- *Documents (*.doc)*
- *Workbooks (*.xls)*
- *Presentations (*.ppt)*
- *Binders (*.odb)*
- *Databases (*.mdb)*
- *Templates (*.dot, *.xlt, *.oft, *.pot, *.obt)*

After selecting the appropriate filename extension, enter the name of the file or files you want to search for in the **Name<u>d</u>**

Finding a file with a different extension

You can't enter any other filename extension; you can only choose from the list. Don't worry about this if you want to search for a different type of file. A little later in this chapter, you'll learn an easy way to accomplish this.

box. If you want to search for just one file and you know its exact name, enter that name without the extension. If you want to search for several files, enter the filenames, separating one from the next by a semicolon.

If you don't know exact filenames, or you want to search for several files with similar names, you can use these *wildcard* characters:

- Use * to represent any number of characters.
- Use ? to represent a single character.

For example, if you enter catfish*, Outlook will find files with such names as catfish, catfish01, catfish02, catfish23, catfishfood, and so on. If you enter *fish, Outlook will find files with such names as fish, catfish, dogfish, and so on. If you enter catfish0?, Outlook will find files with such names as catfish01, catfish02, but not catfish23 or catfishfood. One more example: If you enter *fish*, Outlook will find such names as fish, catfish, fish01, and so on.

What if you want to find a file that's name doesn't have one of the standard Office extensions, such as Readme.txt? In that case, enter the complete filename and extension in the **Named** box. When you enter a filename with an extension, Outlook ignores whatever extensions are in the **Of type** box.

After you've specified one or more filenames, choose **Find Now**. Outlook searches in the folder you specified in the **In** box and in all its subfolders and displays a list of all the files that match the filename and extension you specified. You can double-click any name in the list to open the file.

Narrowing the Search

You can narrow the search by entering a word or phrase in the **Search for the word(s)** box.

To specify where Outlook should search for the words or phrases you've specified, open the **In** list to select

- *any text or property (including contents)*
- *contents only*

By default, the **Ti̲me** box contains **none**, meaning that Outlook doesn't consider times and dates when it searches for files. You can open the **Ti̲me** drop-down list and select **modified**, in which case the adjacent drop-down list is available. Open that list, and select from the following:

- *anytime*
- *yesterday*
- *today*
- *in the last 7 days*
- *last week*
- *this week*
- *last month*
- *this month*

Making More Choices

The **More Choices** tab contains two check boxes and a drop-down list, as shown in Figure 13.17.

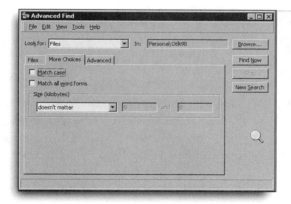

FIGURE 13.17
You can refine your search by using the choices in the **More Choices** tab.

Outlook normally searches for the file contents you specify in **Sear̲ch for the word(s)** (in the **Files** tab) without regard for case. Check **Match Case** if you want the search to be case sensitive.

Outlook normally searches for files that contain exactly the word you specify in **Search for the word(s)**. If you check **Match all word forms**, Outlook locates files that contain variations of the words you specify. For example, if you specify **write**, Outlook finds files that contain variations of write, such as "writes," "wrote," and "written."

You can also specify the size of files you want Outlook to find by opening the **Size** drop-down list and selecting from the following:

- **doesn't matter**
- **equals (approximately)**
- **between**
- **less than**
- **greater than**

After you select anything other than **doesn't matter**, enter the file size in the two adjacent boxes.

Using the Advanced Tab

The **Advanced** tab contains the same elements as the **Advanced** tab described earlier in this chapter for use when finding Outlook items. One difference, however, is that the **Fields** drop-down list contains fields associated with files instead of those in Outlook items. You can choose either **Frequently-used fields** (that contains Created, Modified, and Size), or **All File Fields** (that contains a long list of fields only some of which are associated with any particular type of file). You can select specific fields in documents, and create criteria based on the values in those fields.

Using Find from the Windows Desktop

You can use Outlook's Find feature from the Windows desktop without starting Outlook.

Using Outlook's Find feature from the Windows desktop

1. Choose **Start** in the Windows taskbar to open the **Start** menu.

2. Point to **Find** in the **Start** menu to display the menu shown in Figure 13.18.

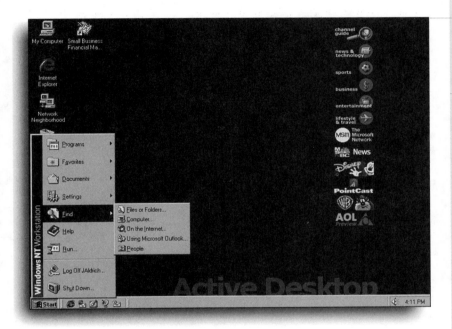

FIGURE 13.18

One of the items in the **Find** menu is **Using Microsoft Outlook**.

3. Choose **Using Microsoft Outlook**. The Advanced Find dialog box is displayed with **Files** in the **Look for** box.

4. Use Find to locate files, as described in "Finding Files" earlier in this chapter.

If you open the **Look for** drop-down list and choose a type of Outlook item, Outlook opens to enable you to proceed.

Using Outlook Templates

Understanding how Outlook uses templates

Using the e-mail templates supplied with Outlook

Creating your own e-mail templates

Saving an Outlook item as a template

Using an Outlook item template to create a new item

What Is a Template?

Outlook 98 Messaging and Collaboration Client uses *templates* in three ways:

- To control the appearance of e-mail messages when you use Microsoft Word to create those messages, and also to create e-mail messages with some standard (boilerplate) text.
- To save Outlook items so those items can subsequently be used as a basis for creating similar items.
- As a means of saving custom forms.

This chapter covers using templates for e-mail messages and using templates to create items based on existing items.

Selecting and Using an E-mail Template

Setting Word as your e-mail editor

To set Word as your e-mail editor, open the **Tools** menu and choose **Options**. Then choose the **Mail Format** tab of the Options dialog box. In the Message format section of the tab, open the **Send in this message format** drop-down list and select **Microsoft Word**.

By default, Outlook uses the Microsoft Exchange Rich Text Format (RTF) or HTML format (depending on which information services you have in your profile) when you create e-mail messages. E-mail templates are available only when you're using Word as your e-mail editor.

By default, Outlook uses the template named EMAIL when you use Word to create e-mail messages. You can also select one of the other templates supplied with Outlook.

Selecting an Outlook template

1. Open the U**se this Template by default** drop-down list shown in Figure 14.1.

2. Choose the template you want to use; then choose **OK** to close the dialog box.

Recipients must use Outlook to see your template

If message recipients use an e-mail client other than Outlook, they won't see the template as you intend.

After choosing a template other than the default EMAIL template, you can use that template to create your e-mail messages. For example, after you choose the URGENT template you'll see that template when you next choose the **New Mail Message** button in the Inbox Information Viewer's Standard toolbar. Figure 14.2 shows the URGENT template.

FIGURE 14.1
The templates shown here are those supplied with Outlook.

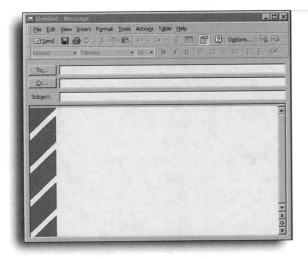

FIGURE 14.2
The graphic design at the left is displayed in red to draw recipients' special attention to the message.

Selecting a template for messages you create using Word has no effect on messages you create using one of the other formats (HTML, Microsoft Exchange Rich Text, or Plain Text). Also, the template you select has no effect on e-mail messages you've already received or will receive in the future.

SEE ALSO
➤ *For more about mail formats, see "Specifying Mail Format" on page 546.*

Creating an E-mail Template

The templates Outlook uses for e-mail messages are Word templates. You can create your own e-mail templates from scratch or by modifying the templates supplied with Outlook. Outlook expects to find these templates in a specific folder. Any templates you create must be in the same folder as those supplied with Outlook.

Finding Where Outlook Looks for Templates

Although a default folder exists where Outlook expects to find templates, Outlook may have been installed on your computer in a folder other than the normal default folder. Before beginning to create your own templates, you must locate the folder in which Outlook expects to find templates.

Finding the default templates folder

1. With any Outlook Information Viewer displayed, open the **Tools** menu and choose **Options**.

2. Choose the **Mail Format** tab and select **Microsoft Word** in the **Send in this message format** drop-down list.

3. Choose **Template Picker** to display the Wordmail Template dialog box.

4. Scroll down the list of template files until you see the name of one of the templates supplied with Outlook, such as Urgent.dot.

5. Right-click the template filename to display its context menu, and then choose **Properties** in the context menu to display the Properties dialog box. Choose the **General** tab, as shown in Figure 14.3.

6. Make a note of the Location of the template file. The location of the file on your computer may be different from the location shown in Figure 14.3.

You must save any template file you create in the location you've just noted. If you save a template file in any other location, Outlook won't be able to use it.

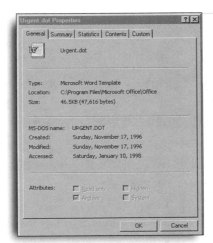

FIGURE 14.3
The General tab tells you the
location of the template file.

Creating the Template

The templates Outlook uses are really Word templates, so it's
not surprising that you use Word to create templates. Close or
minimize Outlook and open Word.

Creating a template

1. Open a new, blank Word document.

2. Use the appropriate Word capabilities to create your template. You can place text, background effects, clip art,
   WordArt, and other graphics on the template (refer to *Using
   Microsoft Word 97* published by Que for information about
   working with Word).

3. Open the **File** menu and choose **Save As** to open Word's
   Save As dialog box.

4. Open the **Save as type** drop-down list and select
   Document Template (*.dot).

5. Replace the default filename (probably Doc1.dot) with the
   name you want to call your new template. You don't need to
   supply the filename extension—Word supplies the extension
   automatically.

6. Navigate in the **Save in** list to find the folder you previously
   noted as the folder in which Outlook looks for templates.

Don't be tempted to save the template in the default folder named Templates.

7. Choose **Save** to save the template.

You've finished creating the template, so you can close Word.

Using the New Template

Use the steps described in "Selecting and Using an E-mail Template" earlier in this chapter to select and use the template you've created.

If you don't see the name of your new template in the **Use this template by default** drop-down list, you probably saved the template in the wrong folder.

Some templates are forms

When you save an item as a template for other items, you're really saving a form. Outlook's terminology is not consistent. When you save a template, Outlook calls it a *Template*; when you subsequently use that template to create an item, Outlook classifies it as a *Form*.

Saving an Outlook Item as a Template

You can save any Outlook item as a template and subsequently use that template as a basis for creating similar items. For example, you may have specific information you always want to include in the Notes box of a task that you create and then assign to someone else. You could create a basic task item with the boilerplate text in the notes box and then save that item as a template.

Saving any item as a template

1. Open the form's **File** menu and choose **Save As**.

2. In the Save As dialog box, open the **Save as type** drop-down list and choose **Outlook Template**.

3. Enter a name for the template and choose **Save**. Outlook saves the template in the same folder as other Outlook templates with .oft as the filename extension.

After you've created a template, you can use that template to create a new item.

Creating an item based on a template

1. In the Outlook Bar, click the icon representing the type of item you want to create, such as Tasks.

2. Open the Information Viewer's **Tools** menu, move the pointer over **Forms**, and choose **Choose Form** to display the dialog box shown in Figure 14.4.

FIGURE 14.4

Open the **Look in** drop-down list in this dialog box to see where forms (including templates) are available.

3. Select **Templates in File System** to see a list of available templates.

4. Select the template you want to use for the task, and then choose **Open**. Outlook opens a new Task form with all the information in the template already in place.

Using Address Books

Creating a Contact List and Outlook Address Book

SEE ALSO

➤ *To learn about some of the ways you can use contact items, see Chapter 17, "Using Contact Items."*

Understanding Contact Items

Contact items contain information about your personal and business contacts, people and organizations. If you have installed Corporate/Workgroup Outlook, your Outlook Address Book contains the e-mail and fax addresses of all your contacts. In the case of Internet Only Outlook, these addresses are in your Contacts list.

Contacts are the people and organizations you interact with. Within the Outlook 98 Messaging and Collaboration Client environment you can

- Send messages to, and receive messages from, contacts.
- Plan meetings with contacts.
- Assign tasks to, and receive task assignments from, contacts.
- Automatically place phone calls to contacts.
- Address letters to contacts.

You can have access to several lists of contacts if you're using Corporate/Workgroup Outlook. These include

- *Contacts folder*. An Outlook folder that contains contact items you create.
- *Outlook Address Book*. A list of e-mail and fax addresses in your Contacts folder.
- *Global Address List*. A list of people who have access to your LAN (Local Area Network).
- *Postoffice Address List*. A list of people with whom you share a Microsoft Mail postoffice.
- *Personal Address Book*. A list of your personal contacts and, optionally, distribution lists.

Internet Only Outlook has only the Contacts folder. You won't necessarily use all the Corporate/Workgroup lists. In the simple situation in which you use Outlook as a Personal Information Manager and as a means to send and receive Internet e-mail messages, you'll probably use only the Outlook Address Book.

If you're a member of a peer-to-peer network, you'll also use the Postoffice Address List to address e-mail messages to your colleagues. Likewise, if you have an account on a LAN, you'll probably use the LAN's Global Address List.

The Personal Address Book serves three purposes:

- Use it to keep a short, quickly accessible list of contacts copied from other address lists.
- Use it for information about your personal friends and other contacts.
- Use it to create mailing and distribution lists.

This chapter focuses on using Outlook to create information about your contacts.

SEE ALSO
➤ *For information about Personal Address Books, see Chapter 16, "Creating a Personal Address Book."*

Creating a Contact Item

In Outlook, a contact item consists of the information you save about a contact, whether the contact is a person or an organization. A contact item consists of many fields of information, only some of which you'll use for any one item. When you create a contact item, you must provide either a person's name or an organization's name (or both). You can enter whatever other information you want to save or leave information fields empty.

Creating a contact item

1. Click **Contacts** in the Outlook Bar to select the Contacts Information viewer.
2. Choose the New Contact button 🔲 in the Standard toolbar (or open the **Actions** menu and choose **New Contact**) to display the Untitled – Contact form with the **General** tab selected, as shown in Figure 15.1.

Outlook's items

Contact items are just one type of item that Outlook saves. Others include Calendar, Message, and Task items.

Moving from one field to another

You can move from one field to the next by pressing Tab. You can move from one field to the previous field by pressing Shift+Tab.

FIGURE 15.1

Use the **General** tab to enter the principal information about a contact.

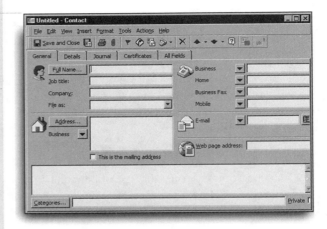

If the information you're entering is about a person, enter the person's name in the **Full Name** box; then enter information into the other boxes as necessary. If the information is about an organization, ignore the **Full Name** and **Job title** boxes and enter the organization's name in the **Company** box.

SEE ALSO

➤ *For general information about creating items, see Chapter 8, "Creating Outlook Items."*

Entering a Person's Name, Job Title, and Company

You can usually enter a person's name in the **Full Name** box in the normal fashion. Enter the first name or initial, a space, the middle name or initial, a space, and then the last name. Figure 15.2 shows the contact form with a typical name entered.

To see how Outlook interprets the name you've entered, choose **Full Name** to display the dialog box shown in Figure 15.3.

When you enter a straightforward name, such as the one in this example, you don't need to check the name in the Check Full Name dialog box. Outlook isn't always smart enough to parse (divide into components) more complex names correctly, however, so it's a good idea to check if you have any doubts.

After you've entered the person's name, press Tab to move the insertion point into the **Job title** text box. When you do so, Outlook automatically displays the person's name in the **File as**

A period should follow all initials

Enter a period after all initials, particularly if you might use Contact items to address letters. You can, of course, omit the middle name.

Entering name components separately

Instead of entering a person's name in the **Full Name** text box, you can choose **Full Name** to open the Check Full Name dialog box and then enter the components of the name in the five text boxes. Click **OK** to close the dialog box.

box, with the last name first (see the following section for more details). At the same time, the title of the form changes—"Untitled" in the title changes to the name of the contact.

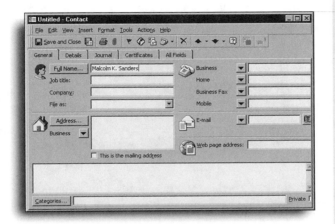

FIGURE 15.2
Enter a person's name like this.

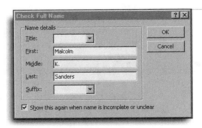

FIGURE 15.3
Outlook separates the name you entered into first name, middle name, and last name fields.

Enter the person's job title in the **Job title** box, press Tab, and enter the person's organization in the **Company** box. These entries are optional.

Selecting a File as Name

The **File as** name for a contact is the name by which contacts are normally alphabetized when you display a list of contacts.

As mentioned previously, Outlook suggests one **File as** name as soon as you enter a person's name. After you've entered an organization name, other **File as** names become available. Open the **File as** drop-down list to see these names, as shown in Figure 15.4.

FIGURE 15.4

You can select a **File as** name from this list.

Instead of choosing one of the **File as** names Outlook suggests, you can enter any name you like (a nickname, for example) in the **File as** box.

SEE ALSO

➤ *For more information on contacts, see "Viewing and Printing Contact Items" on page 261.*

Entering Phone and Fax Numbers

Although the contact form has just four boxes for phone and fax numbers: **Business**, **Home**, **Business Fax**, and **Mobile**, you can use Outlook to save as many as 19 phone and fax numbers for each contact.

To save a phone or fax number, place the insertion point in the appropriate box and enter the number. Consider these hints about entering phone numbers:

- Outlook ignores characters other than numbers. You can use such characters as parentheses and dashes if you want to, but Outlook ignores them. Outlook automatically displays phone numbers in the format used in the region you've selected in the Windows Control Panel Regional Settings dialog box.

- In North America, don't place a 1 before the area code. Your modem's dialing properties should be set to provide the 1 automatically when it's needed.

- Always include the area code, even if it's your local area code that you don't need to dial. If your modem's dialing properties are set correctly, Outlook ignores your local area code. With the area code entered, you can use your contact information to place phone calls from a location outside your normal area, such as when you're traveling or after you move.

- Enter international phone numbers in the format

  +021(982)494-4321

  where 021 is the country code. The parentheses and the hyphen are optional.

- Outlook saves any text after the phone number, but doesn't use that text when placing phone calls. You can, for example, append a contact's extension number after the phone number. When you place a call, the extension number is there for you to refer to.

After you've entered a phone number, press Tab or Enter to move to another box on the form (or click in another box). When you do so, Outlook saves the number in the appropriate contact field.

Entering additional phone numbers

1. Click one of the arrow buttons at the left of the phone number boxes to display a list of available phone number types, as shown in Figure 15.5. Those phone number types that already contain entries are indicated by check marks.

2. Select the phone number type you want to enter. The name of that type replaces the label at the left of the arrow button you clicked in step 1.

3. Enter the number for the type of phone number you just selected.

Continue in this way to enter and save as many phone and fax numbers as you need.

Outlook saves all the phone numbers you enter

Replacing one phone number label with another in this way doesn't affect a phone number previously displayed in the box. That phone number is still saved. You can open the list of phone number types and select one that's checked to see the number.

FIGURE 15.5

It doesn't matter whether the arrow button is next to a phone number you've already entered or next to an empty box.

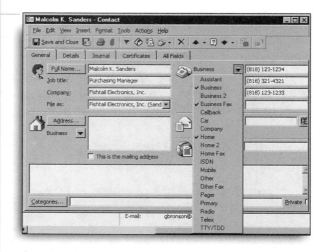

Entering Addresses

Outlook can save three addresses for each contact: Business, Home, and Other. By default, Outlook expects you to enter a business address; if you want to enter a different address, click the arrow button below **A_ddress**, and select **Home** or **Other** from the drop-down list.

Entering an address is similar to entering a contact's name:

- You can enter the complete address in the large address box.
- You can choose **A_ddress** to display the Check Address dialog box in which you can enter the address components in individual text boxes.

For straightforward home addresses, you should normally enter the complete address in the large box.

Entering addresses

1. Enter the street address on the first line, and press Enter.

2. Enter the city name, a comma, the state or province abbreviation, two spaces, and then the postal (ZIP) code. Press Enter.

3. If the address is for a country or region other than your own, enter the name for the country or region and press Enter.

Saving more than three addresses for a contact

Outlook lets you save only three addresses for each contact. If you need to save more than three addresses for a contact, you'll have to create two or more contact items for that contact.

Selecting Outlook Regional Settings

Outlook automatically selects a country or region name according to your Windows Regional Settings. To select Regional Settings, open the Windows Control Panel and double-click **Regional Settings** to display the Regional Settings Properties dialog box. In the **Regional Settings** tab, open the drop-down list of regions and choose your own region. Choose **OK** to save the setting.

After you've entered an address, you can (but don't have to) choose **Ad̲dress** to open the dialog box shown in Figure 15.6 to confirm that Outlook has correctly parsed the address.

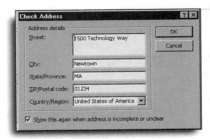

FIGURE 15.6

These are separate fields in which Outlook saves address components.

If the information in any field is incorrect, you can edit that information in the normal way. Choose **OK** after you've made any changes.

To enter more complex addresses, such as many business addresses, you're usually better off to choose **Ad̲dress** and enter the address components directly in the five text boxes.

You can enter as many lines of information as necessary in the **Street** box, but only one line of information in the other four boxes. You can open the **Co̲untry/Region** drop-down list and choose a name, or you can enter a name yourself (either one that's in the drop-down list or one that isn't).

After you've completed the address, click **OK** to close the dialog box and display the address in the Address box on the form. Outlook checks the **This is the mailing add̲ress** box automatically after you finish entering the first address.

Now you can proceed to enter one or two more addresses. All the addresses you enter are saved.

Entering E-mail Addresses

Outlook can save three e-mail addresses—identified with fields labeled as **E-mail**, **E-mail 2**, and **E-mail 3**—for each contact.

You have to provide the country or region name in the Check Address dialog box

When you enter an address in the Check Address dialog box, Outlook doesn't provide a country or region name automatically.

Choose the correct mailing address

When you enter two or three addresses for a contact, make sure the correct one is marked as the mailing address. Choose the mailing address (business, home, or other), and check the **This is the mailing add̲ress** check box.

Accessing AOL and CompuServe directly

Use the address formats listed to address messages to AOL and CompuServe addresses by way of the Internet. You can also send messages directly to these services by adding the AOL and CompuServe information services to your profile.

To enter the first e-mail address, place the insertion point in the **E-mail** box and then enter the address in the normal manner, such as these examples:

- Internet: `essmith@company.com`
- AOL: `essmith@aol.com`
- CompuServe: `99999.999@compuserve.com` or `essmith@compuserve.com`

You can enter an e-mail address that's already available in an address book or list (other than the Outlook Address Book).

Adding an e-mail address already found in the Address Book

1. Choose the book icon at the right of the **E-mail** box to display the Select Name dialog box.

2. Open the drop-down **Show names from the** list, and select the appropriate address book or list.

3. Select a name from the list and choose **OK** to close the dialog box. The contact form now shows the name you selected (underscored to indicate the name is an alias for an e-mail address).

After you've entered one e-mail address, you can open the drop-down list to choose **E-mail 2** or **E-mail 3**, and then enter one or two more e-mail addresses.

Saving more than three e-mail addresses

If you need to save more than three e-mail addresses for a contact, you'll have to create two or more contact items.

Entering a Web Page Address

To save a contact's Web address, place the insertion point in the **Web page address** box and enter the address, normally in the following format:

`http://www.company.com`

Adding Notes and Attachments

You can use the large unnamed text box near the bottom of the **General** tab to enter miscellaneous notes. Also, you can choose the Insert File button 🔘 to attach information to the contact item.

SEE ALSO

➤ *For more information about adding miscellaneous notes, see "Providing Additional Information" on page 146.*

Assigning Categories to a Contact

Choose **Categories** at the bottom of the **General** tab to open the Categories dialog box and assign one or more categories to the contact. Don't omit this step if you want to be able to organize your Contact items by category.

SEE ALSO

➤ *For more about categories, see "Assigning Categories to an Item" on page 147.*

Entering More Contact Details

In many cases, you can use the **General** tab to enter all the information you need to save about a contact. Sometimes, however, you'll want to save more information. You can use the contact form's other tabs for this purpose.

Select the **Details** tab to display it, as shown in Figure 15.7.

> **Keep information where it belongs**
>
> Don't use the large text box in the **General** tab for information that belongs in fields accessible in other tabs.

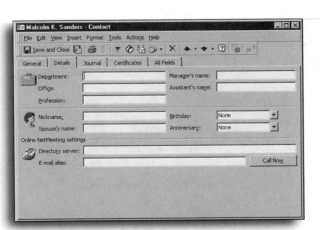

> **FIGURE 15.7**
> The **Details** tab has 11 boxes you can use to save contact information.

Enter information into the five boxes in the top section of the tab; place the insertion point into a box, and then type the information. Use the same method to enter information into the **Nickname** and **Spouse's name** boxes.

You can enter **<u>B</u>irthday** and **Anniversar<u>y</u>** either by typing dates or by opening a calendar and selecting a date. When you enter a birthday or anniversary, Outlook automatically creates a recurring event in your Calendar folder.

The reverse Y2K problem

If you enter **00** for a year, Windows assumes you mean the year 2000. You must enter **1900** if you want your birthdays and anniversaries to be marked for that year. Otherwise, you won't see those birthdays and anniversaries in your Outlook calendar until the year 2000.

One problem with entering birthdays and anniversaries is that Outlook insists on including a year; although you know the month and date, you frequently don't know the year. My workaround for this problem is to use the year 1900 when I don't know the year (none of my contacts was born or married in 1900).

The bottom section of the **Details** tab contains NetMeeting-related information. If the contact is someone with whom you have NetMeetings, and that contact is listed in a directory server, enter the name of the server in the **<u>D</u>irectory server** box. You can also enter the contact's e-mail alias in the **E-mai<u>l</u> alias** box. After you've done so, you can initiate a NetMeeting by choosing the **Call No<u>w</u>** button.

SEE ALSO

➤ *For more information about working with dates, see "Specifying Dates and Times" on page 144.*

Creating Automatic Journal Entries

Outlook can automatically record all your activities relating to a contact, but you have to set Outlook to make journal entries for each contact.

To direct Outlook to make journal entries for a specific contact, open the contact form's **Journal** tab, shown in Figure 15.8.

By default, **Auto<u>m</u>atically record journal entries for this contact** is unchecked. Check this box if you want Outlook to create journal items for this contact.

The remaining part of this tab has to do with displaying existing journal items. See Chapter 29, "Journaling Your Activities," for additional details.

SEE ALSO

➤ *For an introduction to Outlook's Journal, see "Remembering What You've Done" on page 51.*

➤ *For additional information about Outlook's Journal, see Chapter 29, "Journaling Your Activities."*

➤ *For additional information about recording journal entries related to a contact, see "Setting Journal Options" on page 542.*

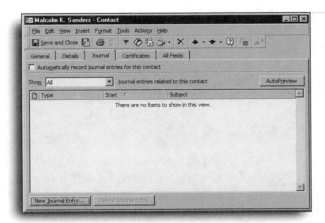

FIGURE 15.8

Use this tab to direct Outlook to make journal entries for a specified contact and to display existing Journal items.

Using Other Contact Fields

Outlook saves each piece of information you provide about a contact in a storage location known as a field. Separate fields exist for each of the five components of a full name, each component of an address, and so on. In addition to these, and other fields you can directly access from the contact form's tabs you've already looked at, there are many more fields. In fact, Outlook has 134 fields for information about each contact.

Open the **All Fields** tab to have access to all of Outlook's contact fields. When you first open this tab, you'll see no fields listed because **User-defined fields in this item** is selected, and you probably haven't created any user-defined fields at this point.

Open the **Select from** drop-down list and select **Frequently-used fields**, as shown in Figure 15.9.

You can scroll down to see many more fields than those shown in Figure 15.9.

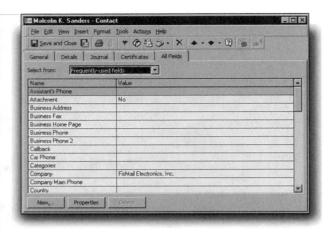

FIGURE 15.9
Outlook displays the contents of **Frequently-used fields** in the selected contact item.

Outlook offers several lists of fields that you can select by opening the drop-down **Se_lect from** list:

- **User-defined fields in this item**
- **Frequently used fields**
- **Address fields**
- **E-mail fields**
- **Fax/Other number fields**
- **Miscellaneous fields**
- **Name fields**
- **Personal fields**
- **Phone number fields**
- **All Contact fields**
- **User-defined fields in folder**
- **All Document fields**
- **All Mail fields**
- **All Appointment fields**
- **All Task fields**
- **All Journal fields**
- **All Note fields**
- **All Post fields**

Select whichever group you need, and then scroll through the list of fields. In addition to seeing what's currently in a field, you can, in most cases, edit the existing value in the field or enter a value into an empty field.

Saving a Contact Item

After you've entered all the information for a contact, save that item by choosing **Save and Close** in the form's toolbar. Alternatively, you can open the form's **File** menu and choose

- *Save*. To save the item and leave the form open with information about the current item displayed in the form.
- *Save and New*. To save the item and leave the form open with all fields cleared, ready to enter information about a new contact item.
- *Save As*. To save the item in a specific format, as described later in this section.

When you choose **Save As**, Outlook opens a dialog box in which you can choose the format in which you want to save the item. Select among these formats:

- *Text only (*.txt)*. Use this if you want to use the contact information in another application that accepts text files.
- *Rich text format (*.rtf)*. Use this if you want to use the contact information in another application that accepts files in rich text format.
- *Outlook template (*.oft)*. Use this if you want to save this item as a template for another item.
- *Message format (*.msg)*. Use this if you want to save this item in a format compatible with a messaging application such as Exchange client.
- *VCARD Files (*.vcf)*. Use this to save the contact in the industry-standard VCARD format.

SEE ALSO
➤ *For information about templates, see Chapter 14, "Using Outlook Templates."*

You can't change Outlook's internal data

Some fields contain internal data that it wouldn't make sense to change. Examples are the **Size** field that contains the size of an item and the **Created** field that contains the date on which the item was created.

Editing a Contact Item

To edit a contact item, open the Contact Information viewer in any view. Double-click the item you want to edit to display it in the contact form.

In the form, you can change the information in fields, delete information from fields, and add new information into blank fields.

Creating Similar Contact Items

Outlook keeps information about each contact as a separate contact item. Although a contact item for a person has a field for that person's spouse, there's only one birthday field. Similarly, a contact item has a field for children's names, but you have to list all the children's names in a single field. For your family contacts, therefore, you'll want to create a separate item for each member of the family.

In the case of contact items for organizations, only one set of fields exists for a person's name. If you have several contacts within an organization, you'll normally want to have one contact item for each person within an organization.

Creating Contact Items for Members of a Family

Some of your contacts are probably members of a family, all of whom have the same address and phone numbers. Each family member, however, has a different birthday.

You probably have better things to do with your time than to create a completely new contact item for each family member. You don't have to. Instead, create a complete contact item for one member of the family, copy that item as many times as necessary, and edit the items so that each has the correct name, birthday, and other personal information.

Creating multiple contact items for family members

1. Create a complete contact item for one member of the family.

2. Display the Contact Information viewer with the Outlook Bar at its left side.

3. Locate the contact item you created in step 1.

4. Duplicate that contact item by holding down Ctrl while you drag the item onto **Contacts** in the Outlook Bar.

5. Repeat step 4 to duplicate the original item as many times as necessary.

6. In the Contact Information viewer, double-click the duplicated items one at a time to open them in the Contact form; then make the necessary changes in each one. Choose **Save and Close** in the form's toolbar to save each item.

Creating Contact Items for Members of an Organization

You can use the method described for creating items for individual members of a family, or you can use Outlook's built-in New Contact from Same Company capability.

Creating contact items for members of the same company or organization

1. Create an item for one contact at the company.

2. In the Contact Information viewer, select that contact item.

3. Open the **Actions** menu and choose **New Contact from Same Company**. Outlook creates a new contact item with the organization name and address already entered.

4. Complete the item by entering the contact's name and whatever other information is appropriate.

Viewing and Printing Contact Items

You can view contact items in any of the standard views provided with Outlook; you can also create your own views. You'll probably find that the views provided with Outlook provide the overall format you need, but don't include all the fields you'd like to see. You can easily add fields to Outlook's views.

By default, Outlook displays contacts in alphabetical order of **File as** name.

When you're satisfied with your views of Outlook items, you can print these views in various formats.

SEE ALSO

➤ *For information about modifying views, see "Changing the Fields in a View" on page 177.*

➤ *For information about printing, see "Printing Your Address Book in Card View" on page 194.*

Only in Corporate/Workgroup Outlook

You can't, and don't need to, create an Outlook Address Book in Internet Only Outlook.

Creating an Outlook Address Book

Outlook saves the contact items you create in the Contacts folder. Although you can display items in the Contact Information viewer and you can print an address book that contains your contact items, you don't necessarily have an Outlook Address Book you can use to address e-mail messages. Some steps must be taken to let Outlook see your Contact items in an Outlook Address Book.

The first important step is to add the Outlook Address Book information service to your profile if you haven't already done so. To see if you already have that information service, open the **Tools** menu and choose **Services**. If you see Outlook Address Book included in your list of information services, it's already in your profile. If it's not already there, you must add it.

The next step is to make sure your Contacts folder is shown as an e-mail Address Book.

Adding your Contacts folder as an e-mail Address Book

1. Choose **View** in the menu bar and then select **Folder List**.

2. In the **Folder List**, right-click **Contacts** to display the context menu.

3. In the context menu, select **Properties** to display the Properties dialog box. Choose the **Outlook Address Book** tab, as shown in Figure 15.10. Make sure that **Show this folder as an e-mail Address Book** is checked.

4. Choose **OK**.

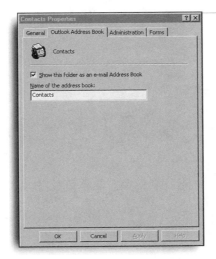

FIGURE 15.10

Use the **Outlook Address Book** tab to designate a folder to be shown as an e-mail Address Book.

The **Name of the address book** box contains the name by which Outlook proposes to identify your Outlook Address Book. The default name is "Contacts;" you can replace this name with another if you want.

SEE ALSO

➤ For information about adding the Outlook Address Book information service, see "The Outlook Address Book Information Service" on page 115.

➤ Learn how to use contacts to address an e-mail message in the section "Creating an E-mail Message" on page 296.

Creating a Personal Address Book

Why use a Personal Address Book?

Creating and managing a Personal Address Book

Creating and using distribution lists

No Personal Address Book in Internet Only Outlook

With Internet Only Outlook, you can create distribution lists by using groups, as described at the end of this chapter.

What Is a Personal Address Book?

A *Personal Address Book* contains names, addresses, phone numbers, and other information about people and organizations that you maintain for your personal use. In Outlook, your Personal Addess Book can contain information copied from other address books and lists, and also information you've entered into it manually. A Personal Address Book is a file that has .pab as its filename extension.

Why would you want to have a Personal Address Book? Consider these four good reasons:

- To save time, particularly if your other address books and lists are large.
- To make it easy to create distribution lists.
- To save information about personal contacts that you don't want to share with other people.
- To be able to specify messaging encoding for individual message recipients.

Saving time requires a little explanation. If you work in a large organization, you probably have access to several address books and lists, each of which contains information about people to whom you send e-mail messages. When you're ready to send a message, you may have to search through several address books and lists to find an e-mail address. You can avoid this time-consuming chore by copying information about the people with whom you frequently communicate into your Personal Address Book. Then you have to look in only one place for most e-mail addresses.

Using a Personal Address Book for distribution lists and as a place to keep information about your personal contacts is covered later in this chapter.

SEE ALSO

➤ *For information about encoding messages, see "Manually Entering Information into Your Personal Address Book" on page 267.*

Creating a Personal Address Book

You create a Personal Address Book by adding the Personal Address Book information service to your profile.

Add the Personal Address Book information service to your profile

1. Open the **Tools** menu and choose **Services** to display the Services dialog box.

2. Choose **Add** to display the Add Service to Profile dialog box.

3. Select **Personal Address Book** in the list of services and choose **OK** to return to the Services dialog box in which Personal Address Book is now listed.

SEE ALSO

➤ *For more information about the Personal Address Book information service, see "The Personal Address Book Information Service" on page 135.*

Manually Entering Information into Your Personal Address Book

You can enter information into a Personal Address Book in two ways: manually and by copying information from other address books.

Manually adding information to your Personal Address Book

1. Click the **Inbox** shortcut in the Outlook Bar to display the Inbox Information Viewer.

2. Choose the Address Book button 📇 in the Standard toolbar to display the Address Book dialog box.

3. Open the **Show Names from the** drop-down list and choose **Personal Address Book** (or the name you gave your Personal Address Book when you created it) to display the dialog box shown in Figure 16.1.

4. Choose the New Entry button in the dialog box's toolbar to display the dialog box shown in Figure 16.2.

You must close and restart Outlook

Although Personal Address Book is listed in the Services dialog box, you must close and restart Outlook 98 Messaging and Collaboration Client before you can use the service.

FIGURE 16.1

The Address Book dialog box contains the names of all existing entries.

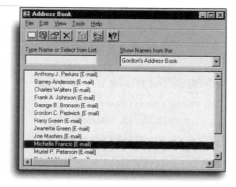

FIGURE 16.2

The New Entry dialog box lists various types of entries.

5. Select the type of entry you want to create. For example, if you're making an entry for a person who has an Internet e-mail address, select **Internet Address**. If you're making an entry for a person who has an address of a type that's not listed, select **Other Address**. Then choose **OK** to display the dialog box shown in Figure 16.3.

FIGURE 16.3

This is the dialog box you see when you're entering information for someone who has an Internet address.

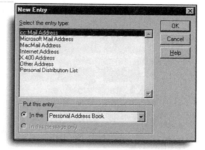

6. Enter the person's name in the **Display name** box and the person's address in the **E-mail address** box.

7. If you want to send e-mail messages in Microsoft Exchange rich text format, click the **Always send to this recipient in Microsoft Exchange rich text format** check box; otherwise, leave the check box unchecked.

8. To provide special message encoding instructions for messages you send to this recipient, choose **Send Options** to show the dialog box in Figure 16.4.

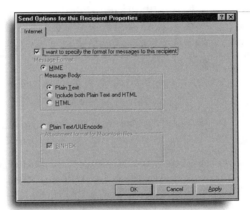

FIGURE 16.4
Use this dialog box to specify encoding instructions for messages to this person.

9. You can, if you like, open the other three tabs in this dialog box to save business information (address, title, company, phone number, and so on), various phone numbers, and general notes.

10. Choose **OK** to save the information in your Personal Address Book.

Editing and Deleting Information

To edit information in your Personal Address Book, display the names in the book, as described at the beginning of the preceding section. Then double-click a name to open the Properties dialog box with information about that name displayed. You can open any tab in this dialog box and select any box to make changes.

To delete information about a person, display the list of names and select the one you want to delete. Choose the Delete button ☒ in the toolbar to delete that person from your Personal Address Book. When you do so, the name is permanently deleted (not moved to your Deleted Items folder).

Importing Information from Other Address Books

You can import information from other address books and lists into your Personal Address Book.

Add names from your Outlook Address Book into your Personal Address Book

1. Click the **Inbox** shortcut in the Outlook Bar to display the Inbox Information Viewer.
2. Choose the Address Book button 📖 in the Standard toolbar to display the Address Book dialog box.
3. Open the **Show Names from the** drop-down list and choose **Outlook Address Book**, **Contacts** (or the name you gave your Outlook Address Book when you created it) to display a list of contacts.
4. Select the names in your Outlook Address Book that you want to copy into your Personal Address Book.
5. Choose the Add to Personal Address Book button in the Address Book dialog box toolbar.

You can use the same method to copy information from other address books and lists into your Personal Address Book.

Importing Your Personal Address Book into Your Contacts Folder

You can import the information from a Personal Address Book (your own or someone else's) into your Contacts folder.

Importing your Personal Address Book

1. Open the Outlook **File** menu and choose **Import and Export** to display the first Import and Export Wizard window shown in Figure 16.5.

FIGURE 16.5

Use the Import and Export Wizard to import information from your Personal Address Book into your Contacts folder.

2. Select **Import from another program or file**; then choose **Next**.

3. In the **Select file type to import from** list, select **Personal Address Book**. Then choose **Next**.

4. In the **Select destination folder** list, select **Contacts**. Then choose **Next** to display the Import a File dialog box.

5. Choose **Finish** to initiate importing information.

Creating a Distribution List

You can use your Personal Address Book to create distribution lists for e-mail messages and faxes.

Creating a distribution list

1. Click the **Inbox** shortcut in the Outlook Bar to display the Inbox Information Viewer.

2. Choose the Address Book button 📖 in the Standard toolbar to display the Address Book dialog box.

3. Open the **Show Names from the** drop-down list and choose **Personal Address Book** (or the name you gave your Personal Address Book when you created it) to display the New Entry dialog box shown previously in Figure 16.2.

4. Choose the New Entry button in the dialog box's toolbar to display the New Internet Address Properties dialog box shown previously in Figure 16.3.

5. Select **Personal Distribution List** in the list of entry types and choose **OK** to display the dialog box shown in Figure 16.6.

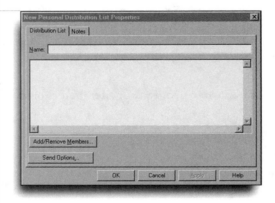

FIGURE 16.6

The New Personal Distribution List Properties dialog box initially contains no names.

6. Choose **Add/Remove Members** to display a dialog box that contains a list of names in one of your address books or lists.

7. Select all the names in this list that you want to include in your distribution list, choose **Members**, and then choose **OK**.

8. If necessary, open the **Show Names from the** drop-down list, select another address book or list, and select names. When you choose **OK**, the names are added to names you previously selected from other lists.

9. Place the insertion point in the **Name** box, and enter a name for the distribution list.

10. Choose **OK** to save the distribution list.

Subsequently, you can open your personal address list and select the distribution list. Use this method to send e-mail to all the names in the distribution list.

SEE ALSO

➤ *For information about using distribution lists to address conventional mail, see "Creating a Form Letter" on page 281.*

Using Groups in Internet Only Outlook

In Internet Only Outlook, you create groups instead of the distribution lists you create in Corporate/Workgroup Outlook.

Creating a group

1. Open the **Tools** menu and choose **Address Book** to display the Address Book dialog box that's similar to the one shown in Figure 16.1.

2. In the Address Book toolbar, choose **New Group** to display the Properties dialog box.

3. In the Properties dialog box, enter a name for the group in the **Group Name** box.

4. Choose **Select Members** to display the Select Group Members dialog box that contains the contact names in your Contact List.

5. Select the contacts you want in the group; then choose **Select** to copy the selected contacts into the Members list.

6. Choose **OK** to go back to the Properties dialog box that now contains the names to the selected contacts.

7. Choose **OK** to go back to the Address Book dialog box that now contains the new group name in addition to the original list of contacts.

After you've created a group in this way, you can select the group name to send e-mail or faxes to all members of the group.

Using Contact Items

Placing a phone call to a contact

Writing and addressing a letter to a contact

Creating a form letter to be sent to selected contacts

Opening a contact's Web page

Initiating a NetMeeting with a contact

Displaying a map showing a contact's location

Using Contact Items for Many Purposes

As described in Chapter 15, "Creating a Contact List and Outlook Address Book," you can create an Outlook Address Book that contains e-mail addresses and fax numbers for all the contacts in your Contacts folder. Then you can address e-mail and send faxes to your contacts.

You can print your contact information in formats suitable for putting in binders of several sizes so you always have it with you.

You can share your contact information (all of it or selected items) with other people by copying items in a folder that other people can use or, if you maintain the information on Exchange Server, by sharing your Contacts folder.

This chapter describes several more ways you can use information in your Contacts folder.

SEE ALSO

➤ *To make printed copies of your contact items, see "Printing Your Address Book in Card View" on page 194.*

➤ *To learn about sending e-mail, see Chapter 18, "Sending an E-mail Message"; to learn about sending faxes, see Chapter 24, "Sending and Receiving Faxes."*

➤ *To copy items to a folder, see "Moving and Copying Items From One Folder to Another" on page 204.*

Placing Phone Calls

Saving records of your phone calls

Automatically saving records of phone calls (including their duration) is particularly valuable for people who bill clients for time spent on projects.

If you have a modem, you can use the Outlook 98 Messaging and Collaboration Client to make phone calls to your contacts. That saves you the trouble of looking up phone numbers and possibly misdialing them. An additional benefit is that Outlook can automatically save a record of when you made the call and its duration in the Outlook Journal.

Setting Dialing Properties

You must, of course, have a modem installed in your computer and you must have Dial-Up Networking installed under Windows. Also, you must have specified the location you're calling from so the number you're calling can be dialed correctly.

You can set up several locations, allowing you to make calls from various places without changing the phone numbers you've entered into your contact items.

Setting your dialing properties

1. Click **Contacts** in the Outlook Bar to display the Contacts Information Viewer.

2. Select any contact and open the **Actions** menu. Move the pointer onto **Call Contact** to display a list of the selected contact's phone numbers, and select any number in the list to display the New Call dialog box shown in Figure 17.1.

FIGURE 17.1
This dialog box displays the number you've selected to call.

3. Choose the **Dialing Options** button at the bottom of the dialog box (be careful not to select **Dialing Properties**) in this dialog box to display the Dialing Options dialog box; then choose **Dialing Properties** (not Line Properties) to display the dialog box shown in Figure 17.2.

FIGURE 17.2
Use this dialog box to control how your modem dials the call.

Dialing properties affect all Windows applications

Each location you set up applies to the way Windows handles phone calls made from Windows itself or from any application that runs under Windows.

You can save your calling card number

You can choose **Change** to open the Change Calling Card dialog box in which you can specify your calling card and your calling card number. If you do that, you won't be asked for a calling card number when you place a call. You probably wouldn't want to do that unless you're confident no one else can access Windows on your computer.

If you're working on a desktop computer that's always in the same place, you'll only need to set up one location. If you have a laptop computer that you use in various places, however, you'll need to set up a separate location for some of those places.

Each location you set up should have a name, such as Home. In addition, each location specifies

- The area code you're dialing from so the area code of the person you're calling is omitted if that person's area code is the same as yours.

- The country or region from which you're calling so country codes are used as required.

- Any numbers you need to dial to access an outside line for local and long-distance calls. Leave these boxes empty if access numbers are not required, as is normally the case when you're calling from home.

- Whether you use a calling card when calling from the location. If you check this box, you'll be asked for the calling card number when you place the call.

- You may have the phone company's call waiting service on the line you'll be using. If you have this service, you can enter the code that disables call waiting, so your modem connection won't be interrupted if a call comes in while you're using your modem. Often, this code is *70, but you should check with your local phone company for the code to disable call waiting.

- Select whether you want to use tone or pulse dialing.

Placing a Call

After you've set up the location, or locations, from which you make phone calls, you're ready to place calls to phone numbers in your Contacts folder.

Placing a call to a contact

1. Display the Contacts Information viewer and select the contact you want to call.

2. Open the **Actio͟ns** menu, choose **C͟all Contact**, and select the number to call, or open the **Autodialer** drop-down list ⌖⏷ in the Advanced toolbar and select the number to call. In either case, Outlook displays the New Call dialog box shown previously in Figure 17.1.

3. If the New Call dialog box displays the correct number to call and you have specified only one location that you call from (very important), choose **S͟tart Call**. Outlook dials the number and tells you to Lift the receiver and click **Talk**. Follow those instructions to talk with the person you're calling.

Before you choose **S͟tart Call**, answer the following questions:

■ *Is the correct phone number displayed?* If your contact has several phone numbers, make sure you selected the correct one in step 2. If the number displayed in the New Call dialog box isn't the right one, open the drop-down **Number** list and select the correct number.

■ *Is Outlook going to use the correct dialing location?* If you've set up only one dialing location, that's not an issue. If you've set up two or more dialing locations, however, you need to check that the correct one is selected. Unfortunately, the New Call dialog box doesn't display the dialing location; you have to choose **Dialing P͟roperties** to see which location Outlook intends to use. In the Dialing Properties dialog box, the **I am d͟ialing from** box contains the name of the currently selected location. If that's correct, choose **OK**. To select a different location, open the **I am d͟ialing from** list box, select the appropriate location, and choose **OK**.

■ *Do you want to create a Journal entry for the call?* If you do, make sure the **Create new Journal Entry when starting new call** box is checked. Otherwise, make sure the box is unchecked.

After you've attended to these questions, choose **S͟tart Call** to place the call.

SEE ALSO

➤ *For information about keeping records of your phone calls, see "Journaling Phone Calls" on page 472.*

Writing a Letter to a Contact

Despite our commitment to the era of electronic communications, there are times when we have to write a letter, address an envelope, attach a postage stamp to it, and drop it in the old-fashioned mailbox. Outlook can help us with that.

Writing a letter to a contact

1. Open the Contacts Information Viewer and select the contact to whom you want to write the letter.

2. Open the **Actions** menu and choose **New Letter to Contact** to display the Letter Wizard window shown in Figure 17.3.

FIGURE 17.3

The Letter Wizard leads you through the steps of creating a letter to a contact.

3. Follow through the series of tabs and windows to create and print your letter, and to print an envelope.

This wizard is a little different from most others. You can go from one window to another either by clicking the tabs or by choosing the **Next** or **Back** buttons. Use the **Letter Format** tab to choose the overall format of your letter, the **Recipient Info** tab to choose how the letter will be addressed, the **Other Elements** tab to choose special elements to be included, and the **Sender Info** tab to choose how it will be signed. When you choose **Finish**, Word opens ready for you to write the letter.

Creating a Form Letter

It's beyond the scope of this book to go into all the details about sending a form letter to some of your contacts. If you need to do so, consult a book that deals with Word's Mail Merge capabilities, such as *Using Microsoft Word 97* by Jane Calabria (published by Que).

Creating a form letter to send to a distribution list involves three steps.

1. Creating a data source that contains the names and addresses of the recipients and, possibly, other recipient-specific information.

2. Creating a main document that contains the text that's included in every letter and placeholders (field codes) for information supplied from the data source.

3. Combining the data source with the main document to create individual, personalized letters.

Creating a Mailing List

You can use your Outlook Contacts list as the data source. That's fine if you want to send a form letter to all your contacts. Most likely, you want to send a form letter to only some of your contacts. You can do this by creating a mailing list consisting of specific contacts.

Creating a mailing list from your contact items

1. With any Outlook Information Viewer displayed, open the **File** menu, point to **Folder**, and choose **New Folder** to display the Create New Folder dialog box shown in Figure 17.4.

2. Enter a name, such as Mailing List, for a new folder in the **Name** box.

3. Open the **Folder contains** drop-down list and choose **Contact Items**.

4. Choose an existing folder, such as **Contacts**, in the **Select where to place the folder** list under which the new folder is to be a subfolder.

FIGURE 17.4

This dialog box shows the names of your currently existing folders. Now you have an Outlook folder that contains the names and addresses of people to whom you want to send a form letter.

5. Choose **OK** to finish creating the new folder. If Outlook asks you whether you would like to have a shortcut to this folder in the Outlook Bar, choose **No**. Outlook displays the folder list with the new folder included.

6. Click **Contacts** in the Outlook Bar to display the Contacts Information Viewer. You can select any view of your contact items.

7. Select the contact items you want to include in your mailing list. You can do this by holding down Ctrl while you click individual contact items.

8. If the Folder List is not already displayed, open the **View** menu and choose **Folder List**.

9. Hold down Ctrl while you drag one of the selected contact items onto the new folder name (Mailing List or whatever you called it) in the Folder List. Although you only drag one item, Outlook copies all the selected items into the new folder.

Creating a Large Mailing List Using Categories

The preceding example shows how you can create a new Contacts folder that contains a few of the contacts in your original Contacts folder. But what if you have a Contacts folder that contains thousands of contacts and you want to send a form letter to a few hundred of them? It would be time-consuming (and prone to errors) to manually select contacts. A better way exists—it's based on using categories.

When you create your contact items, assign a specific category to each contact to whom you want to send a form letter—the category might be "customer." To begin creating the mailing list, follow steps 1 through 5 in the preceding section.

When you get to step 6, choose the **By Category** view of your Contacts folder to see your contacts grouped by category. One of the categories is "customer" (or whatever name you used). Instead of having to hunt through your entire list of contacts, you have all the contacts to which this category is assigned in one place.

You don't have to select these contacts before you can copy them into your new Contacts folder. Instead, just drag the category header (with Ctrl held down) onto the name of the Mailing List folder in the Folder List.

This fast way of creating a mailing list is particularly useful if you want to send periodic mailings to a group of people. You only have to keep your main contact list up to date. Each time you're ready to send a mailing, delete the previous items in the Mailing List folder and then just drag the customer category from your Contacts list into the Mailing List folder. That way, mailings are always based on the items in your current Contacts folder.

Using the Mailing List in a Form Letter

Sending a form letter

1. Open a new, blank document in Word.
2. In Word, open the **Tools** menu and choose **Mail Merge** to open the Mail Merge Helper dialog box shown in Figure 17.5.
3. Choose **Create**, **Form Letters**, **Active Window**.

It's not necessary to close Outlook

You can close Outlook if you like before proceeding, but you don't have to unless your computer has limited resources.

FIGURE 17.5
Use the Mail Merge Helper to step through the Mail Merge process.

4. Choose **Get Data** and then **Use Address Book** to display the Use Address Book dialog box shown in Figure 17.6.

FIGURE 17.6
This dialog box lists your entire contacts list and any subsidiary contact lists, such as your mailing list.

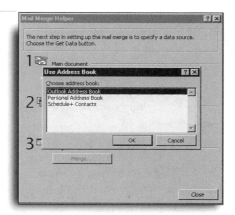

5. Choose **Mailing List** (or whatever name you gave to your mailing list folder) and then click **OK**. If several Outlook profiles are available on your computer, and Outlook isn't already open, you're asked to select a profile. Select a profile and choose **OK**. After a few seconds delay, a message box tells you there are no merge fields in your main document.

6. Choose **Edit Main Document** to display a Word window that includes the Mail Merge toolbar.

7. In the Mail Merge toolbar, choose **Insert Merge Field** to display a list of fields that can be merged from your contacts list.

8. Select a field from the list to place that field into your main document. The field name enclosed in chevrons (<<>>) appears in the Word document.

9. Repeat step 8 as many times as necessary to place additional merge fields in your document. You can insert whatever characters you want between the field names.

10. Choose the Check for Errors button in the Word Mail Merge toolbar to preview the merged documents. This icon appears as a document with a check mark. Note that this toolbar is only displayed when you are creating a mail merge.

Exploring a Contact's Web Page

The **General** tab of the Contact form contains a box in which you can provide a contact's Web page address. You can use Outlook to open a contact's Web page.

Opening a contact's Web page

1. Display the Outlook Contacts Information Viewer and locate the contact whose Web page you want to open.

2. Double-click the contact item to open the Contact form with information about the selected contact displayed in the **General** tab.

3. Choose the hyperlink displayed in the **Web page address** box. Outlook opens Internet Explorer and, if you are currently online to the Internet, attempts to find the Web page. If you're not currently online, a dialog box asks if you want to dial a remote network. Choose **Yes, dial** to create the Internet connection.

Starting a NetMeeting with a Contact

You can start a NetMeeting with a contact, but only if you have entered the contact's directory server name and e-mail alias in the **Details** tab of the Contact form for that contact.

As mentioned in Chapter 2, "Communicating with the World," NetMeeting is not a part of Outlook, it's a separate Microsoft application. It's mentioned here only to draw your attention to the fact that you can start a NetMeeting from within Outlook. For more information on using NetMeeting, see *Special Edition Using Microsoft Internet Explorer 4*, published by Que.

SEE ALSO

➤ *For general information about NetMeetings, see "Holding NetMeeting" on page 36.*

➤ *For information about providing NetMeeting information in a contact item, see "Entering More Contact Details" on page 255.*

Locating a Contact

You can display or print a map showing any contact's location in the United States.

Mapping a contact's location

1. Establish a connection to the Internet in the normal way.

2. Click **Contacts** in the Outlook Bar to display your contacts in any view.

3. Double-click the contact whose location you want to find to display information about that contact in the Contact form.

4. If you have more than one address for the contact, make sure the one you want to see is selected in the form.

5. Open the form's **Actions** menu and choose **Display Map of Address**. Outlook accesses the Microsoft Expedia Maps site on the Internet, finds the map that contains your contact's address, and displays that map, as shown in Figure 17.7.

You can do several things at this stage:

■ Change the scale of the map by clicking the buttons in the **Zoom Level** box at the right side of the map.

Perhaps not 100%

Expedia Maps provides up-to-date coverage of most of the United States. Microsoft is constantly making more maps available. Extended coverage of Expedia Maps is beyond the scope of this book. For additional information, choose the Help button above the map.

- Change the area covered by the map by clicking the buttons in the **Map Mover** box at the right side of the map.

- Obtain the URL of the map. You can insert this URL into your own documents to provide immediate access to the map.

- Choose **Printable Map** (at the bottom-left of the map) to give you a version of the map that can be printed, as shown in Figure 17.8. To print the map, choose the Internet Explorer's **Print** button.

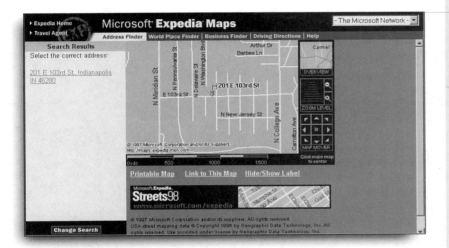

FIGURE 17.7

Your contact's location is shown by a pushpin on the map.

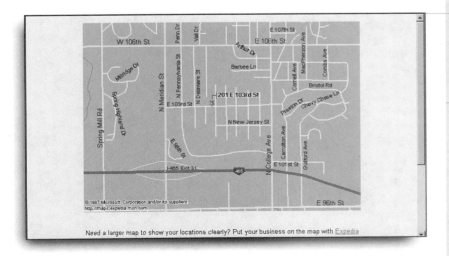

FIGURE 17.8

This map, ready for printing, is at the same scale as the one you chose by clicking buttons in the **Zoom Level** box.

Sending and Receiving Messages

Sending an E-mail Message

Understanding E-mail

Electronic mail (*e-mail*) is probably the most important application in Outlook 98 Messaging and Collaboration Client for many people, whether they work on a corporate network or independently. Many companies have decided to use Outlook primarily for its e-mail features, replacing the e-mail or other messaging systems they already have. Both in the workplace and at home, e-mail is quickly becoming one of the world's most common means of communication.

E-mail lets you send messages to co-workers in your organization, to friends and relatives all over the country and even around the world. You can contact just about any company, as well as most government agencies. Best of all, e-mail is fast, convenient, and relatively inexpensive. You can use Outlook's Inbox to send and receive messages, to attach files to your messages, and to include formatting, such as fonts, colors, and bullets, in your messages.

This chapter explains how to create and send e-mail messages with Outlook, taking advantage of many of Outlook's unique features.

Within a Workgroup or LAN

If you are a member of an organization that uses a *Local Area Network (LAN)*, you can use Outlook to send and receive messages using the e-mail system that is installed on the network. Your network's e-mail system usually gives you access to everyone in your immediate workgroup, and might also give you direct access to colleagues in other facilities or other parts of your organization.

Most corporate networks also have services installed that let you send and receive messages over the Internet. This allows you to keep in touch with your clients, suppliers, vendors, and anyone else who has an Internet e-mail address.

Sending Messages over the Internet

If you are not a member of an organization that provides e-mail services for you, you can use a commercial *Internet service provider* (commonly known as an *ISP*) to gain access to Internet e-mail. The services of an ISP give you the same capability to reach businesses, corporate contacts, or friends and relatives that you would have on a corporate network.

An Internet service provider is a company that can provide connectivity to the Internet, usually for a monthly fee. Many ISPs are local companies that serve a small area. Local ISPs usually provide you with Internet browser software, e-mail service, and the capability to host your own Web site.

Many larger companies also provide Internet service to a large region, or to the entire nation. Larger ISPs include regional telephone companies, and traditional online services such as CompuServe and America Online. These companies sometimes provide additional services beyond those available from local ISPs, such as online information services and forums. Users in some locations, however, may need to use a long-distance call to access the services.

Adding an E-mail Information Service to Your Profile

Profiles are used to store the preferences and configuration for a user in Outlook. Your Outlook profile must contain at least one messaging service for you to be able to send and receive e-mail. The messaging service might be a connection to a Microsoft Exchange Server, a Microsoft Mail Postoffice, Lotus Notes, or some other messaging service. If you are working remotely, the connection might be to an Internet service provider (ISP) or a commercial service such as America Online or CompuServe.

You must also have connectivity to the service you are installing. If you are working on a network, this connectivity is usually provided by a Network Interface Card (NIC) in your computer,

What is an e-mail service, and why do you need one?

Although the Outlook e-mail folders are great for sending and receiving messages, you need to use an e-mail service to actually deliver those messages. Outlook is sometimes called an *e-mail client*, which means that it works together with an existing e-mail service to provide addressing and delivery of your messages.

If you don't install an e-mail service, you can still use Outlook for its Contact, Calendar, and other features, but you won't be able to send or receive messages.

which is connected by cable to the physical network. If you are working remotely, you can connect to your ISP or your network mail service over telephone lines, using a modem.

After you have established your connectivity to your network or other mail provider, you are ready to set up a mail service in Outlook.

Installing an e-mail service in Outlook

1. Open the **Tools** menu and choose the **Services** command to display the Services dialog box, as shown in Figure 18.1.

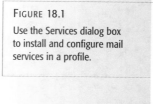

FIGURE 18.1

Use the Services dialog box to install and configure mail services in a profile.

2. Click the **Add** button to display the Add Service to Profile dialog box, as shown in Figure 18.2.

FIGURE 18.2

Use this dialog box to install a new service in your profile.

3. Select the type of service you want to add, and then click **OK** to configure the service.

The configuration options for the service will vary depending on the type of service you selected. Figure 18.3 shows the configuration options for Microsoft Exchange server. This dialog box lets you configure your computer to communicate with your Exchange server while directly connected to the network, as well as when using remote connections and Dial-Up Networking.

SEE ALSO

➤ *To learn how to create and modify profiles, see Chapter 6, "Creating a Profile."*

➤ *For more information on configuring Outlook to work with Exchange, see Chapter 22, "Using Outlook as an Exchange Server Client."*

➤ *For more information on remote mail and Dial-Up Networking, see Chapter 32, "Working Remotely."*

FIGURE 18.3
The Microsoft Exchange Server dialog box shows the properties of this mail service.

Selecting a Message Format

Outlook enables you to create messages in four different formats. You can select one of these message formats based on the features it provides, measured against its compatibility with other e-mail systems:

- *HTML* enables you to include all the elements of the Hypertext Markup Language, which is the primary document format of the Internet. This format supports fonts, colors, and active content such as animations. When you send an HTML message to users whose e-mail editor doesn't support HTML, they won't see all the formatting, and they might see a lot of confusing codes.

Using e-mail accounts with Internet Mail Only

If you have installed the Internet Mail Only (IMO) version of Outlook 98, the process for installing an Internet e-mail service is slightly different than with the Corporate or Workgroup installation. Open the

Tools menu, and choose **Accounts**. The Internet Accounts dialog box appears. The **Mail** tab in this dialog box lists all the Internet e-mail accounts that you already have installed.

- *Microsoft Exchange Rich Text* also supports formatting such as fonts, colors, bullets, and other common document formatting features. This format is supported by a larger range of e-mail editors than the HTML format, including earlier versions of Outlook and the Exchange Inbox.

- *Plain Text* messages include no formatting. Although these messages have the least attractive appearance, they can be read by just about any e-mail editor and also result in small message sizes.

- *Microsoft Word* messages use the formatting and editing capabilities of Word to create and read your messages. If you are an experienced Word user, you might find that you can work most effectively in Word. If you use advanced features such as tables in your messages, these features might not be supported in all e-mail editors.

To select a message format, follow these steps:

Selecting your e-mail message format

1. Open the **T**ools menu, choose **Options**, and then click the **Mail Format** tab.

2. Select an item in the list next to **Send in this message f**o**rmat**.

3. Click **OK** to close the Options dialog box and complete the command.

Creating an E-mail Message

After you have installed and configured an e-mail service in your Outlook profile, you can use Outlook to compose and send messages. You can create a new e-mail message at just about any time while Outlook is running, no matter what Outlook activity you're performing.

Outlook's e-mail features let you send e-mail messages to your coworkers, and to users through the Internet. Your messages can include formatting, such as fonts, bullets, indenting, graphics, and you can attach files of just about any type.

To create an e-mail message, begin by opening the **File** menu, choosing **New**, and then choosing **Mail Message**, or by pressing Ctrl+Shift+M. A new, untitled message window appears, as shown in Figure 18.4.

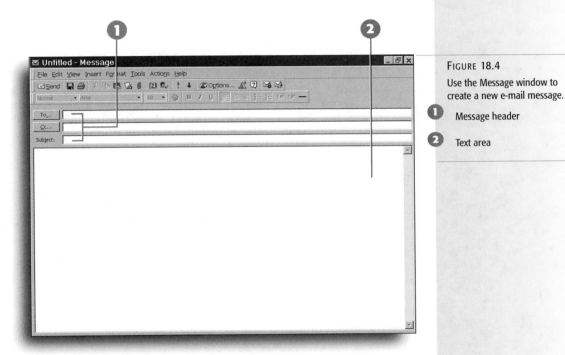

The area at the top of the message editing window, known as the message header, has text boxes for entering one or more addresses for the message, along with the subject of the message. Two basic ways exist to provide an address for your message:

- You can type the address in the **To**, **Cc**, or **Bcc** text boxes.
- You can select names from an address book, such as your Personal Address Book, or your Contacts list. If you are connected to a network e-mail system, you can select from your network e-mail address list.

Make sure you have the correct address

If you choose to type an address directly into the **To** or **Cc** text boxes, you need to make sure the address is correct—Outlook will not be able to check the address before attempting to send it. If you're sending a message to an Internet address, the address is usually in the format user-name@organization. com. For example, one of my e-mail addresses is WilliamRay @Compuserve.com.

Automatic name checking

When you type an e-mail address in the **To** or **Cc** box of a new message, you can use Outlook's automatic name checking feature to help you enter the name more quickly.

To enable automatic name checking, open the **Tools** menu and choose the **Options** command. Then click the **Preferences** tab. Click the **E-mail Options** button, then the **Advanced E-mail Options** button. Check the **Automatic name checking** box, then click **OK** three times to close the dialog boxes.

If you don't have automatic name checking turned on, you can ask Outlook to check names at any time, by opening the **Tools** menu and choosing the **Check Names** command after you have typed the **To** and **Cc** names in a new message.

Of course, the easier method is to select a name from a list. To use this method of addressing and to add a subject line to complete the message header, follow these steps:

Selecting names from an address list

1. Click the **To** button to display the Select Names dialog box, as shown in Figure 18.5.

2. Click a list in the **Show Names From the** drop-down list box to choose the address list that has the addresses you want to use.

3. Select a name from the list at the left side of the dialog box, then click **To** to add the selected name to the list of addressees for this message.

4. If you want to send the message to more than one person, repeat steps 2 and 3 to select additional addressees. You can select more than one name at a time by holding the Ctrl key as you click additional names.

5. To send someone a copy of the message, select a name from the address list, and then click **Cc**; to send someone a blind copy (so other recipients do not see that person's name on the recipient list), select a name and click **Bcc**.

FIGURE 18.5

The Select Names dialog box shows the e-mail address of everyone in your workgroup.

1 Select names from the list here

2 Choose an address list here

3 Click here to add the name to the **Message Recipient** list

4 Click here to copy or blind copy a recipient

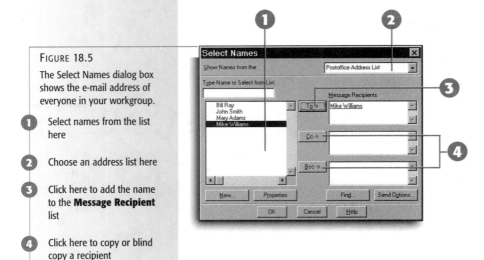

6. Click **OK** to close the dialog box and insert the addresses into the message header.

7. To add a subject line, click in the **Subject** line text box and type the subject.

Now that you've addressed your message, you can type the content of the message. Tab or click into the main text box of the message window, and begin typing your text.

SEE ALSO

➤ *To learn how to install and use a Personal Address Book, see Chapter 16, "Creating a Personal Address Book."*

➤ *To learn how to use a Contacts list, see Chapter 15, "Creating a Contact List and Outlook Address Book" and Chapter 17, "Using Contact Items."*

Adding Attachments

In addition to the text in your message, you can use e-mail to send additional files. You might want to send someone a copy of a financial spreadsheet you've created in Excel, a report you wrote in Word, a graphic image, or even a video clip. Outlook lets you send just about any type of file or object, as an attachment to your e-mail.

To send a file as an attachment to an Outlook e-mail message, follow these steps:

Attaching a file to an e-mail message

1. Create a new message and enter the addressing information, as well as the text of the message.

2. Open the **Insert** menu and choose **File** to display the Insert File dialog box, as shown in Figure 18.6.

3. Select the location of the file you want to attach by clicking the **Look in** drop-down list. Select the file you want to attach by clicking the filename. You can select more than one file by holding down the Ctrl key while you click.

4. On the right side of the dialog box, select **Attachment** in the **Insert As** area.

5. Click **OK** to close the dialog box and complete the command.

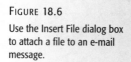

FIGURE 18.6

Use the Insert File dialog box to attach a file to an e-mail message.

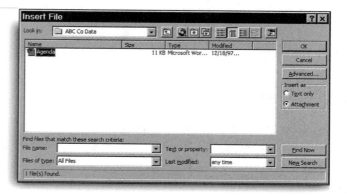

The attachments you have added are displayed at the bottom of the message window. The files represented by the attachments will be sent along with the message.

Keep in mind that attached files might be large. Files such as graphics, audio, video, and other document formats often grow to several megabytes in size. Such large files can take a long time to send and receive. Some mail administrators enforce a limit, such as 1MB (megabyte), on the file size permitted for attachments. Check with your mail administrator for any restrictions that may exist on message or attachment size.

Not all e-mail systems can reliably handle all types of attachments. When you send a message to an Internet address, it's possible that the attachment won't survive the delivery. If you haven't tested sending attachments to a particular destination, make sure you verify that the attachment was sent successfully.

Flagging a Message

Outlook uses *flags* to let you draw special attention to a message. If your recipient is using outlook, he will see the flag when he receives the message. Outlook provides several types of flags to highlight a message.

You can only place one flag on a message, and you also have the option of setting a reminder date for the flag.

1. While you are creating or editing a message, open the **Acti<u>o</u>ns menu and choose <u>F</u>lag for Follow Up**. The Flag for Follow Up dialog box appears, as shown in Figure 18.7.

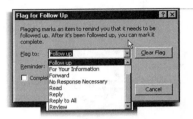

FIGURE 18.7
The Flag for Follow Up dialog box shows the available type of flags for messages.

2. Click the <u>F</u>lag to list to select the type of flag for the message.

3. If you want to select a reminder date, click the **Reminder** list to display a calendar. Select the date for the reminder.

4. Edit the date and time in the **Reminder** list box to make the time more specific.

5. Click **OK** to close the dialog box and add the flag to the message.

Figure 18.8 shows the result of adding a Review flag to a message, with a reminder date included in the flag.

SEE ALSO
➤ *To see the effect of flags when you receive messages, see "Flagging a Received Message" on page 324.*

Setting the Importance and Sensitivity

Because many people send and receive a high volume of e-mail, it helps to prioritize messages according to importance. Each Outlook message is marked with one of three levels of importance: High, Normal, or Low. By setting the importance level of each message appropriately, you will make it easier for the recipients of your messages to recognize the priority you have given to the message.

The quickest way to set the Importance of a message is by clicking the toolbar buttons for this purpose. Click either the

Message importance can be changed

The recipient of your message may choose to change the importance of the message after she has received it.

Importance: High ![] or Importance: Low ![] button to change the importance from the default of Normal importance. After you have clicked either of these buttons, you can click the button again to turn off the special setting, returning the importance setting to Normal.

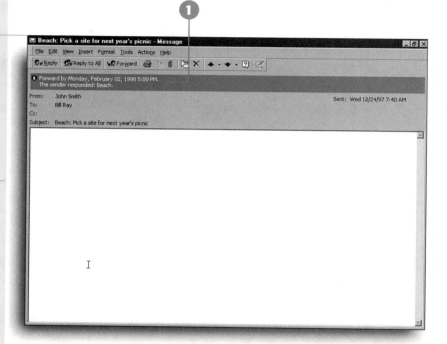

FIGURE 18.8

After adding a Review By flag to a new message, the flagged message and reminder date appear in the Message window.

① Flag information appears in the message header area of the Message window.

Another property you can set for a message is its sensitivity. Outlook has four levels of sensitivity for messages: Normal, Personal, Private, and Confidential. To set the sensitivity of a message to anything other than Normal, follow these steps:

Setting message sensitivity

  1. Click the **Options** button on the toolbar, or open the **View** menu and choose the **Options** command while editing a message. The Message Options dialog box appears, as shown in Figure 18.9.

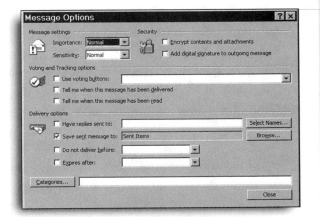

2. Click the **Sensitivity** list to choose the desired sensitivity setting.

3. Click **Close** to close the dialog box and complete the command.

After you have added a sensitivity setting to a message, the recipient of the message will see a notice at the top of the message regarding the sensitivity level you have selected.

Tracking the Delivery of a Message

When you send someone an e-mail message, how do you know the intended recipient received the message? Further, just because they have received the message, does that mean they've read it? Outlook lets you add tracking options to a message to notify you that the message has been delivered to the recipient, and that it has been read.

To set the tracking options for a message, take these steps:

Controlling message tracking

1. Click the **Options** button on the toolbar, or open the **View menu and choose Options** while editing a message. The Message Options dialog box appears, as shown earlier in Figure 18.9.

2. Click the **Tell me when this message has been <u>d</u>elivered** check box to receive a notification of delivery.

3. Click the **Tell me when this message has been <u>r</u>ead** check box to receive a notification that the message was opened for reading.

4. Click **Close** to close the dialog box and complete the command.

After you send your message, if Outlook is able to deliver the message to the address you indicated, you will receive a notification message in your Inbox that the message has been delivered. When you are sending a message to another user on your network workgroup, you are likely to receive the delivery notice quickly, often immediately. This means that the message has arrived in the recipient's Inbox.

If you included read notification, you will get another message when the recipient actually opens the message. Because this is a conscious decision, you can assume that the message has been read.

Setting Delivery Options for a Message

Normally, when you send a message using Outlook, several things happen:

- The message is placed in your Outbox folder, to await delivery.

- The message is generally delivered immediately (or the next time you connect to your mail service, if you are working remotely.)

- A copy of the message is placed in your Sent Messages folder, so you have a record of all the messages you have sent.

- After the message has been delivered to the recipient, it remains in the recipient's Inbox until he gets around to reading it.

- After the recipient reads the message, he can use his **Reply** button to respond directly back to you.

Each of these behaviors can be changed using the Message Options dialog box. The following sections describe why and how you might want to change these options.

Having Replies Sent to a Different Address

What if you send a message to someone, and you want the replies sent to a different address, such as an associate's address or your personal e-mail address? This practice is especially convenient if you are going to be away, and will not be checking your e-mail. Outlook lets you select an address to receive the replies to the message.

Redirecting replies to your messages

1. Click the **Options** button on the toolbar, or open the **View** menu and choose **Options** while editing a message. The Message Options dialog box appears, as shown previously in Figure 18.9.

2. Click the **Have replies sent to** check box and enter the address of the person you want to receive the replies. If you need help providing the address, click the **Select Names** button to select from your address lists. Click **Close** to return to the Message Window.

3. Click the **Send** button to send the message as usual. Any replies will be sent to the address you selected.

Saving the Sent Messages

Normally, a copy of each message you send is saved in your Sent Items folder. You can choose to copy the message to a different folder, or not to save a copy of the message at all:

1. Click the Options button on the toolbar, or open the **View** menu and choose **Options** while editing a message. The Message Options dialog box appears, as shown earlier in Figure 18.9.

2. To save the message in a different folder, click the **Browse** button. The Select Folder dialog box appears. Select the folder where you want to save the message, and click **OK**.

3. If you don't want to save a copy of the message at all, uncheck the box labeled **Save se<u>n</u>t message to**.

Delaying the Delivery of a Message

When you create a message, you might not want the message to be sent until later. Perhaps you want the message to be sent out immediately after a scheduled announcement or meeting has taken place. Outlook lets you send the message and delay the delivery.

Deferring delivery of a message

1. Click the **Options** button on the toolbar, or open the **<u>V</u>iew** menu and choose **Options** while editing a message. The Message Options dialog box appears.

2. Click the **Do not deliver <u>b</u>efore** check box.

3. Click the drop-down arrow to the right of this check box to display the calendar. Select the date on which you want the message delivered.

4. Edit the time of day if you want more precision on the delivery.

Setting an Expiration Date for a Message

When you send a message, you have no control over when the recipient receives the message. In some cases, a message might become irrelevant after a certain time. Suppose, for example, that you send a message inviting a coworker to lunch, but that person is tied up in a meeting all day, and doesn't get a chance to check her messages. When she checks the message at the end of the day, it's too late to be of any use. Outlook lets you set an expiration date and time for a message, so the message will not be available after the expiration time has passed.

Setting a message's expiration date

1. Click the **Options** button on the toolbar, or open the **<u>V</u>iew** menu and choose **Options** while editing a message. The Message Options dialog box appears.

2. Click the **Expires after** check box.

3. Click the drop-down arrow to the right of this check box to display the calendar. Select the date on which you want the message to expire.

4. Edit the time of day if you want more precision on the expiration time.

Assigning Categories to a Message

Outlook messages, like all Outlook items, can have one or more categories assigned. Categories are useful for sorting and filtering your messages for review at a later time.

Setting a message's categories

1. Click the **Options** button on the toolbar, or open the **View** menu and choose **Options** while editing a message. The Message Options dialog box appears.

2. Type one or more categories in the **Categories** text box, or click the **Categories** button to display the Categories dialog box.

3. Select one or more categories from the list, and click **OK** to assign the categories.

You can assign as many categories to a message as you want. If you're selecting the categories from the list, click as many as you'd like. If you are typing the categories in the **Categories** text box, separate them with commas.

SEE ALSO

➤ *For more information on using categories in Outlook, see Chapter 9, "Creating and Using Category Lists."*

Saving a Draft of a Message

Because completed messages are saved in the Sent Items folder, it's not usually necessary to save additional copies of a message. You may want to save a message, however, if you begin composing it, and you need to exit Outlook before you are ready to send. Outlook lets you save a draft of the message, which you can open later to complete your work. You can save a draft while editing a message. Open the **F**ile menu and choose **S**ave 🖫. Then open the **F**ile menu again and choose **C**lose to close the message form. The message is saved in the Drafts folder, as an unread message. You can open the message for further editing by double-clicking the message in the Drafts folder.

Sending a Message

After you have completed the creation of a message, along with all the options that are available for the message, it's time to send it. You send a message by clicking the **Send** button on the toolbar in the message window. If you're connected to your LAN, or to an online e-mail service, that's all you have to do. Outlook sends the message automatically. If you're working offline, the message is placed in the Outbox, and will be delivered the next time you connect to your LAN or other e-mail service.

After the message is delivered, a copy of the message is placed in your Sent Items folder, in case you need to review the message later, or you want to resend the message.

SEE ALSO

➤ *To learn more about working offline, see "Using Offline Folders and Personal Folders" on page 513.*

Using HTML E-mail Stationery

If you are sending your message to another user who can read the HTML mail format, such as another Outlook 98 user, you can make your messages look more attractive and interesting by adding a stationery background to the message. To create a new message with a stationery background follow these steps:

Selecting stationery for an e-mail message

1. Select your Inbox folder, or another message folder, such as Outbox or Sent Items.

2. Open the **Actions** menu and choose **New Mail Message Using**.

3. If the stationery selection that you want to use is listed on the menu, select it.

4. If the stationery you want is not listed, click **More** to display the Select a Stationery dialog box, as shown in Figure 18.10. Select the stationery you want to use, then click **OK** to close the dialog box and continue with the creation of the message.

Remember, not everyone can read HTML formatted messages in their e-mail packages. If you send an HTML message to someone outside your organization, they might not be able to read the message at all, or the message might contain a lot of confusing codes.

You can restrict the format of messages that you send to a particular address by modifying the properties for that address in your Personal Address Book.

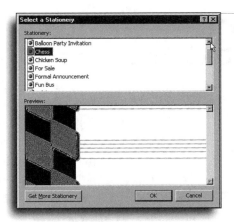

FIGURE 18.10
You can preview and choose stationery for an HTML e-mail message using the Select a Stationery dialog box.

Some of the stationeries included with Outlook provide a colorful background or border, over which you can type. Other stationeries contain some default text, which you probably will want to edit before sending your message.

Editing a Message in the Outbox

If you have sent a message to the Outbox, but have not delivered it, you can open the message for editing, and send it again. This is primarily useful when you are working offline, and you want to make changes to a message that you have sent, but have not delivered by connecting to your mail service.

Revising a message before it is delivered

1. Open your Outbox, displaying any messages that are waiting for delivery.
2. Click the message that you want to edit.
3. Open the **File** menu and choose the **Open** command, or press Ctrl+O.
4. Edit the message.
5. Click the **Send** button on the Standard toolbar to send the message.

Recalling a Message

Did you ever drop a letter in the mailbox, only to wish you could get it back? With Outlook, you can recall messages, preventing them from being read if the recipient has not already opened the message.

Outlook will only be able to recall the message if it has not been read. The recall feature may not work if it is not supported by the e-mail system used by the recipient of your message.

Attempting to recall a message

1. Open your Sent Items folder, displaying the messages you have sent.
2. Select the message you want to recall.
3. Open the message.
4. Open the **Tools** menu and choose **Recall This Message**. The Recall This Message dialog box appears, as shown in Figure 18.11.

FIGURE 18.11
Use the Recall This Message dialog box to take back a message before it has been read.

5. Select **Delete unread copies of this message**, if you want to recall the message without replacing it with a new message, or select **Delete unread copies and replace with a new message**, if you want to create a new message to replace the previous message.

6. Click the **Tell me if recall succeeds or fails for each recipient** check box to receive a notification in your Inbox of the success or failure of the recall.

Resending a Message

It may happen that you send someone a message, and the recipient accidentally deletes the message before reading or responding to the message. Do you have to create the message over again? Fortunately, the answer is no, because you can resend any messages that are still in your Sent Items folder.

Sending a message a second time

1. Open your Sent Items folder, displaying the messages you have sent.

2. Select the message that you want to resend.

3. Open the message.

4. Open the **Tools** menu and choose **Resend This Message**. The message is reopened with the message form as if you were creating a new message.

5. Click the **Send** button to send the message again.

Adding Your Signature Automatically

Many e-mail writers have a customary way of ending all their messages. In a business environment, you might want to include your name, company, phone and fax numbers, and e-mail addresses. You might want to include links to your Web site, or other sites of interest.

Outlook lets you create one or more signatures that you can automatically add to an e-mail message, making your message appearance more consistent and reliable.

Creating an automatic signature for your messages

1. Open the **Tools** menu and choose the **Options** command, and then click the **Mail Format** tab.

2. Click the **Signature Picker** button to display the Signature Picker dialog box.

3. Click **Create** to open the Create New Signature Wizard. Follow the steps in the wizard to create a new signature entry from scratch, or based on an existing file.

4. Select the signature that you want to be the default signature, and click the **Set as Default** button.

5. Click **Close** to return to the Options dialog box.

6. Select your preference in the **Don't use when replying or forwarding** check box.

7. Click **OK** to complete the command.

If you have selected a default signature, that signature will be added automatically to each e-mail message you create.

If you didn't select a default signature, you can add a signature manually when you are creating a message. While you are creating your message, open the **Insert** menu and choose **Signature**, then select the signature you want to use from the submenu that appears. If you have more signatures from which to choose, click **More** to display the Select a Signature dialog box.

Receiving an E-mail Message

Reading your new mail messages

Saving attachments from your incoming messages

Replying to messages

Forwarding messages

Using Outlook Today

The Outlook Today view gives a convenient summary of your activities and messages as you start the day; Outlook Today shows items from your Calendar, Tasks, and Mail. The Mail area shows how many unread messages you have in your Inbox and how many unfinished messages are in your Drafts folder.

To activate your Inbox from the Outlook Today screen, click the word **Mail**, or the word **Inbox**. If any other folder names are displayed on the Outlook Today screen, you can click the name of the folder to activate it.

You can activate the Outlook Today view at any time by selecting the **Go** menu and choosing the **Outlook Today** command. Figure 19.1 shows the Outlook Today view.

FIGURE 19.1

The Outlook Today view shows you a quick overview of your upcoming schedule, and any waiting mail messages.

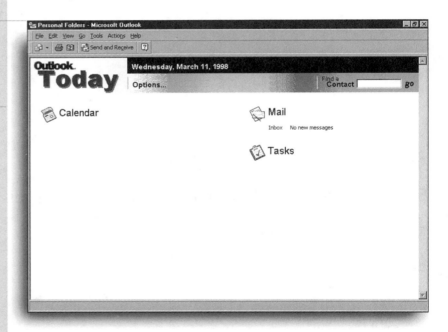

Receiving E-mail Messages

When someone sends you an e-mail message, that message is delivered to your e-mail service. That service might be a post-office on your network using Microsoft Mail or Microsoft Exchange, or it could be a remote service, such as an *Internet service provider* (*ISP*). When you start Outlook 98 Messaging and Collaboration Client, you can have your mail delivered automatically to Outlook, or you can request it manually.

SEE ALSO

➤ *To learn about adding an e-mail service to Outlook, see, "Adding an E-mail Information Service to Your Profile," on page 293.*

Automatic Mail Delivery

If you are connected to a local area network postoffice, Outlook automatically retrieves your new e-mail messages into your Inbox folder when you start Outlook. As long as you keep Outlook running, new messages are also immediately received in your Inbox, according to the instructions in your profile.

To adjust the delivery options for your mail, follow these steps:

Controlling delivery of your mail

1. Open the **Tools** menu and choose the **Services** command. The Services dialog box appears as shown in Figure 19.2.

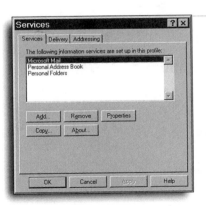

FIGURE 19.2
Use the Services dialog box to add and configure mail services.

2. Select the service whose delivery properties you want to review or modify.

3. Click the **Properties** button to display the properties for the selected service.

Figure 19.3 shows the properties dialog box for Microsoft Mail, with the **Delivery** tab selected. Note that Microsoft Mail is currently configured by this user to automatically deliver incoming and outgoing mail and to check for mail every 10 minutes. The appearance of the properties dialog box is different for each e-mail service you have installed.

Mail Delivery for Internet Mail Only users

If you have installed the Internet Mail Only (IMO) version of Outlook 98, your delivery options are controlled a little differently. Open the **Tools** menu, and choose **Options**. Select the **Mail Delivery** tab to display your options for delivery of your messages. Use the options in this dialog box to control how often to send your messages and how to control your dial-up session.

FIGURE 19.3

The Delivery properties of the Microsoft Mail window show the current settings for sending and receiving messages.

SEE ALSO

➤ *For information on configuring an e-mail service, see "The Internet E-mail Information Service" on page 117.*

Manual Mail Delivery

If you are working offline, you have to connect to your mail service to receive new messages. The new messages that are waiting for you in your postoffice or mail service will be delivered to your Inbox the next time you connect to the service, by logging onto the network or connecting via modem.

Even if you are connected to your mail service, you might want to deliver or receive messages immediately, instead of waiting for the next timed delivery.

To deliver all your mail, sending items that are in your Outbox, and receiving items into your Inbox, open the **Tools** menu and choose **Send and Receive**. On the submenu that appears, select the account for which you want to deliver mail. If you want to deliver mail for all the accounts in your profile, select **All Accounts**.

Clicking the **Send and Receive** button has the same effect as choosing **All Accounts** with the **Send and Receive** command.

Outlook delivers your mail according to the instructions in the profile for each service. If the postoffice for a service is available on your network, the delivery should take place immediately. If the service requires a modem connection, Outlook will attempt to make the connection, by dialing through your modem.

Viewing New Messages: The Inbox, AutoPreview, and the Preview Pane

Outlook displays new messages in your Inbox folder, as shown in Figure 19.4. New, unread messages are in bold type and they have an unopened envelope icon beside them.

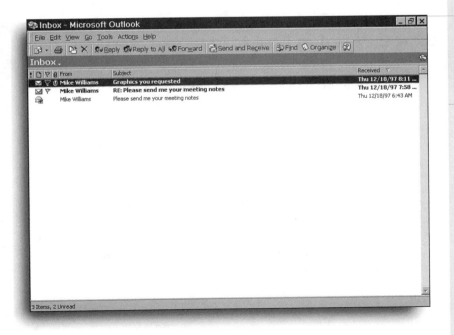

FIGURE 19.4

The Inbox shows your new messages, including the header information for those messages.

This standard viewing option is consistent with the way many e-mail programs work, but Outlook 98 has two features that make viewing e-mail even easier: *AutoPreview* and the *Preview Pane*.

The Preview Pane and AutoPreview features of Outlook 98 speed your e-mail reading process by showing you the actual contents of your messages, without requiring you to open the messages individually. Because many interoffice messages are short, it's not unusual to be able to see the entire content of a message in one or both of these windows.

Using AutoPreview to Browse Your Messages

The AutoPreview feature of the Inbox lets you see up to the first three lines of content of your unread messages as you look through the messages.

To activate AutoPreview, open the **View** menu and choose the **AutoPreview** command. The same command turns the feature off.

Figure 19.5 shows the same folder with AutoPreview turned on. Notice that the text of the unread messages is displayed along with the listing of those messages.

Using the Preview Pane to Read Your Messages

The Preview Pane displays a larger amount of text than is shown by the AutoPreview feature. The Preview Pane also has a scrollbar, so you can use it to read through longer messages without having to open the messages.

To activate the Preview Pane, open the **View** menu and choose **Preview Pane**. Selecting the command again closes the Preview Pane.

You can manually adjust the amount of space that the Preview Pane takes up by dragging the border of the Preview Pane up or down. Making the Preview Pane larger lets you see more of the contents of each message you read, but lets you see fewer messages listed at a time.

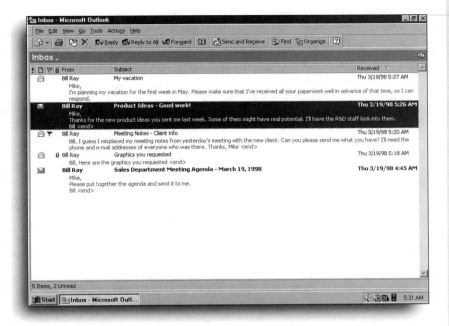

FIGURE 19.5
With AutoPreview enabled, you
can see at least the beginning
of each unread message.

Figure 19.6 shows the Inbox with the Preview Pane displayed.
Note that you can combine the Preview Pane with the
AutoPreview feature, if you want to.

Setting Options for the Preview Pane

The Preview Pane has a few display options that you can adjust
to your preference. Some people like lots of extra information
displayed on the screen at all times, although others like the
screen as simple as possible. It's up to you.

To adjust the Preview Pane's options, right-click the top border
of the Preview Pane. The shortcut menu displays the following
options:

- *Header Information* is a toggle, or on/off setting. When
  header information is displayed, the Preview Pane shows
  you the To, From, Subject, and Cc text boxes.

- *Preview Pane Options* displays the Preview Pane dialog box,
  shown in Figure 19.7. Use this dialog box to control how
  you want to read messages with the Preview Pane.

FIGURE 19.6

You can read an entire message in the Preview Pane.

1 Preview Header

2 Preview Pane

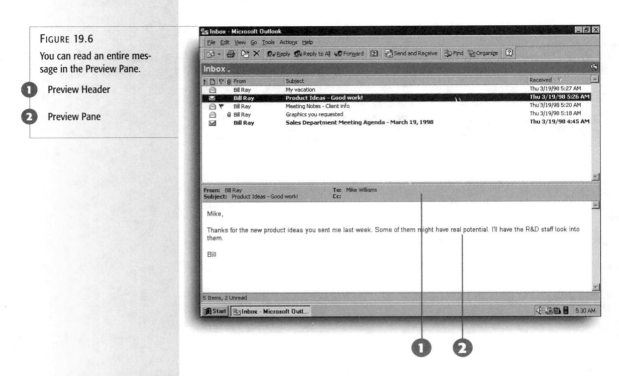

FIGURE 19.7

Use the Preview Pane dialog box to control how you read messages.

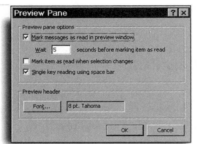

- ***Mark messages as read in preview window***. Checking this box causes each message to be marked as read after you have viewed it for at least the number of seconds you have selected.

- ***Mark item as read when selection changes***. When this check box is enabled, each message is marked as read each time you move from one message to another.

- *Single key reading using space bar.* Check this to let you move from one message to the next by pressing the Spacebar, while reading your messages using the Preview Pane.
- *Font.* Use this button to change the display font for the header area of the Preview Pane.

- *Fonts* lets you select the size of the display font in the Preview Pane.

Reading an E-mail Message

To get the full viewing and editing features of Outlook, you can open the message directly in the Outlook Message window. This gives you as much of the screen area as you want to use for viewing and responding to your messages.

Reading mail in a message window

1. Select the message you want to open in your Inbox folder, or in any other message folder, such as Drafts, Outbox, or Sent Items.

2. Press Enter, or double-click the message, to open a message window, as shown in Figure 19.8.

3. When you are done reading your messages, open the **File** menu and choose the **Close** command.

Moving from One Message to Another

If you have several messages in your Inbox, it isn't necessary to close the Message window to get to the next message. Use the Next Item and Previous Item buttons to move through the messages in the Inbox.

If you are viewing the last item in the Inbox, and you click the Next Item button, the Message window closes and you are returned to the Inbox.

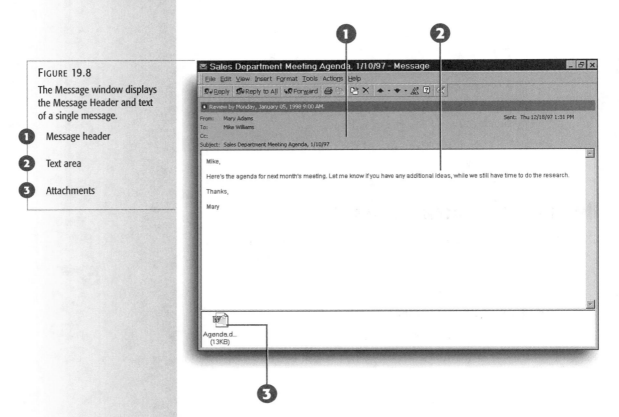

FIGURE 19.8

The Message window displays
the Message Header and text
of a single message.

❶ Message header

❷ Text area

❸ Attachments

Saving the Attachments from a Message

If you receive a message that includes an attachment, you can
save the attachment on your local hard drive or network.

1. Open the **File** menu and choose the **Save Attachments**
   command.

2. If the message contains more than one attachment, the Save
   All Attachments dialog box appears, as shown in Figure
   19.9. Select the attachments that you want to save in the
   same location, then click **OK**.

3. The Save Attachment dialog box appears. Select the location
   where you want to save the attachment, and click **Save**.

FIGURE 19.9
Select the attachments you
want to save in the Save All
Attachments dialog box.

If you have a message with several attachments, you might want
to save them in more than one directory. In that case, you'll have
to repeat the saving process for each directory, electing only
those files you want to store in one directory at a time.

Deleting a Message After Reading It

If you don't need to keep a message after you've read it, you can
delete the message. E-mail messages certainly have a tendency to
accumulate over time, so it's a good idea to keep your Inbox as
clean as possible.

After reading a message in the Message Window, you can delete
the message by clicking the Delete ☒ button on the toolbar, or
by pressing Ctrl+D. The message is moved to the Deleted Items
folder.

Items in the Deleted Items folder are not immediately removed
from your system. You should remember the following things
about deleted items:

- Items in the Deleted Items folder can be recovered by moving them back to the Inbox or another folder.
- To empty the Deleted Items folder, open the **Tools** menu
  and choose **Empty "Deleted Items" Folder**.
- To have Outlook automatically empty the Deleted Items
  folder after each Outlook session, open the **Tools** menu and
  choose the **Options** command. Under the **Other** tab, check
  the box labeled **Empty the Deleted Items folder upon
  exiting**.

After items are deleted from the Deleted Items folder, they can't be recovered. If you have configured Outlook to automatically empty the Deleted Items folder upon exiting, it's up to you to check that no important items are in that folder before you exit Outlook.

Flagging a Received Message

In Chapter 18, "Sending an E-mail Message," you learned to place a flag on a message that you sent using Outlook. You can also use flags when you are reading messages, to call your attention to important messages, and to set reminders for yourself.

Flagging a message for later reference

1. Open the **Actions** menu and choose the **Flag for Follow Up** command. The Flag for Follow Up dialog box appears, as shown in Figure 19.10.

FIGURE 19.10

Select the type of flag for a message using the Flag for Follow Up dialog box.

2. Select the type of flag using the **Flag to** list, and select a reminder date using the **Reminder** list.

3. Click **OK** to close the dialog box and place the flag on the message.

You also can place a flag on a message while you are browsing in the Inbox. Just right-click the message, or open the **Actions** menu and choose the **Flag for Follow Up** command. The Flag for Follow Up dialog box appears and you add a flag just like you did in the previous steps.

Saving Received E-mail Messages

New messages are received in your Inbox, and you can leave your messages in the Inbox if you want to. However, you might want to move a message to a different folder for one of the following reasons:

- As you accumulate more and more messages in your Inbox, it becomes harder to find old messages to which you need to refer.

- Your postoffice or mail administrator might place limits on the total amount of message space that is allocated to you, or to the length of time you can leave a message in your Inbox.

You can move messages from your Inbox folder to another of Outlook's built-in folders, or to a custom folder you have created.

After you have decided where you want to move your messages, follow these steps to move messages from your Inbox folder to another folder.

Moving messages to a different folder

1. Select one or more messages in the Inbox window. Hold the Ctrl key down while clicking to select multiple messages.

2. Click the Move to Folder button [image] on the toolbar. The Move Items dialog box appears, as shown in Figure 19.11.

3. Select the folder where you want to store the messages, and click **OK**.

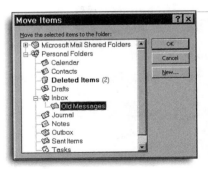

FIGURE 19.11

Select a destination folder for your message with the Move Items dialog box.

An even more efficient technique is to save your messages directly to a specific folder after reading them. This eliminates the extra step of moving the messages to a different folder.

Moving a message to a folder from the message window

1. Double-click a message to open it in the message window.
2. Click the Move to Folder button 🖼 on the toolbar. The Move Items dialog box appears.
3. Select the folder where you want to store the messages, and click **OK**.

SEE ALSO

➤ *To learn how to create and organize your folders, see Chapter 12, "Creating and Using Folders."*

Saving the Sender's Name in Your Contact List

It is not uncommon to receive a message from a client, friend, or other source outside your organization. In many cases, it's convenient to create an entry in your Contacts folder to represent this new e-mail address.

Adding a sender's address to your Contacts folder

1. While you have a message open in the message window, right-click the name of the sender in the message header of the message you are reading. The shortcut menu appears as shown in Figure 19.12.

FIGURE 19.12

Use the shortcut menu to add a new Contact item from an incoming e-mail message.

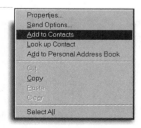

2. Choose **Add to Contacts**. A new Contact form appears.
3. Complete and save the Contact form.

Replying to and Forwarding an E-mail Message

You will often receive messages that require a response or comment from you. Outlook makes it easy for you to reply to the sender of a message, or to forward a message to another party.

Replying to the Sender of a Message

While you are reading a message in the Message window, or while browsing through your messages in the Inbox, you can send a reply to the person who sent you the message, or to everyone who received the message.

Use the following steps to send a reply:

1. Click the **Reply** button to send a reply to the sender only. Click the **Reply to All** button to send a reply to everyone who received the message, as well as to the sender. A new message window appears, with the addresses already filled in, and with the text of the original message included in the message area.

2. Complete the message as usual, typing additional message text, adding attachments, or adding additional recipients or Cc addresses.

3. Click the Send button to move the message to your Outbox when the message is complete.

Forwarding a Message

Some of the messages you receive need to be forwarded to another person. Outlook's Forward command lets you send the message to another person, adding your comments as required.

Forwarding a message to another e-mail address

1. Click the Forward button. A new message window appears, with no addresses filled in but with the text of the original message displayed in the message area.

2. Fill in the **To** text box with the address of one or more persons to whom you want to forward the message.

3. Complete the message as usual, typing additional message text, adding attachments, or adding additional recipients or Cc addresses.

4. Click the Send button 📧 to move the message to your Outbox when the message is complete.

Annotating the Original Message

Normally, when you reply to or forward a message, you'll type your response or comments in the area at the top of the message, and the previous message text is displayed below your comments. Sometimes, however, it is useful to add annotations to the original message.

Suppose, for example, you have received a message that details the directions to your company's annual picnic. In reading the message, you've noticed a mistake in the directions, due to highway construction. You'd like to send a Reply to All message correcting the error. Adding your comments at the end of the directions is not as effective as annotating the message at the point where the directions need to be changed.

To annotate the original message, click in the previous message text where you want your annotation to appear, and then type your annotations. Outlook automatically adds a marker before the text you type, identifying you as the annotator. When you reply to a message you've received or add comments to a message you're forwarding, Outlook attempts to use the same mail format as the original message. If that format isn't available, however, Outlook resorts to the Plain Text format.

Controlling the Appearance of Replies and Forwarded Messages

Outlook provides customized settings for the display of the message text in replies and forwarded messages, as well as for annotation markings.

Customizing the appearance of replies and forwarded messages

1. Open the **Tools** menu and choose the **Options** command. Then, click the **Preferences** tab.

2. Click the **E-mail options** button to display the E-mail Options dialog box, as shown in Figure 19.13.

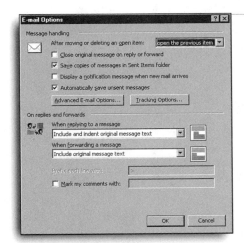

FIGURE 19.13
Use the E-mail Options dialog box to control the appearance of replies and forwarded messages, and to change your comments mark.

3. In the **When replying to a message** list, select the appearance option you prefer.

4. In the **When forwarding a message** list, select the appearance option you prefer.

5. If you want to customize your annotation mark, check the **Mark my comments with** check box, and type the text that you want to appear in the mark next to the check box.

Asking for Opinions

Create messages that let others vote on an answer

Create custom voting buttons

Send and respond to voting messages

Interpret the results of voting responses

What Are Voting Buttons?

When you want to send a message that asks a simple question, you can use *voting* buttons to provide a short list of choices from which the user can select an answer. Outlook 98 Messaging and Collaboration Client has three built-in sets of voting buttons:

- Approve or Reject
- Yes or No
- Yes, No, or Maybe

In addition to these built-in voting button lists, you can design your own lists of buttons. Any short list of items can be used as a set of voting buttons. The following are a few examples:

- Small, Medium, or Large
- Monday at 3, Wednesday at 1, or Friday at 9
- New York, Chicago, or Los Angeles

When you send a message with voting buttons, the user responds to the choices by clicking one of the buttons. Answering the question is quick and easy. It doesn't require any additional typing, although, as you will see, the user can add comments to the reply message, too. Another advantage to using voting buttons is that Outlook automatically keeps track of the results of the voting.

Creating a Message That Contains Voting Buttons

A message that contains voting buttons is no different than any other message, until you add the buttons. You can begin as usual, by creating an e-mail message, addressing it to one or more persons in your workgroup. You can use voting buttons for a message that you send to just one person, or a message that you send to many people.

Using the Built-in Voting Buttons

After you have selected the recipients, and typed the subject and the body of the message, you can add the voting buttons.

Using built-in voting buttons in your message

1. Open the **View** menu and choose the **Options** command, or click the **Options** button on the toolbar. The Message Options dialog box appears, as shown in Figure 20.1.

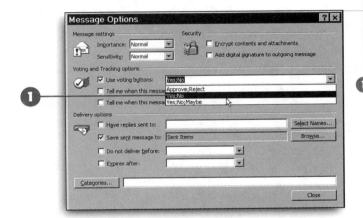

FIGURE 20.1
The Message Options dialog box contains the lists of built-in voting buttons.

1 Voting button lists

2. Click the **Use voting buttons** check box, and click the drop-down list to the right of the button.

3. Select the type of voting buttons you want to use.

4. Click the **Close** button to return to your message.

5. Click **Send** to send the message.

Creating Your Own Voting Buttons

If you don't want to use the built-in voting buttons, you can create your own lists for buttons.

Create and use custom voting buttons in your message

1. Open the **View** menu and choose the **Options** command, or click the **Options** button on the toolbar. The Message Options dialog box appears.

2. Click the **Use voting buttons** check box, and type the list for the buttons directly into the list box to the right of the check box. Separate the items in your list with semicolons, as shown in Figure 20.2.

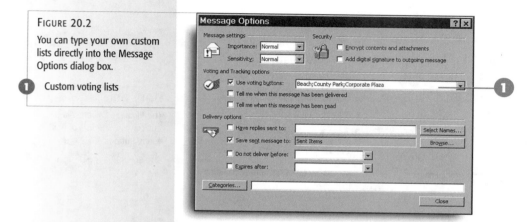

3. Click the **Close** button to return to your message.

4. Click **Send** to send the message.

Replying to a Message That Contains Voting Buttons

When you receive a message that was sent with voting buttons, the buttons appear at the top of the message window, as shown in Figure 20.3. Instead of clicking the **Reply** button to respond to the message, you can click the button that represents your answer.

After you click a voting button, the message box shown in Figure 20.4 appears.

If you want to send your vote without any additional comment, just click **OK** to send the voting response immediately. If you want to add comments to your response, select the **Edit the response before sending** option button, and then click **OK**. A message box appears, allowing you to type additional comments to accompany your vote, as shown in Figure 20.5.

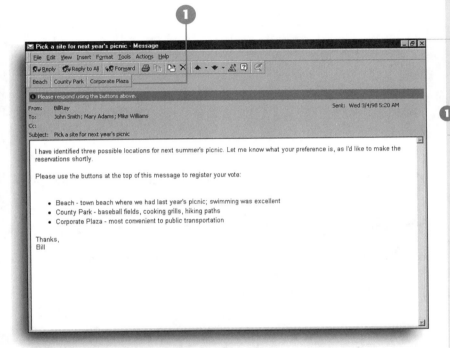

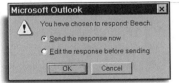

FIGURE 20.3

The recipient of a voting button message can click the buttons to cast a vote.

1 Voting buttons

FIGURE 20.4

You can send your vote without comment, or add some remarks to your choice.

FIGURE 20.5

You can add comments to your vote when you send a response.

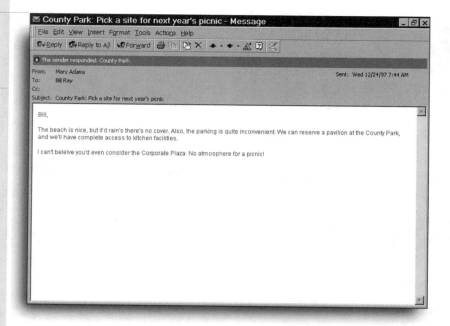

Tracking Responses to Voting Buttons

Each time someone casts a vote with a voting button, a message is returned to the original sender. When you view the messages in the Inbox window, you can see the vote from that person, indicated in the subject line of the message, as shown in Figure 20.6.

That message indicates the voting selection in the message header, as shown in Figure 20.7. Any additional comments that the user added are shown in the message body.

Although you can read the responses individually if you sent the voting messages to a lot of people, you'll appreciate the fact that Outlook counts the votes for you. These votes are tallied in the original message.

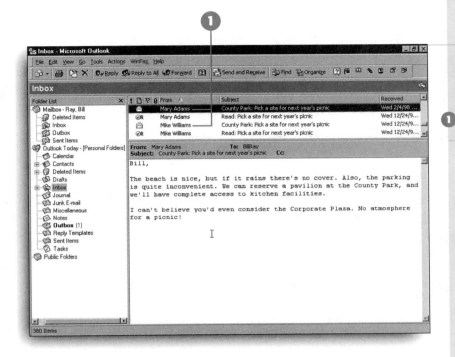

FIGURE 20.6

Incoming responses to voting button messages show the selection of the voter.

① Voting responses

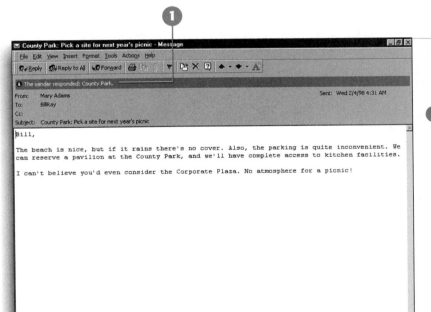

FIGURE 20.7

The message that is returned from a voting button shows the voter's selection.

① Voting response

View the tallied votes

1. Select the folder where the original message is stored. This is the Sent Items folder, unless you told Outlook to store the message somewhere else when you sent it.

2. Open the message by double-clicking it. The message window contains two tabs: **Message** and **Tracking**.

3. Click the **Tracking** tab. The results of the voting responses are displayed, as shown in Figure 20.8.

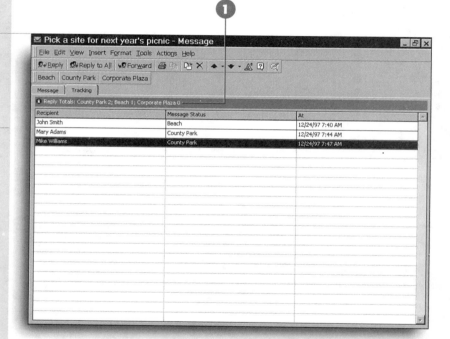

FIGURE 20.8

The Tracking pane of the original message displays the results of the voting responses.

1 Voting totals

The tracking information shows each vote as well as the totals of the responses.

Organizing Your E-mail with the Rules Wizard

Use rules to organize incoming and outgoing messages

Define your own custom rules using Outlook's Rules Wizard

Automatically dispose of junk e-mail and adult content

Organize the rules you have defined

Import and export rules from files

What Is a Rule?

Outlook lets you define rules to help you manage your messages automatically. A *rule* is a set of conditions and actions for processing and organizing your messages. The conditions are used to select, or identify, messages for special processing, and the actions determine what kind of processing you want to have performed automatically.

The following are a few examples of the kinds of rules you might want to define:

- Forward all messages sent to me by Mike Williams to Mary Adams when they arrive in my Inbox.
- Put all incoming and outgoing messages that have the word "Training" in the subject, into my "Training Messages" folder.

You can use Outlook 98 Messaging and Collaboration Client's Rules Wizard to create and edit rules that are applied to the messages you send and receive. The following are some examples of the kinds of rules you can create with the Rules Wizard:

- Perform an action after a message arrives.
- Perform an action after messages are sent.
- Move newly received messages from a specified sender or list to a destination folder.
- Notify me with a message, when certain messages arrive.
- Move messages to a folder based on the content of the subject or text of the message.
- Delete selected messages automatically.
- Assign a message flag to certain messages.
- Automatically reply to messages from a certain sender.
- Notify me when messages to a particular sender are read.

These examples can be combined in complex ways to create an almost endless set of possibilities. For example, you could create a rule such as the following:

Select any incoming messages where all the following are true:

- My name is not in the To box
- My name is in the Cc box
- The message is from Mary Adams
- The word "travel" appears in the header

Perform the following actions with the message:

- Flag the message for review within 1 day
- Mark it as high importance
- Put a copy of the message in my Expenses folder

The rules that you define are applied to incoming and outgoing messages in the order that you specify in the Rules Wizard.

SEE ALSO

➤ *To learn about adding flags to a message, see "Flagging a Message" on page 300.*

➤ *To learn about message importance, see "Setting the Importance and Sensitivity" on page 301.*

➤ *To learn about working with folders in Outlook, see Chapter 12, "Creating and Using Folders."*

Creating Rules to Manage Received Messages

Normally, when you receive a new message, it is placed in your Inbox folder. You're probably used to looking in the Inbox for all your new messages by now. If you receive a high volume of messages, however, you might wish your Inbox was a little more organized. You'll receive business messages, personal messages from friends and family, messages from the mail administrator, and messages in which you're a carbon copy recipient, all in your Inbox.

By organizing your messages in different folders, you can divide the different categories of messages, and give the proper attention to each type of message when you have the time and interest to do so. Of course, it's possible to move messages from one folder to another manually, but it would be even better to let Outlook do this work for you, automatically.

Delivering Messages to a Folder Automatically

You can use the Outlook Rules Wizard to automatically organize your messages. Because no rules are defined when Outlook is initially installed, you'll have to start by creating a new rule.

Suppose you want to save all the messages that Mary Adams sends you in a folder named "Messages from Mary." You can create a rule that automatically moves Mary's messages to this new folder.

Create a rule to move messages to a new folder

1. Activate the Inbox.

2. Open the **Tools** menu and choose **Rules Wizard**. The Rules Wizard dialog box appears, as shown in Figure 21.1.

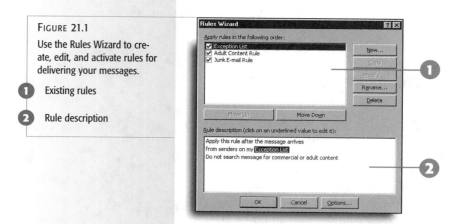

FIGURE 21.1

Use the Rules Wizard to create, edit, and activate rules for delivering your messages.

1 Existing rules

2 Rule description

3. Click **New** to create a new rule. The Rules Wizard shows you the different types of rules you can create, as shown in Figure 21.2.

4. Select the type of rule you want to create. A description of the rule is displayed in the **Rule description** text box, as shown in Figure 21.2. In this example, I've selected the rule

"Move new messages from someone." Notice that the **Rule description** window displays the description, with underlines indicating those values that I need to edit so the Rules Wizard will know whose messages we are moving, and where we want to move them.

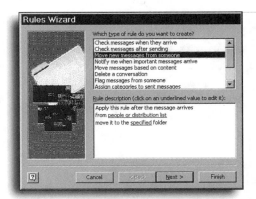

FIGURE 21.2

You can create a rule to move one person's messages to a specific folder.

5. Click **Next** to move on to the next step, selecting the condition for the new rule. Figure 21.3 shows the options for selecting a condition. You can check one or more conditions. If you select several conditions, all of them must be met for a message to be selected for action by the wizard.

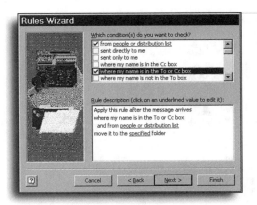

FIGURE 21.3

Select one or more conditions for the new rule you're creating.

6. If the condition requires input values, such as the `people or distribution list` who sent the message, click the underlined value (shown in the **Rule description** area), so you can provide the value for the rule. In this example, the wizard displays the Rule Address dialog box so you can select the e-mail address of the person whose messages you want to intercept, as shown in Figure 21.4.

FIGURE 21.4

Use the Rule Address dialog box to select whose messages this rule applies to.

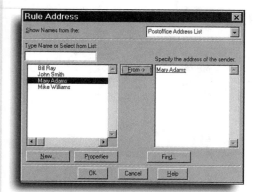

7. Fill in any additional conditional values in a similar manner. Figure 21.5 shows the addition of the condition that my name is in the To or Cc box. After you've finished filling in the values, the modified condition is shown in the **Rule description** window.

FIGURE 21.5

You can select additional conditions which are combined in one rule.

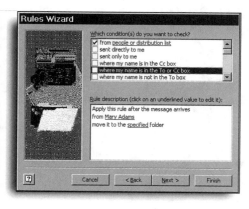

8. Click **Next** to continue with the wizard, so you can specify
    the action that the wizard will perform. In Figure 21.6, we
    have selected (by clicking) the action to move the message to
    a specified folder.

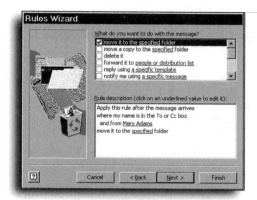

FIGURE 21.6
The Rules Wizard provides
many actions that can be performed automatically.

9. Fill in the input values for this and any additional actions
    you want the rule to perform. Figure 21.7 shows the Rules
    Wizard dialog box for selecting the folder where we want
    to move Mary's messages. If the folder already exists, you
    can just select it from the list. If you haven't created the
    folder yet, click the **New** button to create and name the new
    folder.

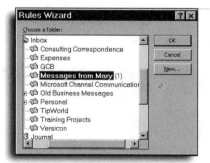

FIGURE 21.7
You can store messages in an
existing folder, or create a new
folder.

10. Click **Next** to move on to the next stage of the rule defini-
    tion, selecting any exceptions to the rule. In Figure 21.8,

we've selected an exception to exclude messages marked with a certain importance.

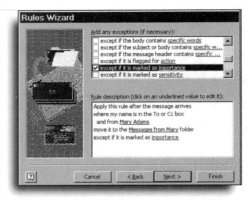

FIGURE 21.8

The third stage of rule definition is the selection of exceptions to the rule.

11. Click the underlined value and fill in the input values associated with any exception you've selected. In Figure 21.9, we've selected **High** importance as the exception to our rule.

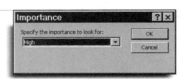

FIGURE 21.9

High importance messages from Mary will be ignored by this rule.

12. Click **Next** when you've selected your actions, to move to the final step of naming the rule. The Rules Wizard dialog box for this action is shown in Figure 21.10.

FIGURE 21.10

The last step in the Rules Wizard is the naming of the rule. Click **Back** if you want to go back and make any changes.

13. Edit the descriptive name for the rule, and click the **Turn on this rule** check box, to activate the rule.

14. Click **Finish** to complete the rule definition. The rule is added to the Rules Wizard list.

From now on any messages that you receive from Mary Adams will be moved to the Messages from Mary folder, unless they are marked with High importance, in which case they will remain in the Inbox.

Creating Rules to Control How Outlook Sends Messages

Just as you can create a rule to automatically process messages that Outlook receives, you can apply automatic processing to the messages you send. Outlook's normal behavior when you send a message is to place the message in the Outbox folder and to place a copy of the message in the Sent Items folder. As you might expect, you can use the Rules Wizard to change these behaviors.

Like the Inbox, the Sent Items folder tends to accumulate a lot of messages after a while. You can determine what becomes of these messages using the Rules Wizard.

Create a rule to organize your Sent Items folder

1. Activate the Inbox.

2. Open the **Tools** menu and choose **Rules Wizard**. The Rules Wizard dialog box appears.

3. Click **New** to create a new rule. The Rules Wizard shows you the different types of rules you can create.

4. Select the **Check messages after sending** type of rule. Notice that the **Rule description** window displays the description, with underlines indicating those values that you need to edit.

5. Click **Next** to select the condition for the new rule. You can check one or more conditions. If you select several

Turning a rule off or on

Some of the rules you create with Outlook's Rules Wizard might be useful at some times, and not useful at others. Suppose, for example, that you occasionally make extended business trips, and that you would prefer to use your personal Internet e-mail instead of working remotely with your office e-mail. You can create a rule to forward all incoming messages to your personal Internet e-mail address. Each time you are about to leave for a trip, you can activate the rule by checking the box next to the rule in the Rules Wizard.

conditions, all of them must be met for a message to be selected for action by the wizard.

6. Edit any input values in the selection conditions for your rule by clicking the underlined value, then completing the dialog box that appears for that condition. Repeat for all conditions that require edited input values.

7. Click **Next** to continue with the wizard, so you can specify the action that the wizard will perform. A list of actions appears in the Rule Wizard dialog box; click an action in this list to select it.

8. Repeating the technique described in step 6, fill in the input values for this and any additional actions you want the rule to perform.

9. Click **Next** to move on to the next stage of the rule definition and select any exceptions to the rule.

10. Repeating the technique described in step 6, fill in the input values associated with any exception you've selected.

11. Click **Next** when you've selected your actions. You move to the final step, assigning a name to the rule. Edit the descriptive name for the rule.

12. Click the **Turn on this rule** check box to activate the rule.

13. Click **Finish** to complete the rule definition. The rule is added to the Rules Wizard list.

For example, you might define a rule to place a copy of all the expense reports you submit into an Expense Reports folder. Each time you send a message with "Expense Report" in the subject, Outlook places a copy of the message in your Expense Reports folder. This rule saves you the work of copying the messages from your Sent Items folder each time you submit a report.

Dealing with Junk Mail

One of the most annoying side effects of the electronic age is the proliferation of junk e-mail. Just as your postal mailbox is often filled with flyers, credit card applications, and catalogs, your

Inbox can also become a target for marketers. Outlook 98 lets you designate the addresses of those who send you junk mail, so you can dispose of this mail appropriately.

Although it's possible to create an individual rule for each junk mailer, you can deal with all junk mailers as a single enemy, by adding addresses to your junk mail list, and specifying what action to take with junk mail messages.

Today's sophisticated junk e-mailers employ more advanced techniques to foil this screening strategy. Often, they supply faked **From** addresses, or suppressed or faked **To** addresses. Some even use your e-mail address as the **From** address. In these cases, adding the sender's address to your junk e-mail list will not work.

In addition to those addresses that you identify as junk e-mail addresses, Outlook can automatically identify e-mail that is suspected of being either junk e-mail or adult content e-mail. See "Setting Rules for Disposing of Junk E-mail," later in this chapter, for identifying what you want to do with these types of e-mail messages.

Editing Your Junk Senders List

Outlook maintains a list of those e-mail addresses that you have designated as junk e-mailers. You can edit the list at any time.

Edit your Junk Senders e-mail address list

1. Activate your Inbox folder.
2. Open the **Tools** menu and choose **Organize**, or click the **Organize** button on the toolbar. Outlook displays the Organize pane as shown in Figure 21.11.
3. Click the **Junk E-Mail** link to display the options for handling junk e-mail, as shown in Figure 21.12.
4. Click the link labeled **click here**, as shown in Figure 21.12, to display additional information about Junk and Adult Content processing, as shown in Figure 21.13. Click **Edit Junk Senders**, to display the list of Junk Senders. Click **Edit Adult Content Senders** to display the list of Adult Content senders.

FIGURE 21.11

Use the Organize window for customizing your folders, colors, views, and junk e-mail.

1   Junk E-mail link

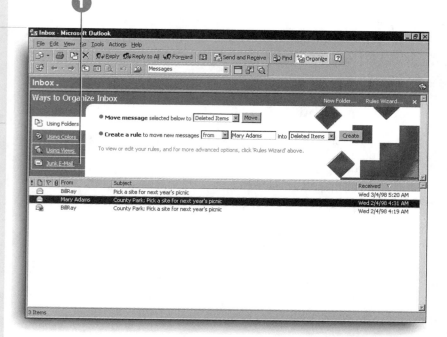

FIGURE 21.11

Use the Organize window for customizing your folders, colors, views, and junk e-mail.

1   Junk E-mail link

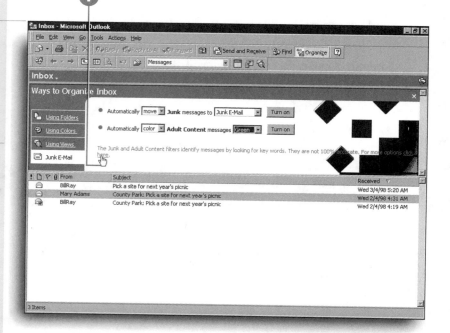

FIGURE 21.12

Use the **Junk E-mail** link in the **Organize** pane to automatically process Junk and Adult Content messages.

1   Link to Junk and Adult Content filters

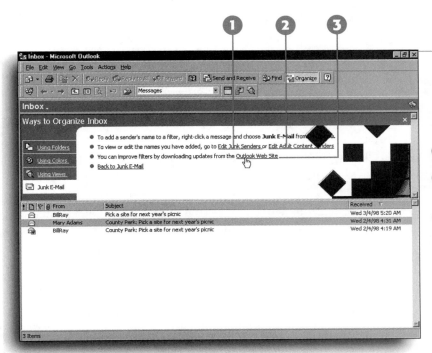

FIGURE 21.13
The Ways to Organize pane
has links for updating your
Junk Senders and Adult
Content lists, as well as an
Internet link for updated filters.

1 Edit Junk Senders link

2 Edit Adult Content Senders
link

3 Update filters link

5. Use this dialog box to add addresses to the list, or to edit
and delete names that are already on the list.

You can quickly add a new address to the Junk Senders list while
viewing messages in the Inbox. Right-click the message, and
select **Junk E-mail** on the shortcut menu. On the submenu that
appears, select either **Add to Junk Senders list**, or **Add to
Adult Content Senders list**.

Outlook uses filtering software to identify potential junk e-mail
and adult content messages. The **Ways to Organize** pane, as
shown in Figure 21.13, contains a link to an Internet site that
has filters that will be periodically updated.

Setting Rules for Disposing of Junk E-mail

After you've begun identifying those who are sending you junk
e-mail, you can decide what to do with the e-mail.

Set Rules to dispose of junk e-mail

1. Activate your Inbox folder.

2. Open the **Tools** menu and choose **Organize**, or click the **Organize** button on the toolbar. Outlook displays the **Ways to Organize** pane.

3. Click the **Junk E-mail** tab to display the options for handling junk e-mail.

4. For each of the categories of junk e-mail (junk e-mail and adult content messages), select from these two options for disposing of these messages (refer to Figure 21.12):

   - Select to **Move** the messages, and select a folder where you want to move the messages.

   - Select to **Color** the messages, and select the color you want to use to highlight the messages.

5. Click the **Turn ON** button next to each category to activate the processing of junk e-mail and adult content messages.

Refer to Figure 21.12 where the Organize pane shows instructions to move my junk messages to a folder named Junk E-mail. Adult content messages will be highlighted in green. These rules will be enabled after the **Turn ON** button for each rule is clicked.

Managing Your Rules

As you define more rules for handling your messages, you can use the Rules Wizard to manage the rules you have created. You can rename rules, turn rules off and on, and change the order in which rules are applied.

Turning Rules On and Off

If you have defined several rules to handle incoming messages, all these rules will be applied to all the messages you receive. Sometimes you might want to temporarily suspend a rule, but reserve the right to turn it on again later.

To change the active/inactive status of rules

1. Activate the Inbox.

2. Open the **Tools** menu and choose **Rules Wizard**. The Rules Wizard dialog box appears.

3. Clear the check boxes of any rules you want to ignore. Check the boxes for those rules that you want to be active.

4. Click **OK** to close the Rules Wizard.

Changing the Order in Which Rules Are Applied

Outlook applies the rules in your list in the order that the rules are displayed in the Rules Wizard dialog box. It's important to recognize that the order in which rules are applied has an effect on their results.

Suppose, for example, that you have a rule that deletes all messages from Mary Adams, and a second rule that stores a copy of all training announcements in a Training folder. If Mary sends you a training announcement, the message will be deleted before a copy of it can be stored. You can correct this problem by changing the order of the rules in the Rules Wizard.

Reorder rules

1. Activate the Inbox.

2. Open the **Tools** menu and choose **Rules Wizard**. The Rules Wizard dialog box appears.

3. Select a rule whose position you want to change in the list of rules.

4. Click the **Move Up** button to move the rule to an earlier position in the list. Click the **Move Down** button to move it to a later position.

5. Click **OK** to close the Rules Wizard dialog box.

A Rule That Stops Further Rules from Executing

A special type of rule that you can create with the Rules Wizard is the "stop processing all following rules" type. When you select this type of rule, the Rules Wizard lets you continue defining the rule as you would any other rule for receiving messages. However, this rule behaves a little differently than other rules. After the rule is applied, any rules further down the list of rules are ignored.

For example, suppose you have defined a rule to place a copy of all newly received messages in a folder named New Messages. Then you decide that you want to define a special rule that puts new messages from your manager in a folder named Management Messages. In that case, you don't want those messages to also be copied to the New Messages folder.

The solution is to create the rule to handle your manager's messages as a "stop processing" rule. Make sure to place this rule earlier in the rules list than the rule for handling all other new messages. After the rule for your manager's messages is applied, it stops further processing of any rules, so the manager's messages are only copied to the Management Messages folder, and not to the New Messages folder.

Exporting Your Rules to a File

The rules you create with the Rules Wizard are stored in your Outlook profile. What if you have more than one profile, and you want to reuse the same set of rules in each profile? Outlook 98 lets you export the rules from your profile to a file, and import those rules into another profile. You can also use this technique to share your rules with another user.

Save the rules in the active profile to a file

1. Activate the Inbox.

2. Open the **Tools** menu and choose **Rules Wizard**. The Rules Wizard dialog box appears.

3. Click **Options** to display the Options dialog box, as shown in Figure 21.14.

FIGURE 21.14

Use the Options dialog box to import and export rules.

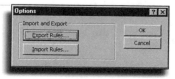

4. Click **Export Rules** to display the Save Exported Rules as dialog box, as shown in Figure 21.15.

FIGURE 21.15

Enter the name and location of the rules file.

5. Select the location and enter the filename for the rules file you want to create.

6. Click **Save** to save the rules in the rules file.

7. Click **OK** to close the Options dialog box, and click **OK** to close the Rules Wizard.

Importing Rules from a File

To complete the process of applying rules from one profile to another, you must import the rules from a previously saved rules file into the active profile. Before importing the rules, make sure you are using the profile into which you want to add the rules.

Import rules into the active profile

1. Activate the Inbox.

2. Open the **Tools** menu and choose **Rules Wizard**. The Rules Wizard dialog box appears.

3. Click **Options** to display the Options dialog box.

4. Click **Import Rules** to display the Import Rules from dialog box as shown in Figure 21.16.

5. Select the file that contains the rules that you want to import.

6. Click **Open** to import the rules into the current profile.

FIGURE 21.16

Select the file that has the rules you previously saved.

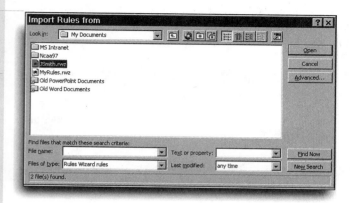

7. Click **OK** to close the Options dialog box, and click **OK** to close the Rules Wizard.

SEE ALSO

➤ *To learn about adding, creating, and modifying profiles, see Chapter 6, "Creating a Profile."*

Using Outlook as an Exchange Server Client

Using Outlook as a client to Exchange Server

Applying Exchange Server Rules to your messages

Delegating control to another user

Sharing Calendars through Exchange

Using Exchange Public Folders

How Does Outlook Work with Microsoft Exchange?

Microsoft Outlook 98 Messaging and Collaboration Client is an e-mail client that requires a separate e-mail service to deliver your messages, both within your workgroup, and to and from Internet e-mail addresses. You can choose from many e-mail services, such as Microsoft Mail, Lotus Notes, or commercial services such as CompuServe or America Online. If you work as part of a workgroup of computers running Windows NT or Windows 95, your network administrator is likely to have selected Microsoft Exchange for your organization's e-mail service.

Microsoft Exchange is a *client/server* messaging system. The server portion of Exchange consists of the Microsoft Exchange Server software that is installed by the network administrator on a special Windows NT Server. On some networks, the Exchange Server is set up as one or more dedicated servers. On smaller networks, the Exchange Server software might be set up on the same server that is used as a file server.

The client portion of Microsoft Exchange consists of software that is installed on your computer to enable you to connect to the Exchange Server. Windows 95 and Windows NT come with a generic Exchange client, which usually appears as the Inbox icon on your desktop. This Inbox icon is replaced by the Outlook icon when you install Outlook 98.

When you use Outlook as your Exchange client, you can take advantage of many powerful features of the Exchange Server. Exchange receives and delivers your messages, and can apply more powerful and flexible rules than those provided by Outlook itself.

Exchange can also be used by remote users, connecting by a modem or the Internet. You can use Outlook as your client for remote connection to your Exchange Server.

SEE ALSO

➤ *To learn about working remotely, see Chapter 32, "Working Remotely."*

Changing Delivery Options for Messages

When you are sending messages through Exchange, you can set several delivery options for your messages. In this section, you'll learn how to have replies sent to someone else, delay delivery of the messages until a later time, and set an expiration date for a message.

Redirecting Replies

Sometimes you'll send a message to an e-mail recipient or a distribution list, but you'll want the replies to be sent to someone else. Perhaps you are asking for input on some matter, but you want a colleague to collect the responses and report on her findings.

You can redirect the replies to a message by setting an option while you are creating the message in the message window.

Redirect message replies

1. Open the **View** menu and choose **Options**, or click the **Options** button on the toolbar. The Message Options dialog box appears, as shown in Figure 22.1.

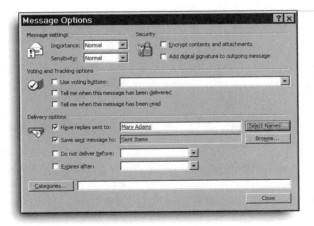

FIGURE 22.1
Use the Message Options dialog box to change the delivery options for a message.

2. In the **Delivery options** section, click the **Have replies sent to** check box to select it.

3. Enter an e-mail address, or click the **Select Names** button to choose names from your address lists.

4. Click **Close** to return to the message window.

When someone receives a message whose replies have been redirected in this way, they won't see anything unusual about the message. The Inbox will show that the message is from you.

When the user replies to the message, however, the message will be addressed to the names you selected using the Message Options dialog box.

Scheduling Messages for Later Delivery

What if you are creating a message, and you want the message to be sent at a later time? Maybe you'll be out of the office, even on vacation, at the time you want the message to be sent. You can have Exchange automatically deliver the message at the time you want it to be sent.

Set a deferred delivery date and time

1. Open the **View** menu and select **Options**, or click the **Options** button on the toolbar. The Message Options dialog box appears.

2. In the **Delivery options** section, click the **Do not deliver before** check box to select it.

3. Enter the date and time, or select the date from a calendar by clicking the drop-down arrow to the right of the check box.

4. Click **Close** to return to the message window.

Messages that you create with deferred delivery are sent to your Outbox as normal when you send the message. However, Exchange will not attempt to deliver the message until the date and time you specified in the Message Options dialog box.

Message Expiration

Some messages become meaningless if they are not read within a certain time. Suppose, for example, that you send a message to someone to invite them to a meeting. If the meeting time has passed without that person reading the message, it's unnecessary for that person to receive the message.

Exchange lets you set an expiration date and time for a message, after which the message becomes unavailable for the recipient.

Set a message expiration date and time

1. Open the **View** menu and select **Options**, or click the **Options** button on the toolbar. The Message Options dialog box appears.

2. In the **Delivery options** section, click the **Expires after** check box to select it.

3. Enter the date and time, or select the date from a calendar by clicking the drop-down arrow to the right of the check box.

4. Click **Close** to return to the message window.

Messages that are sent with expiration dates are delivered to the recipient's Inbox as usual. If the message is not read by the time the expiration date passes, the message becomes unavailable to the recipient.

Granting Delegate Access to Your Mail

One of the most powerful features of Exchange is the capability to delegate access to your folders to another user. You can allow another user to open your folders, read and reply to your messages, and create new messages on your behalf. This allows you, for example, to have an assistant carry out your instructions, or to have someone attend to your matters in your absence.

Choosing a Delegate to Send Your Mail

A delegate can send mail for you in two ways:

- *On your behalf.* The delegate's name appears in the **From** box of the message, and your name appears after the text **Sent On Behalf Of**. You can set this level of delegation using Outlook.

- *In your name.* Only your name appears in the message. Your delegate's name doesn't appear at all. Only your Exchange administrator can grant this permission.

You must be connected to your Exchange Server to make changes to your delegates.

Delegate another user to send mail on your behalf

1. Open the **Tools** menu and select **Options.** The Options dialog box appears as shown in Figure 22.2. Click the **Delegates** tab.

FIGURE 22.2

The Delegates tab shows the delegates you have assigned, and lets you add new delegates.

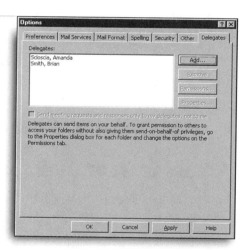

2. Click the **Add** button to select the name of one or more persons to whom you want to grant delegate authority.

3. Click **OK** to close the Options dialog box.

If you want to delegate someone to send messages in your name, contact the Exchange Administrator and request that you be able to grant Send As permission for your delegate. If you do not have this permission, you can delegate others to send messages only on your behalf.

Granting Permissions to Open Your Folders

By giving another person the right to open your folders, you can allow that person to view and edit your messages or other Outlook items. You must be connected to your Exchange Server to change folder permissions. In most cases, logging on to your network automatically connects you to your Exchange Server.

Grant permission to another user to open your folders

1. If the Folder List is not visible, display it by opening the **View** menu and selecting **Folder**.

2. Right-click the folder whose permissions you want to change, and select the **Properties** tab.

3. Click **Add** to select a user to whom you want to grant permissions to this folder.

4. Select the user, then click **OK** to return to the Permissions dialog box.

5. Use the **Permissions** drop-down list to select the role you want to grant to this user, or select the individual permissions.

6. Click **OK** to close the dialog box dialog box.

Exchange has several predefined roles for permission levels you can grant. Table 22.1 summarizes these roles.

TABLE 22.1 Predefined roles for permission levels

Role	Description
Owner	Has all permissions in the folder
Publishing Editor	Can create, read, edit, and delete items, as well as create subfolders
Editor	Can create, read, edit, and delete items

continues...

TABLE 22.1   Continued

Role	Description
Publishing Author	Can create, read, and delete their own items, as well as create subfolders
Author	Can create, read, and delete their own items
Nonediting Author	Can create and read items, but can't edit items
Reviewer	Can read items
Contributor	Can create items
None	No permissions are granted

If you set the default permission of a folder as None, you can then create exceptions for individuals and groups to whom you want to grant some or all permissions.

If you prefer, you can set the permissions individually. The permissions are described in Table 22.2.

TABLE 22.2   Permissions for delegates

Permission	Description
Create Items	User can create or post items in this folder
Read Items	User can read items in this folder
Create Subfolder	User can create subfolders from this folder
Folder Owner	User has all permissions on the folder
Folder Contact	User will be notified automatically when replication conflicts occur, and when messages are received requesting additional changes or permissions on this folder
Folder Visible	The folder is visible to this user
Edit Items - None	User can't edit any items
Edit Items - Own	User can edit his own items
Edit Items - All	User can edit all items
Delete Items - None	User can't delete items
Delete Items - Own	User can delete his own items
Delete Items - All	User can delete any item

It is not necessary to use the individual permissions if one of the predefined roles meets your needs.

Opening Another User's Folders

If you have been granted permission to open another person's folders, you can do this at any time you are running Outlook and you are connected to your Exchange Server.

Open messages to which you've been granted access

1. Select your Inbox folder.
2. Open the **File** menu and choose **Open**; then select **Exchange Server Folder**.
3. Select the folder you want to open, and click **OK**.

   The folder is opened in a separate window.

After the folder is open, you can perform all the actions (that is, read, create, and edit items) for which you have been granted permission.

Displaying Additional Mailboxes in Your Folder List

If you have been granted permission to open someone else's mailbox on the Exchange Server, you might find it convenient to display those folders in your Folder List. After you make this change, the other person's mailbox folders will be opened automatically every time you start Outlook.

Add another user's mailbox folder to your folder list

1. Open the **Tools** menu and select **Services**.
2. Highlight **Microsoft Exchange Server** on the list, then click the **Properties** button. The Microsoft Exchange Server dialog box opens.
3. Click the **Advanced** tab.
4. To add a mailbox, click the **Add** button, and then type the name of the mailbox you want to open.
5. Click **OK** to close the Microsoft Exchange Server dialog box, and click **OK** to close the Services dialog box.

After you have added another person's mailbox to your Folder List, you can open that mailbox and its folders by clicking the folders, just as you do with your own folders.

Removing Previously Granted Permissions

If you have granted permissions to another user to open one of your folders, you might decide at a later time to remove those permissions. For example you might have granted special permissions for the duration of a project, and then decide to remove those permissions upon the completion of the project. In the example that follows, I'll show you how to remove permissions granted to another user to open your Outlook folders.

Removing previously granted permissions

1. If the Folder List is not visible, display it by opening the **View** menu and selecting **Folder**.
2. Right-click the folder whose permissions you want to change, and select the **Properties** tab.
3. Click the name of the person whose permissions you want to remove.
4. Click **Remove** to delete this person's permissions for this folder.
5. Click **OK** to close the dialog box.

In similar fashion, you can remove any delegate authority that you have previously granted to another user.

Remove previously granted delegate authority

1. Open the **Tools** menu and select **Options**; then click the **Delegates** tab.
2. Click the name of the person whose delegate authority you want to remove.
3. Click the **Remove** button.
4. Click **OK** to close the Options dialog box.

Sharing Calendars

In addition to granting permission to another person to work with your Inbox, you might want to give another person, such as your assistant, permission to work with your Calendar folder. As with the Inbox, you can choose to grant a variety of roles or individual permissions to this folder, so some people may be able to view your calendar, and others may be able to create appointments on your calendar.

Grant permission to view your calendar

1. If the Folder List is not visible, display it by opening the **View** menu and choosing **Folder List**.

2. Right-click your Calendar folder, and select the **Properties** tab.

3. Click **Add** to select a user to whom you want to grant permissions to this folder.

4. Select the user, and then click **OK** to return to the Permissions dialog box.

5. Use the **Permissions** drop-down list to select the role you want to grant to this user, or select the individual permissions.

6. Click **OK** to close the dialog box.

Using Public Folders

The Public Folders feature of Microsoft Exchange lets you create folders that anyone connected to your Exchange Server can see and use. Public Folders are commonly used to post messages relating to a particular subject, such as a project that people are working on together. The Exchange administrator can control the rights of each Public Folder; therefore, the capability to post items in the folder, or to open the items that are in the folder, are limited according to security requirements.

SEE ALSO

➤ To learn about creating and using Public Folders, see "Using Public Folders" on page 370.

Sharing Information with Public Folders and Newsgroups

Reading information in Public Folders

Posting information in Public Folders

Creating your own Public Folder

Connecting to a newsgroup server

Reading and posting messages on a newsgroup

Private folders and Net Folders

Public Folders are not available to you unless you are using Exchange Server within your organization. The data in the folders is stored on your company's server, and is not visible outside your organization.

Net Folders let you share information over the Internet or a corporate intranet. To use Net Folders, you don't have to be using Exchange Server, but you must have Internet or intranet access, and you must have the Net Folders add-in installed in Outlook.

Using Public Folders

If you are using Outlook 98 Messaging and Collaboration Client together with Microsoft Exchange Server, you can use Public Folders to share messages and other Outlook items with other people in your organization.

Public Folders are stored on your organization's Exchange Server, where they can be made available to all the users on the network. They can function as electronic bulletin boards for exchanging ideas and announcements, official company documents, and other common information. Storing shared information in Public Folders is more efficient than sending individual messages to each user, and it makes the information easy to find and use.

SEE ALSO

➤ For more information on installing and using Net Folders, see "Using Net Folders" on page 497.

What Is in a Public Folder?

Public Folders can contain Outlook items, such as e-mail messages, contacts, appointments, and notes. Public Folders can also contain other files, such as Word documents, Excel spreadsheets, PowerPoint presentations, or multimedia files.

The owner of a Public Folder might have restricted the type of items that can be placed in a particular folder. For example, if you have a folder that contains the company's client list, you can put contact items in the folder. Most Public Folders are created to store e-mail messages. You can use Outlook to read the messages in a Public Folder, to respond to those messages, and to create, or post, new messages.

Accessing Information in Public Folders

Reading an item in a Public Folder is similar to reading an item in your personal folders.

Reading items in Public Folders

1. If your **Folder List** is not displayed, open the <u>V</u>iew menu and select **Fold<u>e</u>r List**; then expand the folder tree to display the folder with which you want to work, as shown in Figure 23.1.

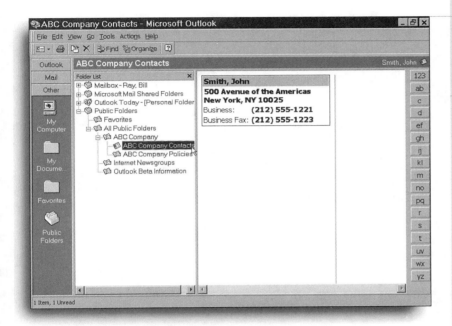

FIGURE 23.1
The ABC Company Contacts folder in this example is used to store information about ABC Company's customers.

2. Select an item in the folder, and double-click it to open it. The item is opened with the default form for the selected folder, as shown in Figure 23.2. In this example, the folder has been designed to use a custom form for editing contacts.

Public Folders work much like your Inbox and other personal folders. You can use many of the same Outlook features for viewing Public Folders as you would use with your other folders:

- Select the <u>V</u>iew menu and choose **Auto<u>P</u>review** to activate the automatic preview of unread messages in a Public Folder.

- Select the **View** menu and choose **Preview Pane** to open the preview pane, displaying a larger amount of the content of each message in the folder.

- Select the **View** menu, and then choose **Current View** and select a view from the list of those available.

FIGURE 23.2

Client information is edited using a custom Contacts form.

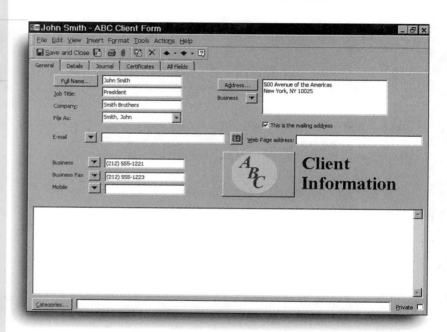

Sometimes you might find an item in a Public Folder that you would like to copy to your own folders. For example, you might want to copy an event from the company's calendar to your personal calendar. This will enable you to add your own comments or notes to the calendar item without sharing them on the Public Folder.

To copy an item from a Public Folder, select the item you want to copy, open the **Edit** menu, and choose the **Copy to Folder** command. Select the destination folder in the dialog box that appears, and click **OK**.

Posting Information in Public Folders

If you have permission to create items in a Public Folder, you can post information to the folder.

The person who created the folder, who is known as the owner of the folder, can grant a variety of permissions to other users of that folder. You might have the permission to post items in some folders, but not in others.

For example, someone from your company's Human Resources department might have created a folder for posting job openings within the company. You would probably have the right to read these messages, but not to post your own messages.

Another common use of a Public Folder is for discussion groups. Folders might be available for posting product ideas, special events, complaints, or other information that might come from anyone in the organization. In this case, you have probably been granted the permissions to create messages, as well as to read them.

Beginning a New Conversation

One of the most common uses of a Public Folder is to contain the messages of a *conversation*. A conversation is a simple exchange of communications about a particular subject. Users can respond to the messages that others have posted, creating a public discussion group for anyone to read. From the back-and-forth nature of these conversations, they have also become known as threaded conversations, or just *threads*.

You begin a conversation by posting a message in a Public Folder.

Posting a message to a Public Folder

1. Select the Public Folder in which you want to post an item.
2. Click the New Post in this folder ⬛ icon on the toolbar. The default form for this folder appears for editing.
3. Fill in the subject and the text of the message, as shown in Figure 23.3. Notice that the **Post To** and **Conversation** lines are filled in automatically with the name of the folder

Posting information

Posting information means placing a message on a Public Folder on a server such as Exchange Server, or on a news server. After a message is posted, other people who have access to the newsgroup or Public Folder can read and respond to your message.

and the name of the discussion, which is the subject of the first message posted in that conversation.

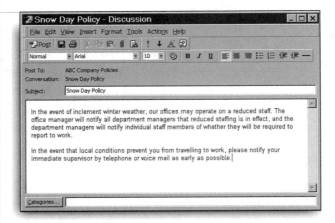

4. Click the **Post** button to close the form and save the message to the selected Public Folder.

Posting a Response to a Conversation

After you read a message in a Public Folder conversation, you can post a response to the message for others to read.

Posting a response

1. Double-click a message in a Public Folder to read it.

2. Click the Post Reply toolbar button. The default form for this folder appears for editing.

3. Fill in the subject and the text of the reply. The **Post To** and **Conversation** lines are filled in automatically with the name of the folder and the name of the discussion.

4. Click the **Post** button to close the form and post the new message in the discussion.

Viewing Messages by Conversation

A Public Folder can contain messages from many conversations. As with any other folder, you can select from a variety of Outlook views for displaying the contents of the folder. The most useful view for reading messages in a conversation is the By Conversation Topic view. Open the **View** menu, choose the **Current View** command, and then select **By Conversation Topic** on the submenu that appears. Figure 23.4 shows the appearance of the Public Folders when viewed by conversation topic. By clicking the plus sign to the left of a conversation heading, you can expand the conversation to see all its messages, as shown in Figure 23.5.

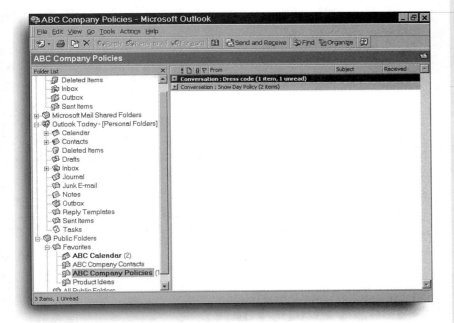

FIGURE 23.4

This Public Folder contains two conversations with individual messages collapsed.

Sending an E-mail Response to a Conversation

Sometimes you might want to send a response directly to the person who posted a message in a Public Folder, without posting a message for everyone to see. Additionally, you might want to forward or copy a message to another user, even someone who doesn't have access to the Public Folders.

FIGURE 23.5

The conversations have been expanded to reveal the individual messages in this Public Folder.

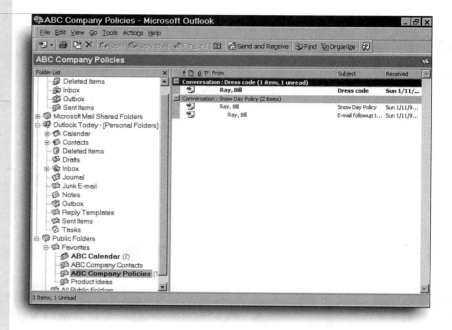

Getting permission to create Public Folders

Only your Exchange Administrator can grant users the right to create Public Folders. Check with your Exchange Administrator to discover your company's policies concerning Public Folders.

In larger organizations that have more than one Exchange Server, a Public Folder can be replicated by the Exchange administrator, making its contents available to users on the other Exchange Servers in the company. If you are creating or proposing a new Public Folder that would be of interest to everyone in the company, you can ask the Exchange Administrator to replicate it to the other Exchange Servers in the company.

To reply to the person who posted the message, click the Reply button while you are reading the message. Outlook creates a new message addressed to the sender of the original message. As with any e-mail message, you can select additional **To**, **Cc**, and **Bcc** addresses for the message before sending it as usual.

To forward the message to another user without replying to the sender, click the Forward button, while reading the message. Outlook creates a new message for you to forward. In this case, you'll have to fill in the **To** address before sending the message.

Creating a Public Folder

If you have been given the right to create a Public Folder, you can use Outlook to create it, just like any other folder. After you create the folder, you are automatically the owner of the folder, and you have the ability to designate the permissions of other users to view, read, create, edit, and delete items in the folder.

Just like personal folders, Public Folders can contain subfolders, so you should first select which folder should be the parent of the new Public Folder.

Creating a Public Folder

1. Display the **Folder List**, if it is not already on your screen.

2. Select the folder that will be the parent of the new Public Folder. To create a top-level Public Folder, select the folder named **All Public Folders**. Right-click the selected folder to display the shortcut menu.

3. Select **New Folder** to create the folder.

4. Type the name for the new folder, and select the type of item that will appear in the folder. Most Public Folders will contain e-mail items. Press Enter to complete the new folder.

Using Forms Within Public Folders

When you create a new Public Folder, you and the other users on your network can use the same *forms* for viewing, editing, and creating items in the folders as you would use in your personal folders. Each time you open an item, Outlook supplies the appropriate form for you.

For example, if a Public Folder is designed to hold e-mail items, you would expect to use the usual forms for creating and reading e-mail messages. In this case, opening an item by double-clicking it opens the appropriate form for the item.

Because Public Folders are often used for special purposes within an organization, such as a discussion of product ideas or company policies, you might want to use custom forms for working with items in a Public Folder. Outlook lets you associate one or more forms with a folder, and lets you designate a default form for a folder.

Viewing and modifying form associations

1. Display the **Folder List**, if it is not already visible.

2. Right-click the folder name whose properties you want to modify; then select **Properties** on the context menu that pops up.

3. Select the **Forms** tab in the Properties dialog box. See Figure 23.6 for an example of the **Forms** tab.

FIGURE 23.6

The **Forms** tab of the Properties dialog box for a folder shows which custom forms you can use with the folder.

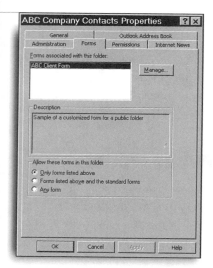

4. In the **Forms associated with this folder** group, select your preference for which forms are available to this folder. In the example in Figure 23.7, the folder has been restricted to enable the use of only the form named ABC Client Form.

5. Click **Apply** to apply your changes, and click **OK** to close the dialog box.

In this example, all items created in this folder will be edited using the custom form that was selected. Figure 23.7 shows a contact being edited using the custom form.

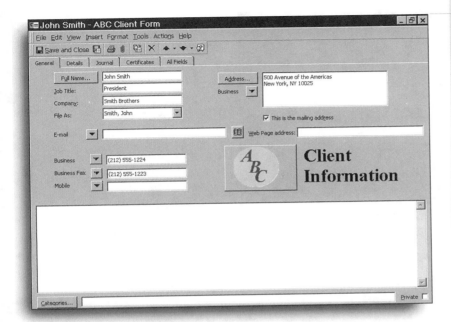

FIGURE 23.7
Client information is edited using a custom Contacts form.

Making a Public Folder Available Offline

Normally, Public Folders are available only when you are connected to your Exchange Server. If you have users who must read from, or post messages to, Public Folders while working remotely, you can make a Public Folder available offline.

Setting permissions for reading a Public Folder offline

1. Right-click the folder, and select **Properties** from the shortcut menu.

2. Select the **Synchronization** tab in the Properties dialog box, as shown in Figure 23.8.

3. Using the **This folder is available** option group, select **When offline or online** to make the folder available for offline use.

4. If a copy of the folder isn't already in your Favorites folder, drag the folder into Favorites to make it available offline.

Synchronizing Public Folders

Copying the content of one folder to another so both folders contain the most recent data is known as *synchronization*. If you have been working with an offline copy of a Public Folder, Outlook automatically synchronizes your offline folder with the actual Public Folder on the Exchange Server.

Adding a Public Folder to your Favorites folder

To view a Public Folder when you are working offline, you have to put a copy of the folder in your Favorites folder, which appears as a subfolder under Public Folders in the Folder List window. You have to do this when you are working online. Drag the Public Folder that you want to use offline into the Favorites folder, creating an offline copy of the Public Folder.

FIGURE 23.8

Use the **Synchronization** tab of a Public Folder to make the folder available for offline use.

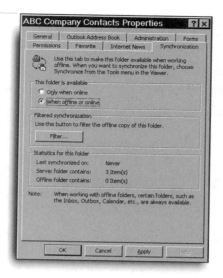

SEE ALSO

➤ *For more information about working offline and synchronizing folders, see "Synchronizing Folders with Microsoft Exchange" on page 529.*

Using Newsgroups

Newsgroups are a feature of the Internet that enable you to enter into discussions with users all over the world. Newsgroups are generally organized into areas of special interest, and thousands of newsgroups exist. You can find a newsgroup to discuss politics, sports, entertainment, medical issues, computer technical support, and many other issues. In most cases, you can find newsgroups covering specific issues, such as fan clubs for individual entertainers, software discussion groups for individual applications, or recreational activities in an individual city.

Newsgroups have evolved to provide a useful, if somewhat undisciplined, forum for users to ask questions, enter discussions, and express opinions. When you want to get a feel for what people are saying about a particular subject, you can visit a newsgroup to read the latest discussion on that topic. A commonly used collection of newsgroups is known as *Usenet*.

What is Outlook Express?

Outlook Express is a separate program that is included with Outlook 98. It is also included with Internet Explorer 4.0. Outlook Express can be used to send and receive e-mail and to work with newsgroups. If you are not interested in using the other features of Outlook, such as the Calendar, Contacts, Journal, Notes, and Tasks, you might elect to use Outlook Express as your primary e-mail editor and newsgroup reader. Because Outlook 98 has no built-in support for reading newsgroups, Outlook Express is included for this purpose.

Outlook 98 provides access to newsgroups through the Outlook Express application that is included in the Outlook installation. You can use Outlook Express to connect to one or more newsgroup servers, where the messages for the newsgroup are stored.

Connecting to a Newsgroup Server

Newsgroups are stored on newsgroup servers, which can be reached via the Internet. It's possible that a newsgroup server is available on your network, but it's more likely that you'll have to connect to the Internet to participate in a newsgroup. You can use Outlook Express to connect to a newsgroup server and to subscribe to a newsgroup. If your company uses Microsoft Exchange Server, and you want to share information within your company, consider using Public Folders, discussed in the first part of this chapter.

You can start Outlook Express by double-clicking the **Outlook Express** shortcut on your Windows desktop, or on your **Start** menu. Depending on your configuration, Outlook Express will either dial your Internet service provider to connect to a newsgroup server, or wait until you want to connect to the server. Figure 23.9 shows the connection message that is displayed when you start Outlook Express.

If you are already running Outlook 98, you can start Outlook Express quickly by opening the **Go** menu and selecting the **News** command.

If you want to connect to the server on your own, click the **Connect** button on the toolbar. Enter your name and password to log on to the server, and click **OK** to start the connection. Outlook Express uses your dial up connection to connect to the newsgroup server.

Reading newsgroups through Exchange Public Folders

If you are working with Exchange Server, you might be able to read your newsgroups without using Outlook Express. Your Exchange Administrator can establish a gateway, which provides access to newsgroups through the Public Folders feature of Exchange Server. Check with your Exchange Administrator to see whether this service is available on your network.

FIGURE 23.9

Outlook Express can automatically dial your online service to connect to a newsgroup at startup.

Configuring Outlook Express

Outlook Express can be configured to dial your Internet service provider automatically, connecting you to the newsgroup servers you have selected.

In Outlook Express, open the **Tools** menu, choose the **Options** command, and select the **Dial-up** tab. If you want Outlook Express to dial automatically, select the **Dial this connection** button, and select the dial-up connection that you want to use from the list. If you don't want Outlook Express to dial automatically, select either the **Do not dial a connection** button, or the **A̲sk me if I would like to dial a connection** button.

If you have not selected a newsgroup server, you need to tell Outlook Express the name of the server to which you want to connect. You can install as many newsgroup servers as you want to use.

Selecting a newsgroup server

1. Open the **T̲ools** menu and choose the **Accounts** command. The Internet Accounts dialog box appears, as shown in Figure 23.10. Click the **News** tab to see the list of news servers that are currently available.

2. If no server is listed or your news server does not appear in the list, click **Add**, and select **N̲ews** to start the Internet Connection Wizard.

3. Enter your name as you want it to appear in messages posted in the newsgroup, and then click **N̲ext**.

FIGURE 23.10

The Internet Accounts dialog box displays the mail and news service that you have installed for Outlook Express.

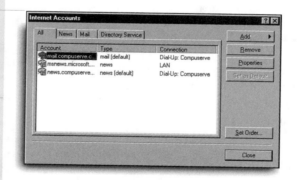

4. Enter your e-mail address, and then click **N̲ext**.

5. Enter the name of the news server that you want to connect to. You should obtain the news server name from your Internet service provider or from your system administrator. Be sure to type the name exactly as your administrator tells you. If you need to log on to the server, click the **My news server requires me to log on** box; then click **N̲ext**.

6. If you selected the **My news server requires me to log on** box, fill in your username and password for the server. Your username (sometimes called userid) and password are supplied by your Internet service provider or your system

What is logging on?

Most computer networks require a process called logging on to gain access to network resources such as shared drives and printers. This requirement provides the security for the network, preventing unauthorized access to company files and programs.

In most cases, your computer is configured to prompt you for a username and password each time you turn on the computer. Check with your network and e-mail administrators for information on the logging requirements for your administrator. As with the news server address, be sure to type it exactly as your administrator tells you. Click **Next**.

7. Type a descriptive name that you want to use for referring to the news server in Outlook Express. This name can be any name that will help you easily refer to your news server (you could name it something as innocuous as News Server). Then click **Next**.

8. Choose the connection type (whether you are using a standard phone line or modem or whether you are connecting at work through a local area network) for the newsgroup. Then click **Next**.

9. If you selected **Connect using my phone line** as your connection method, the wizard asks for the dial-up connection you want to use, as shown in Figure 23.11. Select **U**se an **existing dial-up connection**, or click **C**reate a new dial-up connection. Click **Next** when you have completed your selection.

What is Dial-Up Networking?

Windows 95 and Windows NT use Dial-Up Networking to let you connect to another computer using a modem. You can create a dial-up connection for each computer that you need to call. For example, you might have one dial-up connection to call a commercial service such as CompuServe, and another to dial your company's computer to check your e-mail messages from home.

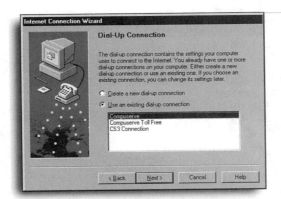

FIGURE 23.11

Select the dial-up connection that you'll use to call your news server.

10. Click **Finish** to complete the connection. The new news server appears in the list of **Internet Accounts**. Click **Close** to return to Outlook Express.

SEE ALSO

➤ *For information on creating a Dial-Up Networking connection, see "Setting Up Dial-Up Networking on Your Computer" on page 509.*

Subscribing and Unsubscribing to a Newsgroup

To receive messages from a newsgroup, you must first subscribe to the newsgroup. Each news server contains a number of newsgroups. Some news servers have only a few newsgroups, although others may have hundreds, or even thousands of newsgroups.

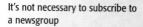

It's not necessary to subscribe to a newsgroup

You don't have to subscribe to a newsgroup to participate in conversations. Subscribing helps you locate that particular newsgroup more quickly later. You may view the messages and reply to any messages you like without subscribing.

Select the server that you want to use by clicking the server name in the list window. If you have already subscribed to any newsgroups on this server, their names are displayed in the message window. Click the Newsgroups button on the toolbar to display a list of the newsgroups available on the server. If the server contains a large number of newsgroups, it can take quite a long time to update the list, depending on the speed of your Internet connection. Figure 23.12 shows the Outlook Express dialog box for selecting newsgroups.

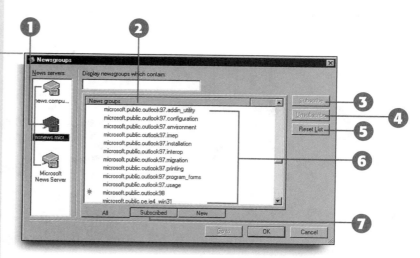

FIGURE 23.12

Use the Newsgroups dialog box to see the available newsgroups on a news server, and to subscribe to the groups that interest you.

❶ Server names

❷ News groups button

❸ Click here to subscribe to a newsgroup

❹ Click here to unsubscribe

❺ Click here to update your list of newsgroups

❻ Newsgroup names

❼ Subscribed newsgroups

Newsgroup names generally are somewhat descriptive, but often can be a bit cryptic. The names usually consist of several words, connected by periods. For example, the name misc.fitness. weights refers to a newsgroup of interest to weightlifters. The first part of the name is used to categorize the newsgroups. The "misc" portion of the weights newsgroup represents miscellaneous newsgroups.

The newsgroup named comp.databases.ms-access contains discussions about the Microsoft Access database. The "comp" portion of the name refers to computer-related topics.

Many newsgroups are hosted by companies or other organizations. Microsoft.public.excel.misc contains miscellaneous information about Microsoft Excel. Bermuda.Sports contains discussions of sports activities in Bermuda.

If you find a name that interests you as you scroll through the list of newsgroup names, you can subscribe to the newsgroup. Click the name of the newsgroup, and click the **Subscribe** button. You can subscribe to as many newsgroups as you want.

After you subscribe to a newsgroup, a small icon appears next to the subscribed group (see Figure 23.13).

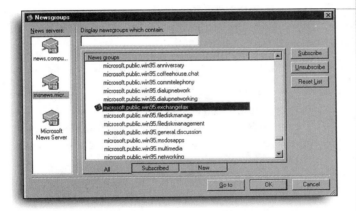

FIGURE 23.13
The Newsgroups dialog box shows that the user has subscribed to the microsoft. public.win95.exchangefax newsgroup.

After exploring a newsgroup, you might decide that you aren't really interested in it. You can end your subscription to the newsgroup by selecting the newsgroup name, and clicking the **Unsubscribe** button. The subscribed icon will be removed from the left of the newsgroup name.

Over time, the operator of the newsgroup server might add new newsgroups. To make sure you have the latest list of newsgroups, click the **Reset List** button to get the latest list of newsgroups available on the server (refer to Figure 23.13).

Reading Newsgroup Messages

After you have subscribed to a newsgroup, you can read the messages posted there. By clicking the name of the newsgroup server in the **Folders List**, you'll see the list of subscribed newsgroups in the message window. To open a newsgroup, double-click the name of the newsgroup. Outlook Express opens the newsgroup, displaying the messages that have been posted on the server.

By default, Outlook Express downloads the 300 most recently posted messages, or the headers representing those messages, when you select the newsgroup. To view the additional messages that might be stored in that newsgroup, open the **Tools** menu, and select **Get Next 300 Headers**. If you want Outlook Express to load more or fewer headers automatically, open the **Tools** menu and select the **Options** command. In the dialog box that appears, select the **Read** tab, and enter the number of headers you want Outlook Express to read at a time.

Figure 23.14 shows the contents of the microsoft.public.win95.exchangefax newsgroup, with a message displayed in the Preview Pane.

Newsgroup messages are organized by conversations (or threads). A conversation thread begins when someone posts a message on the server, and the thread continues as other users reply to the original message. For example, a user might post a question on a Windows newsgroup asking how to adjust the screen colors in Windows. Other users who know the answer will read the message and reply with the solution. Figure 23.15 shows a response to the previous question about automatically printing faxes. Many questions have more than one answer, so the responses of several users to a question can be helpful and informative.

When you are reading the messages in a newsgroup, you'll notice that some messages have a plus sign next to them. That is an indication that responses to this message are on the server, thus indicating a conversation thread. Click the plus sign to expand the thread, showing the responses to the original message.

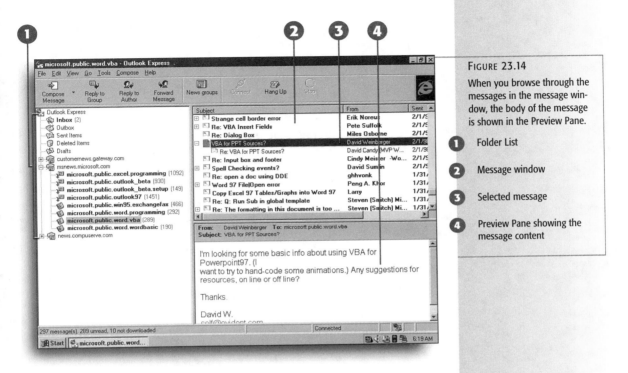

FIGURE 23.14

When you browse through the messages in the message window, the body of the message is shown in the Preview Pane.

❶ Folder List

❷ Message window

❸ Selected message

❹ Preview Pane showing the message content

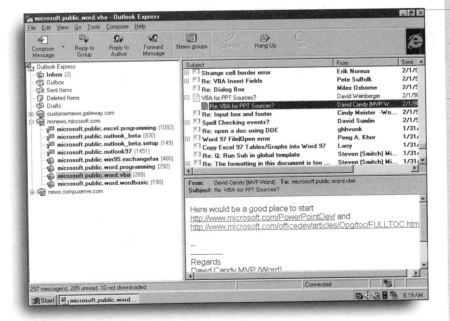

FIGURE 23.15

This message, a response to an earlier question, suggests a useful Internet link for more information.

As you click individual messages, the contents of the messages are displayed in the Preview Pane, on the lower right-hand corner of the Outlook Express window. Because many messages are short, you might be able to see the entire message in the Preview Pane, or you can use the Preview Pane's scrollbar to read through longer messages.

If you prefer to open the message in its own window, double-click the message. A separate message window opens, as shown in Figure 23.16. Because you can maximize this window, you can see more of the message at one time.

FIGURE 23.16

You can open a newsgroup message in its own window for more control over the appearance of the message.

When you are finished reading the message, you can close the message window by clicking the window's Close (**x**) button.

Posting Messages to a Newsgroup

You can learn a lot by reading messages in a newsgroup, but what if you have a question that nobody else has asked? You need to post your question in the newsgroup, thus starting a new conversation thread.

Click the **Compose Message** button. A new message window appears. The name of the newsgroup is already filled in as the destination of the message. Type a subject for your message; then type the body of the message. When you're finished typing

A cautionary note about newsgroups

Before you post a message on a newsgroup, remember that your message can be read by users around the world. Anyone who reads your message might copy it or forward it as they want. Don't divulge any proprietary or personal information, or anything you wouldn't want to have published just about anywhere.

the message, click the **Post** button on the toolbar. Your message is posted on the newsgroup, starting a new conversation thread.

Replying to a Newsgroup Message

While you're reading messages from a newsgroup, you might want to post a response to a message that you've read. You can respond to a message by clicking the **Reply to Group** button. A message window opens, with the name of the newsgroup already entered as the destination of the message. All you have to do is type your response in the message area, and click the **Post** button on the toolbar. Your reply is posted in the newsgroup as a continuation of the conversation thread.

If you want to send an e-mail reply directly to the author of the messages, without posting the reply in the newsgroup, click the **Reply to Author** button. In the message window that opens, the author's e-mail address is filled in automatically. After you type your response in the message area of the window, click the **Send** button on the toolbar. Your message is placed in your Outbox folder, to be sent as an e-mail message. If you are currently connected to your e-mail service, the message is sent immediately. Otherwise the message will be sent the next time you connect to your e-mail service.

Reading Newsgroup Messages Offline

If you want to avoid staying online while you read newsgroup messages, you can download messages for offline reading. The messages are copied to your local hard drive, so you can read them without tying up your phone line, or accumulating charges for an online information service.

To prepare a newsgroup for offline reading, select the newsgroup in the folder list, then open the **File** menu, choose the **Properties** command, and click the **Download** tab. Click the **When downloading this newsgroup, retrieve** check box, then select one of the three options for downloading:

- *New Headers* lets you download the header of new messages, so you know the author's name, subject, and date of

Anonymous authors on newsgroups

You won't always be able to reply directly to the author of a newsgroup message because many authors use fake names and fake e-mail addresses. Some do this to protect their privacy from marketers who scan newsgroups for names and addresses, although others hide their identities because they are the ones doing the marketing.

the new messages that have been posted on the newsgroup. Because the bodies of new messages are not retrieved, the downloading goes faster than downloading the entire message. Later, you can mark those messages that you're interested in reading, and download the bodies of those messages.

- *New Messages* downloads the entire message, including the header and body of the message, for each new message on the newsgroup. Although this takes longer than downloading just the header, it means that as soon as you go offline, you'll be able to read the entire contents of the messages, without reconnecting to the newsgroup.

- *All Messages* downloads not only the new messages, but also the older messages that you've already seen. This is useful if you've deleted some of the older messages from your local system, and you want to refer to an older message. This method will take the longest of the three options to download.

You can set the download method individually for each newsgroup to which you subscribe. This will control the downloading behavior of each newsgroup the next time you perform a download.

After you've set up your folders for downloading, you're ready to perform the download. Three commands for downloading messages or headers from a newsgroup are on the **Tools** menu:

- *Download All* is used when you want to connect to your online service and download all your subscribed newsgroups according to the downloading instructions you have provided.

- *Download this Newsgroup* carries out your downloading instructions only for the newsgroup that is currently selected.

- *Download* **servername** performs your downloading instructions for all the newsgroups on the currently selected news server. This is useful if you have subscribed to newsgroups on more than one server, but you are interested in the messages from one server at a time.

When you select one of the download commands from the **T**ools menu, Outlook Express connects to your news server using your Dial-Up Networking connection, and carries out the download as you have requested. When all your instructions have been performed, you are disconnected from the news server.

If you have downloaded just the headers in a newsgroup, you can review those headers offline. By reading the subject and the author's name, you can decide whether you are interested in reading the body of the message. When you see a message that you would like to read, you can mark the message for downloading, so the body of the message will be available for offline reading. To mark a message for downloading, right-click the message in the message list. On the context menu that appears, select **M**ark Message for Download.

Now that you've marked some messages for later downloading, you can have Outlook Express download the messages. To download the messages for the current newsgroup, open the **Tools menu and choose Download _t_his Newsgroup**. In the Download Newsgroup dialog box, check the **G_e_t marked messages** box. Outlook connects to the news server and downloads the messages for your offline reading.

Sorting and Finding Messages

Because a newsgroup can contain a large number of messages, you might not want to take the time to read every message in the newsgroup. When you want to find specific information quickly, you can use Outlook Express's built-in sorting and search features.

To find a message covering a certain topic, you can search for text that appears in the subject, or for messages from a specific author.

Finding a specific message

1. Open the **E**dit menu, and select **F**ind Message.
2. In the dialog box that appears, enter the text for which you are searching in the **Fr_om_** or **Su_b_ject** text boxes, and select

a date range if you want to limit the age of the messages that are found.

3. Click **OK**. Outlook Express searches the current newsgroup for message headers that match your request. The first message that matches the request is selected.

4. To find the next matching message, press F3. Outlook Express highlights the next matching message.

5. Repeat pressing F3 as long as you want to continue finding matching messages, or until Outlook Express presents a message that no more matches were found.

Searching conversation content is not possible

Although searching newsgroups by the **From** and **Subject** fields is useful, searching for words contained in a message is not possible.

You can use Outlook Express's sorting features to change the order in which messages are displayed in the message window. The easiest way to change the sort order is to click the column heading for the column by which you want to sort. For example, to sort the messages by the author of the message, click the **From** column heading. To sort the messages by the subject text, click the **Subject** column heading. To sort the messages by the date that they were posted, click the **Sent** column heading.

Clicking the selected column heading a second time reverses the sort order. For example, clicking the **From** heading repeatedly alternates between showing the newest messages first, or the oldest messages first.

Sending and Receiving Faxes

Installing Fax Capability in Windows

Microsoft Outlook 98 Messaging and Collaboration Client can work with the faxing capabilities of Windows 95 to let you send and receive faxes from Outlook. If you have installed Microsoft Fax, the menus in Outlook are automatically modified to give you access to the faxing capabilities.

Faxing in Windows 95

When Windows is installed on your computer, Microsoft Fax is usually installed automatically.

Verifying that Microsoft Fax is installed

1. Using the Windows **Start** Menu, select **Settings**, and click **Control Panel**.
2. Double-click the Mail icon.
3. If Microsoft Fax is listed among the services, you don't need to install it. If it isn't listed, continue by clicking **Add** to add the service.
4. In the Add Service to Profile dialog box, select **Microsoft Fax**, and click **OK** to close the dialog box.
5. Click **OK** to accept the changes to your **Services** list.

If Microsoft Fax isn't listed in the Add Services to Profile dialog box, you'll need to install it from your Windows 95 CD-ROM.

Installing Microsoft Fax in Windows 95

1. Insert the Windows 95 CD-ROM in your CD-ROM drive. The Windows 95 CD-ROM window appears.
2. Click **Add/Remove Software** to display the list of components that are currently installed.
3. Check the box next to **Microsoft Fax**, and then click OK to complete the installation.

Faxing in Windows NT

Windows NT does not include a built-in faxing service. Third-party faxing utilities are available commercially, and some can be downloaded from the Microsoft Web site. Some of the popular commercial faxing applications designed to work with Windows NT are WinFax Pro 8.0 by Symantec, OMTOOL Fax by Omtool, Qmodem Pro, and Procom Plus.

At the time of this writing, Microsoft Personal Fax for Windows NT was under development. You can find more information on this product on the Internet at `http://www.microsoft.com/ntworkstation/fax.htm`.

Adding Microsoft Fax to Your Outlook Profile

After Microsoft Fax is installed on your computer, you can add it to your Outlook profile, so Outlook can use the fax service to send and receive faxes.

SEE ALSO

➤ *To learn more about creating profiles, see Chapter 6, "Creating a Profile."*

Adding Microsoft Fax to your Outlook profile

1. While running Outlook, open the **Tools** menu, and choose **Services**.

2. If Microsoft Fax is not listed among the services in your profile, click **Add** to add the Microsoft Fax service to your profile.

3. Select **Microsoft Fax** in the list of available services, and click **Properties**.

4. Complete each of the four tabs in the Microsoft Fax Properties dialog box, as described later; then click **OK** to close the dialog box.

5. Click **OK** to close the Services dialog box.

Use the **Message** tab to set the default values for how faxes will be sent. The **Message** tab is shown in Figure 24.1.

■ Use the **Time to Send** options to select whether faxes should be sent immediately, during discount rate times, or at a specific time.

Adding Microsoft Personal Fax for Windows NT to your profile

This section describes adding Microsoft Fax to your computer when you're using Windows 95. If you are using Windows NT and have downloaded Microsoft Personal Fax for Windows NT, you can use a similar procedure.

- Setting the **Message Format** options determines whether Microsoft Fax will attempt to send an editable fax, or a paper fax only. If you have selected **Not editable**, you can click the **Paper** button to select the paper size and layout for the fax.

- To select a default cover page, check the **Send cover page** button, and select the cover page you want to use. You can also design your own cover pages by modifying the samples, or you can start from scratch with a blank cover page.

FIGURE 24.1

The **Message** tab of the Microsoft Fax Properties dialog box controls the default options for sending faxes.

The **Dialing** tab lets you control how your fax messages will be dialed by Microsoft Fax. The **Dialing** tab is shown in Figure 24.2.

- Click **Dialing Properties** to display the Dialing Properties dialog box, shown in Figure 24.3. Use this dialog box to select what location you are dialing from. This is especially useful if you are traveling, and making long-distance calls that must be dialed differently in your temporary location. You can save each location that you commonly dial from, storing the rules for dialing an outside line, using a phone credit card, and disabling call waiting.

FIGURE 24.2

The **Dialing** tab of the Microsoft Fax dialog box lets you control how faxes are dialed.

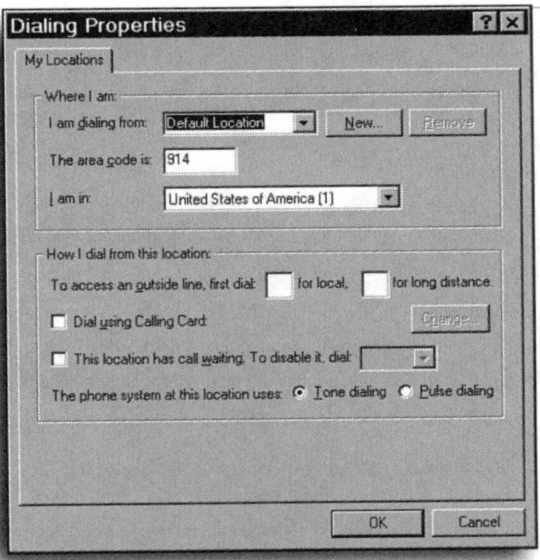

FIGURE 24.3

The Dialing Properties dialog box controls where you are dialing from, and how numbers are dialed from this location.

- Click the **Toll Prefixes** button on the Dialing page to select any 3-digit prefixes within your area code that require you to dial 1 and the area code (see Figure 24.4). Otherwise, Microsoft Fax dials all numbers in your area code without these prefixes.

- Enter the number of times you want to retry dialing a fax number if the line is busy.

- Enter the number of minutes you want to wait between attempts to redial when the line is busy.

FIGURE 24.4

The **Toll Prefixes** dialog box lets you select phone numbers within your area code that require you to dial your area code first.

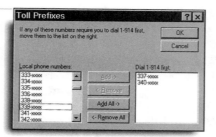

The **Modem** tab is used to select the modem that you want to use to send faxes. Select the modem you will use, and click **Set as Active Fax Modem**, if more than one modem is installed.

FIGURE 24.5

The **Modem** tab of the Microsoft Fax dialog box lets you select a modem and set its properties.

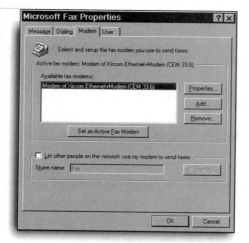

Click the **Properties** button to display the Fax Modem Properties dialog box. Using this dialog box, select the following options:

- Select whether you want incoming calls to be answered manually, automatically, or not answered.

- Set the speaker volume for the modem.

- Select whether you want to wait for a dial tone before dialing, whether you want to hang up if a busy signal is detected, and how long to wait for an answer when the receiving fax machine rings.

FIGURE 24.6
The Fax Modem Properties dialog box lets you control the operation of your fax modem.

The **User** tab lets you enter your name and other information that can be added to your fax pages automatically. If you use the default cover pages, or design your own custom cover pages, this information will be filled into the appropriate locations.

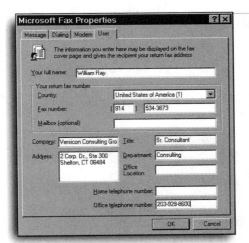

FIGURE 24.7
The **User** tab of the Microsoft Fax dialog box enables you to enter personal information that can be included automatically on the cover pages of your faxes.

Creating and Sending a Fax

After you have Microsoft Fax installed on your computer and have added it to your Outlook profile, you can create and send a fax at any time within Outlook. The Compose New Fax Wizard leads you through the process of creating and sending the fax.

Sending a fax with Microsoft Fax

1. Open the **Act<u>i</u>ons** menu, and select **Fax Message**. The Compose New Fax Wizard appears, as shown in Figure 24.8.

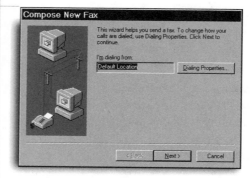

2. If you are not dialing from your default location, click the **Dialing Properties** button. Use the Dialing Properties dialog box, as shown in Figure 24.9, to set your custom dialog information. Click **OK** to return to the wizard.

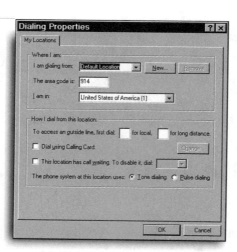

3. Click **Next** to continue and address the destination of the fax, as shown in Figure 24.10. If you want to send the fax to

more than one recipient, Click the **Add to List** button to create the list of those who will receive the fax. You can also click the **Address Book** button to select recipients from your Address Books. Click **Next** when you are ready to continue.

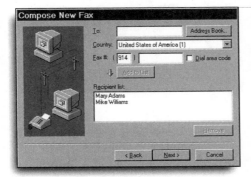

FIGURE 24.10

Enter the names and fax numbers of anyone you want to receive this fax.

4. The next step in the wizard lets you select a cover page for the fax, as shown in Figure 24.11. Select one of the cover pages from the list, or select **No** if you don't want a cover page.

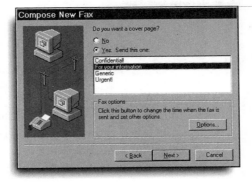

FIGURE 24.11

If you want a cover page for your fax, select it from the list of available cover pages.

5. If you want to change the options, such as when the fax is to be sent, click the **Options** button to display the Send Options dialog box, as shown in Figure 24.12. Select the time that you want to send the message, and other options. Then click **OK** to return to the wizard.

FIGURE 24.12

Use the Send Options for this Message dialog box to send the fax at a later time, or in a different format.

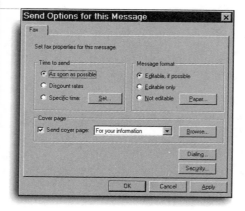

FIGURE 24.12

Use the Send Options for this Message dialog box to send the fax at a later time, or in a different format.

6. Click **Next** to move to the next step. Use the dialog box shown in Figure 24.13 to type the subject and note for the fax. Click **Next** to continue.

FIGURE 24.13

Enter the subject of the fax message, and the note that you want to appear on the first page.

7. To attach files to the fax, click the **Add File** button, and select any files you want to send as part of the fax (see Figure 24.14). Click **Next** to continue with the final step.

8. Click **Finish** to send your fax.

The Fax Wizard sends the fax by dialing the recipient's fax number using your modem and the dialing instructions.

Receiving a Fax

If you are using a dedicated telephone line for your fax modem, you can enable Microsoft Fax to answer incoming fax calls for you. See Figure 24.6, earlier in this chapter, for setting this option.

If you set the **Answer mode** option to answer automatically, Microsoft Fax answers the call and establishes the connection with the calling fax machine. The Microsoft Fax Status window appears to display the progress of the transmission.

If you set the **Answer mode** option to **Manual**, Outlook presents a message box asking whether you want to receive a fax. Answer **Yes** to answer the message.

If you have the **Answer mode** option set to **Don't answer**, Microsoft Fax does not automatically answer incoming calls. You can open the Microsoft Fax Status window by double-clicking the **Microsoft Fax** icon on the Windows status bar. Then you can answer the call by clicking the **Answer Now** button.

Viewing Received Faxes

Faxes that you have received are processed as e-mail messages with the fax as an attachment. You can open the message as you would normally open a message, and double-click the attachment to view the fax in the Fax Viewer.

The Fax Viewer lets you view the fax, zooming in and out to get a better view, as shown in Figure 24.15. Use one of the following buttons on the toolbar to adjust the viewing size.

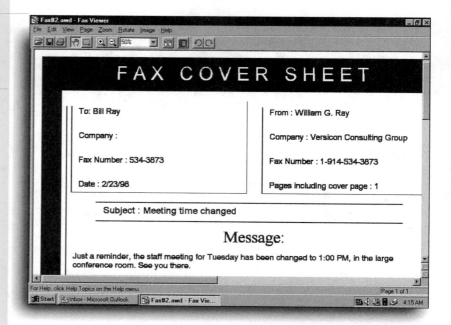

- The Zoom In button makes the fax image larger.
- The Zoom Out button makes the fax image smaller.
- The Predefined Zoom list lets you select from a list of convenient magnifications of the fax image.
- The Fit Width button adjusts the size of the image to fit the width of the screen.
- The Rotate buttons let you rotate the image 90 degrees at a time to the right or left, to adjust for the orientation of the page in the sender's fax.
- The Print button lets you print the fax on your default printer. To customize the paper size, orientation, and margins for the printout, open the **File** menu, and select **Page Setup**.

Because the fax is received as an e-mail message with the image as an attachment, it is easy to reply to a fax message, or to forward the message to others. The same message with the fax attachment is sent to your forwarding addressees. Of course, as with any other e-mail message, you can move the message to another folder, or use Outlook's Categories to organize the faxes you have received.

Creating a Fax Cover Page

Microsoft Fax includes a cover page editor for designing your own fax covers. You can either start from scratch with a blank page, or use one of the included cover sheets as a starting point, and modify it to your preferences.

To start the Fax Cover Page Editor, use the Windows **Start** menu, and select **Programs**, **Accessories**, **Fax**, **Cover Page Editor**. The Fax Cover Page Editor appears.

The Cover Page Editor starts with a blank page. Use the **Insert** menu to add the fields that represent the data items for the fax cover. The fields are divided into four categories:

- *Recipient* fields include **Name**, **Fax Number**, **Company**, **Street Address**, **City**, **State**, **Zip Code**, **Country**, **Title**, **Department**, **Office Location**, **Home Telephone Number**, **Office Telephone Number**, **To: List**, and **CC: List**.

- *Sender* fields include **Name**, **Fax Number**, **Company**, **Address**, **Title**, **Department**, **Office Location**, **Home Telephone Number**, and **Office Telephone Number**.

- *Message* fields include **Note**, **Subject**, **Time Sent**, **Number of Pages**, and **Number of Attachments**.

- *Objects* (such as company logos created in other applications) can be added to your cover sheet.

To insert a field on your new cover page, select the appropriate submenu from the **Insert** menu, and select the field that you want to place on the fax cover. The field is placed in the middle of the cover page. You can then use the mouse to drag the fields into the position you want for the cover page. In Figure 24.16, the Sender's Fax Number field has just been added to the cover page. Several other fields have already been moved to new locations on the cover page.

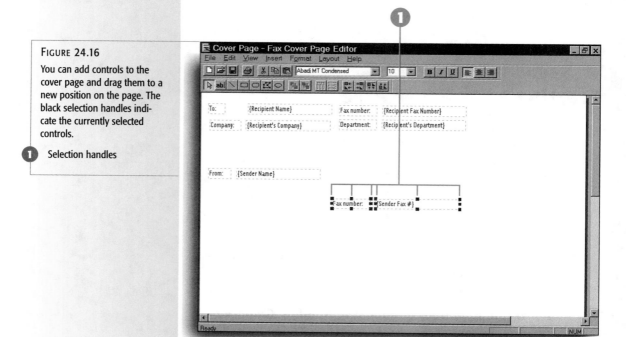

FIGURE 24.16

You can add controls to the cover page and drag them to a new position on the page. The black selection handles indicate the currently selected controls.

1 Selection handles

In addition to inserting the fields, you can add lines, boxes, and text to the form. You can also use the font name and size lists on the toolbar to change the appearance of the text on the cover page.

If you don't want to create a cover page from scratch, you can modify one of the existing pages that come with Microsoft Fax. With the Fax Viewer running, select the **File** menu, and choose **Open**. Select one of the cover sheet files, which are found in your Windows directory:

- *Confidential!*
- *For Your Information*
- *Generic*
- *Urgent*

Figure 24.17 shows the Fax Cover Page Editor with the Generic cover page open for editing.

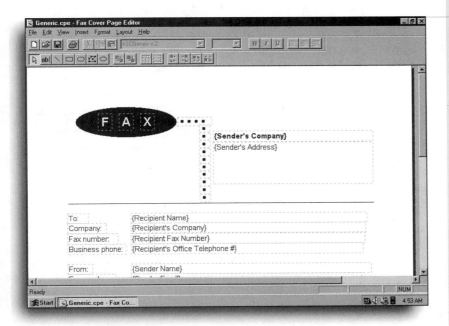

FIGURE 24.17

You can use the Fax Cover Page Editor to customize the cover pages that come with Microsoft Fax.

Modify the cover page by adding controls, lines, or other graphics elements, or by moving and deleting items from the page. When you are finished with your modifications, remember to save the changes. To update the previous cover page, open the **File** menu, and select **Save**. To save your changes under a new filename, open the **File** menu, and choose **Save As**. Type a new filename, and click **OK** to save your changes.

Using WinFax with Outlook

A new feature of Outlook 98 is the inclusion of Symantec WinFax Starter Edition. This software is a simplified version of Symantec's popular WinFax Pro faxing software. At the time this chapter was written, the WinFax Starter Edition features had just been added to Outlook. The final functionality of WinFax and Outlook 98 might be different.

More information on the Web

For the latest information on updated versions of the WinFax Starter Edition, visit the Outlook Web site at `http://www.microsoft.com/outlook`. For the latest information on WinFax Pro and other Symantec products, visit Symantec's Web site at `http://www.symantec.com`.

Faxing with WinFax Starter Edition

At the time of this writing, the WinFax Starter Edition was still under development, and the steps for sending a fax had not been finalized. Indications were that the process of sending a fax would be similar to the process of sending an e-mail.

With the Inbox folder active, you can open the **File** menu, select **New**, and click **Fax Message**. A new message window appears. The **To** and **Subject** boxes of the message are filled out just as you would complete them in an e-mail message, with a fax address or fax number selected as the **To** selection. After typing the body of the message, you click the **Send** button on the toolbar to deliver the fax message.

The WinFax Starter Edition is available only if you have Internet Only Outlook. Corporate/Workgroup Outlook uses Microsoft Fax, as described earlier in this chapter.

To set the options for WinFax Starter Edition, open the **Tools** menu, and choose **Options**. Click the **Fax** tab in the Options dialog box to set your WinFax preferences.

- Use the **Personal Information** section to enter your name, phone, and fax information, which will automatically appear on the cover page that is sent with your WinFax message.

- In the **Cover Page** section, click the **Template** button to select a cover page to be included with your fax massages.

- Use the **Modem** section to select the modem to use for your fax messages, to enable automatic receiving of faxes, and to set the number of rings after which to answer the phone for incoming fax messages.

- Use the **Retries** section to indicate how many times WinFax should try to deliver the fax message if a connection is made, and how long to wait between retries.

Sending Messages to Pagers

Extending Outlook with add-ins

Using Outlook to send messages to numeric and alphanumeric pagers

Installing MobileCHOICE Messenger

Sending messages to your own and others' pagers

Expanding Outlook with Add-ins

Outlook 98 Messaging and Collaboration Client as it comes "out of the box" is a powerful and versatile application. With the capability for creating custom forms and fields, you can tailor Outlook to suit just about all your communication and collaborations needs.

You don't necessarily have to spend your own time and effort to add capabilities to Outlook. A growing number of organizations are creating Outlook add-ins that provide additional facilities for Outlook. You can find up-to-date information about available add-ins on the Slipstick Web site at `http://www.slipstick.com/ exchange/add-ins/outlook.htm#outlook`.

Some add-ins are shareware that's available either free or for a small registration fee. Others are commercial products that have a wide range of prices.

This chapter uses Ikon's MobileCHOICE Messenger as an example of a commercially available Outlook add-in. I've chosen this particular add-in because it offers the type of functionality that could be useful to many Outlook users—sending messages from Outlook to pagers—and also because it illustrates how an add-in can be seamlessly integrated into Outlook. In addition to new functionality, this add-in adds

- An extra tab to the Options dialog box
- Extra buttons in the Message form's toolbar
- Extra menu items in the Message form's **Action** menu

The chapter might also give you ideas about what you can do yourself if you're prepared to spend time with custom programming.

Other pager add-ins

MobileCHOICE Messenger isn't the only Outlook add-in that provides paging capabilities. I'm using this as an example because it's an application I use. If you need paging capabilities, you should evaluate other add-ins.

Finding out more about MobileCHOICE Messenger

To find out more about Ikon's mobile services, go to the Web page:

`http://www.ikon.net`

Numeric and Alphanumeric Pagers

Numeric pagers can receive and display only numbers, such as phone numbers. Alphanumeric pagers can receive text (numbers and letters).

What Does MobileCHOICE Messenger Do?

MobileCHOICE Messenger has a dual personality:

- You can use it to send messages from Outlook to numeric and alphanumeric pagers.

- If you subscribe to Ikon's Mobility Services, you can use MobileCHOICE Messenger to send and receive wireless Internet e-mail, send wireless faxes, and more.

This chapter only covers using MobileCHOICE Messenger to send messages to pagers.

Before you get involved with sending messages, you should understand the protocols involved (*protocols* are the ways messages are formatted). The two significant protocols are

- *Dual-Tone Multiple Frequency (DTMF)*. Used to send messages to numeric pagers, those that can only receive numbers.
- *Telelocator Alpha-Paging (TAP)*. Used to send messages to alpha-numeric pagers, those that can receive text messages.

MobileCHOICE Messenger supports both protocols.

Installing MobileCHOICE Messenger

Ikon supplies MobileCHOICE Messenger on three floppy disks. The installation process is straightforward.

Installing MobileCHOICE Messenger

1. Insert the first floppy disk into your drive.
2. In the Windows taskbar, choose **Start** and in the Start menu, choose **R**un.
3. In the Run dialog box's **Open** box, type A:\Setup; then choose **OK**.
4. Follow the onscreen instructions to complete the installation.

The installation process makes the MobileCHOICE Paging information service available, but doesn't add that service to your profile.

Adding MobileCHOICE Paging to your profile

1. Start Outlook, open the **T**ools menu, and choose Ser**v**ices.
2. In the Services dialog box, choose **A**dd to display the dialog box shown in Figure 25.1.

FIGURE 25.1

MobileCHOICE Paging is among the information services you can add to your profile.

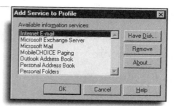

3. Select **MobileCHOICE Paging** and then choose **OK**. The information service is now shown as an information service in your profile, as shown in Figure 25.2.

FIGURE 25.2

Your profile now contains the MobileCHOICE Paging information service.

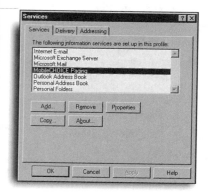

4. Choose the **Delivery** tab in the Services dialog box, select **MobileCHOICE Paging**, and then click the up-arrow at the right side of the box to move MobileCHOICE Paging to the top of the list of information services.

5. Return to the **Services** tab, select **MobileCHOICE Paging**, and choose **Properties** to display the dialog box shown in Figure 25.3.

6. After selecting a modem, choose the **Connections** tab and select the name of your paging service provider, as shown in Figure 25.4.

7. Choose the **Send Options** tab to display the dialog box shown in Figure 25.5.

The **Advanced** tab

The **Advanced** tab lists the paging protocols supported by MobileCHOICE Messenger. You can choose **Add** to add a protocol.

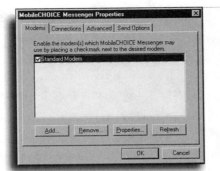

FIGURE 25.3

The **Modems** tab shows the available modems. If more than one modem is listed, select the one you want to use.

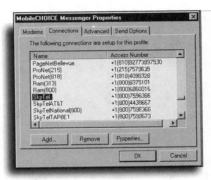

FIGURE 25.4

This tab lists many paging service providers. If yours is not listed, choose **Add** to add it to the list.

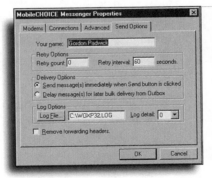

FIGURE 25.5

Use this dialog box to specify how you want to send pager messages and what sort of log you want to keep.

8. Choose **OK** to close the dialog box.

Now you must close Outlook and log on again.

Sending a Message to Your Own Pager

After you've installed the MobileCHOICE paging information service, you can check it out by sending a message to your own pager. To do so, you must have the Personal Address Book information service installed in your profile.

To identify your own pager

1. With any Information viewer displayed, open the **Tools** menu and choose **Options**. Choose the **My Pager** tab (something that wasn't there before you installed MobileCHOICE Messenger), as shown in Figure 25.6.

FIGURE 25.6

Use this dialog box to identify your own pager, which has the name **My Pager**.

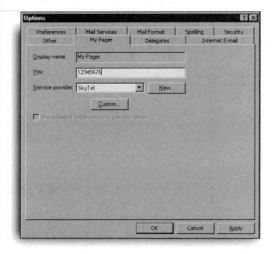

2. Enter your personal identification number (PIN) and select your paging service provider, then choose **OK**.

Now you can check that everything's working by sending a message to your own pager.

Your personal identification number

Your personal identification number is the address to which pager messages are sent.

Sending a message to your own pager

1. Display the Inbox Information viewer and choose the New Mail Message button ![icon] in the Standard toolbar to display Outlook's Message form.

2. Choose **To** to open the Select Names dialog box.

3. Open the **Show Names from the** drop-down list and choose **Personal Address Book**.

4. Scroll down the list of names in your Personal Address Book to find **My Pager** (inserted by MobileCHOICE Messenger).

5. Select **My Pager**, choose **To**, and choose **OK** to return to the Message form with **My Pager** in the **To** box.

6. Enter a subject in the **Subject** box and add some text in the notes box.

7. Choose **Send** in the form's toolbar to send the message.

Depending on the speed of your pager service, you should soon see the message on your pager.

If this works properly, you're ready to start sending pager messages to other people. If it doesn't work, you must resolve the problems before trying to send more messages. Contact Ikon at www.ikon.net for more information.

Sending Pager Messages to Other People

After you've satisfied yourself that MobileCHOICE Messenger is correctly installed, you can get ready to send pager messages to other people. To do so, you need to add pager information for your contacts.

Entering a contact's personal identification number

1. Open the Contacts Information viewer and select a contact for whom you want to add a pager address.

2. Double-click the contact's name to open that contact in the Contact form, as shown in Figure 25.7.

3. Choose the Pager Information button in the toolbar to display the dialog box shown in Figure 25.8.

4. Enter the contact's **PIN**; then open the **Service provider** drop-down list and select the contact's provider.

5. Choose **OK** to close the dialog box.

New menu items

The form's **Actions** menu contains two additional items: **New Message to Contact's Pager** and **Pager Information**.

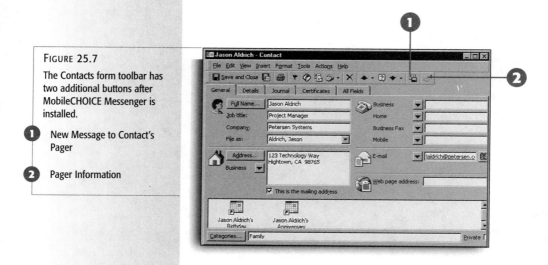

FIGURE 25.7

The Contacts form toolbar has two additional buttons after MobileCHOICE Messenger is installed.

1 New Message to Contact's Pager

2 Pager Information

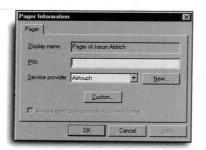

FIGURE 25.8

Use this dialog box to enter a contact's pager information.

Repeat this process to add pager information for other contacts.

Sending a pager message

1. Open the contact in the Contacts form.

2. Choose the New Message to Contact's Pager button in the form's toolbar.

3. Enter the message in the usual way, and then choose **Send**. Outlook sends the message to the pager.

Keeping Your Life Organized

Planning Your Time

Creating One-time Activities

This chapter describes how to enter appointments and events into your calendar. See Chapter 27, "Planning Meetings," for information about scheduling meetings and Chapter 28, "Planning, Tracking, and Assigning Tasks," for planning tasks.

One-time activities are *appointments*, *events*, and *meetings* that occur just once. This is in contrast to recurring activities that happen regularly at specific intervals.

SEE ALSO

➤ *For basic information about viewing Outlook's calendar and entering one-time appointments and events, see "Managing Your Calendar" on page 40.*

Creating a One-time Appointment

You can create a one-time *appointment* (an activity for which you allocate a specific period) on your calendar or in the appointment form.

Creating a one-time appointment on your calendar

  1. Click **Calendar** in the Outlook Bar to display the Calendar Information viewer.

  2. If the **Day** view is not selected, open the **View** menu, point to **Current View**, and choose **Day/Week/Month**.

  3. If the **Work Week**, **Week**, or **Month** view is selected, choose **Day** in the Standard toolbar. You should now see a calendar for the current day (as determined by your computer's internal clock), as shown in Figure 26.1.

  4. To create an appointment on a day other than the current day, select that day on the Date Navigator.

Let's say you want to create an appointment to discuss your project status in your office between 10:00 a.m. and noon.

Point into the calendar's appointment area at, or slightly after, 10:00 a.m., press the mouse button and drag down to select the area between 10:00 a.m. and 12:00 p.m. Release the mouse button. Now those two hours are highlighted in the appointment area.

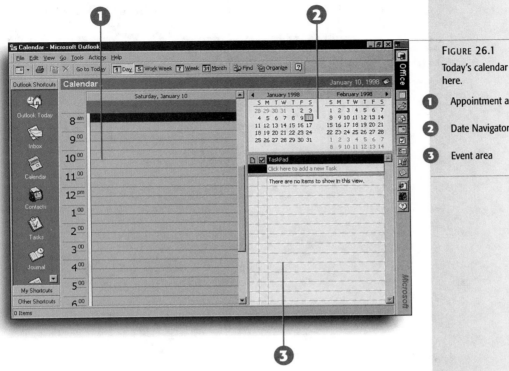

FIGURE 26.1

Today's calendar is shown here.

1 Appointment area

2 Date Navigator

3 Event area

Type Discuss project status and then press Enter. Outlook displays the new appointment as shown in Figure 26.2. The dark blue left, top, and bottom borders indicate you're busy during that time.

That's all there is to creating a basic appointment item. Outlook will subsequently show the appointment whenever the displayed calendar includes the day. Also, the day of the appointment is shown in bold in the Date Navigator.

When you create an appointment in this way, you can't identify a location for the appointment. To do so, you have to use Outlook's appointment form. Double-click the appointment in the Calendar Information viewer to display that appointment in the appointment form, as shown in Figure 26.3.

Using the appointment form to create an appointment from scratch

With the Appointment Information viewer displayed, choose the New Appointment button ▣▾ in the Standard toolbar to display an empty appointment form. Enter information into the form in the normal way.

FIGURE 26.2

Outlook displays an appointment like this.

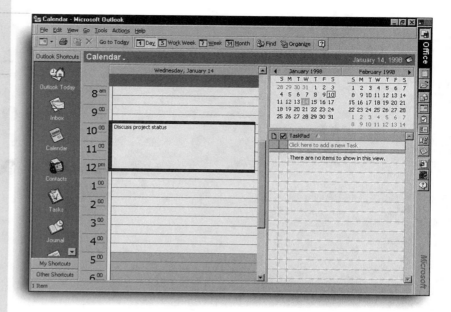

FIGURE 26.2

Outlook displays an appointment like this.

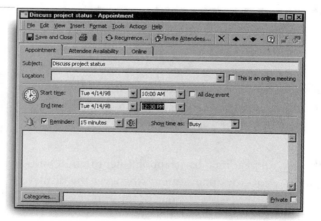

FIGURE 26.3

Use the appointment form to provide more details about the appointment.

You can make additions and changes to information in the appointment form:

- Add a location for the appointment in the **Location** list box. After you do so, the location appears in parentheses in the calendar's appointment area.

- Change the start and end times to other than half-hour increments using the **St<u>a</u>rt time** and **End ti<u>m</u>e** boxes.

- Change the reminder time in the **<u>R</u>eminder** drop-down list to other than the default 15 minutes before the start of the appointment.

- Instead of showing the time as **Busy**, select **Free**, **Tentative**, or **Out of Office** from the **Sho<u>w</u> time as** drop-down list.

- Add notes about the appointment in the large (unnamed) notes box.

- Choose the Insert File button [📎] in the form's toolbar to include attachments that are shown as icons in the notes box.

- Assign one or more categories to the appointment by clicking the **Cate<u>g</u>ories** button.

- Mark the appointment as Private by selecting the **<u>P</u>rivate** check box. If you do so and share your calendar on a network, other people will see only that you have an appointment, not any information about the appointment.

After you've made changes on the appointment form, choose **<u>S</u>ave and Close** in the form's toolbar to save those changes and close the form.

SEE ALSO

➤ *For detailed information about entering information into a form, see "Using a Form to Create a New Item" on page 141.*

Creating a One-time Event

Whereas appointments always have a start and end time, events do not. An *event* is an activity you mark on your calendar without allocating any specific time to it.

Events are created in the same way as appointments, either on your calendar or in a form.

Creating a one-time event

1. Display the Calendar Information viewer and select **Da<u>y</u>** view.

2. Use the Date Navigator to select the day of the event.

3. Click the event area. The area becomes white to show it's selected.

4. Type a short description of the event. The description appears in the event area as you type.

5. Click an unoccupied place in the appointment area.

To supply more details about an event, double-click the event in the Calendar Information viewer to display the event form shown in Figure 26.4.

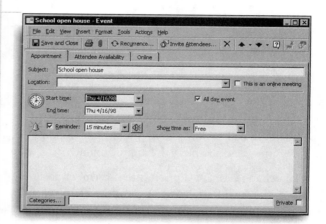

The event form has **All day event** checked. It also has boxes for the start and end dates, but not for start and end times. You can provide additional information about an event in this form.

You can create an event from scratch in the event form.

Opening a blank event form

1. Display the Calendar Information viewer.

2. Open the **Actions** menu and choose **New All Day Event**.

After you've made any changes on the event form, choose **Save and Close** in the form's toolbar to save those changes and close the form.

Changing an Event to an Appointment and Vice Versa

If you have an event marked in your calendar, you might decide to set aside some time for it. You can do that by changing the event to an appointment.

Swapping events and appointments

1. Locate the event in the Calendar Information viewer.
2. Double-click the event to display it in the event form.
3. Remove the check mark from **All day event**. When you do so, **Start time** and **End time** boxes become available and the name of the form in its title bar changes from Event to Appointment.
4. Enter the appropriate times in the **Start time** and **End time** boxes.
5. Choose **Save and Close** in the form's toolbar.

If you look at the day on which the event was previously marked, you'll see the event is no longer there; instead, you'll see an appointment.

Use a similar method to change an appointment into an event. Display the appointment in the appointment form, check **All day event**, and choose **Save and Close**.

Moving a One-time Appointment or Event

You can move an appointment to another time or move an appointment or event to another day.

Moving an appointment to a different time on the same day

1. Display the Calendar Information viewer with the day of the appointment shown in the **Day** view.
2. Drag the appointment up or down to change its time, without affecting its duration.

Moving an appointment or event to another day

1. Display the Calendar Information viewer with the day of the appointment or event shown in the **Day** view.

Changing an appointment's duration

You can point to the appointment's start or end time in the appointment area (the pointer changes to a two-headed arrow) and drag to change the start time without affecting the end time, or to change the end time without affecting the start time.

Using a form to change dates and times

You can, of course, open any appointment or event in a form, and make changes to dates and times there.

2. If the day you want to move the appointment or event to isn't shown in the Date Navigator, click one of the arrows in the Date Navigator's title bar until the month that contains the target date is shown.

3. Drag the appointment from the appointment area, or the event from the event area, onto the target date in the date navigator.

Any change you make to the dates and times by dragging are shown when you open appointment and events in their forms.

Creating Recurring Appointments and Events

As you've seen, appointments and events are similar. The following information applies specifically to appointments. You can use the same information for events, disregarding any mention of times.

When appointments and events occur at regular intervals, it's usually much better to create them as recurring events than to create many one-time events. By doing so:

- It takes much less time to enter a single recurring item than many one-time items.

- A recurring item occupies much less space on your disk than many one-time items.

Don't jump to the conclusion that you can't use recurring items because there are always exceptions, such as when a recurring appointment falls on a holiday. Outlook can take care of exceptions. After you've created a recurring appointment or event, you can easily change individual occurrences, as described later in this chapter.

SEE ALSO

➤ *To change an appointment in a recurring series, see "Changing One Appointment or Event in a Recurring Series" on page 433.*

Creating a Recurring Appointment from Scratch

You can create a recurring appointment from scratch, or convert an existing one-time appointment into a recurring appointment.

Creating a recurring appointment

1. Display the Calendar Information viewer.
2. Open the **Actio_ns** menu and choose **New Recurring Appointment** to display the form shown in Figure 26.5.

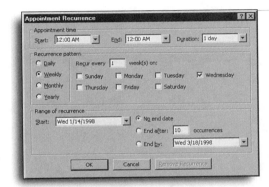

FIGURE 26.5

This is where you define the recurrence pattern. This form shows the recurrence patterns available on a weekly basis.

3. Enter or select the appointment **S_tart** time.
4. Enter or select the appointment **E_nd** time. Outlook calculates the appointment duration and displays it in the **Du_ration** box.
5. Select **D_aily**, **W_eekly**, **M_onthly**, or **Y_early** for the recurrence pattern.

The details of the available recurrence patterns depend on the interval you select. Figure 26.5 shows the available weekly recurrence patterns, Figures 26.6, 26.7, and 26.8 show the available daily, monthly, and yearly recurrence patterns.

After having chosen the appropriate recurrence period, proceed as follows.

Outlook can calculate the End time

Instead of entering the **End** time, you can enter the **Duration**, in which case Outlook calculates the **End** time.

FIGURE 26.6

The available daily recurrence patterns are shown here.

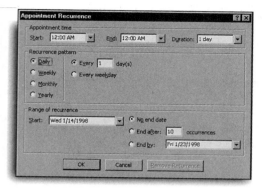

FIGURE 26.7

The available monthly recurrence patterns are shown here.

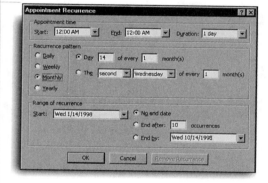

FIGURE 26.8

The available yearly recurrence patterns are shown here.

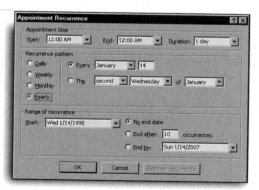

Choosing a recurring pattern

1. Choose the option buttons, check the check boxes, and select from lists to define the details of the recurrence.

2. In the **Range of recurrence** section at the bottom of the form, enter or select when you want the recurrence to start and end.

3. Choose **OK** to accept the recurrence pattern and display the appointment form that's somewhat different from the appointment form you see when you create a one-time appointment, as shown in Figure 26.9.

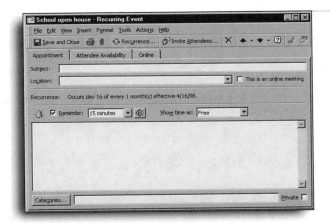

FIGURE 26.9

Instead of the start and end boxes, this appointment form contains a description of the recurrence pattern in the middle of the form.

4. In the appointment form, enter a **Subject** and **Location**. If you want a reminder, check the **Reminder** box, and enter or select the time before the appointment when you want to be reminded.

5. Don't forget to assign one or more categories to the recurring appointment.

6. Choose **Save and Close** in the form's toolbar to save the recurring appointment and close the form.

After you've created and saved a recurring appointment, the appointment appears in your calendar in almost the same way as a one-time appointment. The difference is that a recurring appointment is marked with a pair of curved arrows as you see in Figure 26.10.

FIGURE 26.10

A recurring appointment is marked with a pair of curved arrows.

Creating a Recurring Appointment from a One-time Appointment

An alternative way to create a recurring appointment is to first create a one-time appointment and then convert that appointment into a recurring appointment.

Converting a one-time appointment into a recurring appointment

1. Locate the one-time appointment you want to convert in the Calendar Information viewer.

2. Double-click the appointment to display it in the appointment form.

3. Choose **Recurrence** in the form's toolbar to display the Appointment Recurrence form, similar to that previously shown in Figure 26.5.

4. Select a recurrence pattern and the range of recurrence.

5. Choose **OK** to display the Recurring Appointment form.

6. Make any necessary changes in this form, and then choose **Save and Close** in the form's toolbar.

You can use a similar method to change a one-time event into a recurring event.

Marking Holidays and Other Special Days on Your Calendar

You can mark holidays and other special days on your calendar in two ways:

- *Automatically* by using Outlook's built-in lists
- *Manually* by creating individual recurring events

Usually, I much prefer to do things automatically than manually—I'm all for saving time and effort—but, in this case, I recommend the manual method.

I don't recommend you use Outlook's automatic holidays because

- Outlook adds holidays only over the period from November 1997 to November 2001. That's a problem if you want to find out when a holiday occurred a few years ago or will occur more than just a few years ahead.

- Outlook creates all holidays as individual one-time events, rather than recurring events. That takes up a lot of space on your disk.

- Outlook assigns the category "holiday" to all the events it marks on your calendar. I prefer to reserve the holiday category for events that really are holidays. Groundhog Day isn't a holiday for me; unless your employer is more generous than mine, it's not a holiday for you, either.

One benefit of using Outlook's automatic method of marking holidays is that it provides holidays recognized in many countries and by people of various cultures.

You can add holidays and other special days to your calendar using the method described earlier in this chapter for entering recurring events. The recurrence patterns available in Outlook can be used for most holidays and special days. Some exceptions to that rule include

- In the United States, income tax returns are due on April 15, unless that is a Saturday or Sunday, in which case they are due on the following Monday.

- In the United States, election day is the Tuesday after the first Monday in November.

- Easter Sunday is the first Sunday after the first full moon after the vernal equinox. Other Christian holy days are a certain number of days before or after Easter Sunday.

- Days recognized by various cultures and religions don't match any pattern that Outlook can deal with.

Holidays as one-time events occupy excessive disk space

When you select holidays for the United States, Outlook adds 92 one-time events to your calendar, each of which occupies approximately 350 bytes.

Outlook's recurrence patterns can't calculate dates such as these. You have to enter these dates manually into your calendar.

It's not necessary for everyone in a group to individually enter holidays and other special days into their calendars. One person can create a master calendar and save it as a file. Other people can import this file into their calendars.

Making Changes to Appointments and Events

You can make changes to

- One-time appointments and events
- All the appointments and events in recurring series
- Individual appointments and events in recurring series

Changing a One-time Appointment or Event

The following paragraphs describe how to make a change to a one-time appointment. You can use the same method to make a change to a one-time event.

Changing a one-time appointment or event

1. Display the Calendar Information viewer in any view that contains the appointment you want to change.

2. Double-click the appointment to display it in the appointment form.

3. Make whatever changes are needed to the information on the form.

4. Choose **Save and Close** in the form's toolbar to save the changes and close the form.

SEE ALSO

➤ *For more information about moving an appointment to a different time, and moving an appointment or event to a different date, see "Moving a One-time Appointment or Event" on page 425.*

Changing All the Appointments or Events in a Recurring Series

The following paragraphs describe how to make a change to all the appointments in a recurring series, for example, if a regular meeting scheduled for Monday is changed to Tuesday. You can use the same method to make a change to a recurring series of events.

Changing *all appointments* in a recurring series

1. Display the Calendar Information viewer in any view that contains an occurrence of the series of appointments you want to change.

2. Double-click the appointment. Outlook displays a message informing you that you've selected a recurring appointment and asking whether you want to open this occurrence or this series. To make changes to all the appointments in the series, choose **Open this series**, then choose **OK** to open the Recurring Appointment form.

3. Make any changes to the information on the Recurring Appointment form, then choose **Recurrence** in the form's toolbar to display the Appointment Recurrence form.

4. Make any changes to the information on the Appointment Recurrence form, then choose **OK** to return to the appointment form.

5. Choose **Save and Close** in the appointment form's toolbar to save the changes and close the form.

Changing One Appointment or Event in a Recurring Series

The following set of steps describes how to make a change to one appointment in a recurring series. You can use the same method to make a change to one event in a recurring series.

Changing *one event* in a recurring series

1. Display the Calendar Information viewer in any view that contains an occurrence of the series of appointments you want to change.

2. Double-click the appointment. Outlook displays a message informing you that you've selected a recurring appointment and asking whether you want to open this occurrence or this series. To make changes to all the appointments in the series, choose **Open this occurrence**; then choose **OK** to open the Recurring Appointment form.

3. Make any changes to the information on the Recurring Appointment form, and then choose **Recurrence** in the form's toolbar to display the Appointment Recurrence form.

4. Make any change to the information on the Appointment Recurrence form; then choose **OK** to return to the appointment form.

5. Choose **Save and Close** in the appointment form's toolbar to save the changes and close the form.

Deleting a One-time Appointment or Event

You can delete a one-time appointment or event just as you delete any other item. Display an Information viewer that contains the item, select the item, and then choose the Delete button ☒ in the Information viewer's toolbar. Outlook moves the deleted item into the Deleted Items folder.

Deleting Appointments or Events in a Recurring Series

You can delete individual items in a recurring series, or you can delete the entire series.

Deleting information in a recurring series

1. To delete an individual appointment or event, select the item in the Information viewer. To delete an entire series, select any occurrence of the item.

2. Choose the Delete button ☒ in the Information viewer's toolbar. Outlook displays the Confirm Delete box that asks you whether you want to delete all occurrences or just this one.

3. Choose **Delete all occurrences** or **Delete this one**. Then choose **OK**. Outlook moves the deleted individual occurrence or entire series into the Deleted Items folder.

Viewing and Printing Calendar Items

You can view calendar items in any of the standard views provided with Outlook. You can also create your own views. You'll probably find that the views provided with Outlook provide the overall format you need, but don't necessarily include all the fields you would like to see. You can easily add fields to Outlook's views.

SEE ALSO

➤ For information about modifying views, see "Changing the Fields in a View" on page 177.

Choosing Calendar Views

You'll probably most frequently use the **Day**, **Work Week**, **Week**, and **Month** views of your calendar. Switch from one view to another by choosing the appropriate button in the Calendar Information viewer's Standard toolbar.

You can also select views in the Date Navigator:

- Display the **Day** view of a specific day by clicking that day in the Date Navigator.

- Display the **Day** view for several days by holding down the Ctrl key while you select individual days in the Date Navigator. The days you select can be consecutive or not.

- Display a **Week** view by clicking in the left margin adjacent to a week in the Date Navigator.

- Display a view of several weeks by holding down the Ctrl key while you click at the left of those weeks in the Date Navigator. The weeks you select can be consecutive or not.

- Display a **Month** view by clicking one of the single-letter day abbreviations in the Date Navigator above the month you want to see. Outlook can't display more than one month at a time.

You can also display your calendar information in table views. Open the **View** menu, move the pointer over **Current View**, and choose a view from the list.

One particularly useful standard view is By Category, but it's useful only if you're meticulous about assigning categories to calendar items. For example, if you've assigned the category Birthday to all birthdays in your calendar, this view gives you a quick way to see what birthdays are coming up.

Printing Your Calendar

When you're satisfied with your views of Outlook calendar items, you can print these views in various formats. With a **Day**, **Work Week**, **Week**, or **Month** view selected, you can print handy calendars in various formats.

Open the **File** menu and choose **Print**. In the Print dialog box, choose **Daily Style**, **Weekly Style**, **Monthly Style**, **Tri-fold Style**, or **Calendar Details Style**. Choose **OK** to print your calendar.

SEE ALSO

➤ *To learn more about printing, see "Printing Your Address Book in Card View" on page 194.*

How Outlook Deals with Time Zones

The preceding pages of this chapter have ignored the issue of time zones. You can, too, unless you have to keep track of what's happening in different parts of the world.

Universal Coordinated Time

Universal Coordinated Time (UCT)—previously known as Greenwich Mean Time—is an international, location-independent way of specifying time.

When you enter start and end times for an appointment, Outlook converts those times to UCT. I work in the Pacific Time time zone which is eight hours behind UCT. If I enter 10:00 a.m. (Pacific Time) as an appointment **Start time**, Outlook saves the time as 6:00 p.m. (UTC). Subsequently, when I look at the appointment, Outlook finds 6:00 p.m. and, because my time zone is eight hours behind UTC, subtracts eight hours and displays 10:00 a.m.

It's important to understand this, particularly if you travel with a laptop. After entering the appointment described in the previous paragraph, what happens if I change my time zone, say to Mountain Time which is seven hours behind UTC? When I look at the appointment, Outlook finds that the **Start time** is 6:00 p.m. (UTC); it subtracts seven hours from that and displays 11:00 a.m.

Fortunately, Outlook can display two time zones at once.

Selecting time zones

1. Click **Calendar** in the Outlook Bar to display the Calendar Information viewer.

2. Open the **Tools** menu and choose **Options** to display the Options dialog box with the **Preferences** tab selected.

3. Choose **Calendar Options** to display the Calendar Options dialog box.

4. Choose **Time Zone** to display the dialog box shown in Figure 26.11.

5. If the **Time zone** box isn't showing your correct time zone, open the drop-down **Time zone** list and select your correct time zone.

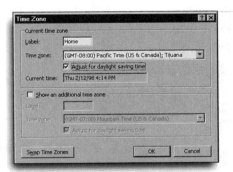

FIGURE 26.11
The Time Zone dialog box shows your current time zone.

6. Enter a name (such as Home) by which you want to identify this time zone in the **Label** box.

7. Choose the **Adjust for daylight saving time** check box.

8. Choose **Show an additional time zone**. When you do so, the boxes in the bottom part of the dialog box become available.

9. Open the **Time zone** drop-down list box (the one in the bottom section of the dialog box), and select a second time zone.

10. Choose the **Adjust for daylight saving time** check box.

11. Enter a name (such as New York) for the second time zone in the **Label** box.

12. Choose **OK** three times to close the dialog boxes.

Now Outlook displays the Day view of your calendar with the two time zones listed at the left, as shown in Figure 26.12.

To return to displaying only your normal times, open the Time Zone dialog box and remove the check mark from the **Show an additional time** zone check box.

FIGURE 26.12

The labels at the top of each time column are those you entered in the Time Zone dialog box.

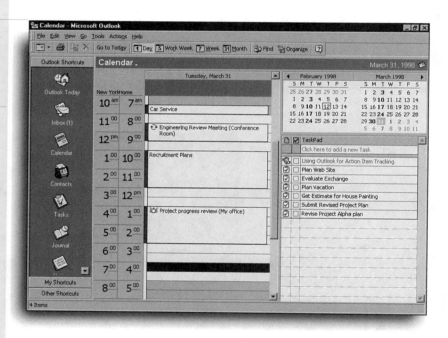

Planning Meetings

What Is a Meeting?

In Outlook's terms, a meeting occurs when two or more people spend time together either face-to-face or at a distance (telephone, online chat, teleconference, and the like). In addition, a meeting can involve the use of certain resources such as a meeting room and audio-visual equipment.

You can use Outlook's calendar to plan meetings by interacting with other people's calendars and also calendars that record the availability of resources (such as meeting rooms and audio-visual equipment). Of course, this only works if everyone in your organization is meticulous about maintaining an up-to-date calendar and if someone maintains a calendar for each resource. This method of planning meetings can save a lot of time compared with the traditional method of sending memos back and forth, or of trying to reach people by phone.

Each person in an organization maintains a personal calendar. In addition, someone has to take on the responsibility for maintaining resource calendars for conference rooms and equipment used in meetings. Each resource must have its own calendar, just as if it were a person. Each meeting room and each piece of equipment that is used in meetings must have an Outlook profile.

Inviting People to Attend a Meeting

You can use Outlook to send a meeting request to one person or to several people. Those people can use Outlook to send back to you an acceptance, tentative acceptance, or rejection of your meeting request.

Sending a Meeting Request

You can use Outlook to schedule a meeting with another person.

Scheduling a meeting

1. Display your calendar in any view, open the **Actions** menu, and choose **New Meeting Request** to display the form shown in Figure 27.1.

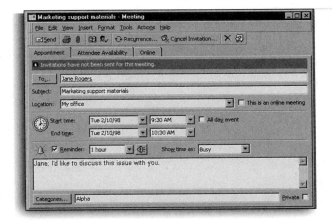

FIGURE 27.1
This is an example of a meeting request form.

2. Choose **To** to display the Select Attendees and Resources dialog box. Open the **Show Names from the** drop-down list and select the appropriate Address Book or list.

3. Select the name of the person to whom you want to send the meeting request, choose **Required**, and then choose **OK**. The person's name appears in the **To** box on the form.

4. Enter information in the remaining boxes of the form, just as you do when creating an appointment.

5. Choose **Send** in the form's toolbar to send the meeting request.

When you send the form, Outlook marks the meeting on your calendar in anticipation that the recipient agrees to the meeting. You see the meeting marked on your calendar with the meeting symbol, as shown in Figure 27.2.

You can double-click the meeting on your calendar to see its details in the meeting form. If you do so before the person to whom you sent the meeting request responds, the form contains the words "No responses have been received for this meeting."

Receiving a Meeting Request

When you receive a meeting request, you see a message in your Inbox, as shown in Figure 27.3.

FIGURE 27.2

A meeting is marked on your
calendar with a special
symbol.

1 Meeting symbol

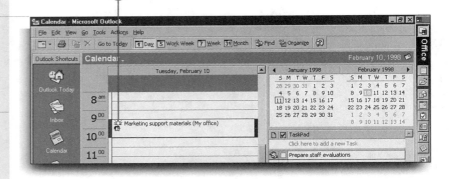

FIGURE 27.3

Your Inbox tells you that you
have a message.

Double-click the message notification in your Inbox to see the
message in the meeting form, as shown in Figure 27.4.

FIGURE 27.4

This form asks you to "Please
respond."

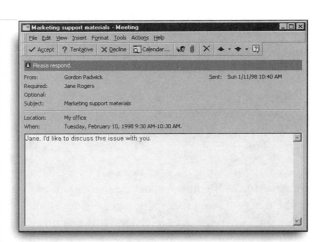

Respond to the message by choosing **Accept**, **Tentative**, or
Decline in the form's toolbar. When you choose the **Accept**
button, Outlook gives you the options shown in Figure 27.5.

Outlook gives you similar options if you choose **Tentative**. After you choose **Accept** or **Tentative**, the meeting is automatically marked on your calendar. If you choose **Decline**, you also have the same options; in this case Outlook moves the meeting request to your Deleted Items folder instead of marking it on your calendar.

Suppose you choose **Tentative**, and then choose **Edit the response before sending**. Outlook displays the Meeting Response form as shown in Figure 27.6.

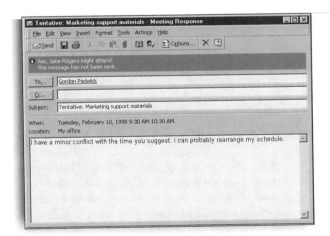

FIGURE 27.6
Use this form to add some comments to your response.

After you've added your comments, choose **Send** in the form's toolbar. Because you chose **Tentative**, the meeting is marked in light blue on your calendar. If you double-click the meeting in your calendar, you can see its details in the Meeting form in which the **Show time as** box contains **Tentative**.

Receiving a Response to a Meeting Request

When you receive a response from the person to whom you sent a meeting request, you receive a message in your Inbox. Double-click the message to see the response, as shown in Figure 27.7.

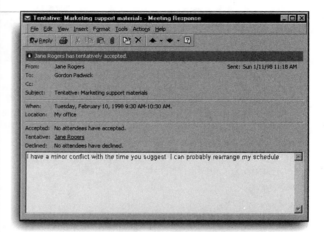

FIGURE 27.7

This form tells you whether the person has accepted, tentatively accepted, or declined your meeting request.

If you had sent the original meeting request to several people, the form tells you how many people have accepted, tentatively accepted, and declined the meeting request.

Sending More Information to Attendees

After you've arranged a meeting, you might want to send additional information to the people who will attend. To do so, double-click the meeting on your calendar to display it in the Meeting form. Then, open the form's **Actions** menu and choose **New Message to Attendees**.

Outlook opens a Message form with the names of the meeting attendees already in the **To** box. You can use this form to create a message just as you normally create an e-mail message.

SEE ALSO

➤ *For information about sending e-mail messages, see Chapter 18, "Sending an E-mail Message."*

Cancelling a Meeting

To cancel a previously scheduled meeting, double-click the meeting on your calendar to display it in the Meeting form. Then open the form's **Actions** menu and choose **Cancel Meeting**. Outlook displays the message box shown in Figure 27.8.

FIGURE 27.8

Outlook asks you if you want to notify attendees about the meeting cancellation.

You probably do want to notify attendees that the meeting has been canceled, so choose **Send cancellation and delete meeting** and then choose **OK**.

Outlook cancels the meeting on your calendar and sends a message to the attendees telling them about the cancellation. The meeting is canceled on the attendees' calendars only when they open your message.

Rescheduling a Meeting

You can change the date and time of a meeting in the same way that you change the date of an appointment.

When you change the date or time of a meeting, Outlook displays a message box in which you are asked "Would you like to send an update to the attendees regarding the changes to the meeting…" You can respond **Yes**, **No**, or **Cancel**:

- If you respond **Yes**, Outlook saves the change on your calendar and gives you the opportunity to send an update message to the attendees.

- If you respond **No**, Outlook saves the change on your calendar, but doesn't send any message to the attendees.

- If you click **Cancel**, Outlook doesn't save the change on your calendar and doesn't send a message to the attendees.

Read your e-mail

Outlook is a powerful information tool, but it only works if you, and everyone in your organization, read it. Reading e-mail should be as regular a habit as brushing you teeth. Read you e-mail at least twice a day: first thing in the morning and right after lunch.

Suppose that you chose **Yes**. Outlook displays the Meeting form with the new time and date displayed. Choose **Save and Close** in the form's toolbar. Again Outlook asks you if you want to send information about the update to attendees. If you choose **Yes**, Outlook automatically sends an update message to the attendees.

Each attendee sees an update message in the Inbox. Initially, the date and time of the meeting isn't changed in the attendees' calendars. Only when an attendee opens the update message is the time and date of the meeting changed in that person's calendar.

SEE ALSO

➤ *For more on making changes to appointments, see "Making Changes to Appointments and Events" on page 432.*

Planning Recurring Meetings

The preceding pages of this chapter have covered only one-time meetings. You can also create recurring meetings in much the same way that you create recurring appointments.

Scheduling a recurring meeting

1. Display your calendar in any view, open the **Actions** menu, and choose **New Recurring Meeting.** Use this form to define the recurrence pattern.

2. Choose **To** to display the Select Attendees and Resources dialog box. Open the **Show Names from the** drop-down list and select the appropriate Address Book or list.

3. Select the name of the person to whom you want to send the meeting request, choose **Required**, and then choose **OK**. The person's name appears in the **To** box on the form.

4. Enter information in the remaining boxes of the form, just as you do when creating an appointment.

5. Choose **Send** in the form's toolbar to send the meeting request.

You can convert a one-time meeting that you've created into a recurring meeting. You can't convert a meeting that you've been invited to. To convert a one-time meeting into a recurring meeting, double-click the meeting on your calendar. Choose **Recurrence** in the Meeting form's toolbar to open the Meeting

Recurrence form and use that form to define the recurrence pattern. Proceed from here in the manner described previously in this chapter in "Sending a Meeting Request."

After you've created a recurring meeting, you can make changes to the entire series of meetings or to individual meetings, just as you can for recurring appointments and events. Any time you make a change, Outlook automatically sends a message to the attendees. When an attendee opens the message, that person's calendar is updated.

SEE ALSO

➤ *To create recurring events, see "Creating Recurring Appointments and Events" on page 426.*

Planning a Meeting to Suit People's Schedules

So far in this chapter, we've taken the approach that one person decides when to have a meeting and then asks other people to attend. If you do this, you can expect that some people will have conflicts and won't be able to accept your invitation. To avoid this problem, you can use Outlook to plan a meeting that doesn't conflict with other people's schedules. This only works, however, if everyone keeps an up-to-date personal calendar in Outlook.

Displaying People's Schedules

Outlook lets you see other peoples' schedules so you can plan a meeting when those people are likely to be available.

Displaying other peoples' schedules

1. Open your Calendar Information viewer and select the date on which you want to have the meeting.

2. Open the **Actions** menu and choose **Plan a Meeting**. Outlook displays the form shown in Figure 27.9.

3. Choose **Invite Others** to display the Select Attendees and Resources dialog box that displays names in your default Address Book or list. If necessary, select the list that contains the name of a person you want to invite to the meeting.

Being the good guy

Your colleagues will appreciate you scheduling meetings to suit their prior commitments, rather than expecting them to change their plans.

FIGURE 27.9

This form initially shows times you're busy on the selected day.

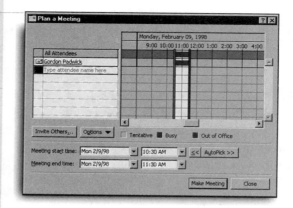

4. Select a person's name, and choose **Required**. The selected person's name is copied into the list of required people.

5. Repeat step 4 to select other people whom you want to attend the meeting.

6. Choose **OK** to return to the Plan a Meeting form that now looks something like the one in Figure 27.10.

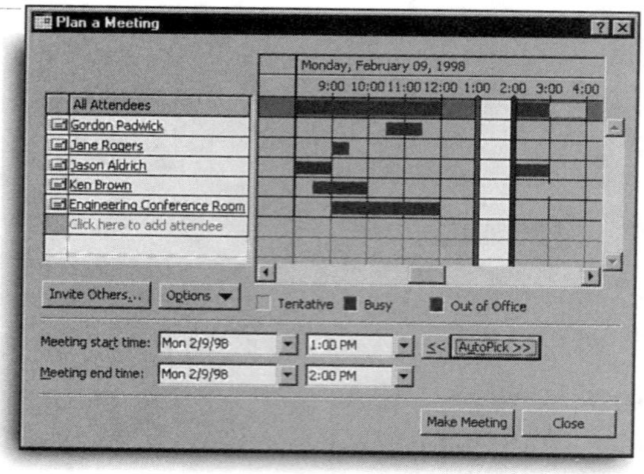

FIGURE 27.10

The form now shows the schedules for all the proposed attendees.

The top row in the chart summarizes the activities of everyone who is to be invited. This is particularly useful if you have a long list of attendees and can't see them all on the chart.

Although you can't see it as it's printed in this book, the various activities on the form are shown in three colors:

- *Dark blue*. Shows activities that are marked Busy on people's calendars.
- *Light blue*. Shows activities that are marked Tentative on people's calendars.
- *Magenta*. Shows activities that are marked Out of Office on people's calendars.

Displaying Resource Availability

In addition to knowing when people are available, you need to know when such resources as a conference room and presentation equipment are available. You add a resource to the Plan a Meeting form in the same way that you add a person.

Setting a Time for the Meeting

You can choose a time for the meeting in three ways. One way is to enter times in the **Meeting start time** and **Meeting end time** boxes. When you do so, the two vertical bars move to indicate the meeting time on the chart.

Instead of entering times, you can drag the bars to the appropriate times. When you drag a bar, the times in the boxes change to correspond with the position of the bars.

Another way to choose a time for your meeting

1. Enter the duration of the meeting by entering start and stop times. The only purpose of this is to define a duration, not the actual time when the meeting will occur.

2. Choose **AutoPick**. Outlook automatically finds the first time when all attendees and resources are available for the duration you defined in step 1.

One advantage of this method is that Outlook will find a time for your meeting even if the first available time is several days in the future.

Figure 27.11 shows the form after a time for the meeting has been set.

FIGURE 27.11

The meeting is set for a time
when no conflicts exist.

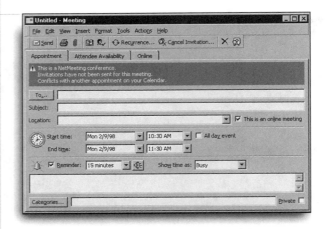

Inviting People to Attend

The next step is to invite people to attend. By default Outlook
expects to send invitations to everyone on the chart. An envelope
symbol appears at the left of each name. You can choose each
symbol to see the options **Send meeting to this attendee** and
Don't send meeting to this attendee. The first of these is
selected. If, for any reason, you don't want to send an invitation
to a particular person, choose the second option.

To send invitations, choose **Make Meeting** to display the
Meeting form shown previously in Figure 27.1. Enter any addi-
tional information in this form and send it, as described in
"Sending a Meeting Request" previously in this chapter.

Planning, Tracking, and Assigning Tasks

Creating one-time and recurring tasks for yourself—your to-do list

Assigning a task to someone else

Receiving a task from someone else

Updating an assigned task

Creating tasks from other Outlook items and from Office documents

Using Microsoft Team Manager to share tasks with two or more people

What Are Tasks?

In Outlook 98 Messaging and Collaboration Client, *tasks* are activities planned for the future but not for a specific date or time; tasks can have a due date and start date, but they don't have a date on which you intend to work on them. This is in contrast to *appointments* that are always for a specific date and time.

A couple of examples will clarify the distinction between appointments and tasks. When you arrange a visit to your dentist, you create an appointment for a specific date and time. On the other hand, when your boss says, "It's time we have a Web site. I'd like you to have it up and running by the end of next month," that's a task. No specific date and time are set when you must work on the project, but there is an end date.

Tasks can be categorized in several ways, one of which is if they have a scheduled due date and start date:

- *Unscheduled tasks.* Tasks that don't have to be done by a specific date—the "when I get around to it" type of thing.
- *Tasks that have a completion date.* Tasks that must be completed by a certain date.
- *Tasks that have a start date.* Tasks you would like to be reminded to start on a specific date.
- *Should have a start date and a completion date.* Tasks for which you want a start reminder on a specific date and which you must complete by a specific date.

Like appointments and events, tasks can be either one-time or recurring.

The next question is who creates a task and to whom it is assigned:

- You can create a task for yourself.
- You can create a task and ask someone else to do it.
- Someone else can create a task and ask you to do it.

Creating a One-time Task for Yourself

You can create a new task for yourself in two ways:

- *In the TaskPad.* You can enter only a title for a task in the TaskPad.
- *In the Task form.* You can enter detailed information about a task in the Task form.

Creating a Task in the TaskPad

When you create a task in the TaskPad, you just create a name for a task.

Creating a task

1. Click **Calendar** in the Outlook Bar to display the Calendar Information viewer. Select the **Day**, **Wo**r**k Week**, or **Week** view.
2. Enter a title for the task in the box immediately under the TaskPad's title bar (where you see **Click here to add a new task**).
3. Press Enter to move the task into the list of tasks in the TaskPad.

Creating a Task in the Task Form

When you create a task in the Task form, you can enter more information than just the name of the task.

Entering detailed information about a task

1. Click **Tasks** in the Outlook Bar to display the Tasks Information viewer. The titles of any tasks you previously entered in the TaskPad are listed in the Information viewer, all with **None** as the due date.
2. Choose the New Task button ☑️ ▾ in the Standard toolbar to open the Untitled - Task form with the **Task** tab selected, as shown in Figure 28.1.

Opening the Task form from the TaskPad

Double-click a task in the TaskPad to open the Task form with information about the task displayed.

3. Enter a brief title for the task in the **Subject** box. Keep the title to only four or five words so there's enough room for it in the calendar's TaskPad.

4. If the task must be completed by a certain date, either enter a date in the **Due date** box or click the arrow in that box to display a calendar and then select a date on the calendar. After you enter a due date, a bar under the form's tabs tells you the number of days from now until the task is due.

5. If you want to be reminded to start the task on a specific date, either enter a date in the **Start date** box or click the arrow in that box to display a calendar and then select a date on the calendar.

6. By default, the task **Status** is shown as **Not Started**—usually appropriate when a task item is created. If you're creating the item after the task has been started, you can open the drop-down list and select among **Not Started**, **In Progress**, **Completed**, **Waiting on someone else**, and **Deferred.**

7. By default, the task **Priority** is **Normal**. You can open the drop-down list and select among **Low**, **Normal**, and **High**.

8. By default, the **% Complete** is shown as **0%**. You can enter a different percentage, or use the spin button to select a different percentage.

There must be a **Due date** if there's a **Start date**

If you enter a **Start date** without having previously entered a **Due date**, Outlook sets the **Due date** to the same as the **Start date**.

Ignore the icon that looks like a Clipboard

The untitled icon at the left of the **Status** drop-down list is for decoration only. It serves no functional purpose.

9. Click the **Reminder** box to check it or uncheck it. When it's checked, you can enter or select a reminder date and time in the adjacent boxes.

10. Click the loudspeaker icon 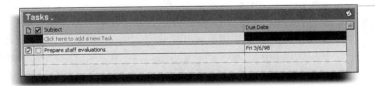 at the right of the reminder time box if you want to choose whether to hear a sound at the time the reminder is due. After clicking this icon, you can select which sound file is to be used.

11. If you want to provide additional information about the task, move the insertion point into the unnamed large notes box that occupies the bottom part of the form and start typing. You can also attach files to the tasks item by choosing the Insert File button 📎 in the form's toolbar. Any files you insert in this way are shown as icons in the notes box.

12. Don't forget to assign one or more categories to the task by choosing the **Categories** button.

13. Choose **Save and Close** in the form's toolbar to save the task item and close the form.

After you create a new task in this way, you'll see the task listed in the Tasks Information viewer, as shown in Figure 28.2. This figure shows the Simple List view. You can, of course, choose other views.

Do you want a reminder?

If you haven't entered a **Due date** or **Start date**, the **Reminder** check box is unchecked. Otherwise, the **Reminder** check box is automatically checked and the adjacent box contains the due date (if there is no start date) or the start date (if there is a start date).

Tasks		
☐ ☑ Subject		Due Date
	Click here to add a new Task	
☑ ☐ Prepare staff evaluations		Fri 3/6/98

FIGURE 28.2

The Tasks Information viewer shows the subject and due date of the task you created. You can edit the subject and due date here.

To see all the information about the task, double-click the task in the Information viewer to display the Tasks form.

SEE ALSO

➤ *For information about categories, see Chapter 9, "Creating and Using Category Lists."*

➤ *For information about views, see Chapter 10, "Viewing Outlook Items."*

Who Owns a Task?

Every task is owned by someone. Only the person who owns a task can change any information about that task.

Initially, a task is owned by the person who created it. If you create a task, you own it, and only you can make any changes to the information about it.

In most cases, you'll see your own name in the **Owner** box in the Task form, as shown in Figure 28.1. This box is gray, which means you can't change the name. Outlook won't let you cheat by pretending that someone else created the task.

In some circumstances, someone else's name appears in the **Owner** box—you might even see the owner listed as **Me**. If several people have profiles on one computer and use Outlook to send e-mail messages, the name that appears in the **Owner** box is the name of the last person who sent an e-mail message. Should you see someone else's name in the **Owner** box, cancel the task you're creating, send an e-mail message to yourself, then re-create the task. This time, your own name will appear as the owner.

Strange behavior!

If you don't have a mail information service in your profile, or if you create a task before you've used Outlook to send e-mail, **Me** appears in the **Owner** box when you create a task.

Updating Task Information

During the period you're working on a task, you'll want to update information in the Task form from time to time. Double-click the title of a task in the TaskPad or in the Tasks Information viewer to open the Task form with the existing task information displayed.

At this time, you can

- Update the task **Status**.
- Change the **% Complete**.
- Add notes about progress in the large notes box.

You can also select the Task form's **Details** tab, as shown in Figure 28.3, to enter supplementary information about the task.

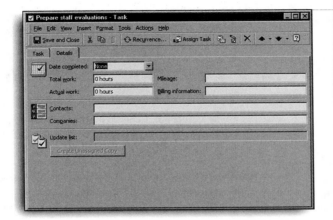

FIGURE 28.3
Use the top two sections of this tab to provide supplementary information about the task.

By default, the **Date completed** box contains **None**. When the task is completed, enter the completion date or open the drop-down calendar and select the completion date. When you select a completion date, the content of the **Status** box in the **Task** tab changes to **Completed**.

Use the other four boxes in the top part of the **Details** tab as follows:

- *Total work*. Your estimate of the total amount of time required to complete the task. You can enter this information at the time you create the task.

- *Actual work*. The amount of time actually spent on the task. You can update this periodically while you're working on the task.

- *Mileage*. The number of miles traveled in connection with the task. You can update this information while you're working on the task.

- *Billing information*. Information related to billing, such as the hourly rate to be charged.

Use the two boxes in the middle part of the **Details** tab as follows:

- *Contacts*. The names of people associated with the task.

- *Companies*. The names of companies and other organizations associated with the task.

New options appear when working with assigned tasks

The **Update list** box and **Create Unassigned Copy** button in the bottom part of the Task form are used when you work with a task assigned to you from another person.

SEE ALSO

➤ *To learn more about the Update list box, see "Updating an Assigned Task" on page 463.*

Creating a Recurring Task for Yourself

Some tasks you do only once; others you have to do regularly. The only way to create a recurring task is by changing a one-time task to a recurring task—Outlook doesn't let you create a recurring task from scratch.

After creating a one-time task, choose **Recurrence** in the Task form's toolbar to display the Task Recurrence form and use that form to define the recurrence pattern.

SEE ALSO

➤ *For an explanation of recurrence patterns, see "Creating a Recurring Appointment from a One-time Appointment" on page 430.*

Assigning a Task to Someone Else

In fact, Outlook doesn't let you assign a task to someone else. What you can do, however, is request that someone accept a task. That person has the option of accepting or rejecting the task. A person who accepts a task becomes the new owner of that task.

You can request that someone accept a task in these two ways:

- You can create a task for yourself and then ask someone else to do it.
- You can create a task request.

Asking Someone to Accept an Existing Task

Suppose you have a new project. The first thing you might do is break down the project into a list of tasks. It becomes clear you haven't the time to work on all the tasks yourself—you need help.

If you've created the tasks in Outlook, you can ask other people to accept responsibility for some of the tasks. You can assign tasks to the people you supervise, and you can ask other people to take on tasks.

Requesting that someone accepts a task

1. Double-click the task in the TaskPad or in the Tasks Information viewer to display the task in the Task form.

2. Choose Assign Task in the Task form's toolbar to display the modified Task form shown in Figure 28.4. Initially, the bar at the top of the form reminds you This message has not been sent.

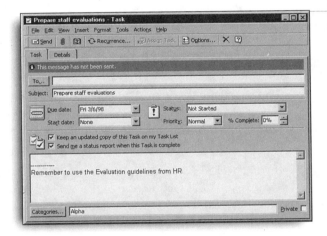

FIGURE 28.4

Outlook reformats the task as a message for you to send to the person whom you want to do the task.

3. Choose **To** to display the Select Task Recipient dialog box that lists names in one of your Address Books or lists. Select the Address Book or list that contains the name of the person to whom you want to send the task, select that person's name, choose **To**, and then choose **OK**. The selected person's name appears in the **To** box in the Task form.

4. By default, the check box labeled **Keep an updated copy of this Task on my Task List** is checked. Uncheck this box if you don't want to keep a copy of the task on your task list. You'll do this only if you want to dump the task on someone else and never hear about it again.

   If you keep a copy of the task on your task list and the person to whom you are sending the task accepts it, any changes that person makes to the task information are automatically copied to the task on your task list. If you uncheck this box, you won't receive notification about changes to the task.

Modifying the task information

Before you send the task request, check the information about the task. You can change any of the information in the text boxes on the form.

5. By default, the check box labeled **Send <u>m</u>e a status report when this Task is complete** is checked. Uncheck this box if you don't want to receive a status report.

6. Choose the **Send** button in the Task form's toolbar to send the task request and close the Task form.

After you send a task request, you have relinquished ownership of the task. The person to whom you've sent the task request becomes the temporary owner. That person assumes ownership by accepting the task. Ownership is automatically returned to you if the person rejects the task.

The task symbol in the TaskPad and in the Tasks Information viewer changes when you send a task request. The original symbol (a clipboard containing a check mark) now has a hand underneath it as an indication that you've given the task away.

You can't change anything in the Details tab

If you choose the **Details** tab, you'll see that all the fields are gray. You can't change these fields after offering the task to someone else because that person is the temporary owner of the task from the moment you send the task request.

If you checked **Keep an updated <u>c</u>opy of this Task on my Task List**, you'll see the title of the task on your TaskPad and in your Tasks Information viewer. But when you double-click the task, you see only a simplified version of the Task form, as shown in Figure 28.5, because you no longer own the task and can no longer make changes to the information about it.

FIGURE 28.5

After you've offered the task to someone else, you can't change the information about it.

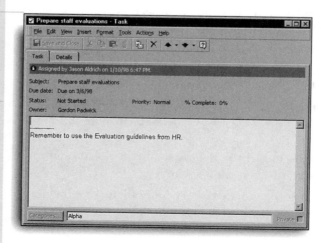

If you unchecked **Keep an updated <u>c</u>opy of this Task on my Task List**, you won't see the title of the task on your TaskPad or in your Tasks Information viewer.

SEE ALSO

➤ *In Outlook, you can offer a task to only one person. For information about working as a team, see "Extending Outlook with Team Manager" on page 466.*

➤ *For more information about addressing a message, see "Creating an E-mail Message" on page 296.*

Receiving a Task Request

Now look at this process from the point of view of the person who receives a request to accept a task. Suppose you sent a task request to Gordon Padwick. When Gordon looks at his Inbox, he'll see a Task Request message. He double-clicks the message to see its details in a Task form as shown in Figure 28.6.

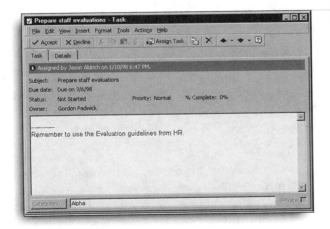

FIGURE 28.6

This is how a person sees a task request.

Notice the **A<u>c</u>cept** and **<u>D</u>ecline** buttons in the form's toolbar. Also notice that the form names Gordon Padwick as the task's owner (although he's only the temporary owner until he accepts the task). Gordon can accept or decline the task. Suppose he is a cooperative fellow who accepts the task.

When Gordon chooses the **A<u>c</u>cept** button, Outlook displays the dialog box shown in Figure 28.7.

FIGURE 28.7

The person who accepts a task can send an automatic or edited reply to the person who sent it.

Gordon has some comments to make, so he chooses **Edit the response before sending** and then chooses **OK**. Another modified version of the Task form is displayed, this time with the insertion point in the large notes box, as shown in Figure 28.8.

FIGURE 28.8

The task recipient uses this form to enter comments or questions about the task.

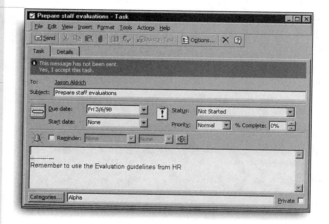

Gordon types his comments and then chooses **Send** in the form's toolbar. Now Gordon owns the task just as if he created it. The task appears in his TaskPad and also in his Tasks Information viewer. He can double-click the task to open the Task form in which he has full access to all the boxes. He can get on with the task himself, or ask someone else to accept it.

The task symbol in Gordon's TaskPad and Tasks Information viewer indicates the task has been received from someone else. The symbol now looks like a clipboard containing a check mark, with a hand receiving the task.

Perhaps Gordon is too busy to accept the task, however. In that case, after he opens the task request in his Inbox, he chooses **Decline** in the Task form's toolbar. As is the case when

Having second thoughts about accepting a task?

A person who accepts a task from someone else can ask the task originator to receive the task back. Of course, the task originator can decline.

accepting a task, Gordon has the choice of replying without comment or of including a comment with his reply. After Gordon declines the task, there's no reference to it in his TaskPad or Tasks Information viewer.

Updating an Assigned Task

When you accept a task request, you own the task. Now you can make whatever changes are necessary to the information in the **Task** and **Details** tabs of the Task form.

If the person who sent the request to you chose **Keep an updated copy of this Task on my Task List**, that person's name appears in the **Update list** box on the **Details** tab of your Task form. This is so you know who is being kept up-to-date with any changes you make to the task information.

Receiving a Task Response and Task Updates

What do you see when a person responds to your request to accept a task? When you open your Inbox, you see a Task Accepted or a Task Declined message, as shown in Figure 28.9.

Where are task messages?

Task request messages are automatically deleted from your Inbox folder when you accept or decline a task. The message you send back to the person who asked you to accept the task remains in your Sent Items folder.

FIGURE 28.9

This is how you see a response to a task request you sent when the person accepts the task.

If the person to whom you send a task request accepts the task, you get a Task Accepted message; if the person declines the task, you get a Task Declined message. You can double-click these messages to open them and read them. When you do so, Outlook automatically removes those messages from your Inbox. At the same time, Outlook changes the content of your Tasks folder. These changes depend on whether you checked the **Keep an updated copy of this Task on my Task List** when you sent the task request. If the person accepted the task:

- *Keep an updated copy is checked*. The task is retained in your Tasks folder, but you are no longer the owner. When you double-click the task in the TaskPad or the Tasks

Information viewer, you see any changes made to it by the new task owner.

- ***Keep an updated copy*** *isn't checked.* The task is deleted from your Tasks folder.

If the person rejected the task, the task remains in your Tasks folder.

Creating a Task Item from Another Outlook Item or from an Office Document

Outlook can create a Task item from another item, such as an e-mail message, or from an Office document.

Creating a Task Item from an E-mail Message

You may receive an e-mail message from your boss that says "Please let me know your thoughts about...". Whatever the subject, you have a task—something you need to spend some time thinking about and then writing. You can easily create a task based on the message so you won't forget to do it.

Creating a task from an e-mail message

1. Display your Inbox Information viewer and locate the message from which you want to create a task.

2. Open the **V**iew menu and choose **Folde**r **List**.

3. Hold down the Ctrl key while you drag the e-mail message from the Inbox Information viewer onto the Tasks folder. When you release the mouse button, Outlook displays the Task form as shown in Figure 28.10.

4. On the Task form, enter whatever additional information is appropriate, such as the start and due dates.

5. Choose **S**ave and Close in the form's toolbar to save the task and close the form.

Now you won't forget to provide the information your boss asked for.

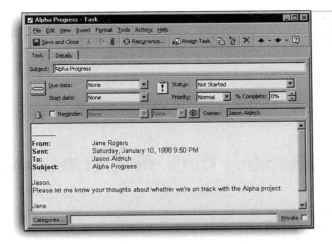

FIGURE 28.10
The Task form opens with the subject of the e-mail message shown as the subject of the task, and with the text of the e-mail message in the large notes box.

SEE ALSO
➤ *For information about receiving e-mail messages, see Chapter 19, "Receiving an E-mail Message."*

Creating a Task Item from a Document

Consider this scenario. Suppose you're reading some text in a Word document and come across text you need to do something about. You can easily use that text to create an Outlook task.

Creating an Outlook task from a Word document

1. Display any Outlook Information viewer and open Word so they are side-by side on your screen.

2. In Outlook, make sure the Outlook Shortcuts section of the Outlook Bar is visible.

3. In Word, display the part of the document on which you want to base a task.

4. Select the text on which you want to base the task, then hold down the Ctrl key while you drag the selected text onto the **Tasks** shortcut in the Outlook Bar. When you release the mouse button, the Outlook Task form appears; the text you selected in the Word document is now in the Task form's notes box.

5. Add a title for the new task in the **Subject** box and also add whatever information is appropriate in the other boxes on the Task form.

6. Choose **Save and Close** in the Task form's toolbar. Exit from Word.

Now you have the text in Word saved as an Outlook task.

Extending Outlook with Team Manager

You can use Microsoft's Team Manager application to extend Outlook's capability to work with tasks. Whereas you can use Outlook to delegate a task to one other person, you can use Team Manager to delegate tasks to a team. To quote from Microsoft's Design Goals for Team Manager, "Microsoft Team Manager is a new workgroup tool that helps everyone on the team stay in sync by consolidating, coordinating, and tracking team activities." As an Outlook user, Team Manager is particularly useful because it can be integrated with Outlook.

For more information about Team Manager, go to the following Web site:

`http://www.microsoft.com/teammanager/`

Team Manager integrates with Outlook by synchronizing task lists. Synchronization occurs when you open or close Team Manager, and when you accept a team member's settings message or a team task update message from the team manager.

Team members can create and track their own tasks using Team Manager, Outlook, or Schedule+; Team Manager keeps the tasks synchronized.

Team Manager has many capabilities, some of which are similar to those in Outlook. Other capabilities unique to Team Manager include

- *Actual Work*. Actual work tracking is included in many project-management applications. It keeps track of and displays work hours, overtime work hours, costs, work completed, and changes in the number of hours worked.

- *Best Fit Scheduling*. Best fit scheduling analyzes workloads to determine whether team members can complete their tasks in the available time, based on priorities and deadlines.

- *Consolidated Status Reporting*. This capability combines individual team members' reports into a consolidated report.

- *Work Calendar View*. This view provides information about what team members are doing by day, week, or month.

- *Workload Graph*. Provides graphical summaries of team members' workloads.

- *Vacation Tracking*. Allows team members' scheduled vacation to be integrated into a project plan.

If you find that Outlook doesn't provide all that you need as far as task management is concerned, consider integrating Team Manager into Outlook.

Journaling Your Activities

What Is the Journal?

Outlook's Journal is a place where you can keep records of your daily activities. The Journal can automatically record such things as

- E-mail messages you send to, and receive from, specific contacts
- Telephone calls you make
- Each time you work with an Office document

In addition, you can use the Journal to manually record other activities, such as

- Letters, memos, and other paper documents you receive
- Telephone calls you receive
- Conversations you have
- Items you purchase
- Anything you do or experience

Outlook 98 Messaging and Collaboration Client saves a record of each activity as a Journal item in your Journal folder. You choose what you want Outlook to record as Journal items. You can see the items Outlook has saved in your Journal folder in the Journal Information viewer.

SEE ALSO

➤ *To see how Outlook displays items in your Journal folder, see "Remembering What You've Done" on page 51.*

Finding files is a real timesaver

I often want to find a Word or Excel file, but can't remember its name or where I saved it. All I'm sure of is that I worked with it around the middle of last month. Outlook's Journal helps me find the file quickly.

Using Automatic Journaling

After you install Outlook, Outlook starts recording work you do with Office files automatically. If you've had Outlook installed for awhile and then open the Journal Information viewer, you'll see items that show each time you worked with an Office file and also files in some other applications that are Office compatible.

Outlook doesn't automatically record e-mail messages you send to, and receive from, contacts, however, unless you explicitly tell it to do so. You have to specify which types of e-mail messages Outlook should record, and also specify the names of the contacts you send those messages to or receive messages from.

Setting Up Automatic Journaling

You can set up Outlook to automatically save Journal items for activities that directly relate to contacts and for the times you work with Office applications.

Set up or modify automatic Journaling

1. With any Information viewer displayed, open the **Tools** menu and choose **Options**.
2. In the Options dialog box, choose the **Preferences** tab.
3. In the **Preferences** tab, choose **Journal Options**.
4. Use the Journal Options dialog box to specify the activities you want Outlook to record automatically.

After you've selected types of e-mail messages and selected names of contacts, Outlook starts Journaling the appropriate items.

You can also set up Journaling for specific contacts when you create or edit a contact item.

Display all Journal items for a specific contact

1. Click **Contacts** in the Outlook Bar to display the items in your Contacts folder.
2. Double-click the Contact item for which you want to Journal items.
3. Choose the **Journal** tab in the contact form.

The bottom section of the contact form, shown in Figure 29.1, shows all the Journal items for the selected contact.

Only future Contact items are journaled

Items you have previously received from, or sent to, a contact are not shown in your Journal.

SEE ALSO

➤ *To set Journal options, see "Setting Journal Options" on page 542.*
➤ *For more information on automatic Journal entries, see "Creating Automatic Journal Entries" on page 256.*

FIGURE 29.1

This is a list of Journal items relating to a specific contact.

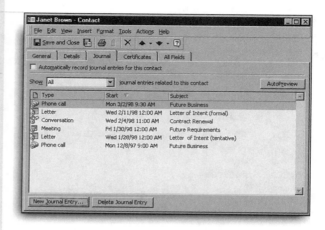

FIGURE 29.1

This is a list of Journal items relating to a specific contact.

Journaling calls must be done manually

Outlook doesn't automatically Journal incoming calls. You have to do that manually. Outlook also can't create Journal items for phone calls you receive, but you can manually create Journal items for these calls.

Journaling Phone Calls

Outlook can automatically create Journal items for phone calls you make, providing you use Outlook to place those calls.

SEE ALSO

➤ *For information about automatically creating Journal records for phone calls you place, see "Placing Phone Calls" on page 276.*

➤ *For information about manually creating records for phone calls you receive, see "Saving Journal Items for Received Phone Calls" on page 474.*

Examples of Automatic Journaling

Keeping things private

Consider password-protecting your Personal Folders file to protect your Journal folder (and other folders) from prying eyes.

After you've been using Outlook for awhile, you'll probably have many Journal items. You can see these items by clicking the **Journal** icon on the Outlook Bar. By default, Outlook chooses the By Type view of Outlook items which is a TimeLine view, as shown in Figure 29.2.

This view shows only the types of Journal items for which items have been saved. For example, if you set Outlook to save PowerPoint items, PowerPoint is listed only if you've worked with PowerPoint files.

A **+** button appears at the left of each Journal type name. Click this button to expand the display to show details of items in the group. For example, if you click **Entry type: E-mail message**, you'll see messages in a timeline similar to those shown in Figure 29.3.

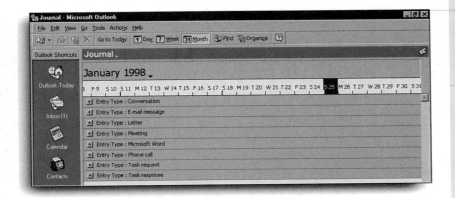

FIGURE 29.2

The By Type view of Journal items initially shows only the types of Journal items.

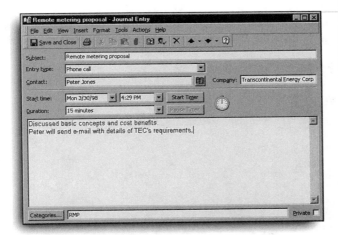

FIGURE 29.3

After expanding E-mail message, you see messages you've sent and received.

You can choose **Day**, **Week**, or **Month** in the toolbar according to the period you want to see in the timeline. Double-click any item in the timeline to open that item in a Journal Entry form in which you can see all the details.

SEE ALSO

➤ *For more information about viewing Journal items, see "Viewing and Printing Your Journal" on page 478.*

Using Manual Journaling

Smart as it is, Outlook can't read your mind. Outlook can only record in its Journal activities it knows about. However, you can manually create Journal items for any of your activities.

Saving Journal Items for Received Phone Calls

If you want to be able to use Outlook to record the time you spend on incoming phone calls, you should always have Outlook running minimized if you're not using it (click the Outlook button on your Windows taskbar to instantly bring Outlook up on your screen).

Add incoming calls to your Journal

1. With any Journal Information viewer displayed, choose the New Journal button [icon] in the Standard toolbar to display the form shown in Figure 29.4.

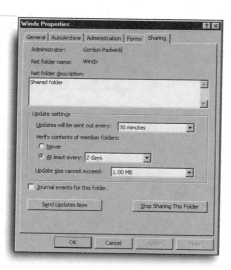

2. If the **Entry type** box doesn't contain **Phone Call**, open the drop-down list and select **Phone Call**.

3. To start recording the duration of the phone call, click **Start Timer**.

While the phone call proceeds, you can click **Pause Timer** to stop accumulating time. When you want to restart timing, click **Start Timer** again. At the end of the call, click **Pause Timer**. During the call, the accumulated time is shown in the **Duration** box.

Enter information in the Journal Entry form during or after the call

1. Enter a title for the item in the **Subject** box.

2. Enter the name of the person who called you in the **Contact** box. Alternatively, you can click the Address Book icon (at the right of the **Contact** box), and select a contact; Outlook places the name you select in the **Contact** box.

3. You can enter the name of the caller's company or organization in the **Company** box (this is optional).

4. Enter notes about the conversation in the large unnamed notes box at the bottom of the dialog box.

5. Click **Categories**, and assign one or more categories to the phone call.

6. Choose **Save and Close** to save the contact item and close the form.

Saving Journal Items for Things You Do

You can create Journal items for any of the things you do or experience. You create these items in much the same way as you create a record of an incoming phone call, as described in the preceding section. One significant difference, however, is that instead of using Outlook to record the duration of the activity, you manually enter or select the duration.

You can use the Notes box in the Journal Entry form to record whatever information you like about the item. This information can be your typed comments or an attachment. As an example, if you're creating a Journal entry to record the receipt of a letter, you could scan the letter and attach a shortcut icon to the image file in the Notes box. Alternatively, after scanning the letter, you could use an Optical Character Recognition (OCR) application to convert the letter into editable text and save that text in the Notes box.

What if the duration isn't significant?

Outlook saves a duration for every Journal item. If the duration isn't significant, I suggest you use 0 minutes.

What is an Optical Character Recognition application?

An Optical Character Recognition (OCR) application converts a picture of text (as received in a fax) into individual characters that can be edited by a word processing application, such as Microsoft Word.

When you open the drop-down **Entry type** list, 21 entry types are available for selection; unfortunately, you can't create additional entry types.

What can you do when you want to create a Journal entry for an activity that's not on Outlook's list? For example, you might want to record a Journal item to record when you bought something. No entry types are available to specifically track purchases. My workaround for this is to use the Notes entry type for anything that doesn't match one of the other entry types, and to assign the category "Purchased," or whatever else is appropriate, to such items.

Adding Appointments and Tasks into Your Journal

Outlook doesn't automatically show appointments and tasks in your Journal. Perhaps a future version of Outlook will enable you to click an appointment that's happened to record it in your Journal. For the present, however, you have to do a little more work.

Record an appointment in your Journal

1. Click **Calendar** in the Outlook Bar to display the Calendar Information viewer and select the appointment you want to record in your Journal.

2. Open the **Edit** menu and choose **Copy** to copy the selected appointment into the Clipboard.

3. Click **Journal** in the Outlook Bar to display the Journal Information viewer.

4. Open the **Edit** menu and choose **Paste**. Outlook displays the Journal Entry form with the details of the appointment already entered.

5. Choose **Save and Close** to save the Journal entry and close the form.

Journaling Net Folder Events

As you'll learn later in this book, Net Folders are folders you can share with other Outlook users by way of the Internet or an intranet.

After you've made a folder sharable as a Net Folder, you can use Outlook's Journal to keep a record of events that affect the folder, such as when someone else adds items to it.

Journaling Net Folder events

1. With any Information viewer displayed, open the **View** menu and choose **Folder List**.

2. Right-click the name of the shared folder to display its context menu.

3. In the **Context** menu, choose **Properties** to display the Properties dialog box. Unlike the Properties dialog box for folders that are not sharable, this dialog box contains a **Sharing** tab. Choose the **Sharing** tab to display the dialog box shown in Figure 29.5.

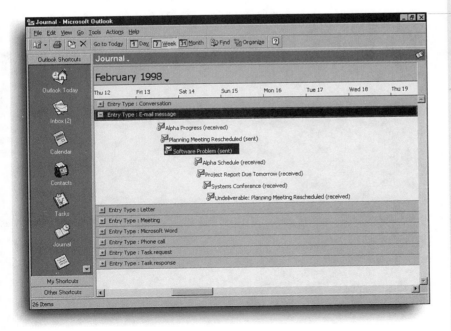

FIGURE 29.5
This dialog box shows the sharing properties of the Net Folder.

4. Check the **Journal events for this folder** check box; then choose **OK**.

From now on, Outlook will record events for the Net Folder in your Journal folder.

SEE ALSO

➤ *For detailed information about Net Folders, see "Using Net Folders" on page 497.*

Viewing and Printing Your Journal

Outlook contains six views you can use to display Journal items; three of these are TimeLines, the others are tables. You can, of course, create your own views.

Display any view of the Journal Information viewer, open the **View** menu, and move the pointer onto **Current View** to see a list of the available views.

You can print Journal items based on a Table view, but not based on a TimeLine view.

SEE ALSO

➤ *For information about selecting and modifying views, and creating your own views, see Chapter 10, "Viewing Outlook Items."*

➤ *For information about printing, see Chapter 11, "Printing Outlook Items."*

Keeping Notes

What Are Notes?

Think of notes in Outlook 98 Messaging and Collaboration Client as the computer equivalent of the sticky, yellow paper notes that decorate your computer monitor and desk in your office, and your refrigerator door at home.

You can use Outlook's notes to jot down reminders, ideas, phone numbers, and suggestions—all those pieces of information you don't want to forget, but can't immediately take the time to file in their proper places. Later, you can review your notes, act on them, or move the information they contain into appropriate Outlook folders or other folders on your computer.

Setting Up Notes

After you install Outlook, you have notes all set up and ready to use. If you want, you can change Outlook's default setting for notes by making choices in the Options dialog box.

By default, notes have a yellow background, are of medium size, and use 10-point Comic Sans MS font for the text. You can change any of these defaults.

SEE ALSO

➤ *To change options for notes, see "Setting Notes Options" on page 544.*

Creating a Note

Previously in this book, I recommended that you always keep Outlook running, probably minimized, while you're working with other applications. If you do so, Outlook is always ready for you to make a note.

With an Information viewer displayed, press Ctrl+Shift+N to open the yellow note form shown in Figure 30.1.

You can display the notes form in two other ways:

- Click the **Notes** icon on the Outlook Bar to display the Notes Information viewer, then choose the New Note button 🗒️▾ in the Standard toolbar.

Outlook creates a note button in the Windows taskbar

Whenever you begin to create a new note, Outlook creates a button for that note in the Windows taskbar. That button remains in the taskbar until you close the note or close Outlook.

- With any Information viewer displayed, click the arrow at the right edge of the New button on the Standard toolbar to display a list of items. Select **Note** in the list.

FIGURE 30.1

The notes form pops up on top of the Information viewer with the current date and time displayed.

After you open the notes form, just start typing your note. Outlook automatically wraps the text within the width of the form. If you type more text than will fit into the height of the form, the text automatically scrolls to provide the space you need.

If you type more text than can be displayed within the form, you can enlarge the form so that you can see everything without having to scroll. To make the notes form wider, move the pointer onto the left or right edge (the pointer changes to a double-headed arrow), press the mouse button and drag. To make the form taller, move the pointer onto the top or bottom edge (the pointer changes to a double-headed arrow), press the mouse button and drag.

Outlook regards the first paragraph of what you type (all you type before you press Enter) as the title of the note. Everything you type after pressing Enter is the content of the note.

When you're finished typing the note, click anywhere outside the notes form to hide it and save its contents in the notes folder. Although the note is hidden, its button is still available on the Windows taskbar—you can click that button to display the note.

Outlook saves the notes you create in the default color and with no categories assigned to them. If you want to change the color of a note or assign categories to it, you must open the Notes Information viewer, as described in the next section.

Using a Note

You can see a note you've created during your current Outlook session by clicking that note's button in the Windows taskbar. To see all the notes in your notes folder, click Notes in the Outlook Bar to display the Notes Information viewer, as shown in Figure 30.2.

FIGURE 30.2

The Notes Information viewer contains icons representing each of your notes.

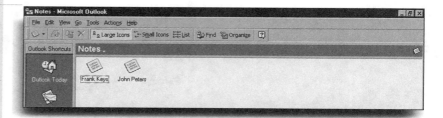

Displaying a Note

By default, notes are displayed in the Icons view in which each icon is identified with the first few words of a note's title. You can choose buttons in the toolbar to modify the way the view is displayed:

- *Large Icons*. Each note is represented by a large icon with the note's title below the icon. Icons are displayed side-by-side in the Information viewer.

- *Small Icons*. Each note is represented by a small icon with the note's title and text at the right of the icon. Notes that have only a few words of text are shown side-by-side in the Information viewer.

- *List*. Each note is represented by a small icon with the note's title and text at the right of the icon. Each note starts a new row in the Information viewer.

Double-click a note's icon to see the complete note, as shown in Figure 30.3.

You can make the displayed note wider or taller by dragging an edge, as described in the preceding section.

FIGURE 30.3
Outlook displays your note.

Outlook provides five built-in views of notes, the first of which was shown earlier in Figure 30.2. These views are

- *Icons*. Notes represented by icons arranged in order of their creation dates.
- *Notes List*. Table view of notes sorted by creation date.
- *Last Seven Days*. Table view of notes you created during the last seven days.
- *By Category*. Table view of notes grouped by categories and sorted by creation date within each category.
- *By Color*. Table view of notes grouped by color and sorted by creation date within each color.

Changing the Color of a Note

By default, all Outlook notes have yellow as the background color. You can change this default color in the Options dialog box. You can also select a color for individual notes.

Changing the color of an individual note

1. Click **Notes** in the Outlook Bar to display the Notes Information viewer.
2. Right-click the note whose color you want to change to display that note's context menu.
3. Move the pointer onto **Color** in the context menu.
4. Select a color: **B**lue, **G**reen, **P**ink, **Y**ellow, or **W**hite.

Assigning a Category to a Note

You can assign categories to notes. Whether you assign categories to notes depends on how you use them. I regard notes as temporary items to be disposed of before I close down Outlook for the day. Using notes in this way, I see no need to assign categories to notes.

You may prefer to use notes for longer-term storage of miscellaneous information. If that's how you use notes, you should assign categories to notes so you can easily find all the information you have that relates to a particular subject.

Assigning a category to a note

1. Right-click the note in the Notes Information viewer.
2. Move the pointer onto **Categories** in the context menu to display the Categories dialog box.
3. Select the categories you want to assign to the note, and click **OK**.

Printing a Note

It's unlikely you'll want to print a note, but you can if necessary.

Printing a note

1. Right-click the note in the Notes Information viewer.
2. Choose **Print** in the context menu. The note is immediately sent to your default printer.

Sending a Note to a Contact

If the information you have in a note is worth sending to someone else, you should normally save that note as an appropriate Outlook item, and then send that item. However, you can send a note if you need to.

Sending a note to a contact

1. Right-click the note in the Notes Information viewer.
2. Choose **Forward** in the context menu. Outlook displays a Message form with the note shown as an icon in the notes section of the form.
3. Choose **To**. Outlook displays the Select Names dialog box in which you can select the names of the contacts to whom

you want to send the note. Select these names in the same way that you do when sending an e-mail message.

4. Choose **Send** in the form's toolbar to send the note.

When someone receives your note, he can double-click the note icon to see what's in it.

SEE ALSO

➤ *To convert a note to an item, see "Converting a Note to Another Outlook Item" on page 485.*

Deleting a Note

Delete a note as you delete any other Outlook item. Select the note in any view, then choose the Delete button ☒ in the toolbar. Outlook moves the note to your Deleted Items folder.

Converting a Note to Another Outlook Item

You can easily create other Outlook items from notes. For example, you can create a Calendar, Contact, or Task item from a note.

Perhaps you've created a note to remind you to do something. You realize that the only way you're going to remember to do it is to create a Calendar or Task item. The following steps explain how to convert a note to a Calendar item.

Converting a note to a Calendar item

1. Display the Notes Information viewer.

2. Drag the icon representing the note you want to move from the Notes Information viewer onto **Calendar** in the Outlook Bar. A calendar form opens with the title and text of the note in its Notes section.

3. Enter whatever information is appropriate in the boxes on the calendar form, then save the form.

Now you have time set aside on your calendar to attend to whatever was the subject of the note. You can drag a note to other Outlook items in this way as well.

Copying a Note into an Office Document

You can copy a note into Word or another Office document by dragging or by way of the Clipboard.

Copying or moving a note into an Office document

1. Display the Outlook Notes Information viewer and the Office document (such as a Word document) side-by-side on your screen.

2. Select the note you want to drag.

3. Hold down the Ctrl key while you drag the note into the Office document to copy the note; hold down the Shift key while you drag to move the note.

Using the Clipboard to copy a note into an Office document

1. Select the note you want to move into the Word document, open Outlook's **Edit** menu, and choose **Copy**.

2. Open the Word document and place the insertion point where you want to insert the note.

3. Open Word's **Edit** menu and choose **Paste**. The note is inserted into the Word document.

Keeping in Touch with the World

Accessing the World Wide Web

Accessing World Wide Web pages

Sending a Web page to a contact

Sharing Net Folders

Connecting to the Web

Internet Explorer doesn't have to be default browser

Although Outlook requires some components of Internet Explorer, Microsoft says, "Outlook 98 does not require that you use Internet Explorer as the default Web browser. You can continue to use whichever default browser you prefer with Outlook 98."

Outlook 98 Messaging and Collaboration Client is tightly integrated with Microsoft's Internet Explorer application. The Outlook installation process looks to see if you have Internet Explorer 4.0 (or later) already installed on your computer; if you haven't, Internet Explorer is automatically installed.

While you're using Outlook, you can easily call up Internet Explorer to access the World Wide Web.

You must, of course, have access to the Internet before you can access the Web. This can be a dial-up connection to an Internet service provider (ISP), or a direct connection provided by your LAN.

Opening Your Home Web Page

Your home Web page

Your home Web page is the page you want to see first when Internet Explorer opens. You can choose this page within Internet Explorer.

Connecting to the Internet

The information provided here is typical of what you might see. You can choose many options in Internet Explorer that affect what you see while connecting to the Internet.

Choosing a dialing location

If you have two or more dialing locations from which you make a dial-up connection, choose the **Settings** button in the Dial-Up Networking dialog box and then select your current location.

To access the Web, open Outlook's **Go** menu and choose **Web Browser**. The Internet Explorer window immediately opens and Internet Explorer attempts to find your home Web page. Internet Explorer's default home Web page is

```
http://www.home.microsoft.com
```

If your computer is already connected to the Internet, you'll normally see your home Web page within a matter of seconds. The time it takes for the page to appear depends on many factors—the speed of your connection to the Internet, how busy the page to which you're connecting is, and the amount of traffic on the Internet.

If your computer is not already connected to the Internet, Outlook displays the Dial-Up Networking dialog box shown in Figure 31.1.

Changing Your Default Home Page

With Internet Explorer running, you can change your default home page—the page you see when Internet Explorer opens.

Changing your default home page

1. Display the Web page you want to use as your home page.

2. Open Internet Explorer's **View** menu and choose **Internet Options** to open the Internet Options dialog box with the **General** tab displayed.

3. In the **Home Page** section at the top of the dialog box, choose **Use Current**. The text in the **Address** box changes to the name of the page you selected in step 1.

4. Choose **OK** to close the dialog box.

Getting started faster

By default, Internet Explorer opens the Microsoft page at `http://home.micro-soft.com`. This is a busy page that sometimes opens quite slowly. By changing to a different default home page, you'll probably find Internet Explorer opens faster.

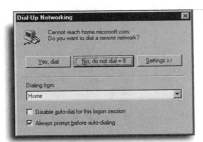

FIGURE 31.1

Choose **Yes, dial** to make a dial-up connection to your Internet provider.

The next time you open Internet Explorer, you'll see the new default home page.

Closing Your Web Connection

To close your connection to the Web, open Internet Explorer's **File** menu and choose **Close**. When you do so, the Internet Explorer window closes and you see your original Outlook window.

Although you're no longer looking at a Web site, you're still connected to your Internet service provider. If this is a dial-up connection, particularly if it's a dial-up connection for which you pay by the minute, you'll want to disconnect. You can disconnect in several ways (including the Windows taskbar option). From within Outlook, however, another way exists to disconnect your Internet connection.

Using Outlook to disconnect from the Internet

1. Open the **G**o menu and choose **News** to open Outlook Express.

2. In the Outlook Express toolbar, choose **Hang Up**.

3. Open the Outlook Express **File** menu and choose **Exit** to close Outlook Express and return to Outlook.

Accessing Web Pages

Every Web page is accessed by its address—also known as a *Uniform Resource Locator* (*URL*). You can see the address of the Web page to which you're currently connected in the **Address** box near the top of the Internet Explorer window.

You can access a Web page in several ways.

Opening a Contact's Web Page

When you create an Outlook Contact item, you can enter a contact's Web page address as shown in Figure 31.2.

FIGURE 31.2

This contact form contains a Web page address. Outlook displays the address in blue on the form.

To directly access a Web page, choose the Web page address on the Contact form. Outlook opens Internet Explorer and attempts to make a connection to the Internet. If a connection isn't available, you'll see the Dial-Up Networking dialog box previously shown in Figure 31.1; choose **Yes, dial**. After a few seconds, you should see the page begin to appear on your monitor.

SEE ALSO

➤ *For more on entering Web addresses, see "Entering a Web Page Address" on page 254.*

Opening a Web Page from an E-mail Message

Quite likely, you'll receive e-mail messages that refer you to Web pages. You can go directly from the e-mail message to the Web page by choosing the Web page address in the message. The process is the same as described in the preceding section for opening a contact's Web page.

Opening a New Web Page

You'll often come across Web page addresses in newspaper and magazine articles and advertisements. You can access these pages by entering the address in Internet Explorer's **Address** box.

For example, I mentioned earlier in this book that Slipstick is one of the best sources of information about Outlook. Slipstick's Web address is

```
http://www.slipstick.com
```

You can access this site by replacing whatever address is currently in the Internet Explorer **Address** box with Slipstick's address.

Saving Favorite Addresses

Some Web pages are so valuable and interesting that you want to return to them frequently—others you'll wonder why anyone would want to look at them.

You don't have to retype a Web page address each time you want to go to it. Instead, save it as one of your Favorites and subsequently choose it from a list.

Be careful when typing Web addresses

When entering a Web page address, be careful to enter it correctly. There is no forgiveness here. If one character or punctuation mark is missing or out of place, Internet Explorer will tell you it can't open the page. Web addresses are not case-sensitive.

Favorites menu and **Favorites** button

Make sure you open the **Favorites** menu. Don't choose the **Favorites** button on the Internet Explorer toolbar.

Save an address as one of your Favorites

1. Open the Page you want to save as a Favorite.

2. Open Internet Explorer's **Favorites** menu and choose **Add to Favorites**. The Add Favorite dialog box appears as shown in Figure 31.3.

FIGURE 31.3

Choose how you want to save the Favorite and also the name you want to give it.

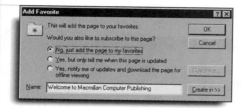

Where to save Favorites

By default, Internet Explorer saves all your Favorites in your Favorites folder. You can save Favorites elsewhere, but that's beyond the scope of this book.

3. Choose **OK** to save the Favorite.

After you've saved favorite Web pages, you can easily open any of them.

Opening favorites

1. With the Internet Explorer window displayed, choose the Favorites button on the toolbar (not the **Favorites** menu). A pane at the left of the window shows the Favorites you've saved, as shown in Figure 31.4.

2. Click the Favorite you want to open and within a few seconds, you'll see the page you selected.

3. Click the Close **(X)** button at the top-right corner of the list of Favorites to hide the pane so the Web page occupies the whole window.

Viewing Your Favorites Folder

To view the Favorites in your Favorites folder, choose **Other Shortcuts** in the Outlook Bar, and then click **Favorites**. You'll see a list of your Favorites similar to that in Figure 31.5.

You can open a Web page by choosing that page in the list.

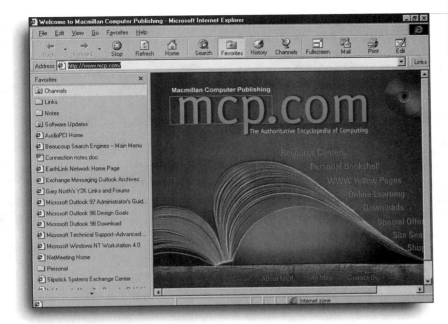

FIGURE 31.4
The pane at the left lists your Favorites.

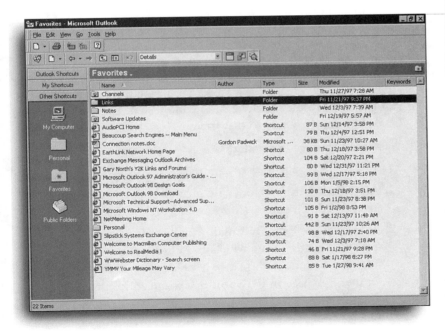

FIGURE 31.5
A typical list of Favorites is shown here.

Subscribing to a page

After you subscribe to a page, you're automatically notified whenever a change is made to that page. You're not notified if you do not subscribe.

To look at detailed information about a Favorite, right-click its name to display its context menu and then choose **Properties**. The Properties dialog box has five tabs if you've subscribed to the selected page, but only three tabs if you haven't subscribed.

These tabs include

- *General*. Such information as the location of the Favorite; its size; the dates on which it was created, modified, and last accessed; and the file attributes.

- *Internet Shortcut*. The target URL (Web address).

- *Subscription*. A summary of your subscription. Contains an **U**nsubscribe button if you have already subscribed; contains a **S**ubscribe button if you have not already subscribed.

- *Receiving*. Only available for Favorites to which you have subscribed. You can determine how you are to be notified about changes to the information at the address.

- *Schedule*. Only available for Favorites to which you have subscribed. You can determine how often your subscription should be updated.

Sending a Web Page to a Contact

You'll probably often come across a Web page that contains information in which a friend will be interested. You can easily send the page by e-mail to that friend.

Sending a Web page to a contact

1. Open the Web page you want to send.

2. Open Internet Explorer's **F**ile menu and move the pointer over **S**end. The menu shown in Figure 31.6 appears.

3. If you choose **P**age by Email, you'll experience a delay of several seconds during which nothing appears to be happening. Then Outlook displays a Message form with the name of the Web page in the **Subject** box and an icon representing the page in the notes box.

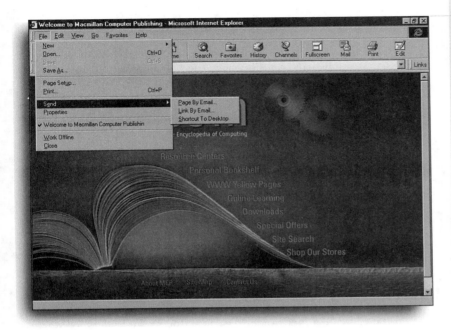

FIGURE 31.6
Choose how you want to send
the Web page in this menu.

4. Choose **To** to open the Select Names dialog box. Select the names of the contacts to whom you want to send the page as you do when sending an ordinary e-mail message.

5. Choose the **Send** button to send the message.

If you choose **Link by Email** in step 3, the only difference is that the message contains only the page's address, not the complete page.

If you choose **Shortcut to Desktop** in step 3, nothing appears to happen. The next time you look at your Windows desktop, however, you'll see an icon representing the page.

Using Net Folders

Net Folders are Outlook folders you can use to share information by way of the Internet or an intranet. If you regularly share information with a group of people, you can use a Net Folder instead of sending e-mail messages.

Possible security problem

Net Folders are not encrypted. When shared over the Internet, data is not secure.

Installing the Net Folders Add-in

To publish a Net Folder, or to receive a Net Folder someone else has published, you must have the Net Folders add-in installed on your computer. To ascertain whether you have that add-in installed, open any Information viewer (not Outlook Today), and then open Outlook's **File** menu. If that menu contains **Share**, you have the Net Folders add-in installed. If **Share** isn't there, you must install it before you can publish or subscribe to a Net Folder.

The remainder of this section assumes you have the Net Folders add-in installed.

SEE ALSO

➤ *For information about installing Net Folders, see "Installing Outlook Add-ins" on page 593.*

Understanding Net Folders

No Exchange Server folders

Net Folders can't be based on Exchange Server folders.

You can create a Net Folder based on one of the folders in your Personal Folders file, but not on your Inbox or Outbox folders.

When you create a Net Folder you are, in effect, publishing or sharing (both terms are used) one of your folders. You identify those people who will have access to the Net Folder and give each person specific permissions. Typically, you give people only the permission to read the folder. After you've created a Net Folder, you are the owner of that Net Folder.

If a person agrees to receive the Net Folder, a copy of the shared folder appears on that person's Outlook folder list. A person who agrees to receive a Net Folder is known as a *subscriber*. At intervals you specify, Outlook sends the contents of your shared folder to subscribers.

You can use Net Folders to share your Calendar, Contacts, Journal, Notes, Sent Items, and Tasks folders with other Outlook 98 users. You can share e-mail messages with people who use other messaging applications; those people receive the shared items as e-mail messages.

The functionality of Net Folders involves sending messages back and forth between the owner of a Net Folder and the recipients.

Although these messages use the same mechanism as e-mail messages, they're not listed in your Inbox and Sent Items folders.

Publishing Your Calendar

As an example of publishing a Net Folder, suppose you want to share your Outlook calendar with some colleagues. The calendar you're going to share must be a folder in your Personal Folders file.

Share your Outlook calendar

1. With any Information viewer (not Outlook Today) displayed, open the **File** menu and move the pointer onto **Share** to see the menu shown in Figure 31.7.

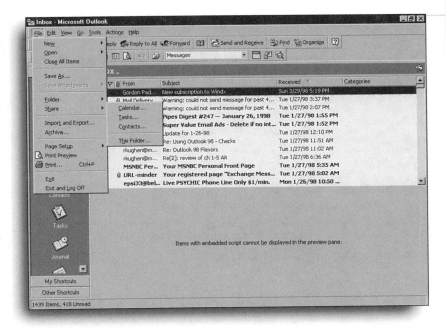

FIGURE 31.7

You can choose to share your Calendar, Tasks, or Contacts folder. You can also share a folder you have previously selected.

2. Choose **Calendar** to display the first Net Folder Wizard shown in Figure 31.8.

FIGURE 31.8

This window confirms the name of the folder you intend to share.

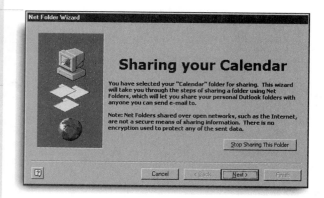

3. Choose **Next** in the wizard window to display the window in which you select the people with whom you want to share your folder, and assign permissions to each person. This window is shown after names have been selected and permissions given later in Figure 31.9.

4. Choose **Add** to display the dialog box shown in Figure 31.9.

FIGURE 31.9

Use the Add Entries to Subscriber Database dialog box to select the names of people with whom you want to share your folder. Each name you choose must be for someone with an Internet or intranet e-mail address.

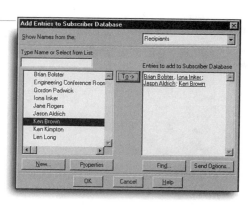

Waiting for response

Waiting for response appears until such time as people accept or decline the shared folder. After a person accepts the shared folder, the phrase is no longer there; after a person declines the shared folder, that person's name is no longer listed.

5. Choose names in the same way that you choose recipient names for an e-mail message; then choose **OK** to return to the wizard. After you've chosen several names, your window will look like the one in Figure 31.10.

6. If you want to change the permissions for a person, select that person and then choose **Permissions** to display the dialog box shown in Figure 31.11.

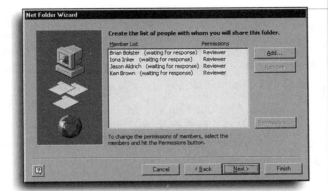

FIGURE 31.10
By default, each person you choose is given Reviewer permission—that is permission only to read the contents of the folder.

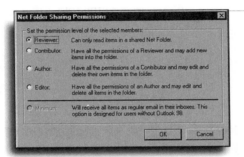

FIGURE 31.11
Choose the permissions you want to assign to each person in the Net Folder Sharing Permissions dialog box.

7. After naming all the people with whom you want to share the folder, choose **Next** in the wizard window to display the window in which you can enter a description of the shared folder, as shown in Figure 31.12.

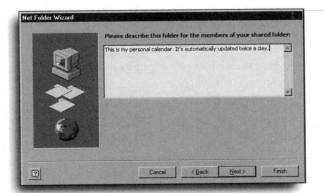

FIGURE 31.12
Enter a description of the shared folder here.

8. Choose **Next** to display the window that tells you you've finished setting up the shared folder. Choose **Finish**. Outlook sends invitations to share the folder and then displays a message telling you the invitations have been sent. Choose **OK** to close the wizard.

When Outlook tells you that it has sent the invitations, what it's really telling you is that it has sent the invitations to your Outbox. As with other e-mail messages, the invitations are sent on their way as soon as a connection to the mail server is available.

You may see a message saying `Message not deliverable`. This could be because the folder you're trying to send is larger than the maximum update size, or it's larger than the message size allowed by your mail server.

SEE ALSO

➤ *To make changes to the properties of the shared folder, see "Setting the Properties of a Shared Folder" on page 503.*

Responding to an Invitation to Subscribe to a Net Folder

Just because someone sends you an invitation to subscribe to a Net Folder doesn't mean you have to accept that invitation. Let's see what happens when you receive the invitation.

When someone sends you an invitation to subscribe to a Net Folder, you see a new e-mail item in your Inbox. That item shows the sender's name and, in the **Subject** column, **New subscription to** followed by the name of the folder to which you are invited to subscribe.

Responding to a subscription invitation

1. Double-click the item in your Inbox to see information about it. You'll see a message as shown in Figure 31.13.

2. Choose **Accept** if you want to be a subscriber to the Net Folder, or choose **Decline** if you don't want to be a subscriber.

No **Accept** and **Decline** buttons?

Recipients see the message whether or not they have the Net Folders add-in installed. If you don't have the add-in installed, you won't have the **Accept** and **Decline** buttons.

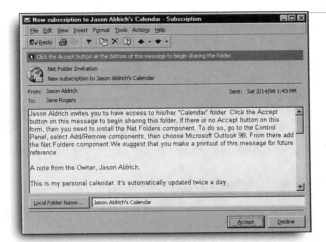

FIGURE 31.13
An example of the message you see when you receive an invitation to subscribe to a Net Folder is shown here. Notice the **Accept** and **Decline** buttons at the bottom-right corner.

If you choose **Accept**, you see a message confirming your acceptance and telling you The contents of the administrator's folder will be sent to you shortly. Your **Folder List** now contains the shared calendar.

Opening a shared calendar

1. Open the **View** menu and choose **Folder List**. Your **Folder List** now contains the name of the shared folder.

2. Select the shared folder to display it in an Information viewer.

If you choose **Decline**, you'll see a message that confirms you don't want to receive copies of the administrators folder.

When a recipient chooses **Accept** or **Decline**, Outlook automatically sends a message back to the person who offered to share the folder. That message appears temporarily in the Inbox with other e-mail. Outlook processes the response automatically and then removes it from the Inbox.

Setting the Properties of a Shared Folder

After you've sent invitations to people to subscribe to a shared folder, you can set certain sharing properties.

Viewing shared folder properties

1. Open the <u>V</u>iew menu and choose **Folder List** to display your **Folder List**.

2. Right-click the folder you shared to display its context menu. Choose **Properties** on the context menu to display the Properties dialog box that has a **Sharing** tab. This tab is not present for folders that aren't shared. Choose the **Sharing** tab to display the dialog box shown in Figure 31.14.

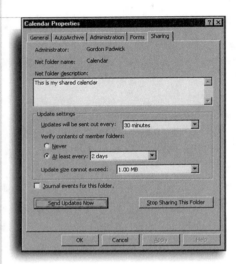

You can use this dialog box as follows:

- *Net folder <u>d</u>escription*. Edit your original description of the folder.

- *<u>U</u>pdates will be sent out every*. Set the interval at which you want to send updates. The default of **30 minutes** is probably much too frequent if you're using a dial-up connection to the Internet.

- *Verify contents of member folders*. Choose <u>N</u>ever, or <u>A</u>t least every (and then choose an interval). When verification occurs, hidden messages are sent between users to verify the contents of shared folders.

- *Update size cannot exceed*. This number affects only items that are sent from the Net Folder on your computer. Your Internet or intranet mail server may impose size limitations that are smaller than the size you specify here.

- *Journal events for this folder*. Check this box to create Journal items for this shared folder in your Journal folder.

- *Send Updates Now*. Choose this button to send immediate updates to subscribers.

- *Stop Sharing This Folder*. Choose this button to stop sharing this folder.

Changing a Subscriber's Permissions

By default, each person with whom you share a folder is given Reviewer permission that allows the person to read the folder but not make changes to it. If you're fortunate enough to have an administrative assistant, you may want that person to be able to make changes to the folder. The dialog box shown previously in Figure 31.11 contains definitions of the four permissions you can give to recipients.

Changing subscriber permissions

1. Open the **Folder List**, and select the shared folder.

2. Open the **File** menu, move the pointer over **Share**, and choose **This Folder** to open the Net Folder Wizard.

3. Choose **Next** to display the window that contains the **Member List**.

4. Select the name of the person for whom you want to change permissions.

5. Choose **Permissions** and then select the new level of permission. Choose **OK** and then choose **Finish**.

You can remove a subscriber by deleting that subscriber's name from the **Member List**.

Stop sharing a folder

To discontinue sharing a folder, choose **Stop Sharing This Folder**.

Learn more about the Internet

There is much more to learn about using the Internet than has been covered in this chapter. What's been covered here should be enough to get you started. Much of the rest is fairly intuitive, but you can save yourself a lot of time and frustration by referring to a book such as *Special Edition Using the Internet* (published by Que).

Working Remotely

What Can You Do While Working Remotely?

In today's mobile workplace, we can't assume that all e-mail will be sent by corporate users directly connected to a physical network. Telecommuting has moved many workers out of the office and into their homes for some or all of their working hours. Business travel adds the requirement to stay in touch with your office while you are on the road. Mobile workers, such as a sales staff, can send messages, submit orders, and send and receive faxes from the field.

Many people who work in corporate offices have computers at home, as well as in the office. You can use Outlook 98 Messaging and Collaboration Client to connect to your company's e-mail system using your modem and Dial-Up Networking.

If you don't belong to a corporate network, you can still use Outlook for sending and receiving e-mail through a commercial service. You can subscribe to a commercial online service such as CompuServe or America Online, or one of many local or regional Internet service providers (ISPs).

Many business users have to stay in touch with the office while they're traveling. Today, you can get your e-mail remotely from around the country, even around the world.

Setting Up Your Remote Computer

The most common way to communicate with your mail system remotely is by using a modem to connect over regular telephone lines. Many different types of modems are currently available:

- *External modem*. Connects through the serial port of your computer to your telephone line. External modems can be used with desktop and notebook computers.

- *Internal modem*. Permanently installed in an expansion slot inside your computer and allows you to plug a telephone cable into the expansion card. Internal modems are primarily used in desktop computers. To use an internal modem with a notebook computer, you generally have to invest in a docking station for the notebook computer.

- *PC-Card modems*. Also called PCMCIA modems, are designed for use in notebook computers that have one or more PC-Card slots built in. The modem, about the size of a credit card, can be installed in the slot, and swapped with other cards that provide such features as network connections, extra memory, and many other expansion features. Although PC-Card modems are primarily designed for notebook computers, you can purchase and install a PC-Card expansion device for a standard desktop computer.

- *ISDN adapters*. Enable you to communicate at much higher rates of speed than with traditional modems. *ISDN* requires a special ISDN line to be installed by your phone company, which usually incurs an installation fee and higher monthly rates than normal telephone service. At the time of this writing, ISDN is not available in all locations.

Due to the increased interest and requirements for mobile communications, many other technologies are under development, including satellite and other wireless communications. Another technology, currently available in some communities, is the service provided by cable television companies. Some local cable companies are now offering Internet and e-mail services.

After you have installed your modem and connected it to your telephone line, you are ready to set up the Dial-up Networking utility that comes with Windows. Consult your modem and computer documentation for setting up your hardware.

Setting Up Dial-Up Networking on Your Computer

Dial-Up Networking is a set of communication components that comes with Windows 95 and Windows NT, enabling you to connect remotely to a network. If Dial-Up Networking was installed with Windows, a Dial-Up Networking icon appears in the My Computer folder.

If Dial-Up Networking was not installed when Windows 95 was installed, you can install it from your Windows 95 disks.

Installing Dial-Up Networking for Windows 95

1. Choose **Start** and select **Settings** and **Control Panel**. Double-click **Add/Remove New Programs**, and select the **Windows Setup** tab.

2. Select **Communications** from the Components list, and then click the **Details** button.

3. Click **Dial-Up Networking** in the Communications dialog box, and then click **OK** to complete the installation.

Installing the Remote Access Service under Windows NT 4.0

1. Go to the **Start** menu, choose **Settings** and click **Control Panel**.

2. Double-click the **Network** applet.

3. Click the **Services** tab.

4. Click the **Add** button.

5. Highlight **Remote Access Service** in the **Network Service** list and click **OK**.

6. Enter the location of your Windows NT 4.0 setup files (typically the I386 directory on the Windows NT 4.0 installation CD-ROM).

7. Click the **Continue** button. Files will be copied from the CD-ROM to your system. Remote Access setup will complete the installation procedure.

8. Click the **Close** button on the Network applet.

9. Restart your computer.

After you have verified that Dial-Up Networking is installed on your computer, you can set up a Dial-Up Networking connection for each service to which you want to connect. For example, you might create a connection for logging on to your office network from home, and another connection for dialing a commercial service, such as CompuServe or America Online.

Creating a new Dial-Up Networking connection for Windows 95

1. Open the My Computer folder on your Windows desktop.

2. Double-click the Dial-Up Networking icon to open its folder window.

Completing initial modem setup

If you haven't previously set up your modem, a dialog box will appear asking if you want to invoke the Modem installer. Click **Yes** and you will be stepped through the Modem Installer (similar to the Windows 95 modem installer). When the Add RAS Device dialog box appears, select your modem in the **RAS Capable Devices** drop-down list and click **OK**. Your modem will show up in the Remote Access Setup dialog box. Click the **Continue** button to resume the Remote Access Service setup.

3. Double-click **Make New Connection** in the Dial-Up Networking window to start the Make New Connection Wizard, which leads you through the process of defining a new connection, as shown in Figure 32.1.

FIGURE 32.1

The Make New Connection dialog box lets you name your connection and select a modem to use.

4. Enter a descriptive name for the connection, and select the modem you will use to dial the service. Click **Next** to continue.

5. Enter the area code and telephone number of the network you are connecting to, as shown in Figure 32.2. If necessary, select the appropriate country code. Click **Next** to continue.

FIGURE 32.2

Enter the area code, phone number, and country for the number you want to dial with this Dial-Up Connection.

6. Click **Finish** on the final screen to add the new Dial-Up Networking connection to your Dial-Up Networking folder.

Hosts for Dial-Up Networking

This chapter covers setting up your computer as a client for Dial-Up Networking. To use Dial-Up Networking, you must have a server, or host computer, that is configured to work as a host to Dial-Up Networking. The server might be a Microsoft Exchange Server or other Microsoft NT Server, an Internet service provider (ISP), or a Novell Netware Server. For information on setting up the host computer using Windows NT, see *Special Edition Using Windows NT 4.0*, published by Que.

Creating a new Dial-Up Networking connection for Windows NT

1. Open the My Computer folder on your Windows desktop.

2. Double-click the Dial-Up Networking icon to open its folder window.

3. If no entries have been created on your machine, click **OK**. If there are existing entries, and you want to add a new one, click **New**.

4. Enter a descriptive name for the connection. Leave the **I know all about phonebook entries and would rather edit the properties directly** check box blank, so Windows NT will prompt you through the connection's properties. Click **Next** to continue.

5. Check **I am calling the Internet**. Click **Next** to continue.

6. Select a modem or adapter to use for the connection. Click **Next** to continue.

7. Enter the phone number of the computer you'll be calling with this connection. If you're using a notebook computer, you'll probably want to check the **Use Telephony dialing properties** box, which lets you enter the area code separately, so you can dial according to your current location. Click **Next** to continue.

8. Fill out the New Phonebook Entry Wizard options, then click **Finish** to complete the operation.

Preparing to Access E-mail Remotely

After you have Dial-Up Networking installed and configured on your computer, you must set up the appropriate software for the service you are connecting to. The following sections describe how to set up your computer for connection to Microsoft Exchange, Microsoft Mail, and the Internet.

You also need a place to store your messages. Outlook data, including e-mail messages, contacts, calendar items and other data, can be stored in a personal folder file (.pst) or an offline folder file (.ost). The following section discusses the difference between these two types of folder files, and how to set them up.

Using Offline Folders and Personal Folders

Outlook has two types of files for storing the messages that you receive when working offline:

- *Offline folders.* Used to create an offline copy of the folders that you normally use when you are working online with Outlook and Microsoft Exchange Server. Offline folders have the extension .ost, and are stored on your local hard drive. You can use the offline folders to store messages when you are not connected to your e-mail system, then synchronize those folders with your e-mail system the next time you are connected.

   By using offline folders and the **Remote Mail** command, you can filter the messages you want to receive by downloading the headers of the messages, and then marking those messages that you want to receive.

   Offline folders are not typically used as your primary delivery location for messages. If you normally receive messages in a .pst in the office, or you normally work online with Exchange Server in the office, you can use offline folders to create a synchronized copy of the folders for working offline.

   Offline folders are a Microsoft Exchange feature

   Offline folders are a feature of Microsoft Exchange, and are not available to users of other e-mail systems.

- *Personal folders.* Also stored on your local hard drive, they have the extension .pst. You can designate your personal folders as the delivery location for your messages. You might want to set up personal folders, even if you don't work offline, so you can keep a copy of your messages on your hard drive. If you use an e-mail system other than Microsoft Exchange, you might be required to use personal folders to store your messages.

To create a set of folders that synchronize with your Microsoft Exchange Server folders when you are working offline, you need to create an offline folder file, or .ost, on your computer.

Creating an offline folder file

1. While running Outlook, select the **Tools** menu, and choose the **Services** command. The Services dialog box, shown in Figure 32.3, lists the services installed in your profile.

FIGURE 32.3

The Service dialog box lists the information services that are installed in your profile.

2. Select **Microsoft Exchange**, and click the **Properties** button. The Microsoft Exchange Server dialog box appears.

3. Click the **Advanced** tab. Check the **Enable offline use** box, and click the **Offline Folder File Settings** button.

4. Select or type the name of the offline folder file. The default name for this file is C:\WINDOWS\outlook.ost.

5. Click **OK** three times to close the dialog boxes and return to Outlook.

To store the messages you receive on your local computer, you can set up a personal folder file, or .pst, on your computer.

Creating a .pst file

1. While running Outlook, select the **Tools** menu, and choose the **Services** command. The Services dialog box lists the services that are installed in your profile.

2. Click the **Add** button to add the Personal Folders service to the services in your profile.

3. Select **Personal Folders**, as shown in Figure 32.4, and click **OK**.

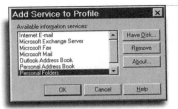

FIGURE 32.4
Select **Personal Folders** to add a Personal Folder file to your profile.

4. In the Create/Open Personal Folders File dialog box shown in Figure 32.5, type a name for the .pst file you are creating, and click **Open**.

FIGURE 32.5
Type a name for your personal folder file, or select an existing .pst file.

5. Use the Create Microsoft Personal Folders dialog box to customize your personal folders (see Figure 32.6). You can enter a name that will appear in the services list, and set your encryption preferences. To establish a password for your personal folders, enter your password in the **Password** and **Verify Password** boxes. Click **OK** to complete the dialog box.

FIGURE 32.6
Use the Create Microsoft Personal Folders dialog box to name your personal folders, and to set encryption and security.

6. The Personal Folders service is added to the list of installed services for your profile. Click **OK** to complete the Services dialog box.

Using a Microsoft Mail Postoffice

If your organization uses a Microsoft Mail postoffice, and has configured the mail server for remote access, you can use your Dial-Up Networking connection to send and receive mail remotely. The messages will be stored in your personal folders file.

To make a connection to the Microsoft Mail postoffice, you must add the Microsoft Mail service to your profile.

Adding Microsoft Mail to your profile

1. While running Outlook, open the **Tools** menu, and choose **Services**. The Services dialog box, shown earlier in Figure 32.3, lists the services that are installed in your profile.

2. Click the **Add** button to add the Microsoft Mail service to the services in your profile.

3. Select **Microsoft Mail**, as shown in Figure 32.7, and click **OK**. The Microsoft Mail dialog box appears, as shown in Figure 32.8.

FIGURE 32.7

Select **Microsoft Mail** as the new service to be added to your profile.

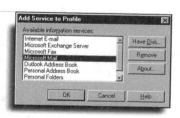

4. Complete the information in each tab of the dialog box, as described in the following section. When you are finished customizing your Microsoft Mail service, click **OK** to close the Microsoft Mail dialog box.

5. Click **OK** to close the Services dialog box.

Use the **Connection** tab, shown in Figure 32.8, to identify the location of your postoffice file. The postoffice is usually stored on your organization's network. Contact your e-mail administrator for the location of this file. You can also use this tab to indicate whether you want Outlook to connect to the network at startup, to connect remotely, or to work offline. If you are working at home and will use Dial-Up Networking, select **Remote using a modem and Dial-Up Networking**.

Use the **Logon** tab, shown in Figure 32.9, to store your mailbox name and password. If you check the box to automatically enter your password, you won't have to enter it yourself when you connect to your postoffice.

FIGURE 32.9
The **Logon** tab is used to enter your mailbox name and password.

With the **Remote Configuration** tab shown in Figure 32.10, you can select how mail is delivered when you connect to your postoffice using Dial-Up Networking:

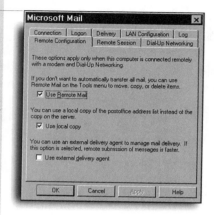

- Check the **Use Remote Mail** box to enable the use of the Remote Mail command. If you uncheck this box, Microsoft Mail automatically downloads all messages immediately after you connect.

- Check the **Use local copy** box to use the address list that is stored on your computer instead of the one on the mail server. If you're working remotely, you'll need this to be activated.

- Check the **Use external delivery agent** box to speed the delivery of remote mail messages.

Use the **Remote Session** tab, shown in Figure 32.11, to control when remote sessions start and finish. If you check **When this service is started**, Dial-Up Networking automatically connects to your postoffice when you start Outlook. Because you might want to write some messages first, most users leave this box unchecked. Use the remaining check boxes to control when a Dial-Up Networking session should be terminated by hanging up the phone line.

The **Dial-Up Networking** tab is used to set additional dial-up preferences, as shown in Figure 32.12. Select which connection you want to use from the list of Dial-Up connections. You'll find it useful to set up more than one connection if your network has more than one modem, and the lines are sometimes busy.

FIGURE 32.11

Use the **Remote Session** tab to control how you start up and end your Dial-Up Networking sessions.

FIGURE 32.12

Use the **Dial-Up Networking** tab to select your Dial-Up Networking connection, and to control how to respond if the connection fails.

After your connection to the postoffice is established, you can download a copy of the postoffice address book, so that you can address messages to your colleagues by selecting their names from the list.

Downloading an Address Book

1. Select the **Tools** menu and choose **Synchronize**.

2. Select **Download Address Book.** Dial-Up Networking connects to your postoffice and places a copy of the global address list on your local hard drive.

Using a Microsoft Exchange Server

If your organization uses Microsoft Exchange for its e-mail service, you can set up the Remote Mail feature of Exchange to work on your local computer. Using Exchange remotely gives you access to the powerful features of Microsoft Exchange Server, such as using rules to control delivery of messages. You can easily add Microsoft Exchange to your profile.

Adding Microsoft Exchange to your profile

1. While you are running Outlook, open the **Tools** menu, and choose **Services** to show the Services dialog box.

2. Click **Add** to add a new Microsoft Exchange Server service to your profile. To modify the service, select **Microsoft Exchange Server**, and click the **Properties** button.

3. Complete the four tabs of the Microsoft Exchange Server dialog box as described later in this section, and click **OK** to complete the command. Click **OK** to close the Services dialog box.

The **General** tab, shown in Figure 32.13, is used to identify the name of the Microsoft Exchange Server, and the name of your Exchange mailbox.

FIGURE 32.13

The **General** tab of the Microsoft Exchange Server dialog box is used to identify your server and mailbox, and to set the connection type when Outlook starts.

Setting the General options for Microsoft Exchange

1. Enter the name of your Microsoft Exchange Server. If you are not sure of the name, check with your Exchange Administrator.

2. Enter your mailbox name. Check with your administrator if you are not sure how names are listed on your Exchange Server. Click the **Check Name** button to verify the mailbox name with Exchange Server. If the name that you entered is found, it will be underlined in the **Mailbox** text box.

3. Use the **When starting** section to control how Outlook determines whether you usually work offline or directly connected to the network. Select **Automatically detect connection state**, if you want Outlook to test for the connection state at startup. If you want to select the connection state yourself, select **Manually control connection state**.

4. If you chose to manually control the connection state, you can further determine how Outlook should start by default. Check **Choose the connection type when starting** if you want Outlook to ask for the connection type each time you start an Outlook session. Select the default connection state that Outlook should select by choosing one of the options in the **Default connection state** group.

5. Enter an appropriate value in the **Seconds Until Server Connection Timeout** text box, for the duration Outlook should wait before presenting an error message if Exchange Server can't be detected. You might want to increase this value if you work remotely, and it takes a while to get a response from your server.

The **Advanced** tab, shown in Figure 32.14, lets you set several advanced options for working with Exchange Server.

Setting the Advanced options for Microsoft Exchange

1. To open additional mailboxes when you start Outlook, click **Add**, and select the names of the additional mailboxes you want to open. You can only open the mailboxes of persons who have given you permission to do so.

2. To encrypt information for greater security, check either the **When using the _network_** or **When using dial-up n_e_t-working** check boxes.

3. Using the **_Logon network security_** list, select the method for validating your username and password. By selecting **NT Password Authentication**, your identity is confirmed for Exchange Server when you log on to your Windows NT Server.

4. Check the **Enable offline _use_** box if you will be using an offline storage file to work with your Exchange messages when you are not connected to the network. Click the **Offline _F_older File Settings** button to display the dialog box shown in Figure 32.15, which lets you customize your offline folder settings.

FIGURE 32.14

The **Advanced** tab of the Microsoft Exchange Server dialog box lets you open additional mailboxes, and control your network logon.

FIGURE 32.15

Use the **Offline Folder File** Settings dialog box to configure your offline storage file.

Enter the filename for your offline storage file and your encryption preferences. Click the **Compact Now** button to reduce the size of your offline storage file by removing deleted items. If you click **Disable Offline Use**, the offline folders will not be opened the next time you start Outlook. Do not select this option if you are using Outlook remotely on this computer.

The **Dial-Up Networking** tab, shown in Figure 32.16, is used to select which Dial-Up Networking connection you want to use. If your organization has more than one phone number for remote mail, it's a good idea to set up a separate Dial-Up connection for each one.

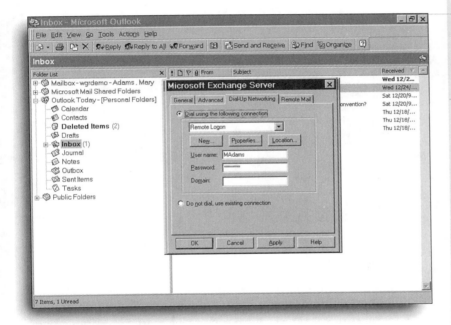

FIGURE 32.16
Use the Dial-Up Networking dialog box select a connection and enter your logon information for dial-up connections.

Configuring Dial-Up Networking for Microsoft Exchange

1. Select the **Dial using the following connection** button if you will get your messages using a modem. Select **Do not dial, use existing connection** if you will get your messages using a network connection.

2. Select the dial-up connection that you want to use from the drop-down list. To create a new dial-up connection, click **New**. Click **Properties** to edit the settings for the current dial-up connection. Click **Location** if you are dialing from a different location than usual, such as from a different area code, or from an office that requires a dialing prefix to get an outside line.

3. Enter your Exchange Server username and password, and the domain name of the Exchange Server. You may have to get the domain name from your Exchange administrator.

Use the **Remote Mail** tab, shown in Figure 32.17, to customize the behavior of your remote sessions.

FIGURE 32.17

Use the **Remote Mail** tab of the Microsoft Exchange dialog box to control what happens in a remote connection.

Setting your Remote Mail options

1. In the **Remote mail connections** group, select **Process marked items** if you want Outlook to retrieve all the messages that you mark for retrieval. Select **Retrieve items that meet the following conditions** if you want to limit the messages that can be retrieved. Then click the **Filter** button to indicate the conditions for receiving messages, such as messages from a specific sender, or with a specified subject.

2. Check **Disconnect after connection is finished** if you want Outlook to hang up the phone after the messages have been processed according to your instructions.

3. Use the **Scheduled Connections** group to instruct Outlook to perform a connection automatically at a predetermined time or interval. Select the options within this group to indicate what messages should be received during a scheduled connection.

To make a Public Folder available offline, drag the folder from the original location to the Favorites subfolder of the Public Folders. This doesn't move the folder in Favorites, but creates a shortcut to the actual folder. Figure 23.18 shows the result of dragging several Public Folders from their original location into the Favorites folder.

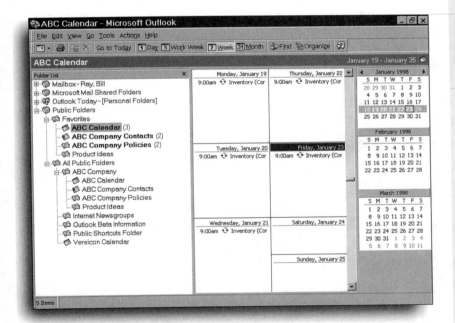

FIGURE 32.18
Use the Offline Folder File Settings dialog box to configure your offline storage file.

Using an Internet E-mail Service

If you don't belong to a network postoffice, you can send and receive e-mail using Outlook through your Internet service provider (ISP).

Setting up Internet services through Outlook

1. While you are running Outlook, open the **Tools** menu, and choose **Services** to open the Services dialog box.

2. Click **Add** to add a new service to your profile. Select **Internet E-mail**, and click **OK**.

3. Complete the four tabs of the Mail Account Properties dialog box as described later, and click **OK** to complete the command. Click **OK** to close the Services dialog box.

In the **General** tab, shown in Figure 32.19, enter a descriptive name for the mail service. This descriptive name will appear on the list of services, and is especially useful if you use more than one ISP. Enter your name, organization, and e-mail address. If you want replies to be sent to a different address, such as your business e-mail address, enter that address in the **Reply address** text box.

FIGURE 32.19

Use the **General** tab of the Local Internet Provider Properties dialog box to identify the name of the provider, and your identifying information.

Use the **Servers** tab to enter information about your ISP's e-mail servers (see Figure 32.20). Enter the names of the servers for outgoing and incoming mail, and your logon name and password.

Use the **Connection** tab to specify that you will connect by modem, and the name of the Dial-Up Networking connection you will use (see Figure 32.21).

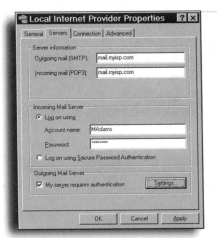

FIGURE 32.20

Use the **Servers** tab of the Local Internet Provider dialog box for the mail server information from you Internet provider.

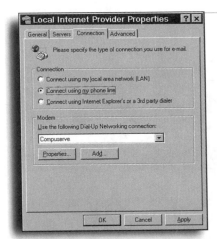

FIGURE 32.21

Use the **Connection** tab of the Local Internet Provider dialog box to select a connection type, and to choose a dial-up connection.

Connecting to Your E-mail Service Using Remote Mail

After you have configured one or more e-mail services, you can connect to your services using Remote Mail in Outlook. You can compose new messages in Outlook without connecting to your services, so you don't incur telephone charges or tie up your phone line. When you are ready to send and receive messages, follow these steps:

Checking your e-mail remotely

1. Click the **Send and Receive** button on the toolbar to send and receive messages using all available services. If you want to select an individual service, open the **Tools menu,** choose the **Send and Receive** command, and select the service you want to use for the remote connection.

2. Outlook connects to the services in the order that they are listed in your profile.

3. Each service presents its own set of screens to report the progress of the connection.

Figure 32.22 shows the dialog box that is displayed after Dial-Up Networking calls your Microsoft Exchange Server, and is waiting for a response from the server. Figure 32.23 shows the logon screen for Exchange Server, which appears after the server responds to your connection. Figure 32.24 shows the dialog box that appears after you have entered your logon information, and you are connecting to Microsoft Exchange Server.

FIGURE 32.22

Outlook has dialed the Microsoft Exchange Server, and is waiting to be connected.

FIGURE 32.23

Microsoft Exchange Server requires a logon and password when you are connecting remotely.

FIGURE 32.24

After the logon is completed, Outlook continues connecting to Microsoft Exchange Server.

Synchronizing Folders with Microsoft Exchange

While you are working offline, your offline folders are likely to become out of synch with your Microsoft Exchange folders. Several events might cause this to happen:

- You have composed and sent e-mail messages to the OutBox folder of your remote computer, but the messages have not been delivered.

- New messages have arrived in your Inbox on the Exchange Server, but they have not been delivered to your offline Inbox.

- You have posted messages to the offline copy of a Public Folder, but those messages haven't been posted to the Exchange Server copy of the folder.

- New messages have been posted in the Public Folders on the Exchange Server, but you can't read them, because they haven't been delivered to your offline copy of the folders.

The process of resolving these inconsistencies is known as *synchronization*. When you synchronize your folders, Outlook uses Dial-Up Networking to connect to your Exchange Server, and copies the waiting items to and from your online and offline folders.

Synchronizing your folders

1. If you want to synchronize just one folder, select the folder first.

2. Open the **Tools** menu and choose the **Synchronize** command. On the submenu that appears, select **All Folders** to synchronize all you offline folders, or **This Folder** to synchronize only the selected folder.

3. Outlook uses Dial-Up Networking to connect to your Exchange server, synchronizing the contents of your offline folders.

Customizing Outlook

33

Setting Outlook's Options

Setting preferences for Outlook folder items

Specifying e-mail options

Choosing a language for spell-checking and adding words to your custom dictionary

Setting up security

Authorizing delegates

Setting up Internet e-mail options

Choosing Your Options

With any Information viewer displayed, open the **Tools** menu and choose **Options** to display the Options dialog box as shown in Figure 33.1. The dialog box shown here is for Corporate/Workgroup Outlook; the corresponding dialog box for Internet Only Outlook is slightly different.

FIGURE 33.1

The Options dialog box initially shows the **Preferences** tab.

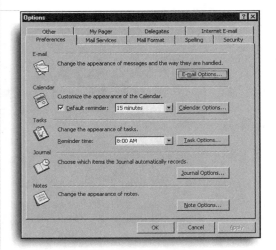

The tabs displayed in the Options dialog box depend on whether you have Corporate/Workgroup or Internet Only Outlook installed. If you are using Corporate/Workgroup Outlook, the tabs also depend on which information services you have in your profile. When you open the Options dialog box on your computer, you may not see some of the tabs shown in Figure 33.1, and you may see some tabs that aren't shown here:

- The **Mail Services** tab appears only for Corporate/Workgroup Outlook. It is replaced by the Mail Delivery tab for Internet Only Outlook.

- The **Internet E-mail** tab appears only for Corporate/Workgroup Outlook and if you have the Internet e-mail information service in your profile.

- The **Delegates** tab appears only for Corporate/Workgroup Outlook and if you have the Microsoft Exchange Server information service in your profile.

- The **My Pager** tab appears only for Corporate/Workgroup and if you've installed the MobileCHOICE Messenger add-in.

- After you install other add-ins, you may see more tabs.

In each Options tab, you can make choices about how Outlook works. This chapter contains information about the tabs you'll see if you have the Internet E-mail, Microsoft Exchange Server, and Microsoft Mail information services in your profile.

SEE ALSO

➤ *For more information about Outlook's faxing capabilities, see Chapter 24, "Sending and Receiving Faxes."*

➤ *For information about adding information services to your profile, see Chapter 7, "Setting Up Information Services."*

➤ *For information about the MobileCHOICE Messenger add-in that lets you send messages to pagers from Outlook, see Chapter 25, "Sending Messages to Pagers."*

➤ *For information about installing add-ins and also for Web pages where you can find out what add-ins are available, see page 593.*

Specifying Your Preferences

Choose the **Preferences** tab of the Options dialog box, shown previously in Figure 33.1, to specify your preferences for **E-mail**, **Calendar**, **Tasks**, **Journal**, and **Notes**.

Setting E-mail Options

Choose **E-mail Options** to display the dialog box shown in Figure 33.2.

The **After moving or deleting an open item** drop-down list at the top of the dialog box contains choices related to message handling. You can specify what you want Outlook to do after you've moved or deleted an open message. The choices are

- *Open the previous item* (*the default*)

- *Open the next item*

- *Return to the Inbox*

Small difference in Internet Only Outlook

The **E-mail Options** tab shown in Figure 33.2 is for Corporate/Workgroup Outlook. The corresponding tab for **Internet Only Outlook** contains an additional check box (described later in this chapter).

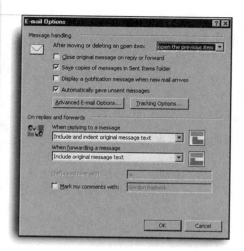

Next, check or uncheck the four check boxes in the dialog box according to your preferences.

- ***Close original message on reply or forward*** *(default is unchecked)*. When checked, a message displayed in the Message form is closed when you choose **Reply**, **Reply to All**, or **Forward** in the form's toolbar.

- ***Save copies of messages in Sent Items folder*** *(default is checked)*. When checked, a copy of each message you send, including attachments, is saved in your Sent Items folder.

- ***Display a notification message when new mail arrives*** *(default is unchecked)*. When checked, Outlook displays an onscreen message whenever a new message arrives in your Inbox folder.

- ***Automatically save unsent messages*** *(default is checked)*. When checked, Outlook saves messages you created but haven't sent (moved to your Outbox folder) in your Drafts folder. By default, Outlook saves unfinished messages every three minutes. You can choose to save unfinished messages in a different folder, and also change the frequency in which Outlook saves unfinished messages, by choosing the **Advanced E-mail Options** button.

The E-mail Options dialog box contains two buttons. Choose the **Advanced E-mail Options** button to open a dialog box in which you can make many choices, including

- Where Outlook should save mail you've prepared but are not ready to send. By default, these messages are saved in your Drafts folder, but you can choose your Inbox, Sent Items, or Outbox folder.

- How often Outlook should AutoSave items. The default is every three minutes.

- Whether you want Outlook to save replies with original messages. The default is to save replies in your Inbox folder. You can choose to save replies in your Sent Items folder (so replies are in the same folder as the messages they reply to).

- Whether you want to save copies of messages you forward. By default, Outlook saves copies of forwarded messages.

- Whether Outlook should play a sound or briefly change the shape of the mouse pointer when a message arrives. By default, Outlook does both.

- Whether you want Outlook to process requests and responses when they arrive. By default, Outlook does process them. This means that Outlook automatically places meeting requests on your calendar as well as responses you receive to meeting requests you've sent in the original meeting request.

- Whether you want Outlook to process delivery, read, and recall receipts when they arrive. By default, Outlook does process them. When you request to be notified when messages you send are delivered or read, Outlook can save these notifications with the original message. To view notifications, open the original message in the Sent Items folder, and choose the **Tracking** tab.

- What importance and sensitivity you want your outgoing messages to have. By default, both are set to **Normal**. You can change the default for importance to **Low** or **High**. You can change the default for sensitivity to **Personal**, **Private**, or **Confidential**.

The pointer changes only briefly

The mouse pointer changes shape very briefly. Unless you're watching closely, you probably won't notice the change.

- Whether Outlook should allow a comma as an address separator in the **To**, **Cc,** and **Bcc** boxes on the Message form. By default, you must use a semicolon between e-mail addresses —a comma is not allowed. If you choose to allow commas, you can use either commas or semicolons.

- Whether Outlook should check names automatically. Automatic name checking occurs by default. Outlook can check the names you enter in the **To**, **Cc**, and **Bcc** boxes on the Message form by comparing them with addresses in your Address Books.

- Whether meeting requests should be automatically deleted from your Inbox when you respond to them. By default, they are automatically deleted. If you accept a meeting request, Outlook automatically enters it in your calendar.

Choose the **Tracking Options** button to open a dialog box in which you can specify message tracking. This dialog box contains three check boxes, all of which are unchecked by default. You can check any or all the check boxes to enable tracking. The check boxes are labeled

- **Tell me when all messages have been <u>d</u>elivered to recipients' Inboxes**.

- **Tell me when all messages have been <u>r</u>ead.** That is, when recipients have opened the messages. That's no guarantee, of course, that the recipients have actually read the messages.

- **D<u>e</u>lete receipts and blank responses after processing.** This means that Outlook automatically moves responses to meeting requests you've sent to your Deleted Items folder if those responses contain no comments. Meeting responses are automatically placed on your calendar. Also, notifications you receive when messages are delivered, read, or recalled, are automatically placed in your Deleted Items folder, but remain available in the Sent Items folder's **Tracking** tab.

For these Tracking options to work, the entire e-mail system (from sender through to recipient) must support them. If the sender and recipient both use Exchange Server, the tracking

Having trouble with Tracking options?

Tracking options depend on the entire e-mail system. They work as explained here in an Exchange Server environment. They may not work if you're using a different messaging system.

options work as intended. Postoffices on other e-mail systems may not support these options.

The bottom part of the E-mail Options dialog box contains choices about replying to messages and forwarding them. When replying to a message, you can choose

- *Do not include the original message*
- *Attach the original message*
- *Include the original message text*
- *Include and indent the original message text* (*the default*)
- *Prefix each line of the original message* (*you can choose the prefix character*)

When forwarding a message, you have the same choices with the exception of the first.

When replying to a message or forwarding it, you can choose to prefix lines of the original message. By default, Outlook uses > as the prefix character; you can specify a different character.

By default, when you annotate original messages in your replies, and when you annotate messages you forward, Outlook automatically marks your annotations with the name of your profile. In this dialog box, you can turn off automatic marking of annotations or, if you leave automatic marking turned on, you can change how Outlook marks annotations (to your initials, for example). This option is not available if you use Word as your e-mail editor because Word uses revision marks to mark your annotations.

If you're using Internet Only Outlook, the E-mail Options dialog box contains a check box that's not available for Corporate/Workgroup Outlook. By default, the **Automatically put people I reply to in** check box is unchecked. If you check this box, Outlook puts the name and e-mail address of the original sender into your Contacts folder (if it's not there already).

SEE ALSO

➤ *For information about setting importance and sensitivity in messages, see page 301.*

➤ *For an explanation of annotations, see page 328.*

Identifying lines in the original message with a prefix character

It's a good idea to prefix each line in your messages (many people choose > as the prefix character) so people who receive your replies and messages you've forwarded can easily identify the original message.

Setting Calendar Options

The **Calendar** section of the **Preferences** tab contains the **Default reminder** check box which, by default, is checked so Outlook automatically sets a reminder whenever you create a Calendar item. Uncheck this box if you don't want reminders to be set automatically. If you leave the box checked, you can choose how long before the start of the calendar event you want to receive a reminder (the default is 15 minutes).

Choose **Calendar Options** in the **Preferences** tab to display the dialog box shown in Figure 33.3.

FIGURE 33.3

Use this dialog box to set your Calendar preferences.

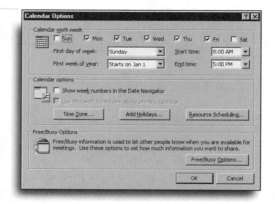

The top section of this dialog box enables you to specify which days of the week are working days. By default, Monday through Friday are working days.

In this section, you can also choose which day Outlook uses as the first day of each week (the default is **Sunday**) and when the first week of the year starts (the default is **Starts on Jan 1**). You can also set the start and end times of the working day (the defaults are **8:00 AM** and **5:00 PM**).

The center section of the Calendar options dialog box contains a check box you can check if you want the Date Navigator to display week numbers. By default, week numbers are not displayed.

You can also choose to use the calendar in Schedule+ 95 instead of the Outlook calendar for group scheduling. This choice is available only if you requested access to Schedule+ when you installed Outlook on your computer.

Three buttons in the center section provide access to more choices. Choose **Time Zone** to display a dialog box in which you can change your current time zone (useful when you travel), and also specify a second time zone (useful when you communicate regularly with people in a time zone other than your local one).

Choose **Add Holidays** to display a dialog box in which you can add what Outlook calls Holidays as events in your calendar. It's usually better to ignore this button and, instead, manually add holidays as recurring events to your calendar.

Choose **Resource Scheduling** to display a dialog box that contains useful options if you're responsible for scheduling resources such as conference rooms and projection equipment. You can choose to

- *Automatically accept meeting requests.* Not a good idea unless you want to have a conference room reserved for several meetings at the same time.

- *Automatically decline conflicting meeting requests.* Choose this to avoid having the same resource reserved at the same time by two or more people.

- *Automatically decline recurring meeting requests.* Use this to avoid the problem of people reserving a resource on a regular basis in case they need it.

The bottom section of the Calendar Options dialog box contains the **Free/Busy Options** button. Choose this button to display a dialog box in which you can specify how many months of your future schedule you want to make available to other people and how often you want to update your published schedule.

SEE ALSO

➤ *For information about marking holidays on your calendar, see "Marking Holidays and Other Special Days on Your Calendar" on page 430.*

➤ *For information about reminders, see "Creating a One-time Appointment" on page 420.*

Sharing your calendar

You can share your calendar with other people in two ways. Exchange Server (accessible only if you're using Corporate/Workgroup Outlook) provides facilities for sharing calendars, as explained in Chapter 22, "Using Outlook as an Exchange Server Client." You can also use Net Folders to share your calendar by way of the Internet or an intranet, as explained in Chapter 31, "Accessing the World Wide Web."

Setting Tasks Options

The **Tasks** section of the Preferences tab contains the **Reminder time** box in which you can set the time of day when you want to receive task reminders (the default is **8:00 AM**).

Choose the **Task Options** button in the **Preferences** tab to display the dialog box shown in Figure 33.4.

FIGURE 33.4

Use the Task Options dialog box to control how Outlook displays tasks.

You can select the colors Outlook uses for overdue and completed tasks. By default, overdue tasks are displayed in red, completed tasks in gray. You can select other colors by clicking either of the drop-down lists and selecting a new color.

SEE ALSO

➤ *For information about tasks, see Chapter 28, "Planning, Tracking, and Assigning Tasks."*

Setting Journal Options

Choose the **Journal Options** button to display the dialog box shown in Figure 33.5.

FIGURE 33.5

Use the Journal Options dialog box to specify the items to be AutoArchived.

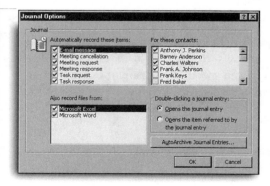

The top part of the Journal Options dialog box is where you specify which types of messages are to be journaled. You can choose any or all of the following:

- *E-mail message*
- *Meeting cancellation*
- *Meeting request*
- *Meeting response*
- *Task request*
- *Task response*

In addition to specifying the types of message to be journaled, you have to specify which contacts those messages are to or from. The dialog box contains a list box in which all your contacts' names are displayed. Check those names for whom you want messages to be journaled.

The bottom-left part of the dialog box lists all the Office 97 (and compatible) applications for which Outlook can create an automatic Journal entry whenever you open and work with those applications' files. By default, all compatible applications installed on your computer are checked. Uncheck those you don't want Outlook to journal automatically.

In the bottom-right part of the dialog box you can choose what will happen when you double-click a Journal item. You can choose to open the Journal entry or to open the item referred to by the Journal entry.

Choose **AutoArchive Journal Entries** to display the **AutoArchive** tab of the Journal Properties dialog box. In this dialog box, you can specify what happens to Journal items when AutoArchiving occurs. You can choose

- The age of items you want to archive (six months is the default, but you can change that)
- Whether you want to move items to a file or delete them

SEE ALSO

➤ *For information about Outlook's Journal, see Chapter 29, "Journaling Your Activities."*

Setting Notes Options

Choose the **Note Options** button in the **Preferences** tab to display the dialog box shown in Figure 33.6.

FIGURE 33.6

Use the Notes Options dialog box to set the default color, size, and font of notes.

You can choose

- The color of notes (default is yellow)
- The size of notes (default is medium)
- The font to be used for notes (default is 10-point Comic Sans MS)

SEE ALSO

➤ *For information about notes, see Chapter 30, "Keeping Notes."*

Specifying Mail Services Options

The **Mail Services** tab is available only if you're using Corporate/Workgroup Outlook. Internet Only Outlook uses only one mail service, so none of the choices in the **Mail Services** tab are applicable.

Choose the **Mail Services** tab of the Options dialog box shown in Figure 33.7 to specify which profile you want Outlook to use on startup and which services it should check for e-mail messages.

Startup Settings

The top section of the **Mail Services** tab is where you specify what happens when Outlook starts. The default is **Prompt for a profile to be used**—you see a message box in which Outlook asks which profile to use. You can then select among the profiles that exist on your computer.

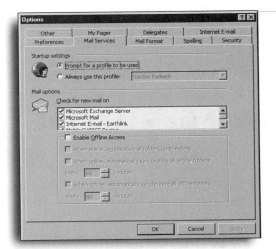

FIGURE 33.7
Use the **Mail Services** tab to specify what happens when you open Outlook. This tab is not available in Internet Only Outlook.

If you always use the same profile, as most people do, choose **Always use this profile** and select the profile you want to use in the drop-down list box. Subsequently, when you start Outlook, it automatically uses the profile you've specified, saving you the step of selecting a profile.

SEE ALSO
➤ *For information about profiles, see Chapter 6, "Creating a Profile."*

Automatically Reading Mail

The bottom section of the **Mail Services** tab contains a list box that contains the names of all the mail services in your profile. By default, all your installed services are checked so Outlook checks all these services for mail on startup. You can select which services you want Outlook to check for mail.

By default, the **Enable Offline Access** check box is unchecked and the check boxes under it are disabled. This is the appropriate choice if your computer is connected to mail services. If you're working offline, check this box to enable the check boxes under it. These boxes let you control when your offline Outlook folders are synchronized with the folders on your mail server.

SEE ALSO

➤ *For information about adding mail information services to your profile, see "The Internet E-mail Information Service" on page 117, "The Microsoft Mail Information Service" on page 122, and "The Microsoft Exchange Server Information Service" on page 130.*

➤ *For information about working offline, see Chapter 32, "Working Remotely."*

Specifying Mail Format

Choose the **Mail Format** tab of the Options dialog box, shown in Figure 33.8, to specify the format for the mail you send, how you want your mail to appear on recipients' screens, and any signature you want to append to your mail.

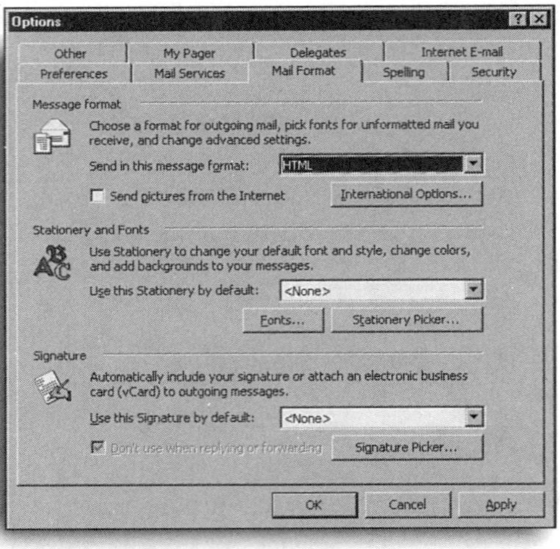

Formatting e-mail

When you consider formatting e-mail, remember that recipients may not see mail as you format it. If you use Word to format e-mail, for example, recipients will see your formatting only if they have Word installed on their computers. Not everyone lives in a Microsoft Office environment.

FIGURE 33.8

Use the **Mail Format** tab to specify how you want Outlook to send your messages.

Formatting Outgoing Mail

Formatting replies to messages

When you reply to a message, Outlook automatically uses an editor that is consistent with the format of the original message, so the original sender can read your replies, regardless of whether he or she uses Outlook.

The top section of the **Mail Format** tab is where you specify the format of messages you create.

You can select from

- *HTML (the default)*
- *Microsoft Outlook Rich Text*
- *Plain text*
- *Microsoft Word*

The **Send pictures from the Internet** check box (available only when the HTML format is selected) is unchecked by default. In this case, Outlook sends only links to pictures, including background images, in your messages. Check this box if you want Outlook to send picture files with your messages.

Choose the **International Options** button to display a dialog box in which you can choose to display the names of header fields in U.S. English, even if you're using another language version of Outlook.

SEE ALSO

➤ *For information about formatting an e-mail message, see "Selecting a Message Format" on page 295.*

Specifying Stationery and Fonts

In the center section of the **Mail Format** tab, you can select *stationery* or a *template* to use for the messages you create. This list isn't available if you've selected Microsoft Outlook Rich Text or Plain Text for your message format.

If you've selected the HTML message format, open the **Use this Stationery by default** drop-down list and select one of the stationeries from the list.

To choose a default font for your messages (when you're using the HTML message format), choose the **Fonts** button. Use the Fonts dialog box to specify the names, sizes, and colors of fonts you want to use when composing, replying to, and forwarding messages. You can also specify HTML fonts. For those stationeries that have specific fonts associated with them, you can specify other fonts instead of using the associated fonts.

If you've selected the Microsoft Word message format, you can choose a Word template in the center section of the dialog box. You can create your own templates by choosing **Template Picker**.

SEE ALSO

➤ *For information about templates, see "Creating an E-mail Template" on page 238.*

What is stationery?

Stationery is a pattern or background Outlook adds to messages you send.

Creating your own stationery

Microsoft supplies several stationeries with Outlook. You can also create your own stationeries. To do so, choose **Stationery Picker** and then choose **Create**.

Signing Messages

In the bottom section of the **Mail Format** tab, you can choose to have Outlook automatically add your signature to messages you send or attach an electronic business card (*vCard*) to them. Before you do so, you must create a signature, or vCard. Create a signature by choosing the **Signature Picker** button to open a dialog box that displays any signatures you have previously created. Choose the **<u>C</u>reate** button to display the Create New Signature dialog box in which you can create a signature.

After you've chosen a signature, Outlook automatically appends that signature to all messages you create. You can choose whether you want the signature to be appended to your replies and to messages you forward.

Specifying Spelling Options

Choose the **Spelling** tab of the Options dialog box, shown in Figure 33.9, to select the spell checking options you want to use. The top section of the **Spelling** tab contains five check boxes. Check or uncheck these boxes according to your preferences.

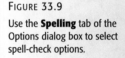

FIGURE 33.9

Use the **Spelling** tab of the Options dialog box to select spell-check options.

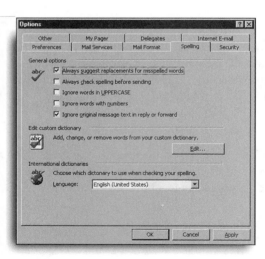

Editing a Custom Dictionary

Outlook provides a custom dictionary with the filename Custom.dic. You can add any specialized words you frequently use into this dictionary so that Outlook doesn't mark those words as spelling errors. When Outlook checks spelling, it compares words in your messages with entries in your principal dictionary and in your custom dictionary.

To add words to your custom dictionary, or to edit words already in that dictionary, choose the **Edit** button in the center section of the **Spelling** tab. Outlook displays your custom dictionary in a Notepad window in which you can add words, delete words, and edit already-existing words.

Choosing Other Dictionaries

The normal process of installing Office includes installing a dictionary appropriate for your location. You can also install dictionaries, separately available from Microsoft, for other locations.

The bottom section of the **Spelling** tab contains a drop-down list box that shows all the dictionaries installed on your computer. Select one of the dictionaries in this list to select the principal dictionary Outlook uses for spell checking. In addition to this principal dictionary, Outlook always uses your custom dictionary.

Specifying Security Options

Choose the **Security** tab of the Options dialog box, shown in Figure 33.10, to specify security options.

Securing E-mail

The **Securing e-mail** section of this tab is where you can select among the security settings you've previously set up.

Selecting a security setting

1. Choose **Change Settings** to display the Change Security Settings dialog box.

Security on the Internet

The subject of keeping things private on the Internet is complex and beyond the scope of this book. For detailed information, refer to *Internet Security Professional Reference*, published by New Riders.

2. Choose **Create New**, and then enter a name for your security setting.

3. In the **Secure Message Format** drop-down list, select **S/MIME**.

4. Check the **Send these certificates with signed messages** check box.

5. Choose **Choose**, and then select your digital ID.

6. Choose **OK** to close the dialog box.

FIGURE 33.10

Use the **Security** tab to specify security options.

Specifying Internet Explorer Security Zones

Use the **Secure content** section of the tab to specify an Internet security zone.

Refer to a book such as *Using Internet Explorer 4.0*, published by Que, for information about Internet security zones.

Setting Other Options

Choose the **Other** tab, shown in Figure 33.11, to access choices that affect the overall operation of Outlook, archiving items, and previewing messages.

FIGURE 33.11
This tab contains three buttons that provide access to detailed choices.

The **General** section at the top of this tab contains the **Empty the Deleted Items folder upon exiting** check box, which means that Outlook permanently deletes the contents in this folder when you close Outlook. If you want to save items in your Deleted Items folder, uncheck this box.

Working with Advanced Options

Choose the **Advanced Options** button to display the dialog box shown in Figure 33.12.

FIGURE 33.12
The Advanced Options dialog box provides control of a variety of Outlook's options.

When Outlook opens, it displays the Outlook Today window by default. If you prefer a different window, open the **Startup in this folder** drop-down list and choose a folder.

Check or uncheck the three check boxes in the **General Settings** section, according to your preferences.

In the middle section, labeled **Appearance options**, you can select

- The font to use in the Date Navigator
- Whether you want notes to show the time and date
- The number of working hours per day and per week to be used for tasks

Use the four buttons at the bottom of the **Advanced Options** tab as follows:

- **Reminder Options** to choose to display a reminder, play a reminder sound, or both.
- **Add-in Manager** to display a list of add-ins installed in Outlook and to install add-ins.
- **Advanced Tasks** to set reminders on tasks with due dates, keep updated copies of assigned tasks on your task list, and send status reports when you've completed tasks assigned to you.
- **Custom Forms** to manage custom forms.

SEE ALSO

➤ *For information about assigning tasks, see "Assigning a Task to Someone Else" on page 458.*

Setting AutoArchive Options

Choose the **AutoArchive** button in the **Other** tab to display the AutoArchive dialog box in which you can specify how you want Outlook to save old items.

Setting Preview Pane Options

Choose the **Pr̲eview Pane** button to display the dialog box
shown in Figure 33.13.

FIGURE 33.13

Use the Preview Pane dialog
box to control the preview
pane.

By default, Outlook marks a message you've received as read
when you double-click the message to display it in the Message
form. If you check the **M̲ark messages as read in preview
window** check box, Outlook automatically marks a message as
read if you display it in the preview pane for a certain period.
After you check this option, you can specify the number of seconds a message has to be displayed before it's marked as read.

You can also set Outlook to mark a message displayed in the
preview pane as read when you select a different message. Do
this by checking the **Mark item as r̲ead when selection
changes** check box.

The normal way to display a message in the preview pane is to
select that message in the Inbox Information viewer. With the
S̲ingle key reading using space bar check box checked (the
default), you can press the Spacebar to move from one message
to the next.

You can use the **Font̲** button to select the font in which preview
headers are displayed.

Authorizing Delegates

If you have Exchange Server information service in your profile,
the Options dialog box has a **Delegates** tab. Select this tab to
display the dialog box shown in Figure 33.14.

Available only in Corporate/
Workgroup Outlook

The **Delegates** tab is available
only if you have Corporate/
Workgroup Outlook installed
and if you have the Microsoft
Exchange Server information
service in your profile.

FIGURE 33.14

Use the **Delegates** tab in the Options dialog box to authorize delegates.

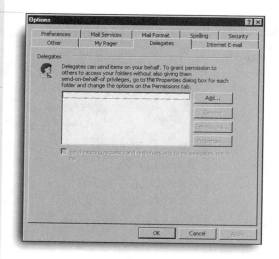

The **Delegates** tab contains a list box that displays the names of any people you have currently authorized to be your *delegates* (the dialog box contains a brief explanation of delegates).

To add delegates to the list, choose **Add** to display the Add Users dialog box that lists the names of people in your Global Address List (the people who have accounts on Exchange Server). Choose one or more names on this list to authorize them as delegates and display their names in the **Delegates** tab.

In addition to authorizing delegates, you can also remove the names of delegates by selecting a name and then choosing **Remove**.

Only in Corporate/Workgroup
Outlook

The **Internet E-mail** tab is available only if you have Corporate/ Workgroup Outlook installed.

Setting Internet E-mail Options

If you have the Internet E-mail information service in your profile, the Options dialog box has an **Internet E-mail** tab. Select this tab to display the dialog box shown in Figure 33.15.

The top section of the **Internet E-mail** tab offers you the choice of using *MIME* or *UUENCODE* for sending e-mail messages. By default, Outlook proposes **MIME** because this format is widely supported by Internet e-mail programs. Select **UUEN-CODE** if your recipients use a text-based e-mail program on a

UNIX system or another e-mail program that doesn't accept MIME.

If you select **MIME**, you can also

- Choose among **None**, **Quoted Printable**, or **Base64** for text encoding.
- Encode headers in MIME, or allow headers to be sent in 8-bit format.

By default, Outlook sends messages in 76-character lines. You can change the number of characters on a line.

The bottom section of the tab deals with how often Outlook checks your postoffices for new messages. By default, Outlook checks the postoffices on your local network every ten minutes. You can uncheck this option if you don't want Outlook to check your postoffices automatically, and you can change the interval at which Outlook checks your local postoffices.

You can check two check boxes if you want Outlook to

- Automatically check Internet Explorer or another third-party dialer
- Automatically dial when checking for new messages

You can check **If using a dial-up connection hang up when finished sending and receiving mail** if you want Outlook to automatically disconnect a dial-up connection when it has finished sending and receiving messages.

Setting Mail Delivery Options

The **Mail Delivery** tab consists of three sections, as shown in Figure 33.16.

Available only in Internet Only Outlook

The **Mail Delivery** tab is available only if you have Internet Only Outlook installed.

FIGURE 33.16

Use the **Mail Delivery** tab on the Options dialog box to choose how you want your Internet e-mail messages to be sent when you are using Internet Only Outlook.

The first section in the **Mail Delivery** tab is Accounts Manager, which contains **Create and update new mail and directory service accounts**. In this section, you can choose **Accounts** to display the Internet Accounts dialog box in which you can examine and change the properties of your mail accounts, delete accounts, or add new ones.

You can use the second section of the tab to choose whether you want to send e-mail messages as soon as you've created them, or to choose an interval at which you want Outlook to connect to the Internet (or your intranet) to send and receive messages.

The third section of the tab contains four check boxes:

- ***Warn* before switching dial-up connection**. This is checked by default. When checked, Outlook displays a confirmation message when you change your dial-up connection. A confirmation is not displayed if you uncheck this box.

- ***Hang* up when finished sending, receiving, or updating**. This is checked by default. When checked, Outlook closes your dial-up connection as soon as you've downloaded waiting messages and sent messages from your Outbox. If you uncheck this box, the dial-up connection remains open after you've sent and received messages.

- ***Automatically dial when checking for new messages***. This is not checked by default. When checked, Outlook automatically dials your default online connection number when you check for new messages. When not checked, you have to initiate the connection.

- ***Don't download messages larger than***. This is not checked by default. When checked, you can set a maximum size for messages to download. When not checked, Outlook downloads messages of any size. Outlook ignores this setting if you're connected to an intranet.

Customizing the
Outlook Bar

Displaying the Outlook Bar

Changing the appearance of the Outlook Bar

Controlling Outlook Bar icons

Modifying Outlook Bar groups

Customizing the Outlook Bar to Your Needs

The Outlook Bar at the left side of Outlook's Information viewers contains shortcuts to Information viewers and other folders. When you first install Outlook 98 Messaging and Collaboration Client, the Outlook Bar appears as described in Chapter 1, "Getting the Feel of Outlook." You may find, however, that the Outlook Bar doesn't contain the items you need to work efficiently, or that it contains items you rarely use.

Outlook displays the Outlook Bar at the left side of Information viewers. You can't change the Outlook Bar's position.

SEE ALSO

➤ *For basic information about the Outlook Bar as it appears when you first install Outlook, see "Using Outlook to Access Your Computer Environment" on page 12.*

Hiding the Outlook Bar

You can hide the Outlook Bar by opening the **View** menu and choosing **Outlook Bar**. Use the same command to display the Outlook Bar if it's not already visible.

You can also hide the Outlook Bar by right-clicking an unoccupied space within the Outlook Bar—don't right-click a shortcut or button—to display the context menu shown in Figure 34.1.

FIGURE 34.1

Choose **Hide Outlook Bar** in this context menu to hide the Outlook Bar.

After you've hidden the Outlook Bar, you can get it back by opening the **View** menu and choosing **Outlook Bar**.

Changing the Appearance of the Outlook Bar

The Outlook Bar you see when you open Outlook has the **Outlook Shortcuts** section selected. By default, Outlook displays the Outlook Bar only about one-inch wide, which might not be wide enough to display some of the section and shortcut names completely. You can make the Outlook Bar wider by pointing onto its right edge, pressing the mouse button, and dragging to the right.

The context menu shown in Figure 34.1 contains several other useful items. By default, the shortcuts in the Outlook Bar are represented by large icons, each with a name under it. If you choose **Small Icons** in the context menu, each shortcut is represented by a small icon with its name next to it, as shown in Figure 34.2.

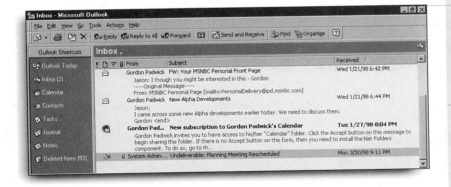

If you prefer large icons, open the context menu again and choose **Large Icons**.

The next three menu items in the context menu enable you to add a new group to the Outlook Bar, to remove an existing group, and to rename a group.

SEE ALSO
➤ *For information about these items on the context menu, see "Modifying Outlook Bar Groups" on page 565.*

Controlling Outlook Bar Icons

You can do several things with the icons on the Outlook Bar to make them more convenient to use.

Changing the Order of Icons

You can change the order of icons so those you use most often are grouped together.

Rearranging icons in the Outlook Bar

1. Point to the icon you want to move and press the mouse button.

2. Drag up or down. As you drag, a black bar appears between icons. Stop dragging when a bar appears at the position where you want the icon you're dragging to be.

3. Release the mouse button. The icon moves into the new position.

Using an Icon's Context Menu

Right-click an icon to see its context menu, as shown in Figure 34.3.

FIGURE 34.3

This is a context menu for an Outlook Bar icon.

Choose an item on the context menu, according to what you want to do:

- ***Open Folder***. Immediately open the Outlook folder represented by the icon to display its contents in an Information viewer.

- ***Open in New Window***. Immediately open the Outlook folder represented by the icon in a new Outlook window. By this means, you can have two or more Outlook folders visible on your screen at the same time.

- *Ad̲vanced Find*. Open the Advanced Find form.

- *Re̲move from Outlook Bar*. Remove this icon from the Outlook Bar.

- *Re̲name Shortcut*. Rename the icon.

- *Propert̲ies*. Display the icon's properties, as explained later.

SEE ALSO

➤ *To conduct even more refined searches, see "Using Advanced Find to Find Words and Phrases" on page 211.*

➤ *For information on adding icons, see "Adding an Icon to an Outlook Bar Group" on page 566.*

Understanding an Icon's Properties

When you choose **Properties** in an icon's context menu, you see the dialog box shown in Figure 34.4.

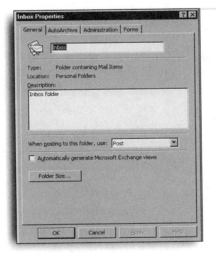

FIGURE 34.4

You can inspect a shortcut icon's properties and change some of them in this dialog box.

In the case of an icon that represents an Outlook folder, the dialog box has four tabs; for all icons except Contacts, these tabs are **General**, **AutoArchive**, **Administration**, and **Forms**. No AutoArchive tab exists for the Contacts icon because Outlook doesn't AutoArchive Contact items; instead there's a tab named **Outlook Address Book**.

You should know the following about these tabs:

- *General*. This tab contains a check box named **Automatically generate Microsoft Exchange views**. Check this box if you want to make the views you create in Outlook available for people who use Exchange Client on their workstations. This is something you should do for Public Folders that are to be accessed by Exchange Client users. You can use the **Folder Size** button to find out the size (in kilobytes) of the folder represented by the icon. This check box has nothing to do with using Exchange Server for e-mail.

- *AutoArchive*. Use this tab to set the AutoArchive properties of the folder represented by the icon.

- *Administration*. You can set the initial view that's displayed when the folder represented by the icon is first opened. You can also set the format for items moved to, or copied from, a Public Folder.

- *Forms*. Provides control over forms associated with the folder represented by the icon.

- *Outlook Address Book* (Contacts only). Use this tab to make items in the Contacts folder available as an Outlook Address Book.

The Properties dialog boxes for icons in the **Other Shortcuts** section of the Outlook Bar are different:

- *My Computer*. Displays the System Properties dialog box, which provides access to various parts of your computer environment.

- *Personal* (*Windows NT only*). Displays information about your Personal Folder and enables you to change its attributes. Also displays the path of your Personal Folder.

- *My Documents* (*Windows 95 only*). Displays information about your My Documents folder and enables you to change its attributes. Also displays the path of your My Documents folder.

- *Favorites*. Displays information about your Favorites folder and enables you to change its attributes. Also displays the path of your Favorites folder.

- *Public Folders*. Displays information about the Public Folders to which you have access.

SEE ALSO

➤ *For more information about Public Folders, see "Using Public Folders" on page 370.*

➤ *To create an Address Book, see "Creating an Outlook Address Book" on page 262.*

Modifying Outlook Bar Groups

By default, the Outlook Bar has three groups, each containing certain icons. You can add icons to, and delete icons from, the existing groups, and create more groups.

To work with Outlook Bar groups, right-click an empty space in the Outlook Bar (not an icon) to see the context menu shown previously in Figure 34.1.

Adding, Removing, and Renaming Groups

To add a new group to the Outlook Bar, choose **Add New Group** in the Outlook Bar context menu. A new group name appears at the bottom of the Outlook Bar. Type a name for the new group and press Enter. Now you have a new group with no icons in it.

- To remove a group, select that group, open the context menu, and choose **Remove Group**. Outlook asks you to confirm that you want to remove the group. Choose **OK** to continue.

- To rename a group, select that group, open the context menu, and choose **Rename Group**. The name of the group is now available for editing. Press Enter after you have renamed the group.

Fast access to disks and folders

Consider adding a new group to your Outlook Bar and dragging icons for disks and frequently used Windows folders into it. Then you can use the Outlook Bar to quickly access those disks and folders.

Adding an Icon to an Outlook Bar Group

You can add an icon to an Outlook Bar group (either one of the original groups or a group you've created).

Adding an icon to an Outlook Bar group

1. Select the group to which you want to add an icon.

2. Right-click an empty space within the group to display the group's context menu.

3. Choose **Outlook Bar Shortcut** in the context menu to display the dialog box shown in Figure 34.5.

FIGURE 34.5

Use this dialog box to select the folder to which you want the new icon to provide access.

4. Initially, the Add to Outlook Bar dialog box shows a list of Outlook folders. If you want the new icon to provide access to a folder in the Windows file system, open the **Look in** drop-down list and choose **File System**; after you do so, the list contains the file system accessible from your Windows desktop.

5. Select the folder you want the new icon to represent, and then choose **OK**. The new icon appears in the Outlook Bar.

You can have the same icon in two or more groups. For example, you might find it convenient to create an Outlook Bar group named E-mail and add Inbox, Drafts, Outbox, and Sent Items icons to that group.

Customizing Toolbars and Menus

Displaying and Hiding Toolbars

The capability to customize toolbars and menus has been available in other Office applications for quite a while, but is new in Outlook 98 Messaging and Collaboration Client. The methods you use in Outlook 98 are similar to those used in other applications.

Outlook Information viewers and forms all have a Standard toolbar that contains buttons providing immediate access to frequently used Outlook operations. In addition, Information viewers have an Advanced toolbar that contains additional buttons. Many forms also have additional toolbars.

The Advanced toolbar

The Advanced toolbar contains buttons that give you access to more Outlook capabilities than the Standard toolbar.

By default, all Information viewers and forms have the Standard toolbar displayed horizontally, immediately below the menu bar. To display additional toolbars, open the **View** menu and move the pointer onto **Toolbars** to display a menu as shown in Figure 35.1.

FIGURE 35.1

This is the **Toolbars** menu for the Inbox Information viewer.

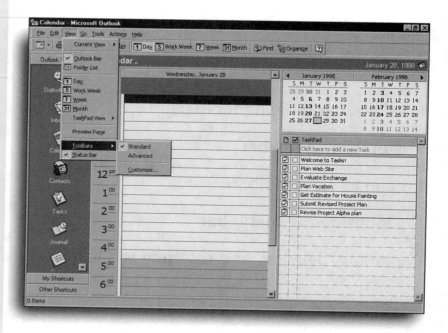

In this case, two toolbars are available: Standard and Advanced. In some cases, more than two toolbars are available. Those toolbars that are checked are currently displayed; those not checked are not currently displayed. Choose a toolbar name to display one that's not displayed or to hide one that is displayed. You can have any number of toolbars, usually one above the other under the menu bar, as shown in Figure 35.2.

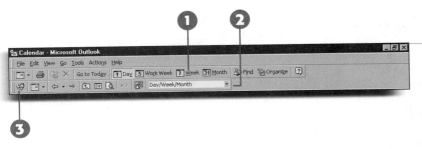

Moving a Toolbar

Toolbars are normally displayed at the top of an Information viewer or form. When they're in this position, they are said to be *docked*. You can drag a toolbar into the Information viewer, in which case it is said to be *floating*. A floating toolbar initially looks like the original toolbar, with the addition of a title bar that contains the toolbar's name.

Each toolbar has two vertical lines at the left end (see the **Drag here** callout in Figure 35.2). To drag a toolbar to a new position, move the pointer onto the vertical lines at the end of one toolbar, press the mouse button, and drag the toolbar to a new position.

After you drag a toolbar onto the Information viewer, you can change its shape. Move the pointer onto one of the edges of the toolbar, press the mouse button, and drag to change the toolbar from a horizontal line of buttons to a rectangular array of buttons, as shown in Figure 35.3.

To return a floating toolbar to its original position, move the pointer into its title bar, press the mouse button, and drag the toolbar into position just under the menu bar.

Saving vertical space

By dragging a toolbar onto the Information viewer, you gain a little more vertical space for information displayed by the Information viewer. Dragging a toolbar into the Information viewer converts that toolbar into a floating toolbar.

FIGURE 35.3

The Calendar Information viewer's Standard toolbar appears as a floating toolbar.

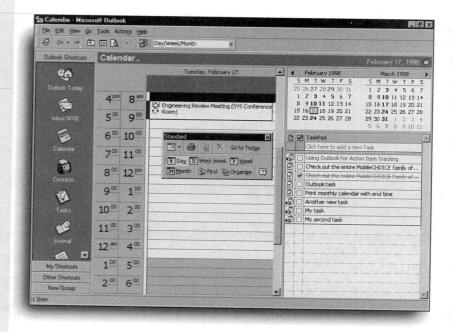

Customizing a Toolbar

You can change the size of toolbar buttons, delete buttons from a toolbar, and add buttons to a toolbar.

Changing the Size of Toolbar Buttons

All Office applications use the same size buttons

After you choose to display large toolbar buttons, this choice affects all Office applications.

By default, all toolbar buttons are small. You can choose to display large toolbar buttons.

Resizing toolbar buttons

1. Open the **View** menu, move the pointer over **Toolbars**, and choose **Customize** to display the Customize dialog box. Choose the **Options** tab as shown in Figure 35.4.

2. Choose the check boxes in this dialog box to enable and disable three aspects of the appearance of toolbars, as described in the following list.

3. Open the **Menu animations** drop-down list and select among the available types of animation, as described later.

FIGURE 35.4
Use this dialog box to modify the appearance of toolbars.

The options available are

- ***Large icons***. Small icons are displayed by default. As soon as you check this box, toolbar icons are enlarged.
- ***Show Screen Tips on toolbars***. ScreenTips are displayed by default. Uncheck this box to disable ScreenTips. You don't see the effect of checking or unchecking until you close the Options dialog box.
- ***Show shortcut keys in ScreenTips***. Shortcut keys are not shown by default. Shortcut keys duplicate the action of some, but not all, toolbar buttons. Check this box to see the shortcut keys as part of ScreenTips. You don't see the effect of checking or unchecking until you close the Options dialog box.
- ***Menu animations***. Menu animations affect the way menus appear. Choose among (**None**), **Random**, **Unfold**, and **Slide**. This has no effect on toolbars.

What are ScreenTips?

ScreenTips are the small flags that appear when you point to toolbar buttons. They provide a brief reminder about the purpose of each button.

Deleting a Toolbar Button

When you are customizing Outlook for other people to use, you might want to remove certain buttons so those people can't use them. For example, you might want to remove the Delete button from the Inbox Information viewer's Standard toolbar so people can't easily delete messages from their Inbox folders.

Deleting a toolbar button

1. Display the toolbar from which you want to delete a button.

2. Point to the button you want to delete; then hold down the Alt key while you drag the button off the toolbar. The button is no longer on the toolbar after you release the mouse button.

Adding a Button to a Toolbar

Restoring a button onto a toolbar

After you delete a built-in toolbar button, you can subsequently restore it. You can't restore a deleted custom button—you can, of course, re-create it.

You can add a button to a toolbar (or restore a built-in button you previously deleted). Suppose that you had removed the Delete button from the Inbox Standard toolbar, as described in the previous section, and now want to restore it.

Adding a button to a toolbar

1. Display the toolbar to which you want to add a button.

2. Open the **View** menu, move the pointer over **Toolbars**, and choose **Customize** to display the Customize dialog box. Choose the **Commands** tab to display the dialog box shown in Figure 35.5.

FIGURE 35.5

This dialog box lists the commands available for adding to toolbars.

3. In the **Categories** list at the left side of the dialog box, choose the category that contains the command you want to add to the toolbar. Figure 35.5 shows the **Standard** category selected. After you choose a category, the commands in that category appear in the list on the right.

4. Scroll down the **Comman<u>d</u>s** list at the right to find the command you want to add as a button into the toolbar. Point to the command, press the mouse button, and drag the command's icon to the position where you want it on the toolbar.

Changing the Position of a Button on a Toolbar

You can change the position of a button on a toolbar by a method similar to the one you use to delete a button.

Moving a toolbar button

1. Point to the button you want to move.
2. Press the Alt key while you drag the button to its new position.

Inserting and Deleting Separators Between Toolbar Buttons

If you look closely at one of Outlook's built-in toolbars, you'll see vertical, gray lines that divide buttons into groups; these lines are known as separators. You can insert separators and delete separators from toolbars:

- To insert a separator at the left of a toolbar button, hold down the Alt key while you drag the button a short distance to the right. The separator appears when you release the mouse button.

- To delete a separator at the left of a toolbar button, hold down the Alt key while you drag the button a short distance to the left. The separator disappears when you release the mouse button.

Resetting Built-in Toolbars

After you've made changes to a built-in toolbar, you can reset it to its original state.

What does a command do?

After you've selected a command in the **Commands** list, you can choose **Description** to see a brief description of what that command does.

Moving a button from one toolbar to another

You can use the same method to move an icon from one toolbar to another.

Returning to the default toolbars

1. Open the **View** menu, move the pointer over **Toolbars**, and choose **Customize**. Display the **Toolbars** tab shown in Figure 35.6.

FIGURE 35.6

This dialog box lists the menu bar and the toolbars available for the selected Information viewer. Those that are displayed are checked.

2. Select the toolbar you want to reset, and then choose **Reset**.

Creating a Custom Toolbar

Only a limited amount of horizontal space is available for buttons in a toolbar. If not enough space is available for all the buttons you need to add, the best solution is to create a custom toolbar for those buttons. Also, if you're customizing Outlook to suit specific needs, you might consider creating separate toolbars that contain buttons useful in specific situations.

Creating a custom toolbar

1. Open the Information viewer or form for which you want to create the new toolbar.

2. Open the **View** menu, move the pointer over **Toolbars**, choose **Customize**, and then choose the **Toolbars** tab shown previously in Figure 35.5.

3. Choose **New** to display the New Toolbar dialog box. Enter a name for the new toolbar in the **Toolbar Name** box. Choose **OK** to return to the Customize dialog box that now contains the name of the new toolbar. In addition, a prototype of the new toolbar is displayed with room for only one button, as shown in Figure 35.7.

FIGURE 35.7

Now you can begin to add buttons to the new toolbar.

4. Choose the **Commands** tab, and select the category for the new button. Then drag the button from the **Commands list** onto the new toolbar, as described in "Adding a Button to a Toolbar" previously in this chapter.

5. Repeat step 4 to add more buttons to the toolbar. The toolbar automatically widens to accommodate the buttons you added.

6. Choose **Close** to close the dialog box. The new toolbar remains displayed as a floating toolbar.

7. Drag the new toolbar to wherever you want it to be displayed.

Customizing the Menu Bar

Outlook handles the menu bar in much the same way as a toolbar. You can add and delete menus from the menu bar; you can add and delete menu items from a menu; and you can change the order of menu items in a menu.

Deleting a Menu Item from a Menu

The following description of deleting an item from a menu uses deleting **News** from the **Go** menu as an example—something you might want to do if you're setting up Outlook for other people to use and you don't want them to spend time in newsgroups.

To delete a menu item from a menu, start by displaying the Customize dialog box, even though you don't actually use that dialog box. The reason for this is that having the Customize dialog box open makes menus available for editing. You can't edit menus without having the Customize dialog box displayed.

Deleting items from menus

1. Open the **View** menu, move the mouse over **Toolbars**, and choose **Customize**.

2. In the menu bar (not in the Customize dialog box), choose the menu from which you want to delete an item. The menu opens with the menu name enclosed by a black box, as shown in Figure 35.8.

FIGURE 35.8

You must have the Customize dialog box displayed to delete a menu item.

3. Hold down the Alt key while you drag the menu item out of the menu. The menu item disappears from the menu when you release the mouse button.

Adding a Menu Item to a Menu

Outlook's menus contain items the application's designers expected to be useful. If you want to add other items to menus, you can.

Adding items to a menu

1. Open the **V**iew menu, move the mouse over **T**oolbars, and choose **C**ustomize.

2. In the menu bar (not in the Customize dialog box), choose the menu from which you want to delete an item. The menu opens with the menu name enclosed by a black box.

3. Choose the **C**ommands tab in the Customize dialog box.

4. Choose the category of the command you want to add to the menu from the **Categories** list.

5. Scroll down the **Commands** list to find the command you want to add to the menu.

6. Drag the command into the menu at the position where you want it to be.

Changing the Position of Menu Items in a Menu

Outlook allows you to reposition menu items and customize them to your satisfaction.

Repositioning menu items

1. Open the **V**iew menu, move the mouse over **T**oolbars, and choose **C**ustomize.

2. In the menu bar (not in the Customize dialog box), choose the menu from which you want to delete an item. The menu opens with the menu name enclosed by a black box, as previously shown in Figure 35.8.

3. Point to the menu item you want to move.

4. Press the mouse button and drag up or down. While you drag, a black horizontal bar appears between menu items. Release the mouse button when the black bar is in the position to which you want to move the item.

Adding a Separator to a Menu

Most menus contain gray, horizontal separator lines to group related items together.

Adding a menu item separator

1. Open the **V**iew menu, move the mouse over **Toolbars**, and choose **Customize**.

2. In the menu bar (not in the Customize dialog box), choose the menu from which you want to delete an item. The menu opens with the menu name enclosed by a black box, as previously shown in Figure 35.8.

3. Point to the menu item above which you want to create a separator.

4. Press the mouse button and drag down slightly. If a black bar appears in the menu, you've dragged too far; drag up a little until the bar disappears. When you release the mouse button, the separator appears.

To remove a separator, point to the menu item immediately below the separator you want to remove. Then press the mouse button and drag up slightly. When you release the mouse button, the separator disappears.

Deleting a Menu

Not necessary to open the Customize dialog box

You don't have to open the Customize dialog box before you drag a menu out of the menu bar.

To delete a menu, point to the menu in the menu bar, and then press Alt while you drag the menu out of the menu bar. You can also drag menus onto toolbars in this manner.

Adding a New Menu to the Menu Bar

Instead of adding items to existing menus, you can create completely new menus.

Follow Office standards for positions of menus

It's standard for **Help** to be at the extreme right in menus. That's why a new menu is placed at the left of **Help**.

Adding a new menu to a menu bar

1. Open the **V**iew menu, move the pointer to **Toolbars**, choose **Customize**, and then choose the **Commands** tab.

2. Scroll to the bottom of the **Categories** list and choose **New Menu**, as shown in Figure 35.9.

3. Drag **New Menu** into the menu bar to the position where you want it to be. It's enclosed in a black box, as shown in Figure 35.10.

FIGURE 35.9
The single item **New Menu** appears in the **Commands** list.

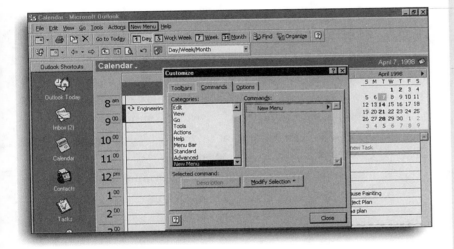

FIGURE 35.10
The new menu is shown here at the left of **Help**.

You can now use the procedure described in the next section to rename the new menu. Then you can use the procedure described earlier in "Adding a Menu Item to a Menu" to add items to your new menu.

Renaming, Deleting, or Resetting a Toolbar or Menu

You can rename or delete a toolbar or menu you've created, but not a built-in toolbar or menu. You can reset a built-in toolbar or menu to its original state.

Deleting a custom toolbar

1. Open the **V**iew menu, move the pointer onto **T**oolbars, choose **C**ustomize, and choose the **Toolbars** tab.

2. Select the toolbar or menu you want to rename or delete in the **Toolbars** list.

3. Choose **Rename** to rename the toolbar or menu, or choose **Delete** to delete it.

Reverting a built-in toolbar to its default settings

1. Open the **V**iew menu, move the pointer onto **T**oolbars, choose **C**ustomize, and choose the **Toolbars** tab.

2. Select the toolbar or menu you want to reset in the **Toolbars** list.

3. Choose **Reset** to reset the toolbar or menu.

Resetting an individual menu

1. Open the **V**iew menu, move the pointer onto **T**oolbars, choose **C**ustomize, and choose the **Commands** tab.

2. Choose the menu you want to reset. The menu name becomes enclosed in a black box.

3. Choose **Modify Selection** in the Customize dialog box.

4. In the menu that appears, choose **Reset**.

Appendixes

Installing Outlook 98

Obtaining Outlook 98

Downloading may take a long time

The Outlook upgrade consists of 26MB (megabytes) of files. Downloading these files can take a long time.

Microsoft offers Outlook 98 Messaging and Collaboration Client as an upgrade to Outlook 97 at no charge to current users of Outlook 97, Office 97, and Exchange Server. The easiest way to replace Outlook 97 with Outlook 98 is to download the upgrade via the Internet. Microsoft warns, however, that you may incur substantial telephone charges and, if you pay by the hour, Internet connection charges.

You can also obtain the Outlook 98 upgrade on CD-ROM from Microsoft. Although the upgrade is free, Microsoft does require you to pay for the cost of the CD-ROM as well as for shipping and handling.

If you don't qualify for the free upgrade, you'll have to purchase Outlook 98 either with Office 97 or as a separate product. After Outlook 98 is released, it's possible that Microsoft will include Outlook 98 with Office 97.

Outlook 98 System Requirements

Upgrade Office 97 before installing Outlook 98

Microsoft recommends that you install the Office 97 SR-1 Patch before installing Outlook 98.

To use Outlook 98, you must have a computer with a 486 or later processor. The recommended minimum speed of the processor is 66MHz, although Outlook will run on a slower computer.

The operating system required is Windows 95 (or later) or Windows NT 4.0 updated with Service Pack 3 (or later).

Memory requirements are

The more memory the better

The memory requirements listed here are the bare minimum requirements. You will see an enormous performance improvement if you have at least double the specified minimum memory. More than double is even better.

- If running under Windows 95, at least 8MB.
- If running under Windows NT, at least 16MB.

The disk space required by Outlook 98 (including the required Internet Explorer 4.01) is

- *Minimum installation—65MB*. Includes all you need to run Outlook and, if it's not already installed, Internet Explorer. Also includes the Microsoft Java Virtual Machine and multi-media enhancements.

- *Standard installation—68MB.* The minimum installation plus Outlook Help files.
- *Full installation—81MB.* The standard installation plus Microsoft NetMeeting, Office Assistants, converters for various Personal Information Management (PIM) applications, system tools, database converters, Outlook development tools, and other Outlook enhancements.

The figures given here are for the beta version of Outlook 98. The final release version may require somewhat less disk space.

These disk space figures are for Outlook itself, and do not include space required for Outlook items. The space required for Outlook items depends on the items you create, receive, and save. The following suggestions for space required by Outlook items are offered just to provide some general guidance about what you might expect:

- If you use Outlook primarily to keep a personal calendar, a to-do list, information about contacts, and for occasional e-mail, you need at least 10MB.
- If you send and receive a lot of e-mail and save messages on the workstation, you need at least 50MB.
- If you save most e-mail messages on the mail server, you need at least 10MB.

To keep Outlook's disk usage under control, be ruthless about archiving or deleting items you no longer need.

Disk space required during installation

During installation, approximately 50% more disk space is required.

Attachments consume disk space

Attachments to items, particularly graphics attachments, gobble up a lot of disk space. If you wonder why Outlook is consuming so much disk space, the most likely culprits are the attachments to your Outlook items.

Understanding Internet Only and Corporate E-mail Services

Before getting started with installing Outlook 98, you need to understand your e-mail options:

- *Internet Only E-mail Service.* Optimized to connect only to one or more Internet service providers or e-mail servers

Corporate/Workgroup replaces Internet Only

When you add the Corporate/Workgroup E-mail Service component to Outlook on your computer, that component replaces the Internet Only E-mail Service.

Outlook requires Internet Explorer components

Although Outlook requires some components of Internet Explorer 4.01, Microsoft says you can use a different Web browser to access Web sites from within Outlook. This book deals only with Internet Explorer within the context of Outlook. For more information about Internet Explorer, consult *Special Edition Using Internet Explorer 4.0* published by Que.

If the CD-ROM doesn't run automatically

Choose **Start** in the Windows taskbar, move the pointer over **Settings**, and choose **Control Panel**. In the Control Panel, double-click **Add/Remove Programs**, choose **Install**, and then choose **Next**. Choose **Finish** to begin the installation.

using Internet standards for e-mail delivery (POP3, SMTP, or IMAP).

- *Corporate/Workgroup E-mail Service*. Optimized to connect to Microsoft Exchange, Microsoft Mail 3.x, third-party e-mail services, or any combination of these, and also Internet e-mail.

The installation process installs the first of these services. If you want to use any form of e-mail other than Internet e-mail, you must add the Corporate/Workgroup E-mail Service component after you've completed the initial Outlook installation.

The advantage of using the Internet Only E-mail Service is that it requires much less disk space than the Corporate/Workgroup E-mail Service. Also, Outlook opens and closes considerably faster when you use the Internet Only E-mail Service.

Installing Outlook 98

You can install Outlook 98 on a computer running Windows 95 (or later) or Windows NT 4.0 (or later). In the case of Windows NT 4.0, you must have upgraded by installing Service Pack 3 for Windows NT 4.0.

The following description of the installation procedure is based on installation from a CD-ROM. You can follow a similar procedure to install Outlook 98 from a server on your LAN or to install it by downloading from Microsoft's server.

Insert the Outlook 98 CD-ROM into your CD-ROM drive. In most cases, your computer automatically accesses the CD-ROM and displays a setup menu. Choose **Setup** to start the installation process. You'll soon see the Outlook 98 Active Setup Wizard's first window, shown in Figure A.1.

Beginning the installation

1. Choose **N**ext to open the second wizard window. Read the license agreement and then choose **I** **a**ccept the **agreement**.

2. Choose <u>Next</u> to open the third wizard window. Enter your **User name** and **Organization**.

3. Choose <u>Next</u> to open the fourth wizard window. Open the drop-down list and choose among **Minimum Installation**, **Standard Installation**, and **Full Installation**.

4. Choose <u>Next</u> to open the fifth wizard window that contains a list of e-mail applications currently installed on your computer, such as the list shown in Figure A.2.

5. Choose <u>Next</u> to open the sixth wizard window. The wizard proposes to install Outlook 98 in the same folder as the previously installed Outlook 97 (if it exists) or in the default path, as shown in Figure A.3.

Moving from Outlook 97 to Outlook 98

You don't have to do anything to move e-mail messages and contact information from Outlook 97 to Outlook 98.

No need to reinstall Internet Explorer

If you already have an up-to-date version of Internet Explorer installed, you don't have to reinstall it.

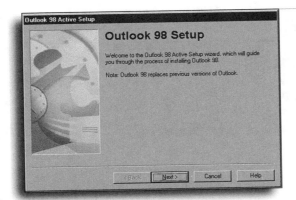

FIGURE A.1

This wizard window confirms that installing Outlook 98 replaces Outlook 97 if it was previously installed on your computer.

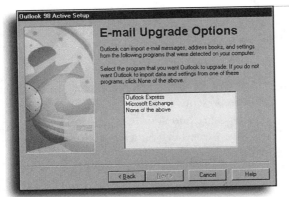

FIGURE A.2

If you want to copy e-mail messages and contact information from any of these applications into Outlook 98, select that application.

FIGURE A.3

Specify the folder in which you want to install Outlook 98.

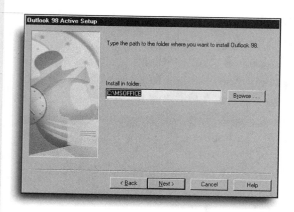

6. Choose **Next**. Outlook asks you about upgrading new items, as shown in Figure A.4.

FIGURE A.4

Choose whether you want to upgrade only newer items or reinstall all components.

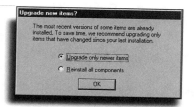

7. Choose **Next**. Outlook tells you it is preparing setup. Wait while files are installed.

At this point, Windows closes down and restarts. You'll see various messages telling you that Internet Explorer, Security, Desktop settings, and Outlook 98 components are being set up. Then you'll be told that your system and personalized settings are being configured.

When all this is complete, you can start Outlook. If, in step 4 of the previous task, you stated that you want to import e-mail messages and addresses from another e-mail system, you'll be asked whether you want to do so now. Choose **Yes** or **No**.

Now you should have Outlook up and running.

Installing Outlook Components

After you've completed the process described previously, you can use Outlook. You may not have all the components you want to use, however. In particular, if you want to use Outlook to exchange e-mail messages in any way other than the Internet, or you want to take advantage of collaboration facilities provided by Exchange Server or another messaging system, you have to add components.

To install Outlook components, you must run Setup again. As when you ran Setup initially, you can run it from your CD-ROM, from Microsoft's Web site, or from your LAN server.

Adding components to your Outlook installation

1. Run Outlook Setup. The Maintenance Wizard window is displayed, as shown in Figure A.5.

FIGURE A.5
You can use this window to add components to Outlook, reinstall Outlook, or remove Outlook.

2. Choose **A**dd New Components. A message recommends that you close all other active Windows applications. After you do so, you're asked whether you want to add new components from a CD or from the Web.

3. Choose **Install from CD** or **Install from Web**. If you chose the latter, Setup checks to see whether you are already connected to the Web. If you're not connected, a connection is established (if available). The Outlook 98 Component

Install Window opens and proposes to determine which Outlook components are already installed.

4. Choose **Yes** to allow Setup to determine which components are already installed. Almost immediately, you see a window that shows which components are already installed. Figure A.6 shows the top part of this window. You can scroll down to see the rest.

FIGURE A.6

The components already installed depend on whether you chose the Minimum, Standard, or Full Outlook installation.

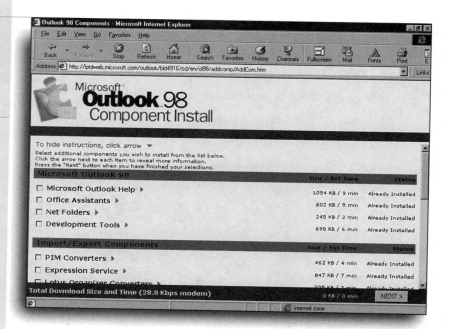

5. Choose the check boxes at the left side of the window to select any components you want to install that are not already installed. Refer to the next section for information about specific components.

6. Choose **Next** and, in the window that appears, choose **Install Now** to start the installation of the components you selected. At the completion of installation, Setup displays a message that confirms what components have been installed. Click **OK** to close the window.

You can return to Setup at any time to add components to Outlook.

Outlook Components You Can Install

The components you can install are listed in several groups.

The Microsoft Outlook 98 components include

- *Microsoft Outlook Help*. Help files for Outlook.
- *Office Assistants*. Sources for help and tips.
- *Net Folders*. The capability to share message, task, and calendar information with other Outlook users by way of the Internet.
- *Development Tools*. The capability to create custom forms, and to debug Outlook Visual Basic code. Also includes Help files for Outlook Visual Basic.

The Import/Export Components include

- *PIM Converters*. Import/export support for various Personal Information Management (PIM) applications.
- *Expression Service*. The capability to create formulas in custom fields.
- *Lotus Organizer Converters*. Utilities for importing information from Lotus Organizer.
- *Export Wizard for Timex Data Link Watch*. The capability to export appointments, phone numbers, and reminders to a Timex Data Link watch and other compatible devices.

The System Tools components include

- *MS Info*. A tool for gathering system configuration information.
- *Integrated File Management*. Provides improved performance for desktop navigation. Also provides the capability to drag files from your desktop onto the Outlook Bar.

The Extra Components include

- *Office Sounds and Animated Cursors*. Adds audio cues to screen elements and visual cues to cursor movements in Outlook and other Office 97 applications.

- *Microsoft Outlook Newsreader.* A news-only mode of Outlook Express.

The Mail Components include

- *Schedule+ Support.* Allows importing information from Schedule+.
- *Internet Only E-mail Service.* Optimizes Outlook to connect only to one or more Internet service providers or E-mail servers using Internet standards for e-mail delivery (POP3, SMTP, or IMAP).
- *Corporate/Workgroup E-mail Service.* Optimizes Outlook to connect to Microsoft Exchange, Microsoft Mail 3.x, third-party e-mail services, or any combination of these, plus Internet E-mail.
- *Microsoft Mail 3.x Support.* Provides support for Microsoft Mail 3.x servers.
- *Symantec WinFax Starter Edition (only if Corporate/Workgroup is not chosen).* Provides WinFax capability if you're using Internet Only E-mail Service.

The Proofing Tools components include

- *Microsoft Shared Proofing Tools–English: US.* A U.S. English spell-checking dictionary.
- *Microsoft Shared Proofing Tools–English: Australian.* An Australian-English spell-checking dictionary.
- *Microsoft Shared Proofing Tools–English: Great Britain.* An English-English dictionary for spell checking.

SEE ALSO

➤ For information about Net Folders, see "Using Net Folders" on page 497.
➤ For information about using Outlook to send and receive faxes, see Chapter 24, "Sending and Receiving Faxes."

Installing Outlook Add-ins

When you install Outlook components as described in the preceding section, those components are installed in the sense that
the appropriate files are copied to your hard drive. They're not
necessarily installed in the sense that Outlook can use them. For
example, you may have installed the Net Folders component. To
make sure Outlook can use this component, use the procedure
described here.

Installing an add-in

1. Open the **T̲ools** menu and choose **Options**. Choose the
    Other tab.

2. Choose **Advanced O̲ptions** and, in the Advanced Options
    dialog box, choose **Add-I̲n Manager** to open the Add-In
    Manager dialog box as shown in Figure A.7.

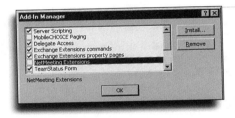

FIGURE A.7
This dialog box lists all avail-
able add-ins. Those that
Outlook can use are checked.

3. To install available Add-ins, check the appropriate check
    boxes and choose **OK** three times.

In addition to the add-ins that become available when you install
Outlook, add-ins are also available from other sources. Most of
these add-ins are available as files with a filename extension .ecf.

Making an add-in available

1. Open the **T̲ools** menu and choose **Options**. Choose the
    Other tab.

2. Choose **Advanced O̲ptions** and, in the Advanced Options
    dialog box, choose **Add-I̲n Manager** to open the Add-In
    Manager dialog box.

3. Choose <u>**Install**</u> to display the Install Extension dialog box. The add-ins that became available when you installed Outlook are listed here.

4. If necessary, navigate to the folder that contains the add-in you want to install.

5. Select an add-in and choose <u>**Open**</u> to return to the Add-in manager in which the new add-in is now listed.

6. Check the check box adjacent to the new add-in; then choose **OK** three times to close the dialog boxes.

Not all Outlook add-ins are installed in this standard way. Some, such as MobileCHOICE Messenger, are installed by using the normal method of installing Windows applications (running Setup).

You can obtain Outlook enhancements and add-ins from several sources. Some from Microsoft are available at the Web page:

`http://www.microsoft.com/office/enhoutlook.asp`

Microsoft also maintains the Outlook Enhancements Library at the Web page:

`http://www.microsoft.com/Outlook/outenharch.asp?prev=314111`

You can find many more enhancements for Outlook and Exchange Server at the Web page:

`http://www.slipstick.com/exchange/add-ins/`

SEE ALSO

➤ *To learn more about MobileCHOICE Messaging, see Chapter 25, "Sending Messages to Pagers," on page 409.*

Web pages change

The Web page addresses given here were current at the time this book was written. They might have changed by the time you read the book, so you may have to search for up-to-date pages.

Glossary

This glossary lists terms and abbreviations you may come across while you're working with Outlook. It doesn't provide broad definitions that necessarily apply in other environments.

Account   See **User account**.

Activity   An appointment, event, or meeting. Activities can be one-time or recurring.

Add-in   A software component that can be added into Outlook to provide extra functionality. Some add-ins are provided with Outlook, others are available from third parties.

Address Book   A folder that contains names of contacts, together with their addresses and other information.

Administrator   The person who controls a workgroup, LAN, or service (such as Exchange Server).

Age   The length of time since an Outlook item was created or modified.

America Online (AOL)   An organization that offers information and communication facilities to computer users.

American Standard Code for Information Interchange (ASCII)   A code that represents letters, numbers, punctuation marks, and certain other characters by numeric values. Standard ASCII code provides for 128 characters; extended ASCII code provides for 256 characters.

AOL   See **America Online**.

API   See **Applications Programming Interface**.

Applications Programming Interface (API)   A set of functions that may be used by programs running under Windows.

Appointment   A period blocked for a specific purpose in an Outlook user's calendar.

Archive   A file containing Outlook items that are older than a specific age. When Outlook archives items, it moves those items from current folders to an archive folder.

ASCII   See **American Standard Code for Information Interchange**.

AT Attachment Protocol Interface (ATAPI)   The protocol used by AT (and later) computers to communicate with CD-ROM and tape drives. Don't confuse the ATAPI protocol with the TAP and TAPI protocols. Also see **TAP** and **TAPI**.

ATAPI   See **AT Attachment Protocol Interface**.

Attachment   A file or object that is linked to, or contained in, an Outlook item. Files and objects may be attached to messages, contacts, appointments, tasks, and so on.

AutoAddress   Outlook's capability to separate an address into street, city, state, postal code, and country fields.

AutoArchive   Outlook's capability to move items of a specific age from the Personal Folders file into an archive file.

AutoCreate   Outlook's capability to automatically convert an item of one type into an item of another type.

AutoDate   Outlook's capability to convert a description of a date into a specific calendar date.

AutoJournal   Outlook's capability to automatically create journal items that record activities involving specific contacts and access to Office files.

AutoName   Outlook's capability to separate a person's full name into first name, middle name, and last name fields.

AutoName Check   Outlook's capability to verify that names entered into To, Cc, and Bcc boxes exist in an Address Book.

AutoPreview   Outlook's capability to display the first three lines of a message without the user having to open the message.

AutoSave   To automatically save data to a file at predetermined intervals.

Balloon   The message box used by the Office Assistant to display information.

Banner   The bar across the top of an Information viewer. The banner contains the name of the folder that contains the items displayed in the viewer.

BASIC   See **Beginners All-Purpose Symbolic Instruction Code**.

Basic Input/Output System (BIOS)   A set of routines, usually in ROM, that support transfer of information among such computer hardware components as the processor, keyboard, disks, memory, and monitor.

BCC   See **Blind Carbon Copy**.

Beginners All-Purpose Symbolic Instruction Code (BASIC)   A high-level programming language initially developed as a means to teach programming. It has subsequently been developed into such programming languages as Visual Basic, Visual Basic for Applications (VBA), and Visual Basic Script (VBS).

BIOS See **Basic Input/Output System**.

Blind Carbon Copy (BCC) A copy of a message that is sent without the recipient's name appearing on the copies other people receive. The word "carbon" comes from the carbon paper that was used to make copies on a typewriter.

Boolean Search A database search that uses Boolean operators (usually AND and OR) to combine words or phrases for which to search. Searching for "cat AND dog" finds items that contain both "cat" and "dog"; searching for "cat OR dog" finds items that contain either "cat" or "dog," or both words.

Browser An application that's used to find information on the World Wide Web.

Calendar A component of Outlook in which users plan their activities. Also, the Outlook Information viewer that displays activities. Outlook saves Calendar items in the Calendar folder. Also see **Activity**.

Carbon Copy (CC) The name of a person to whom an e-mail message is copied. The CC names are included on the messages sent to all recipients. The word "carbon" comes from the carbon paper that was used to make copies on a typewriter.

Card View One of the formats in which Outlook displays or prints Contact information. Resembles an index card.

Category An identifier for an Outlook item. One or more categories can be assigned to each item.

CC See **Carbon Copy**.

Certificate A digital identification used to send secure messages by way of the Internet.

Client A computer, or software running on that computer, that accesses data or services on another computer.

Client/Server A LAN configuration in which one or more computers (servers) provide services to users' computers (clients).

CompuServe An organization that offers information and communication facilities to computer users. Outlook can send and receive CompuServe e-mail messages.

Contact A person or organization. Outlook maintains a list of contacts in the Contacts folder. Each contact item contains information about one contact.

Contact List The list of contacts maintained by Outlook.

Contacts The Outlook Information viewer that displays information about contacts. Items displayed in this Information viewer are stored in the Contacts folder.

Context menu A menu displayed when you right-click an object in a window. One of the most useful items in context menus is Property that you can use to see and change an object's properties.

Control   An object on a form that is used to obtain user input and to display output. Controls available in Outlook are CheckBox, ComboBox, CommandButton, Frame, Image, Label, ListBox, MultiPage, OptionButton, ScrollBar, SpinButton, TabStrip, Textbox, and ToggleButton.

Control Panel   A window in Windows 95 and Windows NT that provides access to the fundamental Window components. To access the Control Panel, choose **Start** in the Windows Taskbar, choose **Settings** in the **Start** menu, and choose **Control Panel**.

Conversation   A sequence of related messages, sometimes known as a thread.

Corporate/Workgroup E-mail Service   An Outlook installation that includes the capability to use other messaging systems, in addition to the Internet, for e-mail. Compare with *Internet Only E-mail Service*.

Data Link   See **Timex Data Link**.

Date Navigator   The section of the Calendar Information viewer that shows one or more complete months. You can use the Date Navigator to move rapidly to specific dates.

Deleted Items   The folder that contains items that have been deleted from other Outlook folders.

Dial-Up Networking (DUN)   Connecting to a network by way of a dialed connection over telephone lines.

Dialog box   A window displayed by an operating system or application that solicits a response from the user.

Distribution List   A list of people to whom a message is to be sent.

Document   Something created in an Office application, such as a table created in Access, text created in Word, a workbook created in Excel, or a presentation created in PowerPoint.

Domain   A group of computers on a Windows NT network that shares a directory database.

Draft   A version of a message that has been prepared to be sent, but may require revision. Outlook saves draft messages in the Drafts folder.

Drafts   An Outlook folder in which drafts of messages are saved.

Drag and drop   The capability to select an object created in one Office application and use the mouse to drag that object into another application.

DTMF   See **Dual Tone Multiple-Frequency**.

Dual Tone Multiple-Frequency (DTMF)   An international signaling standard for telephone digits. When you press a button on your telephone, a dual tone is transmitted. The same dual tone is generated when you use your modem to place a call. Numeric pagers decode DTMF signals to display numbers.

DUN   See **Dial-Up Networking**.

E-mail   A message sent from one computer user to one or more other users. Most messages consist only of text, but messages may include any type of information that can be created on a computer. Users who interchange email messages may use the same computer, may be part of a workgroup, may be interconnected by way of a *LAN* or *WAN*, or may use a messaging service provider.

Embedded object   An object included within another object. The included data consists of the object's native data and presentation data.

Encryption   A means of limiting access to data by converting the data into apparently meaningless form. Only people who have the key to the encryption can reverse the process to make the data meaningful.

Event   In general, something that happens and is recognized by the computer so an appropriate action can be taken. In Outlook, an event is an activity that occupies one or more days but does not require the user to block time.

Exchange Client   The e-mail client in Windows 95 and Windows NT. Provides messaging capabilities similar to those in Outlook, but does not contain scheduling capabilities. Microsoft now refers to Exchange Client as Windows Messaging.

Exchange Server   An e-mail and collaboration server that runs under Windows NT Server. The Exchange Server information service can be added to a profile so Outlook can use the facilities of Exchange Server.

Favorites   A folder that contains shortcuts to items, documents, folders, and Uniform Resource Locators (URLs).

Fax   An abbreviation of "facsimile." A method of transmitting text and graphics over telephone lines in digital form. Outlook can send and receive fax messages.

Fax Viewer   A facility that can display outgoing fax messages.

Field   An area of memory that contains a specific type of information. Also, a space on a form that displays a specific type of information or in which a user can provide information. Outlook uses a separate field for each type of information it deals with; fields are used for such information as First Name, Middle Name, Last Name, Street Address, City, and so on.

Field Chooser   A list of fields which can be used to add fields to a form.

Field Type   The type of data a field can contain. Each Outlook field can contain one of the following types of data: combination, currency, date/time, duration, formula, integer, keywords, number, percent, text, and yes/no.

File   The basic unit of storage on such media as disks and tape.

File Transfer Protocol (**FTP**)   A common method of sending files from one computer to another by way of the Internet.

Filter An Outlook facility used to access information that satisfies certain specified criteria. The specified criteria refers to contents of fields. Filters can be used to find items that contain certain text in text fields, certain dates (or ranges of dates) in date fields, and certain values (or ranges of values) in numeric fields.

Firewall An application that protects a LAN from unauthorized outside access.

Flag An indication in a message that some follow-up activity is necessary. Messages are indicated as flagged by the flag symbol in the Flag Status column of the message list.

Folder A container for information. Outlook uses a file named Personal Folders as a container for folders. This file contains several folders, one for each type of item. Each folder contains either subfolders or items of a specific type. Users can augment the initial folder structure by adding folders and a hierarchy of subfolders.

Form A window used to display and collect information. Outlook provides forms for such purposes as creating and viewing messages, appointments, and contact information. Some of these forms can be modified to suit custom needs. You can create custom forms.

Forward To send a received message to someone else.

FTP See **File Transfer Protocol**.

Function A unit of program code that can be accessed from other code, performs some operation, and returns a value to the code from which it was accessed.

GAL See **Global Address List**.

Gateway A capability to transmit data from one information system to another. For example, a gateway allows exchange of messages between an Internet message server and the CompuServe messaging system.

Global Address List (GAL) A list of e-mail and other addresses maintained on a mail server.

GMT See **Greenwich Mean Time**.

Greenwich Mean Time (GMT) The current time as it is in Greenwich (London, England). Now known as **Universal Coordinated Time**.

Group To separate items displayed in a list or timeline into sections, each of which contain items with a common characteristic. For example, a list of contacts can be grouped by category, company, or other characteristics.

HTML See **Hypertext Markup Language**.

HTTP See **Hypertext Transport Protocol**.

Hypertext Text that contains links to other information in the same document or to information in other documents.

Hypertext Markup Language (HTML) A language used to create hypertext documents for use on the World Wide Web.

Hypertext Transport Protocol (HTTP) The protocol used for sending hypertext documents on the Internet.

iCalendar A format for sending and receiving vcalendar free/busy information by way of the Internet. Outlook supports iCalendar.

IMO See **Internet Only E-mail Service**.

Importance In Outlook and other messaging systems, messages are marked to have high, normal, or low importance.

Inbox The Outlook Information viewer that displays messages received but not moved to another folder. Items displayed in this Information viewer are stored in the Inbox folder.

Information viewer The section of an Outlook window that displays a specific type of item. Each Information viewer displays items from a specific folder or subfolder.

Integrated Services Digital Network (ISDN) A communications system by which many types of information can be transmitted at high speed over telephone lines.

IntelliSense The capability of the Office Assistant to offer assistance with a user's current task.

Internet A worldwide, interconnected system of computers that provides information and communication services.

Internet Explorer An Internet browser available from Microsoft.

Internet Only E-mail Service An installation of Outlook that provides only Internet capabilities. Also known as Internet Mail Only (IMO).

Internet Protocol (IP) The protocol that controls message routing on the Internet.

Internet service provider (ISP) An organization that provides access to the Internet.

Intranet An Internet-like environment accessible only within an organization.

IP See **Internet Protocol**.

ISDN See **Integrated Services Digital Network**.

ISP See **Internet service provider**.

Item A unit of information in Outlook. E-mail messages, appointments, contacts, tasks, journal entries, and notes are all items.

Journal The Outlook facility for creating Journal items that automatically record such activities as working with Office files, and sending and receiving e-mail messages. Users can manually record other activities as Journal entry items. Also the Outlook Information viewer that displays Journal items. Items displayed in this information viewer are stored in the Journal folder.

LAN See **Local area network**.

Legacy   Something passed on from the old days. Legacy applications and files are those designed for old computers, but are still used by people with modern computing systems.

Linked Object   An object included within another object. The included data consists of the object's presentation data and a reference to its native data.

Local area network (LAN)   A computer network limited to a small area, such as one building.

Location   The place where an appointment, event, or meeting is to occur.

Log   A record of specific types of events. For example, Outlook can create an event log that marks the completion of each CompuServe e-mail session.

Mail Client   A computer, or the software running on a computer, that can receive e-mail from, and send e-mail to, a mail server.

Mail Server   A computer, or the software running on a computer, that provides mail services to mail clients. These services include storing messages sent by mail clients until the recipient mail clients retrieve those messages.

Mailbox   The space on a mail server dedicated to storing messages intended for a specific mail user.

Mailing List   See **Distribution List**.

MAPI   See **Messaging Application Programming Interface**.

Master Category List   A list of categories from which a user can choose to assign one or more categories for each item.

Meeting   In Outlook, a period blocked by two or more users for the purpose of a face-to-face or other kind of meeting.

Menu bar   The row immediately under the title bar in a window that contains menu names. The items in each menu are displayed by choosing the menu name.

Message   Any piece of information sent from one person to one or more other people. A message usually, but not necessarily, originates and is received by a computer. E-mail, voice mail, and fax are the principal methods of sending messages. Messages may be received by other devices, such as pagers.

Message Status   An indication, marked by a flag, of something special about a message.

Messaging   The practice of communicating by means of electronic messages.

Messaging Application Programming Interface (MAPI)   A set of API functions and an OLE interface that Outlook and other messaging clients use to interface with message service providers.

Method   An action defined within an object. Each of Outlook's objects contains certain methods.

Microsoft Exchange   See **Exchange Client** and **Exchange Server**.

Microsoft Fax   A set of API functions that Outlook and other Windows applications can use to send and receive fax messages.

Microsoft Mail   A set of API functions that Outlook and other Windows applications can use to send and receive e-mail messages within a workgroup.

Microsoft Network   A system that offers information and communication facilities to computer users. Outlook can send and receive Microsoft Network e-mail.

Microsoft Outlook   A desktop information manager that includes comprehensive messaging, scheduling, and information management facilities.

Microsoft Outlook Express   An application, provided with Internet Explorer, that provides e-mail facilities and allows access to newsgroups.

Microsoft Outlook Web Access   A Web mail client that can access Exchange Server mailboxes and Public Folders.

Microsoft Project   An application used to plan, control, and track the progress of projects.

Microsoft Team Manager   An application used to allocate tasks among team members to coordinate the work of those members.

Microsoft Word   A word processor that can be chosen as Outlook's e-mail editor.

MIME   See **Multipurpose Internet Mail Extensions**.

Modem   A device that converts digital information into analog (sound) suitable for transmission over telephone lines, and also converts incoming analog (sound) information into digital form.

Multipurpose Internet Mail Extensions (MIME)   A protocol for e-mail messages that allows those messages to be formatted and include attachments. Also see **S/MIME**.

My Computer   An icon on the Windows desktop that provides access to folders on any disk on an Outlook user's computer and to disks that other network users have made available for sharing.

My Documents   A folder that contains a list of documents recently created in, or modified by, an Office application running under Windows 95. Also see **Personal**.

Native Data   One of the two types of data associated with an OLE object (the other type is Presentation Data). Native data consists of all the data needed by an application to edit the object. Also see **Presentation Data**.

Navigator   An Internet browser available from Netscape.

Net Folder   A folder that can be shared by way of the Internet, an intranet, or other messaging system.

NetBEUI   See **NetBIOS Extended User Interface**.

NetBIOS   See **Network Basic Input/ Output System**.

NetBIOS Extended User Interface (NetBEUI)   Provides data transport services for communication between computers.

NetMeeting   A Microsoft application that supports communications sessions between two or more Internet users. Also, a name used for that communication. During a NetMeeting, users can exchange text, sound, graphics, and video.

Network   Interconnected computers. In a client/server network, a server provides services to clients (individual users). In a peer-to-peer network, any computer can act as a client or a server.

Network Basic Input/Output System (NetBIOS)   Establishes communication between computers in a network.

Network Interface Card (NIC)   An electronic assembly that connects a computer to a network. Each computer must have a network interface card to be part of a network.

News Server   A computer on which newsgroup messages are stored. Many news servers are open for anyone to access, but some are private and allow access only to people who are registered and can provide a registered username and password.

Newsgroup   A collection of messages posted on a news server. People who access a newsgroup can access the messages and can post their own messages.

All the newsgroups available on the Internet are collectively known as Usenet. Also see **News Server**.

NIC   See **Network Interface Card**.

Node   A computer, printer, or other device connected to a network.

Note   A type of Outlook item. A note consists of data that will be subsequently used for any other purpose.

Notes   The Outlook Information viewer that displays notes. Items displayed in this Information viewer are stored in the Notes folder.

Object   An entity that may contain data, and have properties and methods. OLE associates presentation data and native data with objects. Outlook, and other Office applications, contain a hierarchical structure of objects.

Object Linking and Embedding (OLE)   The technology by which objects may be embedded into, or linked to, other objects. Outlook uses OLE to incorporate various kinds of objects into messages and other items.

Off Hook   The condition in which a telephone or modem is connected to a telephone line.

Office Assistant   The animated icon that may be displayed in an Outlook window to provide help with whatever task a user is attempting.

On Hook   The condition in which a telephone or modem is not connected to a telephone line.

Out of Office Assistant   A facility within Exchange Server that automatically answers or forwards messages. This facility is available only in Outlook when the current profile includes the Exchange Server information service and a network connection to Exchange Server is available.

Outbox   The Outlook Information viewer that displays messages created but not sent. Items displayed in this Information viewer are stored in the Outbox folder.

Outlook   See **Microsoft Outlook**.

Outlook Bar   The bar at the left side of Outlook's Information viewers that contains shortcuts to Information viewers and other folders.

Outlook Express   See **Microsoft Outlook Express**.

Outlook Today   An Outlook window that provides a summary of information relevant to the current day and next few days.

Pane   An area within a window that contains related information. See **Preview Pane**.

Password   A private sequence of characters a user types to gain access to a computer, to specific applications running on a computer, and to specific files. In Outlook, information services can be set up so a password is necessary to use them.

Peer-to-Peer Network   A network in which each connected computer can be a client and a server.

Permission   A permission allows a user to have access to a shared resource such as a disk drive or a printer. Also see **Right**.

Personal   A folder that contains a list of documents recently created in, or modified by, an Office application running under Windows NT. Also see **My Documents**.

Personal Address Book   An address book that contains an Outlook user's personal list of people's names and information about those people. A Personal Address Book can be used to create distribution lists.

Personal Folders   The set of folders in which Outlook stores items. Outlook creates a separate folder for each type of item. Users can add their own hierarchies of folders and subfolders and subsequently move items from one to another.

Personal Information Manager (PIM)   An application used to save and manage personal information including a calendar, an address book, and a to-do list.

PIM   See **Personal Information Manager**.

Polling   The process of periodically connecting to a messaging service to ascertain whether messages are waiting and, if so, to move those messages into the Inbox. At the same time, any messages for that service waiting in the Outbox are sent.

POP3   See **Post Office Protocol 3**.

Post   To place a message on a public folder on a server such as Exchange Server, or on a news server.

Post Office Protocol 3 (POP3)   A messaging protocol commonly used by Internet messaging service providers. Messages you receive are transmitted in POP3 format.

Postoffice   A facility on a network that maintains information—including mailbox addresses—about each user and manages the process of sending and receiving messages.

Presentation Data   One of the two types of data associated with an OLE object (the other type is Native Data). Presentation data consists of all the data needed by an application to render the object on a display device. Also see **Native Data**.

Preview Pane   The area within Outlook's Inbox Information viewer that contains previews of received messages.

Private   Items, such as appointments and contacts, that are marked so they are available only to the person who created them.

Profile   A set of information that defines how a specific person uses Outlook. A profile defines the information services to be used and passwords required to access those services. Each profile may be protected by a password.

Project   See **Microsoft Project**.

Property   A characteristic of an icon, form, or an object on a form. Properties include such characteristics as a name, the position of an object on a form, the font used by the object, and various settings.

Protocol   A set of rules that define how computers communicate. A protocol may contain other protocols.

Public Folder   A folder maintained on a server, such as Exchange Server, that can be accessed by users who have access to the server.

RAM   See **Random Access Memory**.

Random Access Memory (RAM)   The memory within a computer in which currently executing programs and information being processed is stored.

RAS   See **Remote Access Service**.

Recall   Outlook's capability to retrieve a message that has been sent. Outlook can recall messages that recipients haven't read.

Recipient   A person (mailbox) to whom a message is addressed.

Recurring   An appointment, event, or meeting that occurs regularly.

Registry   Windows files that maintain up-to-date information about a computer's hardware and software configuration, and also about users. Outlook's profiles and Master Category List are maintained in the Registry.

Reminder   A visual or audible warning that Outlook gives a certain time before an item is due. Outlook can provide reminders before appointments, meetings, events, and task due dates.

Remote Access Service (RAS)   In Windows NT, the capability of a client computer to access a server by way of a dialed telephone connection, and the capability of a server to be accessed in this way. Also known as **Dial-Up Networking**.

Remote Mail   The facility for working with e-mail at a computer that is not connected permanently to a mail server.

Replication   The process of maintaining up-to-date copies of data in various locations.

Resource   A facility—such as a conference room—or piece of equipment—such as a projector—that can be scheduled for use at a meeting. In some applications, people are referred to as resources.

Rich Text Format (RTF)   A method of formatting text so that documents can be transferred between various applications running on different platforms. Outlook can use RTF.

RichEdit   One of the text editors available within Outlook for creating and editing messages.

Right   A right gives a user access to a domain or a computer. Also see **Permission**.

RTF   See **Rich Text Format**.

Rule   A directive for how messages are to be handled by Outlook or Exchange Server. In Outlook, the Rules Wizard leads you through the process of creating rules.

S/MIME   See **Secure Multipurpose Internet Mail Extensions**.

Schedule+   A scheduling application provided with Office 95 and now superseded by the scheduling facilities within Outlook. Schedule+ was supplied in some versions of Exchange Server.

Search engine   An application that searches the Internet to find pages and newsgroups that contain information that matches specific criteria.

Secure Multipurpose Internet Mail Extensions (S/MIME)   An extension of the MIME protocol that incorporates security provisions.

Sender   The person who sends a message, or the person on behalf of whom a message is sent.

Sensitivity   In Outlook, a sender can mark a message as having normal, personal, private, or confidential sensitivity. A message recipient cannot change the sensitivity.

Sent Item   A message that has been sent to a mail server. Outlook automatically moves Sent Items from the Outbox subfolder to the Sent Items folder.

Sent Items   The Outlook Information viewer that displays messages that have been sent. Items displayed in this Information viewer are stored in the Sent Items folder.

Server   A computer, or the software running on that computer, that provides services to client computers. One server computer may have several server applications; for example, a server computer running under Windows NT Server may provide SQL Server and Exchange Server (and other) services.

Service provider   An organization that provides access to a computer-related service. An Internet service provider (ISP) provides access to the Internet.

Shared Folder   A folder on a server to which several or many users have access for the purpose of sharing information.

Shortcut   A link to information in a folder or to an application.

Signature   Text that Outlook can automatically incorporate into all messages you send. Most often used to sign messages.

Simple Mail Transport Protocol (SMTP)   A protocol used by the Internet for transmitting messages. Messages you send are submitted to an e-mail server in SMTP format.

SMTP   See **Simple Mail Transport Protocol**.

Snail mail   A slang name for conventional mail delivered by a traditional postal service.

Stationery   A pattern or background that Outlook can add to the messages you send.

Status bar   The row at the bottom of a window that displays certain information about what is displayed in the rest of the window. The status bar at the bottom of Outlook's Information viewers displays the number of items in the displayed viewer.

Status Report   Information about the progress of a task assigned to another person.

Store   The location within a server where information is stored.

Subfolder   A component of a folder. In Outlook, a folder may have many subfolders. Each subfolder contains items of a specific type and may contain other subfolders.

Subject   A brief description of an appointment, event, meeting, or message.

Subscribe   To become a regular user of a facility. By subscribing to a newsgroup, you can easily find that newsgroup.

Swap   To move data between memory (RAM) and disk. Swapping allows an operating system to have access to much more memory than actually exists as physical RAM. Also see **RAM**.

Synchronize   To copy data from one folder to another so that both folders contain the most recent data.

Table   Information arranged in rows and columns. In Outlook, a Table view displays items with one item in each row. Each column contains information in a specific field.

TAP   See **Telelocator Alpha-Paging Protocol**.

TAPI   See **Telephone Applications Programming Interface**.

Task   An Outlook item that describes something to be done. A task may have a due date and start date. The person who creates a Task item can assign that task to another person. A person who receives an assigned task can accept or reject the assignment, and can reassign it to someone else.

Taskbar   The bottom row of the Windows Desktop that displays the Start button and buttons representing each active application.

TaskPad   The pane at the bottom-left of the Calendar Information viewer that contains a list of current tasks.

Tasks   The Outlook Information viewer that displays Information about tasks. Items displayed in this Information viewer are stored in the Tasks folder.

TCP   See **Transmission Control Protocol**.

TCP/IP   See **Transmission Control Protocol/Internet Protocol**.

Team Manager   See **Microsoft Team Manager**.

Telelocator Alpha-Paging Protocol (TAP)   A protocol used by alphanumeric pagers. Alphanumeric pagers decode information received in the TAP protocol and display that information on their screens. Don't confuse the TAP protocol with the ATAPI and TAPI protocols. Also see **ATAPI** and **TAPI**.

Telephone Applications Programming Interface (TAPI)   A protocol that controls how Windows applications interact with the telephone system. Don't confuse the TAPI protocol with the ATAPI and TAP protocols. Also see **ATAPI** and **TAP**.

Template   An Outlook item that can be used as the basis for creating other items.

Thread   Related messages in a newsgroup. Also see **Conversation**.

Timeline   A view of Journal and other items plotted in relation to time.

Timex Data Link   A protocol for transmitting information to a Timex Data Link watch and to other compatible devices.

Toolbar   The row (usually under the menu bar) containing buttons that provide quick access to often-used facilities.

ToolTip   The temporary box that appears under a toolbar button to identify that button.

Transmission Control Protocol (TCP)   The protocol that controls delivery of sequenced data.

Transmission Control Protocol/Internet Protocol (TCP/IP)   A combination of the TCP and IP protocols that controls message routing and delivery.

UCT   See **Universal Coordinated Time**.

Uniform Resource Locator (URL) The address of a resource on the World Wide Web (WWW).

Universal Coordinated Time (UCT) An international, geography-independent way of specifying time. UCT was formerly known as Greenwich Mean Time (GMT).

Universal Inbox See **Inbox**.

URL See **Uniform Resource Locator**.

Usenet See **Newsgroup**.

User The person using Outlook or another application.

User account A person having access to a network is said to have a user account.

UUENCODE A utility that converts binary information into 7-bit ASCII characters. After conversion, these characters can be transmitted using a text-only e-mail system. At the receiving end, the UUDECODE utility is used to convert the text back into binary format. This system has been mostly replaced by the MIME format. UUENCODE is also used as a name for the format in which converted messages are transmitted. Also see **MIME**.

VB See **Visual Basic**.

VBA See **Visual Basic for Applications**.

VBS See **Visual Basic Script**.

vCalendar A format by which meeting request information can be sent and received by way of the Internet. Outlook supports vCalendar.

vCard A format by which contact information can be sent and received by way of the Internet. Outlook supports vCard.

View A manner in which Outlook displays information in an Information viewer. A user can select from several standard views and also create custom views. Outlook uses views as formats for printing items.

Visual Basic (VB) A programming environment (much more than a programming language) based on *BASIC* that can be used to create Windows applications.

Visual Basic for Applications (VBA) Dialects of Visual Basic that are tailored for developing applications for Office components (Access, Excel, PowerPoint, and Word).

Visual Basic Script (VBS) A subset of Visual Basic for Applications, originally developed for working with hypertext documents, but now also used for developing extended capabilities in Outlook.

Voting A capability of Outlook and other MAPI-compatible applications for sending a message in which recipients are asked to reply indicating their choice among two or more answers to a question.

WAN See **Wide Area Network**.

Web Page A group of related HTML documents, together with associated databases, files, and scripts accessible by way of the World Wide Web.

Wide Area Network (WAN) A network that covers an area larger than a single building.

Wildcard A character that represents one or more other characters. "$" used as a wildcard represents any one character; "*" used as a wildcard represents any number of characters.

Window An area of a display screen that provides access to an operating system or application and contains information relating to that system or application.

Wizard A sequence of windows that helps a user step through what might otherwise be a complex operation.

Word See **Microsoft Word**.

WordMail A name used to refer to the Word word processor when it is used as the Outlook e-mail editor.

Workgroup Two or more people using Windows 95 or Windows NT Client whose computers are connected to form a peer-to-peer network.

World Wide Web (WWW) Hypertext servers interconnected by way of the Internet that give users access to text, graphics, video, and sound files.

WWW See **World Wide Web**.

Y2000 The year 2000. Due to the way dates are handled in some operating systems and applications, errors can occur when dates after December 31, 1999 are encountered. Also known as *Y2K*.

Zip Drive A disk drive that accepts a removable disk capable of storing 100MB or more of information. Zip drives are supplied by Iomega Corporation.

Zipped file A file compressed in a format introduced by PkWare.

Index